THE CORRUPTION CURE

The Corruption Cure

How Citizens and Leaders Can Combat Graft

Robert I. Rotberg

PRINCETON UNIVERSITY PRESS

PRINCETON AND OXFORD

Published by Princeton University Press,
41 William Street, Princeton, New Jersey 08540

In the United Kingdom: Princeton University Press,
6 Oxford Street, Woodstock, Oxfordshire OX20 1TR

press.princeton.edu

Jacket design by Lisa Force

Library of Congress Cataloging-in-Publication Data

Names: Rotberg, Robert I., author.
Title: The corruption cure : how citizens and leaders can combat graft / Robert I. Rotberg.
Description: Princeton : Princeton University Press, 2017. | Includes bibliographical references and index.
Identifiers: LCCN 2016044328 | ISBN 9780691168906 (hardback : alk. paper)
Subjects: LCSH: Political corruption—Prevention. | Political corruption—Prevention—Citizen participation. | Corruption—Prevention. | Corruption—Prevention—Citizen participation. | Corporations—Corrupt practices—Prevention. | Corporations—Corrupt practices—Prevention—Citizen participation. | BISAC: POLITICAL SCIENCE / Political Process / Leadership. | POLITICAL SCIENCE / Government / International. | BUSINESS & ECONOMICS / Development / Economic Development.
Classification: LCC JF1081 .R683 2017 | DDC 364.1/323—dc23 LC record available at https://lccn
.loc.gov/2016044328

British Library Cataloging-in-Publication Data is available

This book has been composed in Adobe Text Pro and Gotham

Printed on acid-free paper. ∞

Printed in the United States of America

10 9 8 7 6 5 4 3 2 1

For

Linnea and André

the uncorruptibles

CONTENTS

THE CORRUPTION CURE

Introduction

BEATING BACK THE VARIETIES
OF BRIGANDAGE

Nothing will unlock Africa's economic potential more than ending the cancer of corruption . . . [H]ere in Africa, corruption drains billions of dollars from economies that can't afford to lose billions of dollars—that's money that could be used to create jobs and build hospitals and schools. . . .

Only Africans can end corruption in their countries.

—PRESIDENT BARACK OBAMA, ADDIS ABABA, JULY 28, 2015

The places that lose talent, it's where there's a lot of corruption.

—PRESIDENT OBAMA, HO CHI MINH CITY, MAY 25, 2016

The evil of corruption reaches into every corner of the world.

—PRIME MINISTER DAVID CAMERON, LONDON, MAY 12, 2016

I encourage you to work with integrity and transparency for the common good.

Corruption is . . . sweet [so] we like it . . . [But] please, don't develop that taste.

—POPE FRANCIS, NAIROBI, NOV. 25, 27, 2015

Substantially reduce corruption and bribery in all their forms.

—GOAL 16.5., UN SUSTAINABLE DEVELOPMENT GOALS, 2015-2030

Corruption is an insidious cancer of a national body politic. It infects elites, metastasizes harshly across classes and castes, cripples institutions, consumes communities, and cuts deeply into the very structure of people's lives. It destroys nations and saps their moral fiber. Like so many cancers, corruption is invasive and unforgiving. As it spreads relentlessly, it degrades governance, distorts and criminalizes national priorities, and privileges acquisitive rent seeking, patrimonial theft, and personal and family gains over concern for the commonweal. Corruption is the harsh political disease of our era. It must be conquered so that the planet's least well-off peoples can prosper and begin to experience substantially better human outcomes. Combating corruption and beating back the merchants of sleaze are among the better ways to strengthen overall human outcomes.

The corruption malady unfortunately resists easy medicine and other forms of responsible treatment. In too many of the globe's polities it is the default option, an intractable way of organizing daily interactions among powerful persons and between powerful persons and weaker members of national societies. Yet nothing is so ruinous to the body politic of the world's poorest and most fragile countries as the drain of corruption. Only in a few places around the planet have cases of the corruption complaint, even severe examples, been driven into remission. Elsewhere, in nearly all of our continents, the curse of corruption has overwhelmed national immune systems and relentlessly enmeshed more and more wielders of power. This book explains why defenses have been rendered largely powerless—why even modern methods have so often failed to contain the tendrils of corruption and why corruption may be considered in some lights as an effective, if malign, form of governance. But, on the happier upside, this book's main purpose is to demonstrate how and why a few significant nation-states, once riddled with decay, have inoculated themselves against infection by the corrupt political disease and have since produced long infection-free years of stability, probity, and economic growth. Learning from their successes and clinical best practices should give other nation-states new surgical and medicinal treatments capable of improving their own life chances against the incipient harms in their collective midst. This book shows how corrupt infections can be minimized and, in many situations, how the arduous uphill battle against corruption can be won—and won decisively.

But victories will come hard and after very long and carefully considered interventions by the very best practitioners. After all, in its many manifestations, corruption engulfs our everyday defenses. Even infrequent samplers of the media are assaulted by one after another irruption of human greed channeled as corruption. No single day in 2015 and 2016 has gone by without at least three or four instances of illegal, corrupt, harmful large-scale behavior having occurred or having been revealed somewhere in Africa, the Americas,

Asia, or Europe. Four corruption and anticorruption blogs (there may be more) have no shortage of infractions to report daily. Nor do the roughly 11 million documents leaked, 15,000 shell companies enumerated (2,400 of which were American), or the 200,000 offshore entities mentioned in the Panama Papers hint at anything less than a tsunami of questionable, possibly illicit and potentially corrupt, persons and polities.

Some randomly collected examples illustrate the range and variety of corrupt behavior around today's globe and provide glimpses of the extent of the problem; brigandage of many varieties is almost everywhere. Few political jurisdictions are immune. Few political and corporate enterprises are free from temptation. Moreover, the random examples below are as fully banal and prosaic as they are outrageous and perfidious:

- A former president of the United Nations (UN) General Assembly and Antigua's long-time Permanent Representative to the UN took big bribes ($1.3 million and a steady job for his wife) from a wealthy Chinese developer from Macau in exchange for promoting what would have been a UN-sponsored exposition center in Macau. Indicted, but not yet tried in court, he was found dead at his home in mid-2016, allegedly the victim of a weight-lifting accident.
- In a small town in Uttar Pradesh, India, police allegedly burned to death a woman who refused to pay a big enough bribe to release her husband from jail.
- A teenager masquerading as the son of Tajikistan's autocratic president collected $50,000 from a citizen who wanted a protected plot of land. The teenager then called the appropriate government official and asked him to deed the parcel to the citizen.
- In Russia, a creative Siberian artist advertised on Facebook that he was selling special envelopes for delivering bribes, each decorated with the text of the article in that country's criminal code that outlaws bribery. The envelopes sold online like hotcakes, many purchased by state bureaucrats.
- A prominent Canadian petroleum exploration and development firm bribed the Chadian ambassador to Ottawa and his deputy with $34 million worth of company shares to obtain exploration rights in his home country.
- Japan's Hitachi Corporation paid $6 million to a front company for South Africa's ruling African National Congress to obtain two multi-million-dollar power plant contracts. Hitachi was consequently fined $19 million by the U.S. Securities and Exchange Commission for violating the Foreign Corrupt Practices Act of 1977 and the Securities Exchange Act of 1934.

"The Wages of Corruption." The world's most corrupt countries, witness North Korea, Zimbabwe, and Venezuela, are the nations with the least satisfactory economic results for their peoples, largely because kleptocratic rulers systematically and criminally steal from their impoverished citizens. Originally printed in the *Economist*, Aug. 13, 2016. Used with permission of Kevin KAL Kallaugher, *Economist*, Kaltoons.com.

- The mayor of Tokyo resigned after opponents revealed that he had used public funds to pay for an $800 Italian meal, the most expensive suite at an exclusive hotel in London, Chinese silk shirts, comic books, and mystery novels.
- A former chief executive officer of Calpers, the biggest pension fund in the United States, was sentenced to 4½ years in prison for steering $14 million in placement fees to an ex–board member in exchange for cash bribes and gifts. A federal judge called his crime "a dagger in the heart of public trust."
- The mayor of Bucharest skimmed 70 percent of the profits from illicit construction contracts.
- The mayor of Rome resigned after being accused of padding his expense accounts.
- New York State Assembly president and dealmaker Sheldon Silver was indicted for abusing his powerful public position for years, possibly for decades, to amass private gain. After a long trial, he was convicted of seven counts of honest services fraud, extortion, and money laundering, and later was sentenced to twelve years in prison. Dean Skelos, the majority leader in the New York State Senate, was also arrested for the same kinds of offenses and

convicted of bribery, extortion, and conspiracy. He was sentenced to five years in prison.

- The onetime speaker of the Rhode Island House of Representatives went to prison for three years for taking bribes from a Providence restaurant and misusing $100,000 from his political campaign account. He admitted that he had been driven by "greed" and "just plain stupidity."
- A South Korean prime minister resigned after a prominent local construction company executive said that he had given the prime minister and a governor cash in exchange for access to contracts. (The executive committed suicide, but left implicating tapes and documents.)
- In Nepal, after a disastrous earthquake leveled 500,000 buildings all over Kathmandu, local officials admitted that corrupt payments had for years persuaded inspectors to wink at false plans and to "look the other way." This was collusive corruption at work.
- Explosions of sodium cyanide and other dangerous chemicals in Tianjin, China, which killed 145 citizens and injured 700, were traced to illegal permits granted corruptly by a former deputy mayor and a police chief, both of whom were jailed. Yang Dongliang, the deputy mayor and more recently and, ironically, the head of China's National Administration for Work Safety, was investigated for "suspected violations of party discipline and the law," code phrases for corruption. The mayor of Tianjin was also charged with the same kinds of breaches of discipline, and jailed for 12.5 years.
- The chief minister of the Indian State of Goa refused to approve work permits, invoices, and bills until a New Jersey–based international construction firm had paid repeated bribes. The American company ultimately forfeited $17.1 million in penalties to the U.S. Department of Justice for bribing officials in India, Indonesia, Vietnam, and Kuwait to win construction management contracts.
- In Ukraine, two senior officials were arrested in the midst of a televised meeting of the national cabinet for taking construction kickbacks and embezzling funds meant to purchase fuel, and for transferring the proceeds to banks in Jersey and Cyprus. The head of a government-owned railway was fired for stealing from the state. A former regional party leader allegedly "over paid" for coal and abused his power. He, too, was arrested, along with a former finance minister accused of stealing millions of dollars from the state. Another accused leader jumped to his death from a seventeenth-story window.
- Panama's vice president allegedly received a $10 million kickback from a company that won a lucrative contract to construct a huge irrigation

scheme, never completed. Earlier, a former president of the country's supreme court went to prison for five years for falsifying documents and for purchasing apartment houses for $1.7 million in cash without revealing how that amount was obtained.

- Eight Nigerian senior bank employees were sent to prison for defrauding the Central Bank of Nigeria and other banks of the equivalent of $500,000 by stealing huge quantities of high-denomination mutilated naira notes that were intended to be exchanged for fresh, new currency.
- In Kano, Nigeria, an investigator was told that "if you want to win your case, go to the judge with a beautiful girl."
- About 10,000 demonstrators in Budapest demanded the ouster of Hungary's prime minister for employing corrupt officials, especially six tax authority leaders who were alleged to have stolen official funds. Those six were barred from the United States because of corruption.
- In South Africa, a civil society organization published a "what-to-do" guide for citizens approached for bribes by the police, a not uncommon occurrence.
- A big German engineering firm that had paid a large fine in 2013 for massive bribes that sealed a Nigerian natural gas contract revealed in 2015 that its employees had also paid Brazilians to obtain $6.5 million in contracts connected to the 2014 soccer World Cup.
- Gulnara Karimova, daughter of Uzbekistan's late dictatorial president and onetime heiress apparent, was accused of taking at least $300 million in bribes from Swedish-Finnish and Russian-Norwegian multinational corporations in exchange for access to mobile telecommunication contracts. Karimova, once described by the U.S. embassy in her country as a "robber baron" and as "the single most hated person" in Uzbekistan, was put under house arrest in Tashkent in 2014 by her father. (Disclosure: I taught her in a big class at Harvard University in the late 1990s.) Her father was also accused of taking vast bribes from a Russian oligarch, possibly for the same mobile telephone contracts and access. Telia, the Swedish-Finnish company that paid bribes to Karimova, admitted wrongdoing and put aside $1.45 billion to settle claims against it by the U.S. Department of Justice.
- Brazil's ruling party and at least forty parliamentarians, including seven cabinet ministers in an interim government, benefited from at least $3.2 billion in bribes paid by Petrobras, the giant state petroleum company. Those bribes were a part of an even more massive scheme of contract fraud and enrichment involving the search for oil and gas deposits by Petrobras—a scheme or schemes that amounted to

"systematic corruption," according to the federal judge overseeing the investigation. The Petrobras frauds and attempts to limit the political fallout from such discoveries led to the impeachment of Brazil's president, but ostensibly for a different offense, and the installation of an interim president himself deeply implicated in profits from Petrobras. The speaker of Brazil's lower house of Parliament was accused of pocketing a $5 million bribe in the same scheme, and the head of the senate was similarly accused. Brazil's once-popular former president, Luiz Inácio Lula da Silva, was also implicated in the scandal.[1] Separately, a naval admiral was jailed for allegedly running the nation's secret nuclear energy program corruptly.

- Finally, doping. Russian athletes won Olympic and other sporting competitions (including the 2014 Winter Olympics in Sochi) for years despite using illegal performance-enhancing drugs. Russian testing laboratories were both bribed and compelled to cover up the systematic cheating; Russian athletics leaders orchestrated the widespread falsifications.

This list of different and various-sized transnational and national corrupt acts could go on and on. The accounts are each more sensational and alarming than the last. Some are brazen and audacious, others routine and grasping. But the horrific reality is that no one who resides or works in the developing world, engages in finance and commerce in the developing and developed worlds, attempts innocently or naively to bid for contracts, is an ambitious political official or senior bureaucrat in the developing world, operates as a lowly or senior policeman, or tries to get anything done (obtain a marriage license, perhaps) in nearly all developing world settings would be surprised by such revelations of illegality. Nor would citizens of dozens of the globe's obscenely corrupt countries object to characterizing corrupt behavior as criminal behavior; in jurisdictions such as Afghanistan under President Hamid Karzai or Tunisia under President Zine el Abidine Ben Ali, broad and far-reaching criminal-colluding networks operate and operated, top down, to maximize illicit off-takes from entire countries.

Those who know little directly about big-time pilfering endure their own daily abuses. Students often have to buy their promotions to the next grade. Impecunious shanty dwellers are compelled to pay illegally for water or electricity hookups that are rightfully theirs. Obtaining permits, a necessity of a hustled life at the margin, means the crossing of palms with "tea" money, or a payment attached to some other euphemism. All of these abuses of authority and illicit exactions are woven ineluctably into the fabric of daily existence across at least two-thirds of the globe. For billions of the planet's inhabitants, corruption is inescapable.

The Costs of Corruption

Given that the incidents detailed above are merely snapshots, it should be evident that global corruption is alive and well in the middle of the second decade of the twenty-first century. No region, no country, is immune. Arguably, there is more corruption in the world than in 1990, when the Cold War was ending, but real numbers, retrospective or current, remain guesstimates. Two researchers assert that 1.6 billion citizens worldwide are affected by bribery annually. The World Economic Forum suggests that the global annual cost of corruption is about 5 percent of total planetary GDP, possibly $2.6 trillion. It also claims that corruption increases the expense of doing business by 10 percent, on average. Global Financial Integrity estimates that $7.8 trillion was diverted illegally from emerging economies between 2004 and 2013, thanks to tax evasion, corruption, and other criminal activity. The World Bank believes that more than $1 trillion is paid in bribes annually.[2] Whatever the real figures, the number of people involved and the direct wages of cancerous corruption are substantial; the resulting damage to the collective body politic is enormous and debilitating.

Even more debilitating are the indirect costs of corruption. Christine Lagarde, head of the International Monetary Fund (IMF), told London's Anti-Corruption Summit that corruption leads to low growth and income inequality. "A country," she warned, "can be trapped in a vicious circle of corruption and fiscal profligacy, ultimately leading to a debt crisis." She reminded leaders at the summit that corruption helped to determine "some or all drivers" of inclusive growth, including financial stability. It undercut needed private foreign investment.[3]

Corruption is a constant complication in the everyday life of the majority of the world's people, poor and rich. It is with them always, often in their face if they are attempting to accomplish daily tasks like innocently driving an automobile, timorously dealing with bureaucrats, seeking hospital assistance for themselves or a sick child, or engaging in major efforts to begin or build a business. For much of the world, corruption is the norm. It is expected that all forms of governance are manipulated by and for the benefit of ruling elites. As one analyst remarked, "It is entirely routine for the government to distribute public goods and resources on the basis of favoritism."[4]

President Nelson Mandela of South Africa bemoaned predatory elites that use corrupt methods to loot national wealth. President Paul Kagame of Rwanda called corruption "clearly, very largely, behind the problems" of Africa. When James D. Wolfensohn became president of the World Bank, he chose not to mince words: for developing countries to achieve growth and poverty reduction, "we need to deal with the cancer of corruption," he said. "Corruption is the largest single inhibitor of equitable economic development." Jim Yong Kim, the current president of the World Bank, calls corruption "Public Enemy Number One." Secretary of State John Kerry announced at the London Anti-Corruption Summit that he was shocked by the "degree to which I find corruption pandemic in the world today." Corruption, he continued, "threatened governments by encouraging foreign extremism and fomenting domestic dissent." Iranian economist Saeed Laylaz, a confidant of President Hassan Rouhani, admitted immediately after the United States and Europe had agreed to limit Iran's nuclear program that his country's economic problems were caused by mismanagement and corruption, not sanctions.[5]

Fortunately, the popular and academic literature about all manner of corruption is broad and rich. There is no absence of excellent studies of the phenomenon generally and with regard to regions and individual countries, or even concerning sections of particularly notorious nations. The profound and disturbing linkages of corruption to the smuggling of drugs, arms, migrants, and people in general; to nuclear proliferation questions; to money laundering; to the financing of terror and terrorists; and to transnational criminality and criminal gangs are well-known and examined by a wealth of telling and courageous scholars and writers. "How can you solve the problem of violence and organized crime," asked a leading Mexican campaigner for competitiveness and better business conditions, "if you don't solve the problem of corruption?" Violent insurgencies, as well, partially stem from regime corruption and criminal competition over proceeds from illicit activities. "Corruption has helped generate some of today's most dire security crises."[6]

There is no particular need for another book-length analysis of what corruption is (and what it is not), why it persists, how it deters development, and whether and how it should be calibrated. Most of this is old news.

What is novel, however, is the attention that global leaders began to pay to the problems of corruption after about 2010, and especially in 2015 and 2016. Driven by the cascading costs of corrupt dealings, especially in Africa and Asia, by massive dumps of incriminating documents, by newly invigorated American and European law enforcement concerns, and by a realization that the war on terror was a war, equally, on corruption, the leaders of the world began to focus more than ever on how best to lead an anticorruption crusade. Cameron's 2016 London summit symbolized the new awareness. As the leaders at the summit hinted, this coming decade ideally could foster a real reduction in the growth of corrupt earnings for the first time since the early twentieth century.

To accomplish such an objective, we now need a study of how best and most effectively to curb, control, reduce, and diminish corruption, especially in the developing world (where it runs rampantly almost out of control and provides a substitute form of governance). This is that analysis, a how-to book showing what has been done successfully in a few countries and political jurisdictions to bring down high levels of corrupt activity, sometimes to negligible numbers. It includes an articulation of the variety of new methodologies and innovations being developed across the globe to confront corruption. It shows how political movements have battled corruption. It describes how an international anticorruption court could assist in punishing high-level corruption enablers. This is a book of hard-earned lessons—a Baedeker to anticorruption efforts for governments who want to end the scourge within their own public services and national borders, for civil societies that seek to reform their national environments, for corporate executives who wish to control their costs and risks, for donors who want to do good, and for all of us in and out of the academy who want first to understand how to minimize venal and petty corruption and, second, how to avoid the societal decay that accompanies corruption.

This book shows that many things can indeed be done to oppose and contain corruption. Corruption is not inevitable, nor so intrinsic to the offending societies that no amount of scrubbing will remove its stain. This cancer can be cured. Several polities once thoroughly infected with the pathogen of corruption—the former Macaus of the world—are now largely corruption free. The clean countries of the Nordic north and the southern Antipodes were not always without corruption. Several African nation-states have rid themselves of corrupt practices. But, exactly, how?

This book provides myriad answers to the "how?" question. Political will, usually in the form of committed national leadership, plays a major role in ensuring positive change. So does adherence to a robust rule of law and a panoply of legal, judicial, regulatory, and procedural reforms that inhibit bureaucratic discretion. The forging of effective investigative and prosecutorial instruments is essential. Public relations campaigns designed to prevent corruption are critical, as are the kinds of educational endeavors that have been pursued in at least a few of the more successful anticorrupt nation-states. Also necessary are the employment of new technologies such as the versatile mobile telephone, the existence and support of a free and energetic media, the presence of an emboldened civil society, and the actions of an aroused public apprised of its rights and responsibilities. "Without active citizens, free journalists, and independent judges, control of corruption is impossible," one observer noted.[7] These are all massive works in progress, as are the several embryonic and several successful national political party movements against corruption; the efforts of a new wave of brave prosecutors, as in Bulgaria, Croatia, and Romania; and the availability of international protocols and conventions to encourage national initiatives against corruption.

The conquest of corruption will not be achieved solely by the dissemination of the reform ideas discussed in this book. Instead, these innovations should spur to renewed action those politicians, public servants, donors, and international policy makers who care. Those innovations should indicate to lonely anticorruption advocates in some of the hardest-impacted countries that their efforts are neither neglected nor unappreciated.

Each advance in the battle to curb corruption is hard-won, but some places have established formidable beachheads and others are achieving significant advances. This book is a detailed examination of what those pioneers have done (and failed to do) to achieve real forward movement, and how others are trying to keep pace. This book embraces the notion that corruption, as unlikely as it may seem, can be conquered, frontier by frontier and territory by territory. It is full of lessons from the developed and developing worlds for the countries mostly in the developing world about what has been and can be done; it investigates the factors that have permitted the scourge of corruption both to resist and then to succumb to reform.

Pathways to a Cure

This book's opening chapter draws on a very large literature to offer a dissection of the corruption malady—what it is and what it is not. That chapter provides a wealth of definitions ("the abuse of public power and position for private gain," "partiality rather than impartiality," "unfairness," "a lack of transparency," and so on) and parses the differences between those who advocate interpretations devoid of moral content and those who posit corrupt acts as deviations from integrity.

This first chapter examines the several significant ways in which corruption is understood in theory and in practice. It shows how corruption must be examined as a fundamental problem of public service delivery as well as of private and nonprofit sector action and inaction. The corrupt criminalization of states facilitates people- and narcotics-trafficking enterprises and the proliferation of dangerous weapons of war, not to mention the spread of terror.

Corruption is neither culturally relative nor efficient, as some observers once argued. The first chapter carefully considers those propositions and finds that corrupt practices produce no positive good. Nor are they "natural" or anywhere accepted.

The first chapter distinguishes between petty and venal (grand) corruption, showing how pervasive is the first and how destructive the second. It suggests that an embrace of ethical universalism is essential if a nation-state wishes to extirpate corrupt practices within its midst. The chapter also distinguishes among types of states to specify the different kinds of reform interventions that are possible, category by category. It shows how corruption criminalizes states and turns many into top-down looting machines.

Corruption is conceptualized as a problem of collective action, not of reforming agents of the state. Political will, defined in the first chapter, drives that transformation of the collective; enlightened leadership is the primary engine of attitudinal and societal change.

The second chapter of the book examines how we can know what we think we know about corruption. It assesses the many ways in which the amounts and varieties of corrupt practice are now quantified and qualified. The advantages of direct over indirect measurement methods are set out, as are the arguments for perceptions-based approaches. This chapter evaluates the Corruption Perceptions Index and the World Bank's Control of Corruption Indicator, finding both eminently useful, if conceptually compromised. It also examines the new Index of Public Integrity and its use of objective rather than subjective measures of corruption.

The second chapter discusses the role of other indexes in understanding corruption—especially the Global Integrity, Rule of Law, Bribe Payers, Financial Secrecy, Aid Transparency, and Open Budget indexes. Chapter 2 also examines the World Bank's blacklisting of corrupt multinational corporations. Since much of venal corrupt behavior is engendered externally, this chapter further explores the roles of the Extractive Industries Transparency Initiative, Revenue Watch's Resource Governance Index, and rules promulgated by the Securities and Exchange Commission in calibrating and revealing potentially corrupt flows of cash into countries where mineral and petroleum riches are available for the taking and the exploitation.

The second chapter additionally demonstrates what works and what kinds of information will help us learn whether the efforts against the pathogen of corruption are in fact successful. It distinguishes between subjective and objective forms of measurement and shows how each has been employed to illuminate corrupt practices.

Legal barriers against corruption are fundamental in attempting to win any battle against such a scourge. The third chapter samples a variety of legislated mechanisms and systems to examine whether and how they help, and how much they wage war effectively against corruption. It looks comparatively at legislation antagonistic to corruption in Southeast Asia and sub-Saharan Africa, in countries that have been successful in reducing corruption and in other places where equally impressive legal constraints have accomplished little.

The third chapter also scrutinizes the structure and impact of American, British, Canadian, European, and United Nations laws and conventions intended to reduce transnational corruption. It advances the possibility of an International Anti-Corruption Court patterned after the International Criminal Court and examines its potential relevance and importance. This chapter discusses the roles of auditors general and of ombudsmen in revealing and sometimes attempting to remedy the results of corrupt acts. It analyzes the significance of the media and transparency more generally in combating corruption, and underscores the vital importance of independent judges and well-functioning court systems in enabling successful attacks on corruption.

The fourth and fifth chapters discuss the practice of using investigatory commissions to reduce the intensity and predatory nature of corruption, primarily in Asia and Africa, but also in Europe and Central America. The much-touted successes of the Hong Kong model are real, as are the distinctive experiences of the Singaporean and Indonesian examples illustrative of the critical importance of political will in combating corruption. In Hong Kong and Singapore, community attitudes and behavior were altered strikingly, and very swiftly. Well-run commissions supported fully by the political establishment made a signal difference. In Asia and Africa, the effectiveness of capable commissions may have been more repeatedly compromised and undermined by national political failures, but those failures demonstrate how vital it was for successful commissions to have enjoyed high-level national support.

Chapter 5 turns first to the mostly effective African commission experiences in Botswana and Mauritius to show how they prospered because of good internal leadership and the backing of the national executive and legislative authorities. Nigeria's battle, an example of a much more difficult attempt to control corruption, is analyzed, especially the ambitious but ultimately frustrated efforts of the nation's first Economic and Financial Crimes Commission. Ghana's comparable Commission for Human Rights and Administrative Justice accomplished some important gains against corrupt practices but it, too, was hampered by political interference and a lack of meaningful independence. Three well-articulated East African commissions (those of Ethiopia, Kenya, and Tanzania), and a comparable effort in Madagascar, all failed to reduce corrupt practices because of the several ways in which their operations were compromised by political considerations. The Zambian and Malawian commissions similarly suffered, especially after the end of President Kenneth Kaunda's long reign in Zambia and under the wildly corrupt successors to President Hastings K. Banda, whose autocratic tendencies began it all. Taken together, the fourth and fifth chapters suggest that well-established and well-run investigatory commissions can help to reduce levels of corruption, but only if their endeavors are embraced by the full force of the state, as in Botswana, Hong Kong, Rwanda, and Singapore.

The sixth chapter of the book examines the fortunes of the five nation-states that showed the largest scoring gains in reducing corruption between 2004 and 2014. It explains how they changed from horribly corrupt to markedly less corrupt over that decade, according to the Corruption Perceptions Index and the World Bank's Control of Corruption indicator. This "most improved" cohort includes Georgia, Liberia, Rwanda, Macedonia, and Montenegro. But being "most improved" is equated only in the Rwandan case with eliminating corruption; the others just bettered their scores considerably during the decade examined. This chapter discusses exactly to what those countries owe their scoring gains. In all cases, political will mattered considerably. Each country instituted a number of critical regulatory changes and appointed anticorruption commissions with substantial mandates. Each tried to raise police and civil servant salaries, or at least (in Liberia's case) to start paying wages. In a few, legislative and instrumental alterations in the nature of governance were also critical. Overall, improvement occurred because tough-minded leaders introduced institutional innovations and made sure that those innovations helped to bring about measurable reductions in corruption.

The seventh chapter answers a fundamental question. The Nordic nations and such places as New Zealand, now and since the indexes of corruption were invented, have always ranked highest among the noncorrupt. Yet, those nations were desperately corrupt a century or more ago. What moved them from the corrupt to the noncorrupt sides of the ledger? For the globe's ten least corrupt countries, this chapter teases out the variables that can explain such major shifts over time (in several cases over centuries). Political will, again, was important. So were the development of high levels of social trust, the creating of new national solidarities, broad literacy and educational advances, significant attention to religious confessionalism, and the popular embrace over time of ethical universalism.

The eighth chapter examines the critical role of political will. It explains how responsible political leadership is the main ingredient of effective anticorruption achievements in modern times. Hong Kong, Singapore, and Botswana are cases in which determined heads of government and heads of state provided the essential ingredient of major reform. Hong Kong and Singapore were rampantly corrupt before new leadership drastically altered the incentive structure of corruption and rapidly reduced its presence. Botswana's leadership did the same, but from a less infected platform. China and Nigeria are now undergoing the same kind of leader-driven anticorruption alterations. Time will tell whether Presidents Xi Jinping and Muhammadu Buhari succeed in smashing corrupt practices or whether China and Nigeria are too big and too deeply steeped in corruption for reform endeavors to be sustained. This chapter argues, however, that leaders like Xi and Buhari can make a difference no matter the size of their polity, and discusses a Bolivian case and a Tanzanian case that reinforce the notion that political will is absolutely central to anticorruption outcomes.

Chapter 9 examines the various ways in which a concerned civil society, aroused protest movements, social audit initiatives, and political party endeavors have managed to alter public discourse and, in several cases, successfully curtailed the spread of corruption and made its proliferation much more costly. Most notable is the victory of explicitly anticorruption political vehicles in India and Guatemala and the advances against corruption made through the social audit mechanism in such places as the Philippines. This chapter also explores a variety of new technological advances, mostly the imaginative use of handheld devices, which have the potential to expose incidents of corruption and thus help in several important ways to win the fight against that infection. The text messaging capabilities and photographic capacities of mobile telephones are increasingly of great help in the contest; so are dash cam videos that can be quickly uploaded to YouTube or Facebook. This chapter also includes a discussion of how to make improvements to the ethos and management of multinational corporations so that they act more ethically and legally.

The penultimate chapter on lessons learned and best practices reiterates and supports the critical role of political leadership in transforming national political cultures from corrupt to noncorrupt. It also examines many of the other methods that are helpful in destroying the pervasive pursuit of corrupt gains throughout the countries of our planet. It offers a set of best practices for reformers (and donors) ready to do more than just talk about or bemoan the persistence of corrupt practices throughout two-thirds of the globe.

The final chapter offers a fourteen-step program capable of curbing corruption—the overall optimistic goal of this book.

The Nature of Corruption

Greed and taking advantage—self-interest—are hardwired into the human condition. Corrupt acts flow from a natural (rational) desire to improve one's position and one's earning potential. Both the giver and the taker of corrupt exchanges fundamentally attempt to better their position/situation/claim, calculating the extent to which direct or indirect responsibilities and results will flow from an exchange of gratuities, an acknowledgment of influence, and the creation of obligation. All corruption, even the most venal, is fundamentally based on reciprocity, cultivation, and an oiling of whatever wheels permit the vehicle of life to roll faster, roll securely, roll in the right direction, or roll at all. Corruption is a method of allocating scarce resources and of minimizing disadvantages based on status or class.

Corruption, after all, is an ancient phenomenon, known at least from Mesopotamian times. Public notables abused their offices even then for personal gain. Well-born and common citizens have long sought advantage—as citizens, as factions, as participants in business endeavors—by corrupting those holding power or controlling access to permits, perquisites, rulers, and the like. Any exercise of discretion, especially forms of discretion that facilitate or bar entry to opportunity, offers a magnetic opportunity to abuse or take advantage of that power. The privilege of being a gatekeeper under auspicious conditions can reap bountiful returns, especially if the opportunities in question are potentially zero-sum in their impact on individuals or classes of individuals. It is an immutable law of human endeavor that those who seek advantage will approach authorities for recognition or gain and that those who are in positions of authority—those who have it in their office or their function to favor one claim over another—will appreciate the strength of their positions and welcome forms of persuasion to fulfill their responsibilities.

Until avarice and ambition cease being human traits—until integrity triumphs—corruption will flourish. Responding to the pulse of self-interest, favor will be offered and sought. Merit alone will determine outcomes and advancement in only a minority of situations and in a minority of nations. The current of corruption will therefore continue to exist as an undertow even in the most upright and abstemious of nations and societies. Receiving entitlements rightfully, and in a timely manner, will continue to be the global exception rather than the everyday norm. Almost everywhere there will continue to be the presumption, sadly, that the most desirable and beneficial outcomes will be secured through illicitly pressed influence (from connections) or via hard-bought gains—not necessarily from honest attainment.

We see this recognition of the presence of corruption—especially in political life but also in the interactions of citizen and state in the nineteenth century—in the novels of Charles Dickens, especially *Little Dorrit* (1855), and in George Eliot's *Felix Holt, The Radical* (1866), in which Eliot bemoans the fact that British parliamentarians were unashamed "to make public questions which concern the welfare of millions a mere screen for their own petty private ends." Corruption was not felt to be a "damning disgrace" by such figures, and Eliot used the word "corruption" explicitly.

Following Plato, Aristotle, Ibn Khaldun, Hobbes, and nineteenth- and early twentieth-century journalists and authors, this book asserts that corruption is common everywhere, even in traditional societies; that almost no nation-states and few leaders are immune from the temptations of corruption; that we now know more than ever about the mechanisms and the impact of corruption; that corrupt practices are more odious and more disruptive in the world's newer nations than in older ones (which experienced their corrupt eras in times past); and that worldwide corruption is now a pernicious threat to fragile national orders and, as Secretary of State John Kerry and Prime Minister David Cameron both said in 2016, to world order itself.

President Theodore Roosevelt declared that corruption "obliterated" the government of the people.[1] Because corruption is so destructive to the accomplishment of good governance in much of today's world, because corrupt practices deter improved health outcomes and educational opportunities throughout wide swaths of the globe, because corrupt behavior leads indirectly and sometimes directly to loss of life (in Kathmandu, Tianjin, Istanbul, Lagos, and far beyond), because the wages of corruption often lead to civil conflict (as in large sections of sub-Saharan Africa such as Mali, the Democratic Republic of Congo, and the Central African Republic), and because the attractiveness of corruptly acquired benefits undermines the national interest (trading it for personal and special group interests) in one fragile nation after another, the need for a comprehensive and effective anticorruption strategy is more urgent and more imperative than ever before.

Corruption Defined

The standard definition of a corrupt act is some less or more elaborated formula of "the abuse of public office for private gain." In part, that definition, consciously refusing to moralize or to treat corruption merely as a disregard of ethical norms, draws on Nye's key early, still useful but rather cumbersome formulation: "Corruption is behavior which deviates from the formal duties of a public role because of private-regarding (person, close family, private clique) pecuniary or status gains; or violates rules against the exercise of certain types of private-regarding influence." Nye helpfully subdivided corruption into bribery (the "use of a reward to pervert the judgment of a person in a position of trust"), nepotism (a "bestowal of patronage by reason of ascriptive relationship rather than merit"), and misappropriation (illegal appropriation of public resources for private-regarding uses). His definition excluded considerations of whether corruption might, in certain circumstances, be in the public interest, and avoided evaluating whether differing Western and non-Western notions of corruption exist.[2]

Huntington follows Nye in suggesting that corruption is the deviation by public officials from accepted norms to serve private ends. Rapid modernization generates corruption, he asserts, and reflects societal backwardness and the lack of "effective political institutionalization."[3] Scott indicates that corruption is "a deviation from certain standards of behavior." That is, corruption is an undermining of a proper pursuit of the public interest by persons of authority whose roles implicitly commit them to be accountable and to act with integrity.

Corrupt acts are willful "transactions in which one party exchanges wealth," or kinship or friendship, "for influence over the decisions of government." As Scott points out, matter of factly, "were it not . . . that . . . government decisions represent valuable commodities to some citizens, there would be little corruption." Nor would there be much corruption if governments simply auctioned their valuable "things," such as jobs, access to education, and hospital treatment.[4] Noonan, agreeing, says that a bribe is "an inducement improperly influencing the performance of a public function meant to be gratuitously exercised." Moreover, a bribe in classical times was any act that "perverted judgment." A bribe is universally shameful, never acknowledged publicly, and illegal in every jurisdiction.[5]

Bribery is distinguishable from extortion. Bribes, monetary or otherwise, are tendered to gain something—a good or a service. They are given freely, whether intended to hasten or ensure the delivery of documents or services to which the bribe-proffering individuals are legally entitled, or whether intended to deprive someone else illicitly of benefits, services, or property. But payments that are demanded or exacted by officials from persons who would prefer not to pay extra for, say, a notionally free public service, are extorted. Some measure of coercion, often heavy-handed, is involved. Kickbacks qualify as extortion. So do shakedowns, blackmail, and any payments made because of physical or similar threats. The victims of extortion usually include the public interest. Graft is the unscrupulous misdirection of a public good into a private pocket. Embezzlement is theft, from the inside, and usually by virtue of employment in, or the holding of, public office.

Rose-Ackerman began her many important, skillful published contributions to the study of corruption by limiting its expression essentially to bribery by third parties of agents who put their own interests before those of their principals. All payments that were "not passed on to superiors" by agents, and were illegal, were deemed corrupt. She excluded nepotism and embezzlement. Subsequently, she settled on "the misuse of public power for private or political gain" as a working definition. Corruption, she said, is "a symptom that something has gone wrong" in the management of a state. Instead of delivering public services, its institutions are employed for personal enrichment, thus undermining a state's legitimacy as a neutral service provider. Much later, Rose-Ackerman implicitly expanded her definitional universe to include a variety of additional corrupt incentives that appear in any developing state, particularly in postconflict, transitional polities.[6]

Klitgaard agrees that corruption happens when public servants disregard their obligations to perform properly and instead make special arrangements for private profit. For him (and originally for Cicero and many other classical authors), corruption is a question of fidelity, of agents being faithful to the public interest—the key regard of principals; corruption then appears as a divergence between the rational interests of principals acting on behalf of the public and agents maximizing their private interests on behalf of themselves or their families and relations. Corruption occurs when an agent betrays the public interest.[7] Brasz says that corruption is the stealthy exercise of derived power by agents on behalf of principals against the public interest under the pretense that such an exercise is legitimate. He also reminds us that corruption means "the treacherous venom of deceit"—professing loyalty to the public interest while actually benefiting oneself or third parties.[8] Williams believes that corruption is a subversion of the public interest, a notion that accords well with the earlier definitions in this paragraph and is both descriptive and normative.[9]

Harris is quintessentially cynical: Obviously, he says, political corruption is the "exploitation of elected public office for private gain." But that formulation simply describes "normal political behavior." He continues: "Most politicians exploit public office for private gain when given legitimate opportunities to do so. . . . How many decline to benefit personally from office by generous interpretation of perquisites available to them?"[10]

Underkuffler asserts that corruption is "a moral evil." She worries that some corrupt acts may not be illegal, per se, and that all illegal behaviors may not be equally corrupt. She is also concerned that thinking of corruption as an intentional "breach of duty"—as omitted or committed acts, with anticipated private gain—is too narrow, excluding as it does serious ethical and moral lapses. For her, corruption is a special kind of betrayal of trust. Additionally, corruption is more than an act antithetical to the public interest, because such a definition begs the question: who defines the "public interest?" It can include too much and too little. For all of these reasons, Underkuffler prefers a defining concept close to Johnson's eighteenth-century assertion that corruption is "[w]ickedness; perversion of principles," decadence, degeneracy, and decay—the transgression of deeply held universal norms. Heywood and Rose align themselves somewhat with Underkuffler by suggesting that the central issue is not corruption, but a lack of sufficient integrity. Rules-based systems are no substitute for personal integrity. Indeed, corruption is a symptom, the absence of integrity the disease.[11]

Those formulations fit well with Jordan Smith's suggestion that "moral outrage" is much more common in public discourse than some "technical" formulation. The public—especially the Nigerians whom he interviewed at length and observed closely—know that everyone who takes bribes, cheats, extorts, pillages, fails to perform, and contributes to moral decay flagrantly disregards widely accepted notions of equity and fairness.[12] Myrdal essentially agreed that in South Asia, although corrupt practices had preserved the "soft state" and assisted in the persistence of irrationality, such behavior was well known to be wrong and was decried by aroused publics.[13]

Leys, well before Underkuffler, contended that the "rules of private morality," not "public morality," defined corruption, but that those rules were conditioned and modified by rapid social and economic change. The incentive to corrupt, he also reminded us, is especially great in conditions of extreme inequality and considerable poverty. Further, in the new states it is easy to conceal corruption because of poor enforcement and traditions of gift-giving. "The chicken" becomes the "pound note." Or, as Mair wryly notes, "Good men do not practise . . . industry . . . where this would lead to a reduction in piece-rates."

Leys did not excuse corrupt behavior, but he wanted readers to be aware that in developing countries corruption sometimes offered a functional benefit, a position with which Scott agreed.[14] Hoselitz argued that corruption in Asia and Africa was nothing more than a reflection of the "non-rational norms" that regulate official governmental proceedings on those continents.[15] Riggs, too, suggested that group solidarity, poly-communalism, hereditary succession, and other reciprocative practices in developing societies overrode or out-competed Western notions of morality and appropriate behavior.[16]

Johnston argues along with classical authors that a nation-state that has retreated from "goodness" is corrupt. He also says that corruption is "the abuse of a trust, generally involving public power, for private benefit which often, but by no means always, comes in the form of money." But he also believes that corruption may be a term employed generally to describe a range of acts that transcend precise or clear societal limits. Further, for him, the distinctions between private and public corruption are "difficult to draw." It is the absence of an ability to participate in "open, competitive, and fair political and economic processes," and a failure to prevent excesses, that characterize a corrupt society.[17]

Rothstein, Teorell, and Kurer offer the concept of "partiality" as the offense of corruption. Rothstein contends that setting "impartiality" as a specific norm for public officials to abide by enables those who breach the norm for private gain to be held accountable both legally and ethically. For Rothstein and others, the underlying principle, "non-discrimination in the exercise of public authority," is fully in accord with normative theories of justice and democracy.

Kurer believes that states "ought to treat equally those who deserve equally." His impartiality principle demands "rule-bound administration," thus underpinning a "public office definition of corruption with arguments of distributional justice." Public officials therefore act corruptly when they "violate non-discrimination norms that regulate the allocation of a polity's rights and duties in order to derive a personal advantage."[18]

Lee Kuan Yew asserts that fairness is critical. There "must be a level playing field for all. . . . You must have a society that people believe is fair."[19] Lee could have added that legitimacy was also essential. To be regarded by citizens as truly legitimate, a regime has to be viewed as fully fair, as well as transparent, accountable, and honest.

Uslaner thinks the Kurer, Rothstein, and Teorell prescriptions focus too narrowly on governmental corruption. The private sector makes important contributions to corruption, he contends. Instead of fairness or impartiality, Uslaner focuses on transparency and follows Warren in arguing that "political corruption attacks democracy by excluding people from decisions that affect them." Warren makes a powerful case that corruption is particularly problematic in democracies, nominal and otherwise. Democracies by definition are intended to be fair and inclusive. Yet, the corrupt practices that permeate so many "democracies" depend on unfairly excluding groups and individuals—on privileging access to state services to some groups and individuals over others. For Warren, corruption is hypocritical, covert, and duplicitous. So corruption is the absence of transparency and the antithesis of ideal democratic practice. Corruption, Uslaner declares, stems mostly from inequality rather than a simple lack of fair treatment, especially perceptions of economic and social disparities, and from low generalized societal trust. Improvements in institutional structure, especially more democracy and better rule of law instruments, do not diminish corruption if inequality persists. Uslaner's aggregate analysis indicates that "inequality and especially uneven economic development . . . lead to low levels of out-group trust and then to high levels of malfeasance."[20]

These many definitions, and written laws, all capture the essence of the harmful deed as well as its moral opprobrium. To fail to discharge one's public responsibilities faithfully—as the cited authors and many others say—constitutes a dereliction of duty, a refusal to provide good and honest service, and an unwillingness to abide by the norms of behavior (particularly impartiality) that govern civil servants in each and all countries. Corrupt elected and non-elected officials thus put their own interests above the public interest, and assert an (illicit) private morality that trumps agreed-upon and long-established societal norms. "The concept of corruption is universally understood" and not culture bound, *pace* Scott and some others.[21]

"Partiality" becomes a fee for quick or informed service, a natural cost of diligence, or a mere reflection of a nation-state's failure to pay its employees adequately. But this focus, as with the many national laws against corruption, mostly presumes (wrongly) that corruption exclusively concerns interactions between public servants and citizens. Mungiu-Pippidi offers a more inclusive workmanlike definition: "Corruption involves some undue private profit (for someone) due to abuse of an entrusted public authority." Even better is her definition: "the use of public authority to generate private rents detrimental to overall social welfare."[22]

Corruption, in other words, is both a specific private-regarding and personally enriching act by someone capable of offering access to official perquisites as well as a more general abuse of the public trust—a disregard of the state's need to be impartial and to be seen to be impartial. Unfortunately, U.S. Chief Justice John G. Roberts' opinion in 2016 on behalf of the U.S. Supreme Court's majority verdict in *McDonnell v. the United States* almost completely ignored decades of such considered academic and popular opinion. His opinion specified what the U.S. judicial system henceforward could consider corrupt.

Roberts said that only "official acts"—formal and concrete governmental actions—constituted corruption in the United States. Bribes and kickbacks are still corrupt, but offering "ingratiation and access" is not necessarily a conclusive indication of corrupt dealings—at least according to the court's interpretation of the language of the U.S. federal bribery statute (18 USC 201). That statute specifies that it is a crime for an official to receive "anything of value" in return for "being influenced in the performance of any official act." The statute also prohibits giving anything of value to a public official "to influence any official act." For an action by an American public official to be considered corrupt, there must be a solid quo for a supplicant's quid, an improper act in exchange for cash or a reasonable facsimile—"something of value."[23] Moreover, according to the Roberts opinion, all Gov. Robert McDonnell did was arrange meetings with others. According to the Supreme Court, he committed no culpable "official act."

Jack Abramoff, for one, considers the Supreme Court's *McDonnell* judgment naïve. It showed "a regrettable innocence about how things work in the real world." Abramoff, a successful Washington lobbyist, served nearly four years in federal prison for conspiracy, fraud, and tax offenses. His fall from grace also contributed to the conviction of a Republican congressman from Ohio and the downfall of a prominent Republican congressional leader and dealmaker from Texas. Abramoff, reacting to the Supreme Court decision, said that the justices failed to understand that "a little bit of money can breed corruption." Moreover, "When someone petitioning a public servant for action provides any kind of extra resources . . . that affects the process."[24]

Beyond the United States, Roberts' reading of what corruption is and how it operates will seem unusually limiting, even though the *New York Times* cautioned that the *McDonnell* verdict "should not be narrowly construed and need not stop prosecutors from building strong cases against politicians who are abusing their office for personal gain."[25] The decision will find little favor—except among those seeking to influence official decisions and those officials who, by winks and nods, are able to bestow advantages on specific individuals, groups, or corporations.

Facilitating Terror and Criminality; Abridging Human Rights

Not all corrupt actions take place in the public sector. Any trusted office, or any societal position of trust, is also potentially corrupt. This extended definition (as advanced above by Mungiu-Pippidi, Johnston, Jordan Smith, Rothstein, and a few others) allows us to include the misuse of a civil society or corporate position for private gain within our understanding of corrupt behavior; it also permits our definitional universe to accord with popular understandings of what is a corrupt act committed by someone technically not a public servant. According to Mungiu-Pippidi, "People grant a far broader meaning to what pollsters call corruption than lawyers [and most political scientists] do. . . ."[26]

Rose-Ackerman drew attention to private sector corruption shortly after authorities in Hong Kong (see chapter 4) realized that commercial enterprises were prone to buying influence illicitly from other firms, thus subverting the normal laws of supply and demand.[27] Some of those activities were designed to reduce information flows and open competition, that is, to defeat transparency and to gain advantage. Kickbacks and payoffs are just as much the language of corporate-to-corporate dealings as they are the descriptors of corporate-to-public official exchanges. Furthermore, corporate behavior can sabotage the public good by evading taxation, engaging in trade and transfer mispricing, keeping assets offshore (and away from the tax authorities), asset stripping and false bankruptcy, illegal capital flight, and outright criminal smuggling. Some enterprise monopoly or monopsony advantages are secured corruptly, and every practice decried in the public arena has been practiced in the private sphere, to the disadvantage of consumers and citizens.[28]

The International Federation of Association Football (FIFA) soccer scandal makes it perfectly obvious that private, nongovernmental organizations may operate corruptly and be corrupted. Abusing an office, even if a semi-public or fully private one, qualifies as corruption just as much as abuse by a governmental public servant. Nations allegedly bribed leading FIFA decision-makers to obtain World Cup and other sporting championships preferentially for themselves. Deals and counter-deals and almost perpetual conniving took place. Major sums purchased votes for venues and would have continued on and on if the U.S. and Swiss authorities had not arrested some of the central schemers in 2015.

For a long time, in fact, it made sense to understand corruption primarily as a deprivation of citizens' human and political rights, as a set of individual and group economic penalties, and as a serious stain on an individual national society's moral fabric. Obviously, business persons could bribe each other as well as public servants.

Freedom from corruption is also a human right. Arthur Chaskelson, the first president of South Africa's Constitutional Court, in deciding that corruption was "inconsistent with the rule of law and the fundamental values of [the South African] constitution," implicitly made the case that corrupt acts violated individual and group human rights. By undermining a constitutional commitment to human dignity and human rights, corruption was "a serious threat to our democratic state." His opinion echoed the preamble of the Council of Europe's Criminal Law Convention ("corruption threatens . . . human rights") and the Framework for Commonwealth Principles on Promoting Good Governance and Combating Corruption, accepted by the Commonwealth Heads of Government in 1991. It foreshadowed provisions of the UN Convention against Corruption (UNCAC), discussed at greater length in chapter 3, which asserted relief from corruption as a human right.[29] The editor of a prominent anticorruption blog states the case simply: ". . . freedom from corruption is a basic human right, and . . . grand corruption should be deemed a crime against humanity."[30]

Arguably, freedom from corruption is a fundamental human right even if UNCAC does not define corruption precisely. Two authors persuasively and explicitly posit that freedom from corruption is a right that "all persons . . . irrespective of culture or of social position" hold. Governments can violate those inherent rights but cannot take them away.[31] Moreover, corrupt practices undercut noble international efforts to improve the health outcomes, educational attainments, welfare, overall prosperity, and every other basic human right of our planet's inhabitants. A measles or infantile paralysis vaccination campaign may easily be interrupted by corruption. Or, as in Ukraine, corrupt interference with the supply of antiretroviral medicines can doom HIV/AIDS patients to death. So can access to other essential care in medical clinics be denied across the globe. Basic educational opportunities in innumerable villages and towns can be denied by underhanded pilfering or other profiteering by corrupt politicians and officials.

Underappreciated until relatively recently, corruption further constitutes a serious global and national security threat.[32] Building on a fuller appreciation of how corrupt behavior facilitates and drives terror and other major forms of insecurity, we now know that corruption fundamentally compromises world peace and world stability. Terror and terrorists are financed corruptly. Borders become porous because of corruption, enabling the essentially free movement of illicit fissile materials, small arms, and recruits. Even inside a state, the growth of gangs that traffic illicitly in humans and drugs and move laundered money are all greatly facilitated by the venal corruption of the rich and the powerful and by the casual bribing of small-time officials. The sanctity of international frontiers is easily breached by the surreptitious transfer of meaningful amounts of money. Insurgencies depend on networks of smugglers conveying cash and weapons, and sometimes on moving new recruits. None of that can be accomplished without corruptly obtained cooperation and assistance.

Entire countries may be run as noxious, corrupt, criminal fiefs. Governance, from the presidency to the police, is often privatized, with criminalized elements operating under "unofficial license from the civil authority." In these cases, ruling groups focus on maximizing rent-seeking opportunities, eliminating pretensions of judicial independence, and neutering a once free media. Governance becomes entirely a "means of self-enrichment." Virtually "all heads of high-corruption societies may be regarded [as] 'organized criminals.'" They create structures that are designed "to maximize . . . predation." They employ violent enforcement as a facilitator of extensive, "utility-maximizing" corruption.[33] Countries as otherwise distinct as Guinea-Bissau and Uzbekistan belong in this category, but so do such disparate places as Cambodia, the Maldives, and Zimbabwe.

Corruption in one country both affects and infects neighboring nations and regional and global frameworks of order. Corrosive qualities of large-scale political and criminalized corruption have helped to stimulate the rise of such new disturbers of world peace as al-Qaeda in the Maghreb; al-Qaeda in the

Arabian Peninsula; the Islamic State in Syria, Libya, and Iraq; al-Shabaab in Somalia; and Boko Haram in Nigeria. The civil war and atrocities in Mali flowed from corrupt pursuits. So did mayhem in the Central African Republic and South Sudan stem more from avarice and the rewards of corruption than from ideological drivers. The long wars in Colombia are products of reactions to corruption as well as the attraction of drug-growing profits. Likewise, the murderous destruction of large parts of Afghanistan and Pakistan by all manner of insurgents reflects antagonism to official corruption as well as the pull of possible new rich rewards. Corruption drives terror just as the financial benefits of successful insurgencies fuel a perpetuated insurgency. Chayes makes a powerful, persuasive case, for example, that the strength of the Taliban in contemporary Afghanistan builds almost completely on the widespread perception that the state is an irredeemable plunderer intent on sucking the very life juices out of ordinary Afghans. "Afghan government corruption was manufacturing Taliban," she discovered. So did manifest northern Nigerian police corruption help to create Boko Haram. The overthrow of the Hosni Mubarak regime in Egypt in 2011 was in significant part a response to the "corrupt practices perpetrated by an upstart clique of crony capitalists who had captured key levers of the Egyptian state" and were slavishly advancing their own private agendas. "Acute government corruption" lies at the "root of some of the world's most dangerous and disruptive security challenges," she concludes, just as Protestantism arose in large part because of Rome's excessive exactions and luxurious lifestyles.[34]

Secretary Kerry, speaking about the battle against Boko Haram in Nigeria, al-Shabaab in Somalia, and ISIS in Syria and Iraq, forcefully affirmed these very conclusions in Sokoto, Nigeria, in 2016: "The fight against corruption has to be a global security priority of the first order. . . . Bribery, fraud, other forms of venality endanger everything that we hold dear, everything that you value. They feed organized crime. They gnaw away at nation-states. They take away the legitimacy of a nation-state. They contribute to human trafficking. They discourage honest and accountable investment, and they undermine entire communities. . . ."

> Corruption is not just a disgrace and a crime. It is also dangerous. There is nothing more demoralizing, more destructive, more disempowering to a citizen than the belief that the system is rigged against them, the belief that the system is designed to fail them, and that people in positions of power . . . are "crooks"—crooks who are embezzling the future of their own people.[35]

The old corruption persists alongside its novel forms and styles and enables the newer versions and methods to take hold. But the new corruption is sometimes managed by persons who need not be officials, who may be political party operatives, industrialists, traders, and the like, or who may run trans-national corporations. Militaries may act corruptly. So can UN special agencies, UN peace enforcers, regional and sub-regional officials, and more. Globalization in all of its ramifications has made it much easier than ever before to propagate corrupt pursuits, and for corrupt persons to profit from global insecurity, furtive transfers of weapons of mass destruction and conventional arms, sudden food shortages and imbalances, water and other scarcities, and flows of refugees and displaced persons.

Is Corruption Culturally Relative, Sometimes Functional?

In the definitional section above, a number of the commentators implicitly, if not explicitly, assumed that the less developed parts of the world either tolerated corrupt practices more than more modern societies or that their cultures viewed corrupt behavior as more normal than jurisdictions in the West. Yet, there is very little evidence that the nature and practices of corruption vary from culture to culture or that the corrupt act itself is viewed more permissively in some societies than in others. Nor is there much evidence that the presence of everyday grand and petty corruption helps any modern nation to function effectively—that corruption somehow appropriately greases the wheels of commerce, improves official service delivery, and incorporates outgroups into a political, social, or economic environment from which they would otherwise be excluded. Systematically cleansing an infected country of small-scale extortions helps just as much as jailing venal offenders to demonstrate that corruption is dysfunctional and an obstacle to economic and social growth.

Like Leys and Scott, following Furnivall, Klitgaard accepts that corrupt acts may be regarded differently from culture to culture and country to country.[36] Although the majority of nation-states and their peoples decry bribery, fraud, embezzlement, extortion and the like, there may be forms of corrupt behavior that are socially acceptable, even expected. If there are, anticorruption efforts may not be valid in all instances, or may be a Western imposition. Johnston goes farther, suggesting that such key definitional words as "public," "private," "abuse," and even "benefiting from" are contentious in some societies and ambiguously understood in most. How societies respond to the reform of corrupt practices, may, however, be even more significant than how they respond to corruption.[37] Others, such as Underkuffler, believe that corruption is a transgression of deeply held universal norms.[38] Although Johnston and Collier may be right to see varieties of corruption rather than a single "corruption," in the twenty-first century, amid the global village, no nation-state permits bribery, graft, and extortion; a diverse collection of states legally defines private, public, and abuse congruently; and, most important of all, their diverse citizenries have no difficulty knowing the many ways in which their rulers as well as the minor officials with whom they deal, day-to-day, are corrupt. As a pursuit, *pace* Collier, corruption is not culturally determined. "There in fact seems to be decisive moral disapproval of corruption in a majority of countries, including the most corrupt ones."[39] Moreover, in 2016, no groups of citizens anywhere demand more corruption, less transparency and accountability, or more rather than less compromised service delivery. Only multinational corporations with their eyes on a resource prize or wealthy, small countries seeking to host a global sporting championship favor outright covert bidding for services or results that (in theory) should be provided on the basis of merit.

This is not to overlook the traditional practice of gift-giving (in Africa and elsewhere) in gratitude for services rendered. Some consider doing so the fulfillment of a moral obligation, and not only when directed to social superiors. Greeting a chief in some parts of West Africa requires a gift, and in Asia and Africa (and the West) celebrations such as marriages are always accompanied by present-giving. So, too, are gifts given and payments made to ensure positive religious outcomes or auspicious prophecies. Well wishes may come in the form of other special arrangements or the production of evil-spirits-evading amulets. In the eyes of the less well educated, there may be no bright line between such practices and tipping a postal worker or a registry clerk for proper (or for any) service.

Furthermore, from the point of view of the persons with the power to give or deny favors, many African and some Asian officials accept an obligation to provide mutual assistance, to pull strings on behalf of kin and friends of friends. Those are positive social values. The giving of a gift presumes reciprocity and an enduring social bond. Often, if not always, these informal network ties trump formal requirements to serve impartially, even if to do so transgresses the law and oaths of service. A civil servant cannot, by this traditional logic, refuse to profit from any "juicy" postings and fail to "spread the benefit around" to his relatives. "To refuse to grab . . . an opportunity to make a fortune is to make oneself an object of reproach [and] mockery."[40]

Low-level corruption may once have emanated from such contradictions, from a need to satisfy group or lineage expectations despite legal strictures. But, if once that bright line and the distinction between a bribe and a gift were poorly illuminated, increasingly now in urban and middle-class Africa, Asia, and the Americas that demarcating border is fully appreciated, even if adhered to only indifferently.

So, too, do big men know that what in the past might have been their right to appropriate from supplicants and to use their traditional powers to despoil, now, in the twenty-first century, are abuses. Indeed, to "impute corruption in Africa to some kind of 'African culture' . . . would be . . . absurd."[41]

Olivier de Sardan makes the additional, important, point that what we observe in the postcolonial world as corrupt "in no way reflects on 'traditional' or pre-colonial culture. . . ." This is not to say that ancient cultural elements are not amalgamated syncretically with colonial habits and postindependence behaviors. But it is the process of modern state building that produces what we see today as developing world corruption.[42] Nevertheless, he admits that a few postcolonial African societies have not yet internalized a concept called the "public domain." They lack this tradition and a culture of "general interest," and have not acquired one despite years of colonial tutelage.[43]

The functionality argument flows from economic reasoning: corruption provides an understandable method of allocating scarce goods, like a birth certificate, a medical practitioner's permit, a driving license, public jobs, or even a massive construction contract. Who gets served in a bureaucrat's queue, in a clinic, or boarding an aircraft—who has priority—therefore depends on who values the service the most, especially at that time and place. Corrupt payments therefore are competitive and "efficient," and in that last sense supposedly socially as well as economically useful. Conceivably, too, corruption could serve a political purpose by defining and aggregating interests and aligning interest groups. It gives participation to minorities (if they can pay) and more fairly distributes perquisites and other state-controlled resources. Corruption buys representation for otherwise ethnically disenfranchised groups. It overcomes official systems that are clogged, unworkable, dense, and obstacles to progress and modernization. Leff and Huntington believe that a little corruption improves efficiency and enables growth.[44] Rigidities, outdated practices, inertia, and indifference may be overcome by facilitation inducements, by thus encouraging bureaucrats or even fire protection personnel to do their jobs. (Rose and Peiffer remind us that in communist societies, corruption was culturally acceptable if it made individual household outcomes better than they would have been by abiding by regulations.[45])

Marquette and Peiffer additionally suggest that corruption is the means through which many persons solve real problems that have deep social, structural, economic, and political roots. They echo Scott, and his conclusions from field work in Thailand, when they rightly indicate that for citizens, engaging in corrupt activities may be the best (or perhaps the only) way to gain access to services that are rightly theirs, but are inaccessible without cash: "no cash, no service." Marquette and Peiffer also tell us that politicians in weak states face problems of political mobilization and redistribution of benefits to constituents that are facilitated by corrupt rents. Functionally, corruption may enhance stability, especially in fractured societies.[46] But these are not new arguments, and as true as they are, they still are manifestations of inefficiency, distorted priorities, and political systems centralized upon narrow, rather generalized forms of leadership. There is no added functionality in dysfunctionality.

This functionality perspective argues that when governmental machinery grinds to a halt because of outdated work practices or old fashioned bureaucratic pursuits, illicit payments are necessary and justified to unclog systems that retard progress and block development. Perhaps in those many places where markets are imperfect and services inefficient, corruption helps to open the relevant machinery. Corrupt action theoretically could enable distortions to be avoided and development and modernization to proceed, as in Scott's Thailand, contemporary India, China before Xi Jinping's crusade, and in a host of African dictatorships or quasi-democracies. But contemporary citizens prefer to accomplish their daily business without exaction and, as their protest movements across the developing world demonstrate, are no longer content to purchase what is theirs by right.

From a national budgetary perspective, bribery (but not embezzlement) and some forms of graft substitute for acceptable levels of pay. As in Soviet times, a government may pretend to pay its public servants (and pay them too little) and they, in turn, either pretend to work, or they steal. Poorly paid policemen on many beats feel that extorting "contributions" from automobile drivers and passersby is their right, and their obligation to their families. Or public servants may not cheat just the random public; instead they clock in to work and then leave to drive taxis, run shops, or tend their fields.

None of these arguments is persuasive. For a time, it seemed that scholars might support the culturally relative argument, but given the outrage with which every nationality today reacts against reports of corruption or even rumors of corrupt activity, it is contrary to nearly all comparative findings to conclude that "bribery" is not "bribery" everywhere (as Noonan opined), and that "graft," "extortion," "nepotism," and other breaches of social norms are not universally regarded today with equal opprobrium everywhere, even in semi-literate or highly insulated societies. Some communities may be inured to practices by their national or local rulers that are corrupt, or feel powerless to stop them, as in such a place as Zimbabwe, but they never accept them or excuse them as being beneficial.

Nor does the efficiency argument make much analytical sense now that we know the extent to which corruption is socially and economically unproductive. Where corruption exists, politicians and public officials seek all manner of ways not to serve the public but to benefit themselves. An occasional corrupt act, in isolation, may be efficient, but routinized corruption never is, and is always distortive. Bidding in the form of corruption for scarce permits, like licenses, sounds economically reasonable, but not when the license is to practice medicine or open a clinic, or when that piece of paper with the necessary stamp allows a shoddy building to be erected (and later to collapse). Rather than efficiency, corruption produces inefficiencies by allocating scarce resources and services in ways that often fail to serve the public interest. In the most basic terms, too, a nation's budget is depleted if, with kickbacks, its exchequer pays more than the world market price for submarines, tanks, school textbooks, penitentiary food and supplies, medicines and sutures, and the like. When Somali insurgents pay border guards fifty shillings to cross into Kenya, and then attack quarry workers or university students, no efficiency is served. Likewise, the Afghan battle against the Taliban has for years been hindered by private gain at the expense of the official war effort, as a news report quoted: "There is a huge demoralization at all levels that derives from corruption, from nepotism, because a bunch of corrupt commanders are selling ammunition, selling the fuel."[47]

Scott argues that redistribution occurred in Thailand—that those who would not have been served by the ruling regime gained from their ability to bribe—and that Thai society thus functioned more successfully. But most of the time "redistribution" through corruption benefits ruling classes, impoverishing the already poor and disadvantaged, and skews rather than enhances income and other societal reward structures.

Scott also suggests that the lubricating varieties of corruption at least permit those who could not readily receive official services—because of their ethnicity or their class, or because of red tape—to obtain them, and to function more fully in their communities. This aligns with the argument that many societies traditionally tolerated, some even enshrined, the notion that good service deserved good tips, cash in envelopes, or other special returns. But paying money for speedy service also usually leads to ever upward spiraling rounds of extortion, with minor speed payments becoming routine and obligatory (and inefficient). Baker, a businessman with abundant experience over many decades in the developing world, is forthright: "Contrary to the views of some experts, bribery and corruption . . . do not have redeeming social value. . . . There is no good side to corruption."[48]

Klitgaard concludes that the existence of corruption adversely "enhances people's uncertainties about the likely benefits of their productive activities," creating pervasive moral decay and driving at least some citizens into less productive pursuits.[49] Societal cohesion suffers, as does overall output. Crime may rise correspondingly. Where rent seeking is the norm, honesty is a hollow virtue and a society becomes more and more anomic, citizens are cynical and disengaged, social trust is absent, and belief in the cohesive nature of the nation becomes forfeited. Such negative externalities cause safety and environmental crises, prolong civil wars (as in Afghanistan, northern Nigeria, and Uganda), retard educational advances, and endanger health (as in the Democratic Republic of Congo, Malawi, and Zimbabwe).

Moreover, no modern nation-state, and no known district within a modern polity, prefers corruption. That is, rulers and avaricious politicians and bureaucrats would likely opt to play by norms that give preference to rent seeking and that oblige ordinary persons to pay for the privilege of receiving what a regime or a government owes them. But nowhere do the citizens, as distinct from the overlords, cherish corrupt practices. They endure them, yes, and often shrug off the burden, but quietly and sometimes noisily rage against extortion, being solicited for bribes, and what they know or learn of venal corruption in high places. Citizens everywhere are positive about anticorruption initiatives, and about reducing corrupt behavior as rapidly and as fully as possible. "There is no culture or political regime without some claim to integrity and fairness in government," Mungiu-Pippidi believes, and "no culture on record values dishonesty and unfairness."[50]

Venal versus Petty Corruption

The corruption that most citizens experience, and which is most disruptive on a daily basis, is frequently called "petty," as distinct from "venal" or "grand" corruption. Petty corruption is annoying, but for people in a hurry or for people who don't want to stand in the same queue over and over, it is expedient. That is why petty corruption is often labeled "lubricating" or "speedy" corruption.[51] If everyone, public official and consumer alike, expects transactions to be lubricated with an inducement or a consideration, then petty corruption becomes customary, sustainable, and endurable. Daily activity may be punctuated by the necessity of making a series of small payments to procure permits or hospital treatments, or to evade a major fine for running a motor vehicle without headlights or brakes, but once such payments are firmly woven into the fabric of everyday society, life simply moves on. Petty corruption is inescapable; people accept it because they see no way to avoid it.[52]

That is the daily ordeal—the handing over of small sums for governmental acts that should by right be available freely. But even if such forms of corruption may be judged less developmentally destructive in aggregate than venal corruption, the total cost to society in cash and time wasted is still significant and damaging economically. The practice also undermines the very structure and trust of every society so riddled with routinized petty bribery.[53]

It is true, too, that as baleful as are the consequences of venal corruption, petty corruption equally rends a society's and a nation's sense of itself and its sense of moral legitimacy. Where there have been country and community micro-studies, as in Kenya, the toll on ordinary household incomes attributed to the cult of bribery is immense.[54] "The entire state has been captured to an extent by corrupt interests," reported Kenya's Transparency International director. "Nearly every institution of governance and service delivery is working in the interest of a small group of people who profit from it," as the bribes and other payments are passed up from the policeman to the police inspector, each taking a cut, and from the man or woman behind the permitting window upward to their bosses.[55] In Sierra Leone, offenders on trial routinely negotiate lighter sentences by paying fees to the clerks and magistrates. In its government hospitals, even after the Ebola epidemic, nurses' handbags become illicit pharmacies from which drugs are sold illegally to patients.[56] People have few options; there are no complaint mechanisms and, in practice, those who have to bribe have traditionally had few easy ways of protesting against such lubricating exactions.

In Nigeria, touts working in cahoots with personnel who slow down the other queues sell access to airport fast-track security channels for $10. Jordan Smith says that Nigerians pay extra for basic services but think of those bribes as "dash"—as a "sociable and socially acceptable" way of gaining favor and accomplishing tasks. Larger payments, say for gaining university admission or being allowed to use government vehicles privately, in Nigeria are regarded as extortionate and not petty.[57] In Cambodia, "it was a common sight to see truck drivers crossing the main bridge into the capital, Phnom Penh, throwing the equivalent of a dollar or two out their windows to police so they wouldn't be stopped and asked for a larger bribe." More distressing, parents in Phnom Penh gave money to their children to bribe teachers to "let them into classrooms each day."[58]

In Bangladesh, 71 percent of households surveyed reported that they paid bribes to obtain official services: "no money, no service." A further 27 percent said that they bribed "to avoid harassment and complications." More than 77 percent of Bangladeshi households also declared that they had paid a bribe to obtain a passport, 75 percent to appease the police, 61 percent to obtain a school place, 48 percent to influence judges, and 32 percent to obtain electrical power. Overall, 68 percent of households were victims of corruption in Dhaka and other Bangladeshi cities and towns in 2015, spending much more than these same households had spent on bribing officials in 2012, when another household survey was released.[59]

Indeed, not only are some forms of petty corruption extortionate across the globe, many such transactions humiliate and now and then actually cause physical harm. Sometimes, for example, when times are unusually tough, groups of policemen or thugs pretending to be police officers set up roadblocks on city streets and rural roads, use regulations or supposed regulations to find fault with vehicles or licenses, and demand payment immediately. A car's mandatory reflective triangle may be "the wrong size" or a mirror may be broken; a small payment, especially if it is dark and the police or pseudo-police are menacing, will suffice to permit the automobile or bus to proceed. Everywhere in much of Africa and Asia, even in some of the more rule-abiding countries, such harassment occurs nightly.

Venal corruption, by contrast, hardly interferes in these immediately destructive ways with the day-to-day activities of citizens. The latter go about their daily business, lubricating and providing speed payments whenever they absolutely need to, but not always appreciating or being immediately aware of how their rulers are enriching themselves. Venal corruption is the large-scale stealing of state resources—the conversion of the patrimony of the nation into private gain. The UN Office on Drugs and Crime, following Rose-Ackerman, calls "grand" corruption, venal by another name, "corruption that pervades the highest levels of a national government, leading to a broad erosion of confidence in good governance, the rule of law, and economic stability."[60] Venal corruption, therefore, is far more directly antagonistic to a nation's economic, social, and political progress than is petty corruption. There is a direct statistical connection, Uslaner shows, between venal or grand corruption and perceptions of inequality.[61]

In Nigeria, at least before the 2015 election, the entire machinery of state existed almost solely to "siphon off cash." At one point the speaker of the House of Representatives "borrowed" more than 18 billion naira ($90 million) from the House's allowance account. One consultant said, "Nigerian politics is one big bun-fight over . . . money."[62] In South Africa, frigates and aircraft were purchased from France and Sweden by a postindependence government; healthy percentages of each contract were negotiated to be paid to the ruling African National Congress (ANC) and its leaders, two of whom subsequently became president, and one of whom built himself a $25 million house with state funds (see also chapter 3).

President Robert Mugabe of Zimbabwe made sure in 2001 that the contract for the construction of his country's principal new international airport was awarded to a consortium led by his nephew. In Gabon, a close aide to former President Omar Bongo reported that Bongo generously sent "briefcases stuffed with millions in cash" to gain favor with French politicians (to protect Gabon and Bongo's rule). Bongo and his family (his son now rules after a rigged election) "shamelessly" looted its oil-derived wealth and stashed the proceeds in Paris. Burundi, one of the globe's poorer countries, was pillaged by a president who demanded cash for all cabinet and bureaucratic appointments and converted the procurement process into a vehicle for easy and profitable enrichment.[63] Tanzania's cabinet in 2014 and 2015 siphoned off very large amounts of cash from the national electricity monopoly's reserve fund, depositing the proceeds in private bank accounts overseas. Gulnara Karimova, daughter of the ruler of Uzbekistan, for a time controlled its mobile telephone licensing, ritzy restaurants, nightclubs, prostitution rings, and the trafficking of women, all of which obtained her illicit profits.[64]

Oil and gas riches are the big distorters of African (and global) economies. Wealth of that kind, seemingly obtained without much of a struggle or any productive efforts on the part of ruling cliques, has occasioned graft on a scale dwarfing most other venal and certainly all forms of petty corruption combined. Without so much as lifting an entrepreneurial finger, the jurisdictions in which oil and gas have been found and exploited have embraced their unexpected bonanzas and found innumerable clever ways to channel petro and gas dollars into more private than national accounts. In Angola, Africa's largest exporter of oil along with Nigeria, President José Eduardo dos Santos and the men and women (including a daughter) around him have systematically pocketed $3 billion to $4 billion a year; over the last two decades very little of that wealth has trickled down to the least well-off Angolans. In tiny Equatorial Guinea, where oil and gas are also abundant, President Teodoro Obiang Nguema Mbasogo and his family regularly accrue about $3 billion a year while the welfare of the country's inhabitants is mostly neglected. One international nongovernmental organization (NGO) called Equatorial Guinea callously corrupt.[65] In Zimbabwe, the country's unexpected diamond wealth was distributed to consortia controlled by the first lady, the security chiefs, and the former minister of defense and current vice president, with hardly any royalties arriving in the national treasury. Later, when the trove of alluvial diamonds was exhausted and Grace Mugabe, the first lady, sought new plunder, she held an elaborate birthday party and compelled attendance, but at steep prices, unwittingly reminding connoisseurs of corruption of the many methods of flouting power employed by Tunisian President Ben Ali's second wife. A fourteenth century writer warned English King Edward III about the courtiers who hungered for wealth: "The covetous are always grasping . . . and are never sated . . . the more they possess the more they desire."[66] Grace Mugabe is known colloquially among the members of the Zimbabwe cabinet as "grasping Grace."

Abundant opportunities exist in every developing and even some developed countries for those who are politically or bureaucratically influential to abuse their public positions for immense private gain, sometimes over and over. Greed never stops at the edge of a presidential palace or a prime ministerial residence. And it is this high level of venal corruption that saps a nation's resources, diverts tax and royalty revenues from national needs to personal pockets (and ultimately to bolt holes overseas), and robs ordinary citizens of schooling prospects and medical supplies. It also facilitates unnecessary tragedies; witness the shoddily constructed blocks of flats in Kathmandu that collapsed in an earthquake, the firetraps of Dhaka that immolated textile workers, and the lives lost in Tianjin when improperly impounded chemicals exploded. In Alexandria, Egypt, a supervising state engineer took payoffs to favor particular contractors, and then, for comparatively paltry sums, "he'd let them use cheap copper wire for electrical installations, or a shoddy Chinese water pump, instead of the more expensive Japanese one that was budgeted."[67]

It is impossible to quantify overall or country by country how much of a nation's gross domestic product is diverted by petty and venal corruption. In aggregate, the in-country amounts of venal corruption presumably vastly overwhelm what is collected at the local level through petty corruption. It is also a fundamental assumption in the literature that venal corruption does far more damage to a state economically than does petty corruption, especially if construction contracts are awarded to substandard bidders, if other official procurements never materialize, if the textbooks purchased by a Malawian minister of education could not be used for classroom teaching and could not be replaced, if the expensive presidential jet aircraft hardly ever flies because of maintenance issues, and if bridges collapse because of shoddily manufactured concrete. In some cases, the pursuit of corrupt gains has led to widespread hunger; to the onset of debilitating diseases, like Ebola, and an inability to pursue them vigorously; and to diminished life chances.

Incoming President Muhammadu Buhari of Nigeria asserted in mid-2015 that Nigerian governments and officials had stolen $150 billion from the Nigerian people over the previous ten years. Large overseas loans were diverted away from official projects into private hands. He asked President Obama of the United States to help Nigeria find and repatriate from overseas the immense amounts that had been pilfered from the national coffers. Buhari said that the particularly difficult part of his new reforms would be ending a "crooked culture" deeply engrained in many government departments.[68]

Big-time corruption, Olivier de Sardan contends, in terms of scale, social space, and type of protagonist, has nothing in common with petty corruption. In venal corruption, political aristocracies drain public resources with much greater economic consequences than does the whole of petty corruption. Venal corruption is practiced by hidden mechanisms "according to procedures that are impervious to the non-initiated."[69]

Studies show that together, venal and petty corruption reduce average annual GDP attainments by at least 1 percent.[70] Thus the growth in employment and the reduction in poverty that African and Asian nations desperately need are often swallowed up by thefts from the public treasury, over-priced contracts that yield kickbacks more than results for the people, and a pervasive criminalization of the offices and functions of the state. In the process of gaining rents rather than productive income-generating activity, priorities are distorted, the foreign direct investment that is so desperately needed flees, and government legitimacy is diminished and undermined. The wages of corruption ultimately deprive citizens of what is rightly theirs.

Ethical Universalism

Corrupt practices become less common as communities transition from accustomed patrimonial and particularist modes of operation punctuated by acquisitiveness and zero-sum mentalities toward an inculcation of ethical universalism. Since corruption, behaviorally, is a default allocational activity that drives much of the developing world and parts of the developed world, the adoption of stronger and stronger rule-of-law regimes, coupled with successful investigations and prosecutions, potentially helps to reduce societal levels of corruption. But, in order to shift the mindset of a nation-state from accepting the inevitability of corruption as a pervasive informal practice to regarding incidents of corruption as disruptive normative breaches, the concept of ethical universalism must gradually replace what Banfield long ago termed "amoral familism." The latter is a lack of public spiritedness, a prevailing condition when individuals "maximize the material, short-run advantage of the nuclear family . . . and assume that all others will do likewise."[71] Amoral familists are culture-bound (as in so many developing societies) to behave corruptly on behalf of their close networks. The major movement toward ethical universalism, the antithesis of amoral familism, takes place as political cultures evolve, as active political will guides a society or a country toward an acceptance of those new values.

Ethical universalism presumes that all inhabitants of a jurisdiction will be treated fairly, equally, and tolerantly—that minorities are entitled to the same privileges and opportunities as majorities, and that groups large and small can anticipate receiving similar rights and privileges. Particularism, the lot of too many of the globe's citizens, treats individuals and groups differently, not congruently. Corruption goes hand in glove with particularism, as an enabler and as a motivator.

Embracing a collective good such as ethical universalism comes not after a widespread epiphany or in answer to evangelical fervor. Rather, where ethical universalism has arisen as a rejection of corrupt behavior, it has often followed enhanced notions of societal and individual self-interest. In the Nordic and other exceptional countries, the transition from accepting to forbidding corruption as a community value took centuries (see chapter 7). This transition built upon a growing awareness of public and personal integrity, strengthened rules of law, serious prosecutions and convictions, and a growing official intolerance of corruption. But a reformation in behavior also depended on increasing levels of civic participation (through democratic elections and other means) and educational attainments and greater involvement of whole populations in setting and improving rules, in checking executive and legislative actions, and in demanding better performance of bureaucrats and all public servants. This reformation also relied upon a growing sense of the value of judicial probity.

In the modern era (see chapter 3), this altering of norms has been compressed into a matter of decades, not centuries. The leaders of Hong Kong and Singapore, among other once wildly corrupt entities, employed the usual sticks of prosecution and punishment to make corruption less profitable and much more risky. However, using similar but different methods, they also emphasized how corruption was societally disruptive and collectively harmful, and how it was a major obstacle to national prosperity and modernity. The leaderships of both jurisdictions educated and acculturated their citizenries to reject participation in corruption. In a matter of decades, a new sense of ethical universalism guided both polities, as it did and has in much of the rest of the modern, developed world and in scattered pockets in the developing world.[72]

Corruption as an informal operating code within a nation-state in today's world is replaced by ethical universalism when rulers, ruling classes, and the functioning of the postcorrupt state are perceived as legitimate. This legitimacy is accompanied by a generalized belief in the fundamental equity of the regime of governance that embodies and is practiced by the state, and by a widespread acceptance that intolerance of corruption is valued more than preferments obtained by gifts or influence. This fundamental legitimacy cannot occur, naturally, if the state is abusive and corrupt. Satisfying the self-interest of individuals directly and openly obviates speed payments, lubrication, procurement through the side door, and "pay for play" kickbacks for access to contract awards. Efficiency, impartiality, social trust, and transparency accompany this "practical ethic of the public services," the benefit thereof for all to see individually and collectively.[73]

That amounts to an embrace of a norm of ethical universalism. "Ethical universalism becomes an institution . . . rather than a mere ideology . . . when a significant part of society shares the belief in the superiority of ethical universalism over particularism."[74] That is how enduring norms are made.

The broad socialization of the norm of ethical universalism is the ultimate goal of all anticorruption crusades. That is, the only sustainable method of curbing corruption relies on altering societal modes of behavior and expectation. Dramatically changing the incentive structure and shifting the expectations of ruling elites are key components of this shift; since societal expectations are greatly influenced by the behavior of those on top, replacing personal profit with an ethic of service is critical in spreading the norm of ethical universalism.

Hong Kong, Singapore, Botswana, Cape Verde, Mauritius, and Rwanda all show that it is not cultural determinism that prevents corruption so much as it is the development (gradual in the older democracies, rather abruptly in the newer states) of a new political culture of ethical universalism. New institutions are welcome, as are improved constraints, but to remove corrupt practices (or make them a less common pursuit) attitudes must be altered and a new positive norm substituted for older modes of behavior.

Criminal Enterprises and Clusters of Corruption

Developing world corruption flourishes in distinct political and economic environments; controlling corruption depends on a full appreciation of the varieties of corruption. Johnston, a strong advocate of distinguishing different syndromes or clusters of corrupt behavior, asserts that sustainable reform depends on an appreciation of how each mechanism of corruption within the categories ("the ideal types") promotes or inhibits meaningful and lasting change. Open, legitimate societies with autonomous bureaucracies, the democracies—those countries that Johnston labels Influence Market States— usually combine robust political parties with various forms of influence- peddling amid a legalization of the role of wealth in politics and political life. Singapore and the United States are among the strong polities in this cluster.

In Elite Cartels, which are market economies and mostly open political systems, leaders collude behind a façade of competition and colonize and control the apparatus of the state and much of its economy. Johnston places South Korea and Botswana among the Elite Cartel states, along with Italy, Mexico, and Paraguay at earlier moments in their histories. Enhancing transparency in these kinds of states depends on the rise of political competition and the empowering of civil society. Elite Cartel countries "have not so much controlled corruption as found a way to withstand its effects for a time."[75]

In characteristic Oligarch and Clan societies, the elites are "insecure." They construct bases of personal support from which to exploit the state and the economy, and thereafter protect their gains "by any means necessary." This describes the criminalized post-Soviet Russian and Central Asian polities, as per Legvold, and the Philippines and Mexico, where ruling elites use violence and other nefarious methods to assert themselves in states with weak institutions. "Corrupt deals proliferate but lack guarantors, making them disruptive, unpredictable, and prone to violence."[76] Calling for strengthened political will as a remedy in such places is unrealistic and risky; institutions hardly exist that can be built up, much less reinforced.

Official impunity reigns in Official Mogul societies. Institutions are very weak, popular participation in political decision-making is highly limited and manipulated, the civic space is largely closed, popular inertia or at least defeatism is apparent, and local moguls or magnates specialize in extracting rents from whatever resources are available and within reach. It is in such nation- states that outside pressure may prove crucial, permitting successful reformers to rise. Likewise, in such contexts, blocking the export of corrupt cash to safe hiding places overseas is an easy and excellent option. Sometimes, too, new official moguls have replaced old official moguls, and, as in contemporary China, one ruling class removes an earlier cadre of corrupt players and takes back their ill-gotten gains (see chapter 8). But corruption may still survive in new ruling hands and perpetuate its destructive quality in a society long inured, as most have been, to large-scale forms of corruption.

These last two categories of nation-state facilitate criminality. What Chayes calls a Malign Actor Network, orchestrates, from the top (the head of state) down, an enterprise that behaves criminally to extract the riches of the nation and to transfer it to a hierarchy of individuals intent on and motivated from above to keep cash ascending from peasants and workers to middle managers and on to military and political elites, all reporting to and being protected by the national chief executive.[77] When the entire bureaucratic and security apparatuses of a state exist primarily to extort and not to serve, and to facilitate all manner of brigandage, then a nation-state can be considered both thoroughly corrupt *and* criminalized, as in Afghanistan, Azerbaijan, Bulgaria, Equatorial Guinea, Guinea-Bissau, Guatemala, Honduras, the old Myanmar (Burma), Romania, Russia, Tajikistan, the old Tunisia, Uzbekistan, and Zimbabwe.

Consider, too, Cambodia, where massive strong man and Prime Minister Hun Sen has been in charge since 1985, despite losing an election in 1993. He has relied on brutality and intimidation to remain in power. Meanwhile, twenty-one of his close family relatives, especially his eldest daughter, control or have major stakes in 114 local companies or foreign subsidiaries (many American) worth at least $200 million. They have secured distribution rights to cell phones and other major consumer goods and clearly have their tentacles into all sectors of the Cambodian economy. According to Global Witness, an investigative NGO, Hun Sen's family holdings "span the majority of Cambodia's most lucrative business sectors as well as those characterized by high levels of corruption."[78]

Collapsing corruption in these criminalized places implies nothing less than the kind of regime change that revolutionized Georgia after 2002 or Tunisia after 2011. Altering institutional arrangements will prove insufficient remedies for such extreme (and for most other) cases of kleptocratic state capture. "In kleptocracies risk is nationalized and rewards are privatized."[79]

Another optic through which to view these criminal and criminalized states, where various orders of venal corruption are functionally integral and deeply embedded, is to regard them as competitive particularists. That designation acknowledges that a goodly number of the criminal and criminalized entities hold regular sham elections. "Competitive particularism," Mungiu-Pippidi reminds us, "is characterized by the coexistence of rulers spoiling the state despite some form of institutionalized pluralism. . . ." That is, these kinds of polities thrive off corruption but pretend to operate as if they were "normal" nations. They honor rule of law in the breach and focus on enriching the few rather than serving the many. "The social struggle . . . is to belong to the privileged group rather than to challenge the rules of the game."[80] These are predatory entities, and they display nearly all of the characteristics of very weak or failed states.[81] These kinds of polities rank, furthermore, at the bottom of the various scales of corruption (see chapter 2); they are perceived as rampantly corrupt and have, in recent years, been the locales of serious forms of protest.

Understanding Corruption

Globally, more countries harbor at least medium levels of corruption than exhibit little corruption. Employing the rough guidelines of the Corruption Perceptions Index and the World Bank's Control of Corruption Indicator, that means that of 168 nations ranked by the first and 212 by the second, the first fifty on both lists are arguably considered minimally corrupt, the next fifty somewhat corrupt, and the final seventy-five or more fully corrupt. Botswana, ranked 28th in 2015, is thus corrupt only a little; Ghana, in 56th place, is rather but not wildly corrupt; and Nigeria, 135th, is thoroughly corrupt. (These rankings are all on the CPI.)

A key question is why in but a comparatively few places is there so little corruption, not why there is so much corruption everywhere else. This is not to suggest that corruption is the new normal as it may well have been the old normal. Furnivall, in examining Burma in the 1930s and 1940s under British administration, indicates that the colonial administration there, in India, and he could also have said in Singapore and Hong Kong, not to mention throughout Africa, tolerated practices which were corrupt but which it believed (falsely) were culturally approved, even expected.[82] But even if corrupt behavior transgresses the law everywhere, in many jurisdictions it is difficult to conclude serious, wealth-providing, business transactions without promising special consideration to those who have it within their power as responsible ministers or government officials to confirm or deny such privileges. Likewise, at the lubricating or petty level, minor officials guard access. Expediency suggests that they should be assisted or encouraged by a gift.

Societally, corruption is clearly harmful. It distorts priorities, produces manifest class and personal inequalities, impedes economic growth, and often creates direct harm (physicians without proper licenses, fire-trap factories without safe exits, roads that crumble, high-speed railways that cause derailments, the proliferation of drug- and people-smuggling and gun-running, and the illicit transfers of fissionable material).[83] Corruption drives people away from their home societies, inducing migrancy, brain drain, and, in very recent times, huge flows of people from corrupted (and impoverished) zones such as West Africa and the Horn of Africa across the Sahara desert and then the Mediterranean Sea to Europe, there joining refugees from insecure sections of the Middle East. But those who ask why corruption persists despite its clear harms fail to appreciate how rational choice dictates a scramble for corrupt rewards. If corruption seems to be the prevailing national or regional norm—if everyone is doing it, why not? For many, that is sufficient moral justification.

Some suggest that the regular workings of price and market mechanisms should eliminate corruption. If a public position offers bribe revenue, Jain asks, "Why would . . . competition not lower the wages for the job [so that] corruption . . . would become unprofitable?"[84] Demand is high and supply is limited and controlled. Perfect competition is impossible, moreover, without transparency, knowledge, and a market that is accessible to all. In most settings and circumstances, corruption takes place in casino-like surroundings where the house controls the odds.

For a long time, the very best scholars of corruption framed that malady as a persistent principal-agent dilemma where the agent—the person behind the window, the permitting authority, the police persons at the barrier, the judge who could decide to acquit—betrayed the supposedly benevolent principal representing the public interest. When the administrators of the Danish king disloyally accepted bribes, all he had to do in theory to eliminate corruption was to locate those deceivers (his agents) and oust them. Likewise, in a modern setting, the seeking and creating of the right kinds of safeguards supposedly helps to prevent agencies and individuals from behaving badly. All the principal has to do is to curb the nefarious instincts of his agents and then all will be well. Corruption could be compelled to disappear, in other words, if it could be disincentivized—"by fixing the incentive structure of the institutional setting within which it occurs."[85] The discretion of public officials may also be limited, and a number of other institutional reforms introduced.[86] But those and many other clever administrative ways of constraining agents has not done much to alter behavior. Corrupt practices persist and are growing despite such endeavors. Indeed, in those many jurisdictions with high levels of corruption, wholesale societal reorientations are necessary, not simply a re-education of agents.

Even if the principal were not a ruler or a leader to whom the agent owed fealty, and all citizens acting together were considered for theoretical purposes the principal whose communal interests the agents were subverting, the proposition still works incompletely. The principal may be corrupt and may not choose to act in the public good. Further, defining the precise public interest of an inchoate citizenry is difficult, especially in those states that are not yet nations and that are ethnically fractured. Corruption, after all, rewards certain elites and not others, and it often benefits privileged minorities over majorities or other minorities. Corruption is unfair, consciously discriminatory, and permits persons holding power (large or small) to decide without competition, and through covert considerations, who gets what he or she wants or needs.

True, the misbehaving agents, when they choose to solicit bribes and so on, defy the norm of ethical universalism that should guide all of us and all societies.[87] Ethical universalism could be the supreme principle. The least corrupt contemporary societies have come to abide by the principles of ethical universalism after earlier eras when they did or could not. Thus, it is the transition from universal avarice to ethical universalism that marks the shift over time from mostly corrupt to mostly not corrupt. The principal and agents do not change so much as the society as a whole; they come to regard corrupt practices as inefficient and unacceptable (and shame-making). Everyone involved becomes conditioned over time to a prevailing norm that eschews corruption except in (mostly) rare instances. That is the goal of anticorruption efforts—to transform wholly the fundamental ways in which a society deeply regards the pursuit of corrupt gains as unacceptable or aberrant. New political cultures are required.

More democracy might cleanse a corrupt system on its own, but many democratic states are rife with corruption, and most of the available research shows that improved governance (especially strengthened rules of law and accountability) matters more than fair and frequent elections in curbing corrupt tendencies. Although more of the world's nations embrace democratic ideals in this century than in the last, there is no less corruption now than before. More democracy need not mean less corruption. Likewise, improved GDP per capita does not reliably lead to reduced corruption. Angola, Equatorial Guinea, and many other oil exporters have experienced great rises in gross domestic product in this century without corrupt practices becoming any less odious or index scores improving. Improvements in equality are much more indicative; fairness and strengthened approaches to ethical universalism translate into higher (better) ratings. Nigerian voters in 2015 ousted President Goodluck Jonathan in part because his regime had behaved particularistically and unfairly.[88]

What is necessary to reduce corruption (as we shall see in chapter 8) are long-term efforts on the part of leaders (principals), electorates, independent judiciaries, and legislators to persuade entire citizenries that they are better off without the scourge of corruption and that the state will serve them effectively and well without lubrication. Agents are less the problem than the prevailing ethos within which they serve, and their perceptions of where and how rewards will be richest, as well as the risks of taking rewards. Certain public positions are sought (as they were in Europe in earlier centuries) because they provide the best opportunities for persons with entrepreneurial tendencies.

Another aspect of the principal agent problem is that most principals are themselves often enemies of ethical universalism. There are few "principled principals."[89] Political and other ruling elites "are often the ones who stand to gain the most from rents in a corrupt system." They obviously would have little incentive to alter the system.[90] That is, many principals from heads of state on down the prevailing governmental hierarchies come to office wanting a zero-sum share. From a rational choice perspective, they are self-interest maximizers. It is their turn "to eat." Thus, much of the odious corruption of twenty-first-century Africa is leader-determined if not leader-led. The huge sums of cash (in the billions of dollars) stored abroad by Zaire's Mobutu Sese Seko, Nigeria's Sani Abacha, Kenya's Daniel arap Moi, and others hardly came about by accident. With such corrupt principals, the national interests of the state and its citizens receive short shrift. For them, by no means a tiny minority, ethical universalism hardly exists as a useful concept.

Rothstein, one of the most thoughtful of the new scholars of corruption, proposes along with several influential other researchers to conceptualize and understand corruption as a collective action problem.[91] Where it exists, corruption is an informal institution that feeds off and reinforces itself. Benevolent individual behavior by a single or several agents rarely makes a difference. Everyone in the game (principals, agents, clients, citizens) expects it to continue and operates knowing its informal rules. If an economy has a high average level of corruption, it is bound to move "toward the high-corruption stable equilibrium."[92] The collective can only rid itself of corruption when and if new leaders impose ethical universalism, there is a gradual widespread public acceptance of and socialization to ethical universalism over time, and procedures and institutions are developed that provide credible hints that corrupt behavior is no longer normal. To achieve this transformation, there must be a spread of trust or social capital. There must also be a belief that citizens individually and collectively can achieve their goals and fulfill their lives without enabling or indulging in corrupt pursuits. "We need a population of autonomous and critical citizens capable of collective action, not a mass of citizens merely conforming to the corrupt rules of the game."[93]

For Rothstein and others, because systemic corruption is a collective action problem, not primarily a principal-agent issue, to reduce or eradicate it requires strikingly new solutions. There are too few principled principals, too little political will, and too many who benefit directly or indirectly, actively and passively, from an ethos permissive of corruption. Too many anticorruption regimes become themselves entangled in "the very corrupt networks that they were meant to fight."[94] The principals cannot or refuse to control the actions of agents, investigation and prosecution efforts are minimal, and voters even re-elect politicians whom they know to be corrupt.

Corruption becomes embedded in a society when it is common and is the default amoral norm. When being corrupt is the expected behavior, deviating and refusing bribes, refusing kickbacks, and refraining from assisting kin is difficult, even irrational. "Public officials who refuse to take advantage of their positions to enrich themselves are regarded as stupid and may even face ridicule." Moreover, as Persson et al. indicate, the costs of being honest in corrupt settings are high, since behaving ethically "will not change the game."[95] This is the same sentiment that was expressed at the beginning of this chapter: If everybody is partaking, why not me? To break the grip of such a collective vise, everyone engaging in systemic corruption would have to trust that every other corrupt principal would simultaneously cease being "on the take"—a perilous undertaking, but one that is achieved by strong leaders who can impose their will or who can gradually inculcate a move away from corruption. Breaking out of the collective "social trap" of corruption requires committed leadership and problem-solving of a high order (as discussed in chapters 8 and 10). Leaders can dismantle the trap or destroy the trap—create a revolutionary "big bang"—that sets a moral order for principals and thus makes probity in public office a collective good.[96] Good institutions can assist, and newly enabled and aroused middle classes can insist on new institutions, but only after those citizens, public officials, and corporate executives who are the collective problems have their actions redirected.

The tough task of anticorruption reform efforts is to show a society that corruption is no longer an acceptable collective pursuit. That is, by disrupting the informal communal network that hitherto accepted corruption as a fact of life, by cleansing governmental hierarchies from the top down of corrupt and corrupted persons, by relentlessly pursuing and prosecuting major and minor offenders, by showing cynical citizens that official services can be obtained speedily and without service charges, by emphasizing transparency and accountability (the last two being principal-agent betterments), and by educating a broad public to expect and demand good governance, reforming regimes can reduce, sometimes greatly reduce, the capture of their nation-states by the destructive forces of corruption. But to accomplish such tough tasks—to disrupt corrupt equilibria (which are at the root of the collective action problem)—takes high orders of political will and committed, visionary, leadership. It cannot rely on external inducements. Fortunately, and as later chapters in this book demonstrate, dramatic shifts from wide-open corruption to societal integrity have occurred in the past and in modern times. The lessons of those accomplishments can be transferred elsewhere to transform developing countries. That is a message of this book.

Political Will

Rarely do effective, sustainable, remedial actions against the scourge of corruption occur without the exercise of consummate political will on the part of a national or regional political chief executive. As will be shown in the remainder of this volume, many differences in outcomes, from positive to negative, depend on whether persons in positions of political power were and are ready to commit themselves to pursuing politically unpopular, even danger-ous, acts—exercising political will on behalf of one or another important ideal.

Critics say with some validity that "'political will' is commonly used as a catch-all concept, the meaning of which is . . . vague."[97] But, in what follows, "political will" is defined as a specific core quality that leaders in charge of countries or regions employ to attempt to transform existing political cul-tures—to try to inculcate new, uplifting norms. Political will is the exercise of political leadership to influence, direct, or alter public choice outcomes within particular contextual situations. Leaders mobilize governments or followers to pursue particular policy directions that, if consummated, dramatically alter the direction and thrust of governmental accomplishments. So there is a col-lective political will. But political will ultimately is employed by a leader (or a leadership) on behalf of, and as a guide to, that national collective will.

Three influential critics, however, prefer that political will should more properly be considered a governmental, not a personal, attribute. "We argue against an approach that equates political will with individual volition," they say, believing instead that a leader's personal policy proclivities and "willing-ness to act do not constitute 'political will.'" Only dictators, they say, can force their preferences on entire polities. But this argument misses the point. As they themselves write, political will involves "aggregating preferences in such a way that it is meaningful for outcomes in political processes."[98] Only a politi-cal leader or leaders can guide a government or a nation of citizens in thus aggregating preferences. Someone (and associates and a cohort) has to dem-onstrate the capacity to show direction and attempt to mobilize peoples be-hind new ideas. That is among the qualities of leadership.[99] The definition offered by Post and her coauthors, in fact, puts a leader at the center of any action: she arouses "committed support among key decision makers for a par-ticular policy solution to a particular problem."[100] Exactly.

Brinkerhoff suggests a definition that is consonant with Post, and also with the thrust of this section. Political will is "the intent of societal actors to attack the manifestations and causes of corruption in an effort to reduce or eliminate them." Further, it is the "commitment of actors to undertake actions to achieve . . . anticorruption policies." Successful anticorruption actions de-pend, he also says, on political will manifested by elected or appointed lead-ers—"the political will to initiate the fight against corruption . . . and to sustain the battle over time."[101] Brinkerhoff's actors and leaders are, in his formula-tion, "reformers" and "reform teams." Open democratic regimes more easily produce such key actors with political will.

Someone has to motivate the actors. Kpundeh's approach is similar to that of Brinkerhoff: "Political will . . . refers to the demonstrated credible intent of political actors (elected or appointed leaders, civil society watchdogs, stake-holder groups, etc.) to attack perceived causes or effects of corruption at a systemic level. It is a critical starting point for sustainable and effective anti-corruption strategies and programmes."[102]

Consummate transformative political leaders articulate an enlightened vision of how they might deliver better human outcomes. They demonstrate a determination to pursue specific policy goals beneficial to the largest number of citizens. That is political will. As Nelson Mandela told a potentially riotous assembly of supporters in an embattled town near Johannesburg, "Listen to me . . . I am your leader [and] I am going to give you leadership." Mandela was exercising political will—a determination to do what was right in his eyes and to instruct his followers appropriately. "As long as I am your leader, I will tell you, always, when you are wrong."[103] In contrast, Thabo Mbeki, who followed Mandela as president of South Africa, failed on several critical occasions to exercise political will. Mbeki refused to lead his country and Africa against HIV/AIDS. Equally, Mbeki passed up a golden opportunity to quell creeping (now rampant) corruption in his country about 2002 when many of his ruling party's provincial heads were just starting to feed openly at the public table. Mbeki failed South Africa and failed the battle against corruption by forfeiting the use of political will then, and over and over since, as his and President Jacob Zuma's colleagues have indulged themselves.

Persson and Sjöstedt rightly and powerfully caution against such simplistic post hoc analyses of failures to exercise political will. They argue against mere voluntarism as an explanatory variable, preferring to view at least some (if not most) failures of political will and failures of responsible leadership as contextual—as the product of particular bundles of political circumstance, and of incentives skewed against positive leadership. Leaders may lack the ability rather than the will to oppose corruption and pursue a reform agenda.

The same authors suggest that a lack of political will may more properly be diagnosed as either a moral hazard problem or a result of adverse selection. Leaders who refuse to pursue reforms (even if they previously pledged to do so) have greater incentives to "engage in moral hazard." Moreover, "bad leaders manage to come to power due to adverse selection."[104] The authors then indicate that positive political will can only be exercised in states that are legitimate and that have a sense of a shared social contract. (Adverse selection is more likely in states lacking social contracts.) In other words, illegitimate states with deficient social contracts between rulers and the governed rarely permit leaders to exercise political will. The context prevents responsible leadership. Thus, their argument echoes our earlier insistence that the expression of political will—of transformative leadership—emanates from and depends upon political leaders or civil society reformers creating or remaking a positive political culture. That exercise of political will, especially in pre-institutional societies, forges new social contracts and establishes the legitimacy of a state or a government.

Voluntarism need not be the issue. Some modern leaders choose unconventional paths, where a conventional path in much of the world would lead to self-enrichment, the embrace of grand corruption, and the condoning of widespread plunder. Moreover, for many heads of state and heads of government, refusing to exercise a reforming political will has a purpose: those leaders think that they need to provide opportunities to loot—patrimonial privileges—for their associates and their followers in order to secure their own tenure and authority. They believe that they have little choice, whereas the unconventional leader—the leader capable of exercising positive political will—analyzes her or his options rather differently. This leader is not merely "conditioned by underlying social contracts" but in fact (contrary to Persson and Sjöstedt) does have an ability to choose policy paths that shape the social contract.[105]

Exercising political will means leadership from in front, not from behind. It means diagnosing societal ills and articulating solutions that, after careful analysis and broad explanation, can be sold to skeptical publics and opponents. Political will is active, not passive, leadership. Often it is bold and courageous, politically risky. It puts a leader at any level squarely behind public policy choices that may not immediately be popular, may be difficult to accomplish, and may ultimately fail. Exercising political will exposes vulnerabilities.

To enunciate a novel policy direction for a state or a region is one thing. But to put the full weight of high public office or to stake the legitimacy of a presidency or a premiership on an unproven proposition for societal reconfiguration, and to threaten established interest groups in such a manner, constitutes the essence of political will. Additionally, political will encompasses resolve. The national or regional leader telegraphs a determination to do everything within her power to bring about significant change, say to revamp American voting rights laws in the 1960s or to introduce single payer health insurance and a national pension plan in Canada, also in the 1960s.

Expressing what amounts to political will is never enough, however. No amount of bluster and exhortation can translate a change agenda into an acceptable and operational national program. The goals of an energetic political will are only achieved as a result of deep teaching, committed persuasion, and the effective mobilization of large arrays of peoples behind a clearly defined and intelligible project attractive to whole communities and legions of voters. Post et al. are right to emphasize common commitment (and a common or at least consensus agreement as to the nature of a problem, such as gun violence) as key components of effective political will. Accountability to an electorate is also critical. "Accountability mechanisms facilitate a bottom-up convergence of public opinion and political will, which is very different from the top-down 'convergence' sometimes observed in authoritarian regimes."[106]

"Political will" is shorthand for a leader's full attention, for her full backing of a set of actions that might threaten the financial or other interests of important stakeholders or introduce the kinds of societal improvements that reduce the prerogatives of key groups. Political will also means that a leader sets standards, adheres to them, and attempts by a variety of means to overcome opposition. Further, political will means that an innovative leader fully supports those of her subordinates who are attempting to advance her goals.

President Lincoln's Gettysburg Address was a forceful statement conveying political will. It was a beacon of purpose that mobilized northerners behind antislavery goals and the Union. President Wilson was determined to create world peace and to mobilize Americans behind his well-developed political will. But illness intervened before he could make his case convincingly to the people and overcome opposition in Congress.

Specifically with regard to corruption in America, President Theodore Roosevelt demonstrated consummate political will when he, a pioneer in this realm, consciously began to alter the United States' then prevalent political culture. Railing against personal indulgences and political felonies, he declared that corruption struck "at the foundation of all law." Bribers, he boomed, were worse than thieves, for thieves robbed individuals but corrupt officials plundered cities and states. They "assassinate[d]" the commonwealth and obliterated the government of the people.[107]

Roosevelt's administration successfully prosecuted the first federal senators ever to be jailed for taking bribes and abusing their office. He decisively shifted the national perspective on corruption. Roosevelt further promoted the Tillman Act of 1907, which prohibited corporations from contributing to political campaigns. Passage of the Federal Corrupt Practices Act, which limited party and candidate spending in all Senate races, followed in 1910. These Progressive Era reforms, initiated and forcefully promoted by Roosevelt, long governed the manner in which American elections, and election spending, were organized and controlled. His exercise of political will reoriented American political culture as it contemplated and came to disdain corruption.

As we shall soon see, wherever in the modern world success has accompanied anticorruption crusades, political will has been central to accomplishing such disruptive policies. Paul Kagame, Seretse Khama, Lee Kuan Yew, and others in this arena exercised political will in consummate ways that were foreign to so many of their fellow political leaders in the developing world. They were among the successful anticorrupters. And it is the crafting of a successful anticorruption strategy that this book is about.

II

Measuring and Assessing Corrupt Behavior

Corruption is everywhere and nowhere. Stealing directly from the public purse—taking from a bureaucratic petty cash drawer or pilfering from government coffers by authorizing cash transfers to nonexistent private businesses—may be observed or later traced. So can the open embezzlement of significant sums, falsified accounts, payments to "ghost" employees, and many ingenious over-invoicing systems ultimately be uncovered. But it is much harder to gather direct evidence by firsthand observation of bribe soliciting, bribe giving, and bribe taking; of favors exchanged either immediately or promised for some future occasion; of extortion, whether systematic or episodic; of contract (tender) awards distorted by gifts or the expectation of gifts; of nepotism; of jobs given or appointments made without merit and because of "consideration;" of payments proffered to influential persons for "services" rendered; of exceptions made or queues jumped out of gratitude or special preference; or of illicit nonmonetary exchanges to perform or fail to perform any duties. (Chapter 3 sets out the legal frameworks that attempt to prohibit these serial manifestations of corruption.)

When I asked the manager of a high-end safari lodge in the remote bush of eastern Zambia whether, in the past fifteen days, he had bribed anyone, he responded with alacrity. "Yes, of course." He had needed to renew the governmental permits for his vehicles. So he went to the regional licensing offices, paid a large number of kwacha (the local currency) to the man in charge, and avoided hanging about for hours in a long queue. Then, a few days later, he invited the district official responsible for granting the lodge's tourist operating permits to spend a free weekend enjoying the lodge's good food, excellent refreshments, and opportunities to see abundant big game. Nothing was said explicitly, but the manager of the lodge expected to obtain his vital permits without any difficulty or delay. Unless an observer or a camera had seen the manager's palm meeting the palm of the licensing official and had noticed the kwacha notes that passed, little could have been recorded. As for the weekend, who was to count or know since the quid pro quo was unspoken?

No accurate way exists as yet to assess absolute levels of corruption in countries or territories on the basis of hard empirical data. Several researchers have, however, attempted to use various kinds of proxy data to estimate amounts of corruption by listing all bribes reported, counting the number of prosecutions initiated, or studying court cases linked to such criminal acts. Unfortunately, those data might instead show how effective prosecutors, the courts, or the media are in investigating and exposing corruption rather than how much real corruption exists.

It is possible to evaluate the larger question of governance—or its components such as the rule of law, transparency, security and safety, and economic and human development—using locally supplied statistical (usually proxy) data, but not so for corruption. To declare a nation-state better governed than its neighbors, for example, one can determine whether its people are more secure and safe than their neighbors or some other peer group by gathering proxy data such as per capita deaths in intrastate conflicts per year or homicides per 1,000 persons annually. For health outcomes per capita, official national results for annual life expectancy per 1,000 persons offer a reasonable proxy. For sustainable economic opportunity, GDP per capita provides a standard snapshot number, and for educational attainments, the number of students persisting in school offers a better approximation of reality than national literacy rates.[1]

Reasonable ways of employing proxy data to evaluate broad and contested existential phenomena such as freedom, democracy, judicial independence, transparency, regime and bureaucratic individual probity, and overall accountability are also available.[2] But for corruption, those interested in ranking and comparing countries and in estimating degrees of peculation and chicanery are compelled to rely on less satisfactory methods such as public opinion surveys (including the several "barometers"), polls of so-called country or functional category experts, anecdotal observational arrays, and other subjective or essentially qualitative methods.

For nearly all aspects of corruption, universally accepted objective measures are virtually nonexistent, transnational proxies are largely unavailable, and quantification of any comprehensive results at all is virtually impossible. Few receivers of bribes keep accurate books (or books at all). Since the giving or taking of bribes and favors, accepting gifts as quids pro quo, and stealing from the public are all serious offenses, quantified data derived from direct observation of corrupt practices or compilations of reports of corrupt behavior are bound to be rare. Moreover, "The moment at which corruption occurs [often is] fleeting."[3] Bribery is a shadowy endeavor and, whereas one can measure the length of a paved road, the total number of mobile telephone subscribers, the rate of maternal mortality, and so on, hardly anyone has managed effectively to enumerate the myriad facets of corruption—the multiple manipulations and machinations that keep corrupters and corruptees in business.[4]

Nevertheless, several ingenious attempts have been made to obtain objective measures of corrupt behavior, by both direct and indirect methods. For example, it is possible to count the number of criminal convictions of public servants for crimes that are either obviously corrupt or corruption-tainted. This has been done for convictions in the United States, but because minor bribe taking may be mixed with large-scale schemes and because even across these United States prosecutors in various jurisdictions may treat corrupt acts differently, this direct method has its obvious limitations. To employ a similar aggregating device across countries would also suffer from flaws of incomparability, different legal definitions, and questions about judicial independence. In certain places, the lack of convictions could result from corruption itself.[5]

Indirect but objective data could prove helpful. Data about the incidence of corruption have been gathered, for example, in Italy, by comparing total public investment in each region with its total existing infrastructural inventory and thus finding the number of "missing" bridges, roads, railways, and public buildings in each region. That missing number may then be attributed to corruption.[6] Some regions, admittedly, may simply be less competent than others in constructing public works. But the Italian method is at least immensely suggestive, even if employing it across many nations with many different kinds of governmental construction payment modalities is daunting and problematic.

Opinion polls can also ask, say, Kenyans, managers of firms responding to the World Bank's Environment and Enterprise Performance inquiries, and persons interrogated by the International Crime Victims Survey whether in the past week, month, or year they have paid or been asked to pay bribes. This is very helpful and useful information, and more objective rather than subjective in content. From this, it is possible to derive reasonable approximations of corrupt behavior in a city or a country, but since the answers are often collected after or well after the reported event(s), they suffer inevitably from the flaws of retrospective recall. (My inquiry in Zambia covered only the most recent fifteen days in 2015 before the questions were asked.)

All of these nonperceptual, objective, and quasi-objective ways of approximating the extent of corruption in a nation-state or some other political entity provide stronger benchmarks than those derived purely from perceptions—

from impressions, beliefs, feelings, and the like. Yet, definitions of corrupt practices may differ from place to place, as may notions of "serious" versus "trivial" kinds of corruption—issues that bedevil both objective and subjective measuring methods—and can confound results. Even employing clever mathematical deviations from expected distributions as evidence of corruption depends on the same kinds of problematical assumptions. Estimating the real extent of corruption in a country, and being able year after year to demonstrate less or more corruption, ultimately will depend on devising incontrovertible objective measures capable of capturing, probably by proxy, the extent of what are notably clandestine and hidden pursuits. But that is work for the future.

Given the great and understandable difficulty of objectively estimating the real amount or incidence of corruption in the world or in individual countries, provinces, and cities, those who rightly seek to compare levels of corruption across nation-states or regions have so far been compelled to do so subjectively—by soliciting the opinions of so-called country or regional experts and by surveying the opinions of other in-country citizens and external observers. Consequently, perceptions rule. Nation-state X "feels"—to those asked to rank polities—more corrupt or less corrupt than nation-state Y, its neighbor or rival. Such methods of measurement are, *faut de mieux*, now common and, depending on the protocols developed to gather such perceptions, perfectly reasonable in the absence of any better way of obtaining reliable, comprehensive, comparative data. Fortunately, too, it appears that laymen and experts perceive corruption in a complementary fashion.[7] "There seems to be something like a national context of control of corruption that people perceive, which is . . . quite consistent across years and variations in experience."[8]

Another important consideration, however, concerns whether the existence and persistence of corruption is well measured by composites of data derived from myriad existing sources created for separate purposes or from data, possibly original, developed uniquely. The long-established Corruption Perceptions Index (CPI) and the World Bank's Control of Corruption (WBCC) section of its World Governance Indicators are both aggregations of scores provided by disparate third parties. Each mines complicated lodes of relevant or near-relevant information, combines and standardizes the revealed array of nuggets, and helps to make both of those aggregated results useful for activists, politicians, and researchers.

Within the CPI are bundled scores provided for ninety-nine countries by the World Justice Project's Rule of Law Index (WJI); the WJI in turn elicits perceptions of corruption by surveying citizens and by obtaining the opinions of in-country experts. The Global Integrity Index (2004–2011) also relied on opinions. The Afrobarometer does so by survey, too, although the extent to which a selection of its questions may, in any given year, provide answers helpful to anticorruption activists varies greatly. The same caution should be given to the utility of tangential instruments such as the Open Budget Survey and Index, the Financial Secrecy Index, the Anti–Money Laundering Index, and the Aid Transparency Index. In addition to the CPI, Transparency International (TI) helpfully also issues a Bribe Payers Index and a Global Corruption Barometer.

Each of these indexes is based on some kind of compilation of opinions. In turn, none of the indexes is able effectively to control for the manner in which built-in attitudes may influence responses. Urban residents may perceive corruption differently than rural dwellers, and unemployed youths may provide survey answers differently from their settled elders. Beneficiaries will also reflect differently than victims.

Yet, capturing perceptions of corruption from those in a position to offer assessments of public sector venality remains the most utilized and possibly the most effective method of comparing relative corruption levels across countries, despite legitimate questions about whether such perceptions effectively measure actual experience. Is the extent and impact of corruption in a society fully measured by external perception? Is the amount of total corruption (whatever that means) effectively captured by a perception score? But, as has been postulated by others, the CPI and some of the other instruments "are the best we have and they perform rather well for something that is so difficult to measure."[9]

The Corruption Perceptions Index

The best known and most widely used measure of corruption is Transparency International's Corruption Perceptions Index (CPI). As its name indicates, it is fully subjective in method and intent. In 2015, 168 of the world's 194 countries were ranked against each other according to their perceived levels of corruption, using a 1–100 point scoring formula that has steadily been more finely calibrated since its first compilation (and accidental release to the press) in 1995.[10] (The CPI's scoring method was altered in 2012, so, longitudinally, countries technically cannot accurately be compared to each other from 1995 to 2016 and beyond, only from 2012 to 2016.)

In 2015, the CPI ranked the world's ten least corrupt nation-states in descending order as Denmark, Finland, Sweden, New Zealand, the Netherlands, Norway, Switzerland, Singapore, Canada, and Germany, Luxembourg, and the United Kingdom (the last three tied), with raw scores ranging from 91 to 81. The United States ranked 16th, with a score of 76. The ten perceived most corrupt places in the world, in descending order, were Venezuela, Iraq, Libya, Angola, South Sudan, Sudan, Afghanistan, North Korea, and Somalia, with scores ranging downward from 17 to 8 (on a 100-point scale).

Transparency International's official view of why perceptions are the appropriate way to examine comparative levels of corruption is: "Corruption generally comprises illegal activities, which are deliberately hidden and only come to light through scandals, investigations or prosecutions. There is no meaningful way to assess absolute levels of corruption in countries or territories on the basis of hard empirical data. Possible attempts to do so, such as by comparing bribes reported, the number of prosecutions brought or studying court cases directly linked to corruption, cannot be taken as definitive indicators of corruption levels. Instead, they show how effective prosecutors, the courts or the media are in investigating and exposing corruption. Capturing perceptions of corruption of those in a position to offer assessments of public sector corruption is the most reliable method of comparing relative corruption levels across countries."[11] "Relative" is a key word in that last sentence. (See also the discussion of the differences between perceptions, and the actuality of, corruption, below.)

The Corruption Perceptions Index each year is derived from the aggregated opinions of experts and corporate executives. For 2015, those opinions were collated and processed by twelve institutions and index sources: the African Development Bank Governance Ratings 2014; the Bertelsmann Foundation Sustainable Governance Indicators 2014; the Bertelsmann Foundation Transformation Index 2014; the Economist Intelligence Unit (EIU) Country Risk Ratings 2014; Freedom House Nations in Transit 2013; the Global Insight Country Risk Ratings 2014; the IMD World Competitiveness Yearbook 2014; the Political and Economic Risk Consultancy Asian Intelligence 2014; the Political Risk Services International Country Risk Guide 2014; the World Bank's Country Policy and Institutional Assessment reports, 2013; the World Economic Forum's Executive Opinion Survey (EOS) 2014; and the World Justice Project Rule of Law Index 2014.[12]

The persons responsible for constructing each year's CPI rely on each of the above organizations to supply expert opinions that are truly "expert" and surveys of business opinions that are based on representative samples. The experts are known to the source entities, possibly to TI and the CPI, but certainly not to the public. Their qualifications may be examined annually by TI, or not. Moreover, because perceptions of corruption in a country are theoretically based explicitly on corruption in the public but not the private sector, confusion is possible. The perceptions are provided as numerical scores and the scores are standardized across the sources and ultimately computed and published as simple averages of all of the available scores.[13]

What is striking, and not widely known, is that each of the perception-evaluating organizations answers somewhat different questions. That is, Bertelsmann in 2014 was asked by TI and the CPI to determine whether or not public office holders were prevented from abusing their positions for private gain. High scores were hence awarded to those countries where "legal, political, and public integrity" mechanisms prevented abuse.

By contrast, the Economist Intelligence Unit was requested to determine whether the nation-states assessed had clear procedures for the allocation and accountability of public funds, whether public funds were (not "had been") misappropriated by public officials, whether an official body audited public finances, whether the judiciary was independent, and whether bribes were "traditionally" paid to secure contracts and gain favors. The EIU's experts were based in London, New York, Hong Kong, Beijing, and Shanghai and were supported by a network of in-country specialists. Each expert was responsible for reporting on two or three countries.

Country economists in the African Development Bank offered information obtained from "local contacts" and peer discussions within the bank to assess overall transparency, accountability, and corruption in the public sector in forty African countries in 2014, each factor being weighed separately over three or more years. Final ratings for African polities were decided by "open discussions between country teams and reviewers."

The World Bank and its Country Policy and Institutional Assessment team was also asked about transparency and accountability, but more specifically whether executives and public employees generally were held accountable by electorates, legislatures, and the judiciary. Eighty-one countries were scored by World Bank country representatives and experts in 2013 (and the scores used for the 2014 CPI). Apparently, the bank first "benchmarked" a sample of countries and then rated the remaining countries by using the "derived benchmark ratings as guideposts."[14]

The World Justice Project's Rule of Law Index regularly polls 2,000 experts and 68,000 individuals around the globe about justice and rules of law. In recent years, it has asked its respondents to answer sixty-eight questions on corruption, viz., do executive branch officials, legislators, judges, and police and military officers in your country use or do not use public office for private gain? It contributed to the CPI the results of its survey on ninety-nine countries in 2013–2014, but dating in some cases from 2011.[15]

Obviously, the questions posed by Transparency International to the providers, and the results received for the CPI in any year, depend on the responses of a great range of citizens who are asked specific short-survey questions or on considered replies by different kinds of experts who may sometimes not even reside in the nations being assessed. The ratings are scored together and later standardized, even though the questions being asked are similar rather than identical. As evaluated below by a number of powerful statistical tests, these differences in what might be considered inputs, and the ultimate scores, may not (but could) undermine the authenticity of what is the leading and best-regarded method of ranking the countries according to their perceived levels of corruption.

Of the dozen sources aggregated in 2014, some inform the CPI more than others. In 2014, the commercial risk assessment firm IHS, through its Global Insight Country Risk Ratings, provided ratings for every country. The Political Risk Services provided data for 140 polities, the Economic Intelligence Unit for 140, and the Bertelsmann Index for 129. But data gathered by the geographically bound Asian Intelligence was used to rate fifteen Asian countries only, the Freedom House Nations in Transit survey for twenty-nine mostly Central European nations, and the African Development Bank for forty (not the full fifty-four) African states.

The makers of the CPI prefer to rely on as many of the dozen information-supplying organizations as possible. But the minimum required for inclusion in the CPI is three institutional providers of results. In 2012, only six countries were assessed by as many as ten organizations; nineteen countries were evaluated for corruption on the basis of three sources only. Scores for the majority of the 174 entities on the CPI list in that year were developed on the basis of information from but seven or eight of the contributing institutions.[16]

Each organization reports on the overall extent of corruption, i.e., the frequency and size of corrupt transactions, which amounts to an institutional perception of corruption for their target countries. By aggregating the perceptions of three or more institutional assessments, Transparency International gains greater authority and reliability for the CPI than would be obtained by the use of a single source. But, depending on the predilections and experiences of the raters within each organization, the entire process is obviously prone (as all subjective methodologies must be) to selection bias.

Moreover, the CPI and other perceptions-based evaluations do not differentiate across sectors or between different varieties of corruption—whether within a nation the judges are more or less corrupt than the civil servants or the health workers, or whether the public sector is clean and the private sector dirty. Indeed, as presently constructed, the CPI may overemphasize financial expressions of corruption.[17] Heywood and Rose were able to show, too, not only that the CPI scores are generated annually using data that are sometimes old and previously employed, but more significantly and damagingly that scores from more than a decade before explain nearly 90 percent of contemporary ratings of both the CPI and the WBCC (discussed below). That means that there has been no substantive change in the CPI and the WBCC over time, a finding that undermines their utility, analytically. As another study shows, "The order of reputations is based on already preconceived reputations." Additionally, for both of the main subjective indexes (and others), Heywood and Rose cite a serious statistical objection: a large margin of error is created "when subjective indicators are used to produce complex statistical constructions that can easily create an illusion of quantitative sophistication."[18]

The statisticians Saisana and Saltelli nevertheless suggest that the high correlations between CPI ranks and each of the institutional ratings should be expected, since each of the sources attempts to measure the same phenomenon. They further agree that the CPI "efficiently differentiate[s]" levels of corruption among countries because it manages to reconcile many different points of view (or perceptions) across its sources. Additionally, by applying a statistical test to the country-ratings common to the institutions covering the most polities in the 2012 CPI, they show that no one of the six major "perceptions" providers is more significant or more essential than another. No one source dominates the index. They also demonstrate that the ultimate CPI rankings are not affected by the number of sources (three to ten) that are employed to evaluate an individual country. Being assessed only by a handful of evaluators did not change the validity of the results. Finally, these two accomplished researchers concluded that because the CPI covered more countries than any of its component sources, it was more reliable than any of the individual sources alone. The CPI was indeed a "robust" assessment of perceived levels of corruption.[19] However, Saisana and Saltelli were not asked and did not examine how close a perception of corruption might be to some to-be-constructed measure of actual corruption—which no one has as yet devised for the reasons set out above.

World Bank Control of Corruption Indicator

Since 1996 the World Bank's World Governance Indicators (WGI) have annually rated the governance of the globe's countries (in 2015, 215 countries). Governance as defined by the authors of the WGI "consists of the traditions and institutions by which authority in a country is exercised [and] the process . . . by which governments are selected, monitored and replaced; the capacity of the government to effectively formulate and implement sound policies; and the respect of citizens and the state for the institutions that govern economic and social interactions among them."[20]

The WGI subdivides governance into six categories or "broad dimensions": Voice and Accountability, Political Stability and Absence of Violence, Government Effectiveness, Regulatory Quality, Rule of Law, and Control of Corruption. It is this last segment of the WGI that is relevant to this chapter and this book, particularly since this part of the WGI is as often referred to and cited as the CPI when donors (such as the Millennium Challenge Corporation), international financial institutions, scholars, and others seek to conceptualize and intervene to reduce corruption globally. The World Bank's Control of Corruption indicator "captures perceptions of the extent to which public power is exercised for private gain." It further purports to measure the "capture" of the state by predatory elites and private interests. This Control of

Corruption measure is as authoritative as the CPI and is as equally developed from a series of subjective and qualitative data sets.

The sources for the entire WGI are thirty-two indicators and surveys that "report the views and experiences of citizens, entrepreneurs, and experts. . . ." The WGI uses nine surveys of households and firms, including Gallup's World Poll, the Global Competitiveness Report, and Afrobarometer survey responses; four commercial business information providers such as the Economist Intelligence Unit, Global Insight, and Political Risk Services (all also employed in the CPI); eleven reports produced by NGOs such as Global Integrity and Freedom House; and eight data sets produced elsewhere in the World Bank, in regional development banks, and in such special entities as the French Ministry of Finance.

For corruption per se, the WGI's Control of Corruption indicator relies on information from experts in a large variety of institutions, such as the African and Asian Development Banks, and from published accounts such as the Bertelsmann Transformation Index, the Afrobarometer and the Latinobarometro, Freedom House, Global Insight, Global Integrity, Political Risk Services, the World Justice Project Rule of Law Index, the International Budget Index and many more, for a total of about twenty-four providers. Its list of feeding organizations is much longer than CPI's, but includes an overlapping ten or so sets of institutions. For Rwanda, for example, from 1996 to 2013, the WBCC component of the WGI based its scores and judgments on just twelve sources in its final year and on fewer providers in earlier years.

The questions that the WGI asks its cooperating data sources to answer, and which it incorporates in its annual index, are similar to those posed by the CPI, and to which the organizations that work with both indexes presumably respond similarly. The WBCC therefore aggregates what the many respondents say about corruption among public officials; public trust in politicians; any diversion of public funds; and irregular payments to customs officers, to public utilities, to tax collectors, and to influence contract awards. The WBCC reflects the extent of a nation's corruption, venal and petty; business corruption; the amount of corruption involving foreign firms; and whether a country's bureaucracy is intrusive and tied up in red tape.

The WGI further requires some of its information providers to indicate the number of elected leaders, parliamentarians, judges, tax and customs officials, and bureaucrats who are involved with corruption. It uses a survey to inquire whether commercial enterprises in a country have to pay to "get things done;" to estimate the percentage and frequency of total annual sales devoted to "unofficial payments" to public officials; and how problematic corruption is for business growth. From Transparency International's Global Corruption Barometer survey, the WBCC wants to know the frequency of household, political party, parliamentary, media, judicial, and other public service bribery.

From one Asian source, the WBCC seeks to discover whether corruption detracts from the business environment for foreign companies.[21]

At no point are "corruption" and other critical terms defined, but that apparent omission in the public documentation may well reflect a belief that all responding parties surely must know what the relevant words mean. Certainly, too, "corruption" covers a broad range of illicit and compound behaviors. Experts reporting on country X may regard certain kinds of normative breaches more seriously than observers examining country Y, and prevalence and frequency may be counted differently, nation to nation. But, from WGI's point of view, the careful and comprehensive aggregation of so many replies and sources helps to guarantee both accuracy and representativeness. Critics complain, however, that the WGI is muddled and some of its detailed constructs are "meaningless."[22] WGI employs an "Unobserved Components Model" to construct a weighted average for each indicator and each country.[23]

The WGI warns, as does the CPI, that short-term comparisons among countries or scores for a single country year-to-year are less meaningful than shifts over considerable time. The significance of the WGI results within single countries and between countries are also reduced, because from year to year it introduces new data sources and new questions, and alters the weights given to aggregated replies. Nevertheless, as with the CPI, these subtle imperfections in the smoothness of the micro-data provided by the WBCC need not detract from the utility of its macro-findings. More simply, both the CPI and WBCC scoring methodologies suggest the intrinsic difficulty involved in quantifying corrupt practices, country by country, and the inherent improbability, no matter the complexity and data-deep nature of both state-of-the-art enterprises, of them fully representing the range and quality of such illicit, but common, practices.

Index of Public Integrity

The Index of Public Integrity (IPI), released for the first time in 2016 and funded by the European Union, seeks to measure corruption more objectively than the subjective and perception-based CPI and WBCC. Its rankings are developed from six closely related indicators: judicial independence, administrative burden, trade openness, budget transparency, e-citizenship, and freedom of the press. Each of these variables, the creators of the IPI assert, is "significantly associated with control of corruption."[24] The makers of this index believe that it is more transparent, more straightforward, and much more responsive to national policy and contextual shifts than the perception-informed and expert witness–informed indexes. Its makers claim that it does not lag behind abrupt alterations in governmental circumstances.

Nevertheless, a close examination of this new index shows that it, too, bases many of its results as much on expert opinion and perception as the older and better-known indexes. Its judicial independence indicator scores come from the results of the World Economic Forum's Expert Opinion Survey, a compendium of subjective responses. Its administrative burden component is based more objectively on a combination of scores derived from the World Bank's Doing Business Data reports on the number of procedures required to begin a business in a country, the time it takes to do so, the number of times taxes are paid by businesses each year, and the time it takes to pay those taxes. Trade openness is rated using data from the same World Bank source for the average number of documents required to export and import and the time required to complete export and import procedures. Scores for budget transparency stem from questions in the Open Budget Survey (discussed below) that reflect transparency in preparing national budgets. That survey is a subjective compilation. The e-Citizenship category reflects an innovative counting of the percentage of a national population that has fixed broadband subscriptions, uses the Internet, and has Facebook pages. Freedom of the Press is based entirely on the subjective results of the annual Freedom of the Press ratings prepared by Freedom House (discussed in chapter 3). Overall, the Index of Public Integrity correlates closely with the CPI and the WBCC; it uses several of the same underlying data sources and, although developing scores in some cases from objective numbers, also derives half of its scores from subjective public opinion results. "More than 75% of the variation in control of corruption [as compared especially to the WBCC data] across 105 countries can be explained by the IPI."[25] A laudable advance, the IPI complements the CPI and the WBCC, but hardly supplants them as a definitive designator of the amount of corruption within a country. Moreover, it is not immediately obvious why, say, high Facebook usage correlates with the ability to control corruption.

In 2016, the IPI's highest ranked (least corrupt) countries were similar to those highly rated by the CPI and the WBCC. Norway was first (score 9.68), Denmark second (9.56), and Finland third (9.43)—all on a 1–10 scale. New Zealand, the Netherlands, the United Kingdom, Sweden, Ireland, Luxembourg, and the United States rounded out the top ten. Germany and Estonia were tied for eleventh place. The most corrupt of IPI's 105 states, with scores in the 2.16 to 4.18 range, were Venezuela, Chad, Myanmar, Cambodia, Zimbabwe, Tajikistan, Bolivia, and Nepal, reading up from the bottom.[26] These 2016 scores are based on data from 2012 and 2014. The IPI website implies that the index will be kept up to date every other year.

Global Integrity

Another method of gauging cross-country corruption was advanced, from 2004 to 2013, by the Global Integrity Index based in Washington, DC. It eschewed the detailed aggregation of existing approaches to measuring corruption, as employed by the CPI and the WBCC, preferring to combine qualitative, journalistic, impressionistic, "thick" descriptions of corrupt practices within target countries together with, for the same countries, a quantitative-type (but still impressionistic) assessment of a nation's laws, institutions, and mechanisms that are capable in theory of preventing or minimizing corruption. (Some of those indicators included different varieties of accountability, budget methods, electoral integrity, business licensing, forms of regulation, whistleblowing permissiveness, the work of ombudsmen and auditors, tax and customs procedures, and whether and how the rule of law was respected.)[27]

Global Integrity gathered data on corrupt practices in three countries in 2013, two countries in 2012, thirty-one in 2011, thirty-nine in 2009, fifty-eight in 2008, and twenty-six in 2004, its first year of index publication after opening as an organization in 1999. The index (but not Global Integrity) ceased its existence with its 2011 iteration, although individual country reports were compiled in 2012 and 2013. The index data for the years between 2004 and 2011 were obtained from about 200 in-country experts tasked with assessing both de jure and de facto corruption prevention methods, following a coding protocol devised by Global Integrity.[28] A report on each of the different countries assessed in different years (not all countries were rated in each of the index years) emphasized preventive measures rather than descriptions of corruption. That is, Global Integrity focused particularly on the role in battling corruption of a nation's civil society, its media, its oversight and regulatory mechanisms, and its rule of law institutions. Global Integrity reports also assessed accountability across each government and its civil service, and the manner in which elections had been contested. Additionally, Global Integrity was especially concerned with the transparency of public procurement processes, asset disclosure requirements, and conflict of interest laws—a total of 320 "actionable" indicators. It weighed the official legal arrangements curtailing corruption versus what actually happened in practice.

Global Integrity took pride not in measuring corruption directly, but in assessing citizen access to key anticorruption mechanisms—accountability, transparency, and oversight. Global Integrity's reports did not estimate corruption levels and amounts. Rather than examine the "cancer" of corruption, the reports investigated the "medicine" applied against it. In particular, Global Integrity's assessments focused on what it usefully called the "implementation gap"—the difference between a nation's legal framework against corruption and the actual day-to-day and year-to-year enforcement of anticorruption legislation. Exposing that gap was intended to indicate how well existing laws and regulations against corruption were, in fact, being employed to reduce the scale of a country's corruption. Global Integrity was much more concerned with outputs than inputs, in other words, and its country assessments provided scores developed from a legal framework quality number minus an actual performance number. The resulting "implementation gap" indicated whether perfecting good governance in the country under examination would be improved by stronger political will or by purely technical means. The larger the gap, the greater the difficulty in reducing corruption.[29]

In 2011, the last year of the Global Integrity Index, Ireland topped the list of its least corrupt countries. Germany, the United States, Burkina Faso, and China followed. At the bottom of the ratings were Zimbabwe, Uganda, Armenia, Nicaragua, Azerbaijan, Venezuela, and Bosnia, all rated on twenty-three variables. In 2012, Global Integrity produced new scorecards for Cambodia and the Solomon Islands, and in 2013 it had new reports for Indonesia, Vanuatu, and Timor Leste. As an organization, Global Integrity regrouped under a new director in 2015, intending to continue to produce Global Integrity reports on selected countries and to work with the Mo Ibrahim Foundation to assess "key social, economic, political and anticorruption mechanisms at the national level in over 50 African countries" in order to generate and manage data for the foundation's proposed Africa Integrity Indicators.[30]

World Justice Project Rule of Law Index

The Absence of Corruption indicator constitutes one of the eight components of the World Justice Project's Rule of Law Index (WJI). It is based on the views of in-country experts (as few as six and as many as thirty for most of the African countries included in the index) and a survey annually of roughly 1,000 citizens in the three most populous cities of each country. The WJI's ratings of corruption nationally supplement and complement, and are checked against, those produced by the CPI and the WBCC, but for far fewer countries in Africa and Asia. The expert and citizen opinions are obtained through responses to written questionnaires. In 2016, the WJI covered 113 countries only, including twenty-two in Africa and seventeen in Asia.

Defining corruption in the usual manner, the Absence of Corruption indicator focuses especially on "bribery, extortion, improper influence by public or private interests, and misappropriation of public funds or other resources." Within these broad rubrics, the indicator concentrates on the abuse of position by government officers, judges, legislators, and members of the police and military establishments. Four "sub-factors" (the executive, the judiciary, police and military, and legislators) draw their results from answers by the polled "qualified respondents" to sixty-eight relevant questions. One sample question, for example, in 2014 was: "How frequently do people (or private companies) have to pay bribes, [make] informal payments, or [provide] other inducements to register . . . title over immovable property / register a new private business / expedite the delivery of a construction permit / clear goods through customs / obtain a driver's license . . . ?"

The first sub-factor seeks to measure how much bribery exists in the public service and among the executive, and whether public procurement and public works contracts are awarded honestly and through competitive bidding. It also asks whether members of the executive branch refrain from embezzling public funds. The second covers the extent to which judges solicit bribes and whether their rulings are influenced by criminal organizations. The third inquires whether police and military officials accept bribes to do their jobs. The fourth measures whether legislators accept inducements "in exchange for political favors or supportive votes."[31]

Saisana and Saltelli determined that the manner in which the WJI was constructed and its polling conducted was "statistically sound, coherent, and balanced." Overall, they found the WJI in 2014 (as in its earlier iterations) "efficient and parsimonious" despite the reality that the WJI was built upon answers to about 500 survey questions separately administered by a variety of polling firms across the globe. Within each dimension of each sub-factor, a "single latent" answer was scored appropriately, weighted equally against the other replies, and averaged arithmetically in a simple and straightforward aggregation. The Absence of Corruption dimension, they say, "is especially coherent and robust."[32]

In 2016, according to the WJI, the least corrupt countries in the world were Denmark and Norway, Finland and Sweden, the Netherlands, Germany, Austria, New Zealand, Singapore, and Australia, the United Kingdom, and Canada (the last three tied) in that order. The ten most corrupt places reading up from the bottom were Venezuela, Cambodia, Afghanistan, Egypt, Cameroon, Zimbabwe, Ethiopia, Pakistan, Uganda, and Bolivia. South Africa, Ghana, Botswana, and Senegal were the highest ranked African countries, in places 43 through 46. The placement within the index of all 113 countries supported many of the judgments and rankings of the CPI and the WBCC, as well as the IPI. Indeed, the CPI now incorporates the WJI results.

Bribe Payers Index and World Bank Enforcement Efforts

Another obviously relevant instrument to assess the amount and kinds of corruption in the developing world is Transparency International's Bribe Payers Index (BPI). Last issued in 2011, it ranked the world's wealthiest twenty-eight nations—the ones most likely to "export" corruption, and to bribe governments and commercial entities in Africa and Asia and elsewhere in order to gain contracts and favorable business deals. Before 2011, the BPI had been issued four times since 1999. South Africa is the only sub-Saharan African state among the twenty-eight.

This index collected information in 2011 from 3,000 senior business executives globally through a Bribe Payers Survey that essentially inquired whether, to their knowledge, firms in country X or country Y solicited and accepted bribes. In 2011, it revealed which industrial sectors (construction and transport) were the worst offenders, showed clear evidence that private companies commonly bribed, and indicated that Russian and Chinese firms were most likely to offer inducements. The Netherlands, Switzerland, Belgium, Germany, Japan, Australia, Canada, Singapore, and Britain bribed the least. The United States, despite the impact of the 1977 Foreign Corrupt Practices Act, was only tenth on this "good performer" list. Slightly above China and Russia at the bottom of this list of poor performers were Mexico, Indonesia, the United Arab Emirates, Argentina, Saudi Arabia, and Turkey.[33] (But see also chapters 3 and 9.)

A complementary World Business Environment Survey conducted in fifty-eight countries by the World Bank and the European Bank for Reconstruction and Development in 1999–2000 asked business executives the percentage of firm revenues paid annually in bribes to public officials. Swedish executives reported spending 0 percent on bribes, Georgian business leaders a full 7.9 percent.[34]

After World Bank President James D. Wolfensohn in 1996 decried corruption's adverse impact on economic development, he set up the bank's first internal investigative unit to audit loans for evidence of corruption. He also established a telephone hotline to receive calls about corruption around the clock and a sanctions committee to investigate the allegations that arrived over the transom. That committee subsequently became the bank's Department of Institutional Integrity. From 1999, in other words, the bank and its managers have tried to curtail opportunities for graft and rent seeking in connection with its projects or loans or within the bank itself. Paul Wolfowitz, when he presided over the bank in 2005–2006, cancelled major loans and debt relief packages because of suspected recipient corruption.[35]

Today, the World Bank's Integrity Vice Presidency (INT) blacklists specific corporate enterprises if it discovers that they engage in fraud, especially participating in shady practices involving World Bank–sponsored projects. By 2006, the bank had thus disbarred more than 330 firms and individuals from participating in World Bank–sponsored contracts, usually for three or more years, for perpetrating or engaging in corrupt practices while involved in operations backed by the bank. In 2010 alone, the list of admonished corporations, open to public inspection, included 161 companies and individuals from twenty countries. Thirty-eight were from the United Kingdom, thirty from Bangladesh, fourteen from Indonesia, twelve from the U.S., and eleven from Sweden. A German firm had been blacklisted for seven years and a Canadian firm for three years for bribing those responsible for approving bids for the Lesotho Highlands Water Project (which supplies water to Gauteng Province in South Africa and hydropower to Lesotho and South Africa). In 2010, the bank also blacklisted a major British publisher that had hoped to win a lucrative contract to print school curriculum materials for Sudan. Siemens, the big German industrial conglomerate, was sanctioned in 2009 for bribery and attempted bribery in several jurisdictions, most notably Russia, and was obliged to contribute $100 million to fund the bank's anticorruption activities as well as being barred from bidding on contracts paid for by bank funds for two years. Note that decisions to blacklist are made by a bank committee, not in any court of law.[36]

In 2015, Canada claimed the dubious honor of having the largest number of corrupt blacklisted concerns. Among more than 600 multinational companies barred from doing business with the bank, 117 were Canadian, but a full 115 of the 117 were all in some way affiliated with SNC-Lavalin, a construction firm involved in selling nuclear reactors, building rapid transit systems, and erecting bridges (including a questionable one over the Ganges River in Bangladesh).[37] Earlier, SNC was accused of corrupt links to the ousted regime of Libya's Muammar Qaddafi and to the Algerian single-party state. The Royal Canadian Mounted Police (RCMP) charged a former SNC executive with bribery of a foreign executive under the Canadian Corruption of Foreign Public Officials Act (see chapter 3). In 2014, SNC's former boss was arrested by the RCMP, also for corruption overseas. He was again nabbed by the RCMP in 2015 for bribing to secure a contract to build a health center in Montreal.

In 2015, the World Bank expanded its blacklist by adding 250 companies globally. After Canada, the U.S. was in second place on the list with forty-six concerns. Indonesia and Britain followed with forty-three and forty cases respectively. The director of the bank's Integrity Vice Presidency said that the bank was not a "global policeman." But it could "facilitate the global conversation against corruption."[38]

The bank allows multinational corporations to evade possible blacklisting if they enter its Voluntary Disclosure Program. To do so means, in a sense, privately confessing that they previously engaged in fraudulent activities overseas but now promise to cease such behavior, reform themselves, and confidentially disclose the nature of their misconduct to the bank. Having done so and satisfied the bank committee, such firms are then allowed, after further internal investigation by the bank, to bid on World Bank–backed projects without fear of being disbarred. They are also required to adopt a robust best-practices compliance program and to employ an outside monitor.

These bank practices help to reduce corporate bribe paying and other illicit activities in developing and other receiving countries. As the World Bank blacklists are shared with the regional development banks, the European banks, and the IMF, there is a common mechanism to inhibit the kinds of malpractices that the Extractive Industries Transparency Initiative (see below) has been created to limit and the Bribe Payers Index has been developed to highlight. National export credit agencies may also use this information, as do private firms that investigate business operations and supply compliance data. The existence of blacklist data also strengthens the codes of corporate conduct that are discussed in chapter 9.

Global Corruption Barometer

According to the last (2013) Global Corruption Barometer (GCB), also a product of Transparency International, 53 percent of people surveyed said that in their own country corruption had increased over the previous two years; 27 percent had paid a bribe when trying to obtain services from a public institution; globally, the police and the judiciary were the most bribe prone, with 31 percent of respondents having paid a bribe to a policeman during the previous year and 24 percent to a judge or a judicial official. The majority of people polled said that governments were lax in fighting corruption. Moreover, 54 percent believed that governments act in the interest of ruling elites and not in the interest of citizens. To get something vital done in most countries, a person had to know someone.[39]

These findings reflect the survey responses of 114,000 persons in 107 countries. The survey instrument, administered by a collection of commercial agencies, was designed to capture an individual's direct experience with corrupt practice, especially being asked for and delivering bribes. Since a majority of citizens polled acknowledged interacting with corrupt officials, the barometer survey also showed how corruption affects the loss of fundamental human rights. In many societies the need to pay bribes on a regular basis constitutes a heavy societal burden. Refusals or failures to provide such payments or inducements often mean the failure to thrive, to eat, to access basic services, and so on. Paying a bribe in some circumstances may be a priority greater than the nurturing of a child, the obtaining of school fees, or the possibility of wearing shoes.

In 2013, the highest national personally reported bribery rates were in Sierra Leone (84 percent), Liberia (75), Yemen (74), Kenya (70), Cameroon (62), Zimbabwe (62), Libya (62), Mozambique (62), Uganda (61), Senegal (57), Cambodia (57), and Tanzania (56). At the opposite end of the spectrum were Australia, Denmark, Finland, and Japan (all 1), Spain (2), and Norway, Uruguay, Portugal, and New Zealand (all 3). The Maldives and Malaysia also were credited with 3 percent scores, but those are implausibly low numbers. Mexico (33), Indonesia, Kazakhstan, and Pakistan (all 34), Nigeria (44), South Africa (47), Bangladesh (39), and the Solomon Islands (34) likewise reported impossibly low bribery numbers, so a large shadow must be cast over the findings of the last Global Corruption Barometer.

UN International Crime Victims Survey

In an influential paper, Donchev and Ujhelyi show how perceptions of corruption may not accord perfectly with the actual experience of corruption in most countries—that cultural, economic, and political factors may bias results.[40] They further demonstrate that most indexes are sensitive to the absolute number of corrupt occurrences rather than to the relative levels of corrupt behavior, implying that larger countries, with more corrupt transactions, will be perceived as more corrupt than smaller ones. On the other hand, they explicitly do not claim that corruption perception indexes are methodologically flawed, merely that their results are sometimes misinterpreted.

A survey conducted in 1996 and 2000 by the United Nations Interregional Crime and Justice Research Institute—the International Crime Victims Survey (ICVS)—used a standard questionnaire in fifty-eight countries, yielding 82,662 observations in 2000. It asked, as many Global Corruption Barometer and in-country Transparency International opinion surveys do, whether the respondent had paid a bribe or had been solicited for a bribe. The authors suggest that the answers show that "experience" with corruption equals a country's relative level of corruption. Overall, 10 percent of the respondents did experience corruption in this way, ranging upwards from negligible in Britain to 36 percent in Uganda. More experience of corruption came from interactions with police than with other government officials. They also found that perception is influenced more by economic, cultural, and institutional factors than by the kinds of experiences revealed by the survey results. Overall, the authors conclude, "Using corruption perception indices as a measure of corruption experience [is] problematic."[41] Such indices may say more about levels of public trust than about the amount of corruption within a society. Unfortunately, their paper, and several other appropriate and well-reasoned critiques of the indexes of corruption, suggests no immediately usable alternative measures.

Financial Secrecy Index

How open companies are—how fully they reveal what they do and how they do it—and how efficiently and effectively countries collect taxes from their citizens and their corporate entities are considerations that greatly influence the extent of corruption within a state. One way of examining these factors and potential influences on economic and political behavior within a country is to examine its financial secrecy arrangements and practices.

Britain's Tax Justice Network tries to do just that by producing the Financial Secrecy Index. Launched in 2011, it seeks to combat tax evasion by ranking political jurisdictions according to the degree of their secrecy and scale of activity. Qualitatively, this index examines the laws and regulations and international treaties that determine how secretive a country appears to be. Quantitatively, the index weighs a jurisdiction's size and overall importance in global financial markets. Combining both measures, the index overemphasizes secrecy and de-emphasizes the importance of weighting.

Fifteen "secrecy indicators" are constructed by the network's staff from 49 of 202 criteria. Transparency of company ownership is important. So is banking secrecy, the ability to inspect company accounts easily, the efficiency of a jurisdiction's tax administration, and whether it has effective rules against money laundering. In 2015 (before the release of the Panama Papers), the index covered ninety-two countries and dependencies, plus nine other jurisdictions without full information. Switzerland, Hong Kong, the United States, Singapore, and the Cayman Islands were the most successfully secret in 2015. The most open among jurisdictions with full information were Andorra, Slovenia, Dominica, Finland, the Cook Islands, and Montserrat (ranking 87 through 92). The Organisation for Economic Co-operation and Development (OECD) and its Global Forum on Taxation are, this index claims, much too lenient.[42]

Anti-Money Laundering Index

Money laundering often goes hand-in-hand with corruption. It is difficult to conceive of a transaction that launders receipts that is not somehow linked to drugs, arms, and people smuggling or a host of other illicit activities that ultimately depend on "profits" being legitimized or "washed."

The Basel Institute on Governance and an expert team from the International Centre for Asset Recovery annually prepare an Anti–Money Laundering Index (AML), which covered 152 countries in 2015. Designed also to measure terrorist financing across the globe, the AML includes indicators on counterterrorist financing regulations, financial standards, transparency and disclosure, and political risk. High risk scores on the AML obviously suggest lax standards, low institutional capacities, lack of financial and public sector transparency (all of which relate directly to the degree of societal corruption), and a jurisdiction that cares little for scrutiny or regulation. The index further suggests how vulnerable a country is to transnational crime and to all kinds of related criminal activity.

The Basel Index aggregates data from internationally available suppliers and sources such as the World Bank, the World Economic Forum, and, especially, the Financial Action Task Force's (an intergovernmental body) Mutual Evaluation Country Reports. That last source details the compliance of states with anti–money laundering and asset recovery regulations. The AML is a composite index that assesses the likelihood of money laundering and terrorist financing in a country, since those activities cannot be measured directly or quantified. The AML also examines banking secrecy and corruption and financial regulations. Judicial strengths and civil rights are factored in as well.

In 2015, the globe's countries at highest risk of money laundering and terrorist financing according to the AML were Iran, Afghanistan, Tajikistan, Guinea-Bissau, Mali, Cambodia, Mozambique, Uganda, Swaziland, and Myanmar (Burma). In sub-Saharan Africa, Kenya and Guinea joined the nations already listed as money-launderers or terrorist financers.[43] In each of the listed polities, and more, corruption flourishes, as per the CPI, WBCC, WJI, and many other indicators, including the Panama Papers.

Open Budget Survey and Index

The International Budget Partnership within the Center for Budget and Policy Priorities (Washington, DC) has compiled an Open Budget Survey and Index (102 countries in 2015) since 2006. Open national budgets help to minimize corrupt practices and diversion of resources by placing national budgets, at least, before the public for open inspection. Thus, the survey and index measure "the overall commitment of countries to [budgetary] transparency." By "transparency," the partnership means the extent to which a country gives its citizens access to budget information and enables critics or supporters to participate in the budgeting process each year.[44] In 2015 (its most recent published year), the survey (compiled by the partnership in cooperation with in-country local civil society partners) asserted that the national budgets of seventy-eight states were nontransparent, according to standards developed by the partnership. Sixteen countries had failed to publish their budgets and many more gave their citizens too few opportunities to involve themselves in the budgetary process.

The survey based its conclusions in 2012 on the results of a 125-question survey administered in each country, completed by independent researchers. Ninety-five of the questions dealt directly with the public availability and comprehensiveness of the eight key budget documents that governments publish at various points of their budget cycles. The remaining thirty questions related to opportunities for public participation in the budget process and to the roles played by legislatures and supreme audit institutions in budget formulation and oversight (see chapter 3). The survey claims to measure observable facts related to budget transparency, accountability, and participation, but in fact it often measures opinions about those facts, i.e., whether a budget and its presentation are compatible with international standards.

Most of the questions posed inquire about the amount of budget information in eight essential national budget documents. The answers, aggregated, create an Open Budget Index score and rankings. The Open Budget Index is based on policy indicators relating to specific policy components in one of the seven policy areas. For each answer, there are three options. A maximum of three points is awarded without any obvious rationale when policies meet the highest standards for equal treatment.

In 2015, the Open Budget Index gave the highest marks to New Zealand, Sweden, South Africa, Norway, and the United States, in that order, and the lowest marks (ranks 90 to 102) to Egypt, Fiji, China, Sudan, Venezuela, Cambodia, Chad, Equatorial Guinea, Iraq, Lebanon, Myanmar, Qatar, and Saudi Arabia, in descending order. Following New Zealand's 88-point rating and Sweden's 87-point showing, Malawi (where widespread fiscal fiddling was discovered in 2016) was sub-Saharan Africa's top scorer, with 65 of 100 points, and Ghana was next, with 62 points. In Asia, South Korea registered 65 points and the Philippines 64.

Aid Transparency Index

Although aid transparency by major donors ostensibly is only peripherally related to the larger problem of in-country corruption, the less transparent the amounts and utilization of foreign assistance within targeted countries, the more corruption may flourish. Publish What You Fund is a British nongovernmental organization that has campaigned since 2008 for transparency and open disclosure regarding the provision of aid from donor nations. It sponsors the International Aid Transparency Initiative and, since 2011, the annual Aid Transparency Index. Publish What You Fund asserts that, within recipient countries, it is often difficult to know how much aid is invested, on what it is spent, and to whom it goes. This last aspect sometimes enables corruption and corrupt individuals to flourish. Indeed, in Africa, where foreign assistance in a number of instances indirectly and directly funds large proportions of national budgets and many freestanding projects, opportunities for peculation and mismanagement are rife (and very often employed ingeniously).

In 2016, the Aid Transparency Index (ATI) reviewed sixty-eight donor agencies within seven countries, plus the World Bank. Even within a sending nation, donor organizations may vary by the degree of information that they provide, by their level of opacity, and by the extent to which their operations are publicly accessible. In 2016, the index rated the openness of donors by examining thirty-nine variables that accounted for a donor agency's commitment to transparency and the frequency and fullness of the publication of information. The index results are weighted heavily toward the latter question; higher ratings go to those agencies that disclose what they are doing in formats that are readily accessible. The ultimate high marks are decided by a panel of about a dozen reviewers.[45]

In 2016, the index rated most highly the UN Development Program, the U.S. Millennium Challenge Corporation, UNICEF, the British Department for International Development, the Global Fund, and the World Bank's International Development Association. A raft of countries and agencies, such as Italy, Japan, France, China, and the United Arab Emirates performed "very poorly," the lowest category.[46]

Resource Governance Index

The globe's most corrupt countries, especially in Africa, are resource rich—Angola, the Democratic Republic of Congo, Equatorial Guinea, Nigeria, South Sudan, and Zimbabwe, to cite a few examples. Ruling elites there and elsewhere live off the rents that flow from mining and other asset-stripping activities, often undertaken by foreigners. It makes perfect sense, therefore, to keep a close eye on the off-take from such ventures.

Revenue Watch (New York) and its Natural Resource Governance Institute produce the Resource Governance Index (RGI). It measures the quality of governance in the oil, gas, and mining sectors of fifty-eight countries worldwide. Together, these nations produce 85 percent of the world's oil, 90 percent of diamonds, and 80 percent of copper, generating trillions of dollars annually. The RGI focuses in particular on governance issues in the forty nations that profit primarily from hydrocarbon revenues and on the eighteen where rents are predominantly derived from the exploitation of minerals.

In 2013, the RGI's forty-six researchers (with their work reviewed by fifty-eight experts and Revenue Watch staff) employed a detailed 173-item standardized scoring sheet to assess the quality of four key components of resource governance: a nation's institutional and legal environment, the degree to which laws and regulations facilitate transparency and fair competition; its reporting practices, the actual disclosure of information by official government agencies; its industrial safeguards and quality controls, the checks and oversight arrangements that mandate integrity and prevent conflicts of interest; and its "enabling" environment—a country's general governance and rule of law ratings, as provided by TI, the EIU, and the WGI. The RGI's examination separately scrutinized the three ways in which petroleum, natural gas, and minerals are usually exploited—via state-owned companies, national natural resource funds, and subnational transfers.

In 2013, the RGI found that only eleven of the fifty-eight nations assessed had "satisfactory" transparency and accountability mechanisms. The others all lacked fundamental information about arrangements in their critical resource sectors. In 2013 (the RGI is produced every three years), Norway, the United States, the United Kingdom, Australia, and Brazil (since embroiled in a massive corruption scandal) were at the top of the list, while the poorest performers, in descending order from 50th place, were South Sudan, Zimbabwe, Cambodia, Iran, Qatar, Libya, Equatorial Guinea, Turkmenistan, and Myanmar (Burma). Ghana, in 15th place, was the highest positioned African country, followed immediately by Liberia and Zambia. South Africa was ranked 21st.[47]

Complementing the initiatives of Revenue Watch and the Extractive Industries Transparency Initiative (below) to enhance transparency across those sectors of commerce most prone to corruption—the resource extractive domains—in 2016 the powerful U.S. Securities and Exchange Commission (SEC) ruled that all American and non-American petroleum, natural gas, and mining companies would have to disclose exactly (starting in 2018) how much they pay foreign governments in each fiscal year in taxes, royalties, bonuses, dividends, social responsibility assessments, and other types of fees to further exploration, extraction, and other commercial development activities. The rule was announced four years after being mandated by the Dodd-Frank Wall Street Reform Law.[48]

Extractive Industries and Fisheries Transparency Initiatives

In the same vein and with similar goals as the RGI, the Extractive Industries Transparency Initiative (EITI), headquartered in Oslo, seeks to strengthen transparency in the resource sector, specifically by persuading countries to disclose all of their revenues from multinational corporations. The countries are also expected to work closely with civil society in their countries to implement the EITI arrangements. "When poorly managed," the EITI website declares, extraction of a country's natural resources "too often lead[s] to corruption." Openness, it says gently, helps to ensure that hydrocarbon and mineral wealth "benefit all citizens."

EITI may be too gentle. Economically viable oil and gas deposits are so rare and so valuable, as are mineral deposits, that a prospecting concern and its executives have immense commercial incentives to obtain concessions and access at almost any reputational and monetary cost. Government control of that access, in turn, makes that which is underground or undersea vulnerable to high levels of extortion by host country political leaders. Outside petroleum and mining firms are among the most likely of all business operations to pay bribes and promise munificent rewards to cooperating officials. Great fortunes can be made by shady, predatory investors willing to operate in conditions of great risk and high potential reward.[49]

In order to inhibit the shadowy activities that inevitably defraud citizenries, the EITI created a special standard that commits countries, when they agree to adhere to its requirements, to disclose all taxes and other payments made by resource extraction industries to governments so that citizens and civil societies may monitor how those revenues are utilized to benefit the nation or, sometimes, to fill the rent-collecting pockets of their national leaders. The EITI founders and its current directors hope that greater transparency improves developing-world country investment climates, reduces lingering intrastate propensities to conflict, and produces enhanced economic and political, and therefore social, stability.[50]

Nations with resources first submit work plans committing themselves to the transparency required by the EITI standard. They become candidates, are investigated and validated by an independent board, and, if certified, are listed officially as "compliant" candidate countries within EITI. Those countries have to be revalidated every three years. Among other certification issues, the EITI protocol requires that candidate countries submit timely publication of resource receipt reports, arrange plausible auditing methods, and present all of the relevant data to its public. In 2013, EITI also began a pilot project with eleven of its member nations to identify the real owners, the true beneficiaries, of those entities that extract revenues from under the soils or the nearby seas of its countries. The end result of EITI efforts through 2017 might be a much-needed registry in each member country of the beneficial, not the paper, owners of the corporate entities that bid for, operate, or invest in extractive in-country assets.[51]

The potential power of EITI, and its local affiliates, was demonstrated in Nigeria. In 2014, monitors from the Nigerian branch of EITI estimated that the nation could be losing about $8 billion annually thanks to swap deals exchanging crude oil for refined products—a superb source of enrichment for arbitrageurs. In 2015, after the election of President Muhammadu Buhari and his sacking of a raft of holdover officials responsible for distributing official petroleum revenues, the EITI confirmed that "Nigeria's oil industry [was] riddled with corruption and lacking in transparency." EITI admonished Buhari and his new administration to integrate EITI best principles into their economic policy agenda.[52] Subsequently, Buhari decided to be his own oil industry minister and clean house. He also dissolved the Nigerian National Petroleum Corporation, previously the country's official oil operations controller.

In 2016, twenty-seven nations were fully compliant with the EITI requirements, forty-three had publicized the revenues that they were receiving from resources extracted, and sixteen nations were implementing the EITI standard and were candidate members. Cameroon, Chad, the Democratic Republic of Congo, Ghana, Guinea, Liberia, Mali, Mauritania, Sierra Leone, Togo, Trinidad and Tobago, and Zambia were among those certified as compliant, along with Norway. Zambia was the first mining-dependent nation in eastern and central Africa to meet the EITI requirements, meaning that it annually has to disclose and reconcile all revenues from its extractive sector; its citizens could henceforward themselves monitor what their country receives from those who exploit its sub-soil riches. In 2016, Ukraine, the United Kingdom, the United States, Colombia, Ethiopia, Madagascar, Myanmar (Burma), Senegal, and the Seychelles were still candidates for membership. Suspended from the EITI roll of honor were the Central African Republic, Guatemala, Indonesia, Tajikistan, and Yemen.[53]

Given EITI's success in focusing international and host country attention on precisely those sectors of the global economy that are most prone to large-scale corruption, it is not surprising that the president of an African country reliant on revenues from off-shore fishing should have asked EITI's founder to help him launch a Fisheries Transparency Initiative (FITI). In 2015, President Mohamed Ould Abdel Aziz of Mauritania, a desert land on the northwest coast of Africa largely dependent on revenues from oceanic industrial fishing, wanted his impoverished nation to spearhead a new global effort to make revenues from fishing transparent.

Most developing countries with control of fishing zones are taken advantage of by foreign fishing fleets (now especially China's and Spain's) that either under-report their catches or ignore any responsibility to follow on-shore regulations. The fishing sector of the global economy has long been typified by "bribery and crooked deals."[54] Foreign entities routinely bribe local officials up and down western Africa and throughout the island states of Oceania for "licenses" while abusing those permits and vastly depleting fish stocks. If it spreads as a set of procedures to be observed to other nation-states dependent upon fishing revenues, and if Chinese and European fleets comply, FITI could at least bring attention to one more resource-rich arena, and thus to the measurement and possible reduction of corruption in a behavioral zone long obscure.

Crony Capitalism Index

Complementing the intent and efforts of Revenue Watch and the EITI, the *Economist* constructed an index of crony capitalism to test whether "robber barons" were exploiting or living off relations with governments that were inappropriately cozy. The weekly suggested that over the past two decades, "crony fortunes had leapt relative to global GDP and as a share of billionaire wealth." These fortunes were being made particularly in such industries as construction, petroleum, and casinos.

Rent seeking, the notion that owners of inputs of production (land, labor, machinery, or capital) extract more wealth from government-protected and government-facilitated market arrangements (often monopolies and cartels) than they do from competitive markets, is at the heart of crony capitalism and the corrupt dealings that inevitably accompany cozy relationships with those officials and politicians who control permits and perquisites. For example, "We classify deposit-taking as a crony industry," reports the *Economist*, "because of its implicit state guarantee."

The *Economist's* index compares crony wealth to total GDP. Developing economies, it says, account for 43 percent of global GDP but 65 percent of crony wealth. China has the most extensive concentration of crony wealth ($360 billion worth) despite President Xi Jinping's attack on casinos and casino moguls (see chapter 8), but new billionaires in other protected rent-rich enterprises have taken their place, and still live off state contacts.

Overall, in the 2016 running of the Crony Capitalism Index, Russia was the worst, with a level of billionaire wealth as a percentage of GDP that far exceeded second place Malaysia and third place Philippines. Singapore was fourth, because, despite its probity, it was "an entrepôt for racier neighbors."[55] Ukraine, Mexico, Indonesia, Turkey, India, and Taiwan round out the list of the ten jurisdictions most infected by crony capitalism—a list that may also reflect levels of resource-infected corruption. The other twelve nations on the index range from China (11th) and the United States (16th) to Germany (22nd).

Means and Measures

To curb corruption sustainably, reliable knowledge is essential. What all of these indexes and ingenious proxy methods of measuring the comparative levels of corruption, country to country and region to region, provide are targets—goals to be chased, accountabilities to be raised, transparencies to be perfected. Additional measurement methods, and there are several, include the Milken Institute's Opacity Index, which through 2011 estimated some of the hidden costs that are attributed to corruption and poor governance; various Public Expenditure Tracking Surveys that reveal the diversion of public resources; and the several social audit techniques discussed at length in chapter 9. An additional database of enormous potential is the ID Search, a product of the Organized Crime and Corruption Reporting Project and its investigative dashboard. Released for the first time in 2016, it was developed by a nonprofit network of investigative journalism centers in Europe and Eurasia, and contains more than 3.6 million documents derived from business gazettes, company records, court cases, confirmed and unconfirmed leaks of information, and more. The platform is searchable, updated daily, and contains a comprehensive open source list of so-called "politically exposed persons."

Such databases, disclosures, rankings, and ratings enable governments, civil societies, international organizations and lenders, and national donors to diagnose developmental issues and concerns and, conceivably, to recommend and implement potential remedies capable of lessening the impact of corruption on peoples and nations.

Perceptions of corruption, country to country, are more than an exercise. So are levels of financial secrecy or extents of moneys laundered. Each of these indicators helps to illuminate the dimensions of corrupt behavior globally and nationally, but also informs us on how best to reduce, or attempt to reduce, corrupt practices across all nations and within targeted states.

These many indicators collectively also produce a baseline of corruption. From the baseline it is possible to advocate and experiment with the kinds of reforms that have been shown elsewhere to make a difference, and might once more do so in targeted countries. Hence, in a later chapter, this volume examines those nation-states that improved their anticorruption scores most dramatically between 2004 and 2014 and finds out how. Another chapter looks at the laws and altered governmental practices that in some places have helped to reduce perceived levels of corruption. Without such baselines, it would be difficult to demonstrate that certain kinds of initiatives have had positive returns and others have not. Evidence-based endeavors, in other words, are impossible without the existing calibrations of corruption, no matter how flawed technically they might or might not be.

These various ways of employing gimlet eyes of oversight to the sleazy, shadowy business of corruption permit civil societies within countries, and donors and world powers outside a target nation-state, to possess the scores, ranks, and indictments of the kind that lead to helpful pressure on governments to do better, to battle corruption more strenuously, and to institute the kinds of reforms that could be decisively pathbreaking in the global and local struggle against the curse of corruption.

Before the 1990s, when controlling corruption first became a serious international pursuit, subsequently endorsed by the World Bank, the OECD, the UN, and a number of powerful nations, few believed that developing-world corruption could be moderated or that whatever the phenomenon was, that it could be quantified, examined, campaigned against, and occasionally reduced in scope. The battle is not close to being won, but it is being waged skillfully. Some salient victories have been achieved—as future chapters suggest and describe—in large part because numerical methods of expressing the impress of corrupt practices are easily available.

Strong Laws and Other Watchdogs

Corruption is never banished by chance. Essential to any attempted eradication of corrupt practices are:

- political will;
- national and international laws that define a range of improper and illegal acts as corruption;
- an aroused populace that has been educated about the ills of corruption and is opposed to and vocally unhappy with bureaucratic and political decisions that are influenced by corruption;
- a media and a civil society that are sufficiently observant, investigative, and courageous to discover and report corrupt acts;
- functioning ombudsmen and auditors general;
- a national commission or some similar body charged specifically with the detection of corruption and the investigation of individuals accused of illegal corrupt activity;
- diligent prosecutors or attorneys general willing to try offenders, no matter their political heft; and
- a fearless judiciary sufficiently independent to try cases of corruption fairly.

The addition of an international anticorruption court to this armory of weapons against corrupt practices would provide a further institutional method of attacking the scourge. (See also the discussion in chapters 10 and 11.)

Domestic Legal Frameworks

Good domestic laws are at least a start. The best ones define corrupt acts and corrupt behavior clearly, spelling out in some detail what is permitted and what is not. In some cases, specific limits on what may be given and what may be received by a public servant, and under what sets of conditions, are described at length. Many legal frameworks, however, are excessively general, vague, too broad, or poorly drafted. Potential offenders may envisage loopholes or pathways to fortune despite the intent of the relevant legislation. Or, potential offenders may twist weak or fuzzy laws to suit their illicit purposes.

Aware that poorly drafted regulations might prove incapable of regulating avarice and other related human weaknesses among public servants, a few exemplary nation-states have struggled, usually after bouts of trial and error, to write tight, tough laws that—appropriately repugnant as their permissive provisions might be to civil libertarians—ease the pursuit and prosecution of acts or behaviors that approximate or hint at corruption. A few nation-states have discovered, moreover, that legislation written with a long reach and a wide ambit can help to deter corruption.

Some nation-states allow circumstantial evidence of corrupt dealings. Others permit investigation and prosecution merely because someone appears to be living beyond her or his means. Such inclusive laws make it easier to arrest alleged offenders and, after forensic or other investigatory work, to indict them in a convincing manner. The more legal provisions curtail (unfortunately) a potential defendant's civil liberties, the easier it is for the prosecutors. Indeed, in several nations that have successfully reduced corruption, prosecutors have possessed broad powers of search and seizure, have been permitted to enter hearsay evidence, and have been allowed by law and judicial practice to infer guilt merely from suspicious actions or appearances. In some critical nation-states, hard proof or direct evidence has not been required.

Prosecuting corrupt behavior is obviously easier if a defendant can be shown to have assets that greatly exceed his or her regular earnings, or if he or she has made purchases of very expensive houses, motor cars, or yachts. In one Malawian case from the late 1990s, corrupt practices would have continued for years if the culprit, the head of a critical state commission, had not abruptly purchased a wildly expensive car that no one on his puny official salary plausibly could have afforded.

Several nation-states with systematic successes in reducing corruption have relied on tightly written and draconian laws and, naturally, on the employment of robust legal frameworks to ease the work of investigating and prosecuting perceived miscreants. Good laws, no matter how well written, are never sufficient in the battle against corruption. Yet they are necessary to proceed effectively against accused offenders, and to constrain corrupt behavior.

Nation-states that have largely succeeded in reducing corrupt behavior, such as Hong Kong, Singapore, South Korea, Botswana, and Ghana, possess complementary codes of conduct and legal provisions. But so do states where corruption today runs wild, such as South Africa, Tanzania, and Zambia. Legal codes may be similar, but it is how those strictures are brought to bear on conditions of corruption—how political leaders choose to use whatever legal armaments they possess—that determines the extent to which corruption flourishes or subsides.

Singapore and Hong Kong crafted their original modern bars against corruption, and later strengthened them, to give their national administrations the upper hand against those who succumbed to corrupt temptations. Singapore's anticorruption legislation reaches farther and is far more punitive than most. Certainly, Singapore's laws in this area deny a number of protections that are essential to common law regimes and that are fundamental to rights in the United States. But that is the way Prime Minister Lee Kuan Yew, a British-trained lawyer, and his associates, wanted them. For Lee and his colleagues, the struggle against corrupt practices was unremitting, with no plausible legal avenue barred.

British-governed Singapore was rife with rampant corruption before it became self-governing in 1959. "Corruption was a way of life . . . perceived by the public as a low risk, high reward activity." The city-state's 1960 far-reaching Prevention of Corruption Act defined corruption in terms of various forms of "gratification."[1] Both givers and takers were equally culpable. It imposed stiff monetary fines and five-year terms of imprisonment for convicted offenders. A member of Parliament or a member of a public body could receive a longer sentence—up to seven years. So could anyone who had been involved in an official contract. Civil servants could lose their jobs, their benefits, and their pensions. Moreover, a person found guilty of accepting an illegal "gratification" had to repay the full amount of the bribe in addition to the initial $10,000 fine per offense (increased to $100,000 in 1989). Section 17 of the 1960 legislation empowered Singapore's public prosecutor to investigate any bank statement or other financial accounts of suspects. Section 18 enabled the perusal of any accounts belonging to civil servants, their wives, children, or agents.[2]

Singapore's civil service instructional manuals and its regulations prohibited any public servant from borrowing money or financially obligating themselves to any person with whom they did or could have official dealings. They could at no time possess unsecured debts or substantial liabilities. They were barred from using official information for private gain. As in many other jurisdictions, they were required to declare their assets annually. They could not engage in any trade or business or take up part time outside employment (restrictions that would cripple poorly paid African civil servants), or receive shares in public or private companies. They had to refuse to be entertained in any manner by members of the public.[3]

Singapore curtailed the rights of alleged offenders. From 1963, the state's anticorruption bureau could require witnesses to present themselves for questioning. In 1966, an amendment to the 1960 act permitted an accused to be found guilty of corruption, even though that person had never received a bribe, if it were clear to a magistrate that he or she had intended to commit the offense. Persons employed by Singapore could also be prosecuted beginning in 1966 for offenses committed outside the country in embassies or similar bodies.

Beginning in 1981, Singaporeans convicted of corruption could receive stiffer prison sentences if they were unable to repay money embezzled or received as an illegal gratification. In 1989, after a cabinet minister was questioned at length and then committed suicide, laws changed to allow the estate of a corrupt person to be confiscated. So could the estate of any suspect who fled the country and who could not be extradited.[4] In other words, Singapore systematically over several decades legally increased the risk and reduced many of the incentives for corrupt behavior. It did so by enacting and then strengthening tough, even punitive, laws and then by developing efficient and effective means of uncovering and prosecuting corrupt persons. Clearly, when Singapore chose (and wanted) to punish corrupt actions mercilessly, tightly and broadly drawn laws facilitated prosecution.

In 2015, the chief justice of Singapore's Supreme Court decided that it had come time to handle convicted corrupt officials even more mercilessly than before, and to do so even though the accused were, technically, private persons performing governmental functions only under contract. The chief justice increased a ship inspector's jail sentence from two to six months for soliciting bribes in exchange for lenient vessel inspections. "Clean and honest dealings," declared Chief Justice Sundaresh Menon, were one of Singapore's "key competitive advantages." Corrupt behavior, he said, "compromises the predictability and openness which . . . investors have come to expect." The chief justice did not want that "hard won prize" to be forfeited. He also cited a well-known academic study showing that corruption reduced growth considerably. The chief justice did not want Singapore to grow more slowly, hence the increased sentence.[5]

In 2016, in another exemplary Singaporean case, a local corporate executive received bribes from a Malaysian businesswoman in exchange for advancing the interests of the latter with a transport and logistics company. Together they falsified invoices and payment vouchers, and the Singaporean purchased a condominium and a fancy car with the proceeds. Singapore's Corrupt Practices Investigation Bureau (see chapter 4) said this case showed that it still had a "zero tolerance approach" toward corrupt criminal activity.[6]

Hong Kong's colonial rulers faced problems similar to those Singapore confronted in the 1960s and addressed them in a congruent fashion. By the early 1970s, Hong Kong under British control had long been corrupt. Venal as well as persistent petty corrupt acts were accepted modes of behavior. As in contemporary Singapore and other British holdings on the periphery of Asia, high levels of corruption among officials, particularly within police forces, were tolerated provided that they did not threaten British hegemony unduly and did not occasion large-scale citizenry protests. The colony's laws against all recognizable forms of corruption, public and private, dated to the nineteenth century, with little discernible impact on total corruption or on diminished mendacity levels.

Especially egregious examples of corruption, many involving the British-run constabulary, finally led to the revamping and tightening of longstanding laws against bribery and other forms of corruption after 1971. Central was the 1974 amended version of the 1971 Prevention of Bribery Ordinance, an updated Corrupt and Illegal Practices Ordinance, and the Independent Commission against Corruption Act, which established what soon became the most effective of the many attempts to corral corruption through Hong Kong's Independent Commission against Corruption (ICAC) (see chapter 4).

As a result of these legislative actions in 1974, it became illegal in Hong Kong to obstruct justice, steal government resources, engage in blackmail or deception, bribe anyone, make false accusations, or conspire (which could mean anything and everything) with others to commit an offense. Hong Kong, followed by many African jurisdictions, criminalized "any act or omission in the discharge [of a public official's duties] for the purposes of illicitly obtaining benefits for himself or herself or for a third party."[7] Possession by a civil servant of wealth in excess of his or her official salary was prohibited— "living beyond known means." Likewise, in the private sector, anyone who gave or refused favors "in relation to his principal's affairs or business" became guilty of dishonesty, an offense. Kickbacks, unauthorized rebates, commissions capable of undercutting corporate endeavors, and other nefarious "takings of advantage" were deemed illicit. Moreover, in keeping with the Singaporean template, the new commission and prosecutors were permitted to conduct searches, examine bank accounts and safe-deposit boxes, subpoena witnesses, audit private assets, prevent monies from being transferred out of the colony, and detain putative offenders. The authorities could seize passports and property and imprison suspects to prevent border crossings into China or escape elsewhere.[8]

Despite such prosecutorial-friendly, broad-ranging, and punitive legislation, corrupt practices may still flourish in today's Hong Kong and elsewhere.

It is not the tough character of the laws themselves, obviously, but the ways in which those laws are observed, infractions scrutinized, and offenders interrogated and punished. Indeed, legal provisions against corruption, no matter how harsh and far reaching, and the existence of active anticorruption commissions, matter little if political will is lacking and if police investigators, prosecutors, and judges are all compromised by habit or circumstance. Good legislation is never enough, especially in those parts of the globe where legal restrictions are often honored in the breach and where prosecutions and judicial outcomes can be influenced by executive action or further forms of corruption.

South Korea is another Asian case. Even after decades of slimming the levels of corruption that were typical in the twentieth century, South Korea was still not confident that its reduction was sustainable. Thus, in 2015, South Korea, plagued by recurring corruption scandals and some major tragedies probably caused by corruption, made it illegal to accept cash or gifts worth more than 1 million won (about $900). Not only were civil servants prohibited from receiving "presents," but so were journalists and teachers, all of whom were culturally accustomed to receiving envelopes filled with cash at least annually. Moreover, South Korean businessmen and government officials routinely hosted expensive dinners, sent gifts to mark holidays, and provided thick envelopes at weddings and funerals. The obligations of social etiquette could easily be confused with bribery; the new law construes anything over 1 million won as presumptively corrupt, and promises punishment for taking large "gifts," with or without any proof of influence peddling or any direct evidence that the payments are being made in exchange for a specific favor. Under the new law, spouses of presumed inducement recipients are also covered under the ban, with a three-year jail sentence prescribed for convicted culprits.[9]

African Examples

Much of the legislation enacted in sub-Saharan Africa to combat corruption is derived either directly or secondarily from the Hong Kong and Singaporean codes. The legal frameworks, therefore, are strong and well-drafted and give investigators and prosecutors sufficient grounds for effective action. But the experiences of at least several of the African cases over a number of years show that legal frameworks are less important in the battle against corruption than are the attitudes of those who administer and utilize those instruments. The different outcomes in Africa (further discussed in chapter 5) reflect political will (or its absence) and the results of collective action, not necessarily the quality of national laws.

Under its first two presidents, Sir Seretse Khama and Sir Ketumile Masire, Botswana remained largely free of corruption. Khama had worked hard to establish a political culture antithetical to behavior that could be construed as corrupt (see chapter 8). Both men prided themselves on their integrity, their modesty, and their intolerance of the kinds of questionable, self-serving decisions that were common in nearby African countries. Under their leadership, Botswana built strongly upon its precolonial and colonial traditions of honest dealing. But, during Masire's third term in office—in the early 1990s—more and more public servants appeared to be abusing their positions for private gain. Among the cavalcade of misuse of power discovered in that era were the allocation of excessive numbers of ranches to prominent persons under the tribal grazing land program; the awarding of dubious contracts for primary school teaching materials; the selling of land illegally in peri-urban towns; over-invoicing on big construction projects; flagrant excessive rent-seeking arrangements by the heads of the Botswana Housing Corporation; and the plundering by politicians of the Botswana National Development Bank, the Botswana Cooperative Bank, and the Agricultural Marketing Board. Leaders of the ruling Botswana Democratic Party, but not Masire, were directly implicated. There had been "a failure in the entire government system," and of its upper echelons. Yet, a leading critic could not regard this sudden irruption of corrupt behavior as systematic (as in then contemporary Zaire) or as epidemic (as in then militarily managed Nigeria). There was as yet no "culture of corruption."[10]

It was in reaction to these scandals—Botswana was unaccustomed to such culpable political activities—that Botswana sent a high-level delegation to London and Hong Kong and returned home from Hong Kong determined to draw directly on that Crown colony's experience and laws. The Parliament of Botswana subsequently passed the Corruption and Economic Crime Act. It provided for the establishment of the Directorate on Corruption and Economic Crime, modeled on Hong Kong's ICAC. The Ombudsman Act of 1995 also authorized the president, in consultation with the leader of the opposition, to appoint an ombudsman to answer complaints from the public.

Botswana's 1994 legislation outlawed obtaining or receiving a "valuable consideration" and defined it as any gift, benefit, loan, or reward; any office, employment or contract; any payments or discharges of obligations or loans; "any other service"; "the exercise of forbearance" regarding obligations; any promises or undertakings; and the giving of special favors or permits to preferred individuals.[11] Without resolving any contradictions between the provisions of the act(s) and the country's toughly written penal code, it also created new categories of offenses, modified existing legal rules of evidence, and gave the Directorate on Corruption and Economic Crime wide-ranging powers to examine the conduct of any person who may be "connected with or *conducive to* corruption." In an equally vague manner, the directorate was required to assist other governmental agencies in pursuing persons and institutions believed to be dishonest or cheating government revenue authorities. The directorate was empowered to search, seize, and arrest suspects almost at will. It could further require anyone to produce documents, records, and data no matter how or where stored, to provide information, to answer questions, and to proffer a statement detailing all moveable and immoveable property and how each item had been obtained and why and when.

As in Singapore, Botswana was thus empowered to investigate whether and as a result of what specific good fortune an official or a politician was living well above her or his ostensible means. Such legislation permitted anticorruption bodies and prosecutors to discover whether an individual was indeed benefiting from access to resources beyond those commensurate with his present or past regular sources of income or assets, and how those living standards came to be realized. Under section 40 of the act, the existence of "unexplained or disproportionate" resources could be used to corroborate the testimony of witnesses about the illicit transfer of "valuable considerations." Witnesses might be compelled to violate oaths of secrecy.[12] The directorate further was permitted access to all confidential documents.

Singapore's and Botswana's anticorruption acts override fundamental common law principles: individuals may not remain silent and may not be permitted to refuse to incriminate themselves. The evidence of accomplices may be heard without corroboration. Persons "reasonably suspected" of being corrupt may be arrested without a warrant and with the use of any and all necessary force. Aggressive forms of search and seizure are allowed. In other words, both countries (and Hong Kong to some considerable extent) have eroded the civil liberty protections normally afforded to citizens of democracies in favor of easing the investigation and prosecution of corruption. Investigators and prosecutors enjoy remarkable levels of discretion. Furthermore, those affected by such anticorruption legislation are unable to prevent the misuse of executive or legislative powers by invoking the checks and balances afforded in other democracies.

Tanzania has had a robust legal framework capable of countering corruption since at least 1971, but in 2016 corruption still infected every corner of its society (and had without surcease since the 1970s and before). The nation's 1971 Prevention of Corruption Act, amended in 2002 and 2007, makes illegal a broad range of activities in the governmental sector and also bans private sector corruption. The Anti–Money Laundering Act of 2006 (amended in 2012) curbs capital flight and the financing of terrorism. The 2004 Public Procurement Act prohibits bribe-receiving and other illegal methods of influencing tendering procedures. The Elections Expenses Act of 2010 inhibits the illegal mobilization of financial and other resources (and the naked buying of votes) during elections. The 1995 Public Leadership Code of Ethics Act mandates that all public officials file statements of assets annually. Finally, the 2007

Prevention and Combating of Corruption Act protects public-sector employees (whistleblowers) who report instances of corruption.[13]

In neighboring Zambia, the 1996 Anti-Corruption Act made illegal the soliciting of, proffering, or accepting of bribes by public officers and those attempting to bribe public officers in exchange for doing something or not doing it. The act further made it a criminal offense to falsify receipts and other documents, to take or give bribes to influence votes or other official acts by public bodies, to exercise influence regarding contracts or tenders in exchange for inducements, and so on.

As provided in most of the other national anticorruption legal frameworks, the Zambian Anti-Corruption Commission (see also chapter 5) was allowed to investigate any public officer about whom there were "reasonable grounds" to believe that he or she had abused his or her position for private gain, that he or she was living above his or her means, had accumulated property or other assets in excess of his or her present or past emoluments, or was in receipt of services obtained corruptly. Increased assets in the hands of family members made a public officer culpable. Further, it was no defense that a suspect accepted a gratification "without intending to do so." Nor could an accused claim that a bribe was a "customary" payment. As in Singapore, no matter where Zambians resided, they were subject to the act. Those convicted of offenses in Zambia were to be imprisoned for five to twelve years, be fined, and were obligated to pay back the full amount of any bribes received.[14]

In 2010, under President Rupiah Banda, Zambia rewrote all of its anticorruption legislation. Bringing its laws into concert with the Southern African Development Community Protocol on Corruption, the African Union Convention on Combating and Preventing Corruption, and the UN Convention against Corruption (see below), Zambia's Parliament passed the Anti-Corruption Commission Act, the Forfeiture of Proceeds of Crime Act, the Public Interest Disclosure (Protection of Whistleblowers) Act, the Plea Bargaining Act, the Financial Intelligence Act, and the National Prosecution Authority Act, and thoroughly amended the Prohibition and Prevention of Money Laundering Act. This assemblage of laws gave Zambia, almost uniquely among sub-Saharan nations, very strong arms with which to pursue embezzlers, bribers and bribe-takers, and other abusers of authority and position. Supporting the effort of the existing Anti-Corruption Commission (ACC), open for business in 1982 and reauthorized in 1996, the 2010 enactments specify about a dozen illegal forms of corruption, including gratification, concealment, conspiracy, and abetting. They penalize false testimony, falsification and alteration of documents, and obstruction by offenders. They specifically provide for the recovery of assets. But section 47 (4) (b) allows decisions on whom to investigate to be made in consultation with "any appropriate authority," a dangerously politically permissive element. Section 59 further undermines the independence of the ACC by giving the director of public prosecutions discretionary powers over which suspects the ACC is permitted to prosecute. As we shall see in chapter 5, these two sections eviscerate the legal independence of the Zambian (and other similarly worded) anticorruption commission mandates.[15]

South Africa technically has among the best-drafted bodies of contemporary anticorruption legislation in Africa. Its Prevention and Combating of Corruption Act of 2004 forbids public and private persons and, specifically, legislators and judicial officers, from giving or accepting any gratification, whether for self-enrichment or for the benefit of another; bans the misuse or selling of material or information acquired while performing official duties; prohibits abuses of authority or breaches of trust; and equally makes criminal "any ... unauthorized or improper inducement ... not to do anything." Nor are officials allowed to expedite or prevent the performance of an official act. South African legislation specifically bans bribing foreign officials or their surrogates. It seeks to penalize false testimonies in court, the altering or mutilation of official records, and the withholding of information. Auctioneers are not allowed to accept gratifications to alter bidding processes or outcomes. Nor are those involved in sporting events and in running casinos.

As in other national anticorruption endeavors, the South African authorities may arrest suspects without notice, seize their assets, summon anyone as a witness, and make suspects or witnesses produce account books and other forms of evidence of corruption. It is no defense under this same South African law to claim that he or she never had any intent to use influence or perform acts illegally. Moreover, convicted participants in corrupt schemes may be fined heavily, have illicit proceeds confiscated, and be incarcerated for life.[16]

In Ghana, to observe one more African case, it is an offense for anyone holding public office to abuse that position for private profit or benefit or to allow himself or herself to be influenced by gifts, promises, or "valuable considerations." Equally guilty is the person who attempts to influence an office holder, whether or not that office holder is already in a position to provide some return to the bribe giver. "A police officer," Ghana's Criminal Code (Amendment) Act of 2003 proclaims, "is guilty of extortion [if] under colour of his office," if he or she demands any "money or valuable consideration."[17]

Laws Are Never Enough

These many elaborate legislative safeguards of probity are not unusual in the developing world. Many countries have enacted similar laws and have similar regulations. From time to time, in the enduring combat against corruption, parliaments pass tough anticorruption acts or the executive sets down rules and regulations that ministers and civil servants are meant to follow. But in only a very few cases (such as Hong Kong, Singapore, Botswana, Mauritius, and Ghana) have these well-drafted legal instruments plausibly combated corruption with a high degree of success.

The presence of fine laws does not necessarily lead to the discovery, prosecution, or conviction of offenders. Tanzania is a case in point. Tanzania's Prevention and Combating of Corruption Bureau was created to arrest, investigate, and prosecute perpetrators of corruption. But it does so only rarely. It also fails to act on complaints. The judiciary is politically influenced.[18] The Registrar of Political Parties has been unable to monitor fundraising and election expenditures by political parties. The Public Procurement Regulatory Authority has largely failed to prevent fraudulent tendering practices; there have been a number of scandals regarding construction projects. Nor is the Ethics Act enforced: many government officials falsify their declarations or simply refuse to disclose their assets—without effective punishment. In other words, Tanzania's anticorruption legislation has been widely ignored, evaded, and abused (see chapter 5).

In the Tanzanian case (which is similar to many others), none of the impressive available legal instruments works effectively to prevent corruption. Politicians pay no notice to the Election Expenses Act and ignore the Leadership Code, frequently failing to file disclosure forms. Whistleblowers are in great danger; retaliation has occurred often and has been damaging. More significantly, according to public opinion surveys and anecdotal evidence, official efforts in Tanzania against corruption are ineffective.[19] Hardly any corrupt office holders have been prosecuted, even those directly implicated in an Air Tanzania leasing scandal, those who shifted funds illegally from the central bank overseas into private accounts, those who sold overpriced electricity to the government, or those deeply enmeshed in poaching and the illicit sale of ivory. Often the decisions of prosecutors or judges are overruled for political reasons and because of a fundamental lack of political will.[20]

Tanzania's latest major scam cost three cabinet members their positions in early 2015, the energy minister quitting to "bring an end to this debate on the scandal." He insisted, roundly, that he was "not a thief." In late 2014, Parliament's Public Accounts Committee learned that $122 million in central bank funds had been paid fraudulently into private overseas accounts using the cover of energy contracts. Implicated in the scheme, which to some extent echoes Kenya's earlier Anglo-Leasing initiative, were Tanesco (the nation's state-owned electrical monopoly), the attorney general, the minister of energy, the minister of lands, and several other senior politicians and officials. The Public Accounts Committee also accused Prime Minister Mizengo Pinda of knowing about the looting of the Reserve Bank and doing nothing.[21]

New Tanzanian President John Magufuli seemed determined in 2016 to change his national political culture, but the extent to which his leadership actually is being translated into transformative positive action is discussed in chapter 8.

Auditors, Parliamentary Committees, and Ombudsmen

The office of auditor general, often as head of an audit commission, exists in forty-one African countries. In the best of circumstances, that office and the auditor general scrutinize all government operations, especially contracts, to ensure that they conform to proper procedures and regulations. Such activities come to greater popular notice when auditors discover unauthorized actions and expenditures, false tendering, fraud, and systematic corruption. In such cases, the best auditors general document their discoveries and follow usually circumscribed routes to report what they have found. As Liberia's General Auditing Commission reminds readers on its website, it is "the defender and promoter of the Liberian people's interest"—the first line of integrity in government.[22]

In most cases, the reports of auditors general are destined, by law, to be delivered to the relevant parliament. In such a venue, inconvenient findings of auditors general have languished, pigeonholed for political reasons. In some countries, however, auditors general report to the president, or to the public, and their findings may be publicized. In Brazil, auditors' reports are rapidly put on the web, for all to see.

In 2015, Sierra Leone's national auditor revealed that government ministers had "lost track" of more than $3 million in funds that were meant to be devoted to the ongoing battle against the Ebola virus and disease. The fate of another $2.5 million that was disbursed from an emergency fund was documented only incompletely. This $5.5 million in misspent or purloined funds constituted a sizable percentage of the $19 million that had supposedly been allocated to the Ebola battle between May and October 2014, when the epidemic raged fiercely, and had been raised internally from institutions and individuals. (Donor funds were not included.) As the auditor general reported somberly to Parliament, such accounting lapses resulted in "a reduction in the quality of service delivery in the health sector"—services desperately needed and sorely missed.[23]

South Africa has an active and well-staffed audit office. In 2014 alone, Auditor General Thembekile Makwetu reported to the South African Parliament's Public Accounts Committee that parts of the national government had wasted more than R2 billion (then about $200 million) over the previous year while simultaneously incurring R26 billion in irregular expenditures, up by a third from the 2013 reporting year. At the municipal level, the auditor general also discovered that employees had been rewarding themselves (or suppliers with which they had a close interest) with substantial contracts worth at least R850 million (then about $8.5 million) in 2012–2013. Nearly R12 billion of irregular expenditures were uncovered at the local level. Only 9 percent of municipalities received clean audits. As the auditor general concluded, "When government business is conducted outside the controlled environment . . . it becomes [a] free for all. . . . As a result, opportunities for realization of service delivery objectives are lost."[24]

Similarly, in Kenya, a 2015 report of the national auditor general, covering the 2013–2014 fiscal year, concluded that only 26 percent of the government's financial statements were "true and fair." A full 16 percent were "misleading." The government essentially could not account for the largest proportion of its $16 billion budget; there were "persistent and disturbing problems in collection and accounting for revenue." The auditor general cited empty offices for which the police were paying, numerous faulty military vehicles, and the transfer of $2 billion illegally to an offshore bank.[25]

In the more effective African parliaments, a public accounts committee receives and acts upon the reports of auditors general. At least, these committees (often chaired according to parliamentary custom by an opposition-nominated figure) may question the government of the day about irregularities noted by the auditor general. If the auditor general has found discrepancies in official accounts, in tendering, in misappropriated departmental budgets, or in particular expenditures, members of the committee may cross-examine the relevant cabinet minister or heads of statutory bodies. Done right, and brightly, the combination of a vigilant auditor general and an active committee can expose fraud and corruption—which has a laudable preventive effect.

Ombudsmen, called public protectors in South Africa, operate differently, but, by turning complaints from the public into investigations and cases to answer, may have an equally salutary impact on the spread of corruption. The world's first so-called ombudsman was designated by Swedish King Charles XII in 1713 to ensure that judges and bureaucrats behaved justly and appropriately, that is, that they remained loyal to the king during his exile in Istanbul. A century later, Sweden's Riksdag in 1809 established the Office of the Supreme Ombudsman to watch over the interests of citizens who might be oppressed by the chancellor of justice, the king's enforcer. But this early ombudsman, as most subsequent ones, could notice and expose abuses and make recommendations but had no power to right wrongs directly. However, in Sweden the ombudsman was able to proceed legally against those who acted improperly and to urge Parliament to legislate necessary legal changes. In Sweden in the nineteenth century there was a "high demand for accountability" and a desire to control corruption.[26]

Finland installed an ombudsman in 1920, Denmark in 1954, and New Zealand in 1962. Those functions of giving citizens access to legal redress, hearing complaints against officials and finding remedies, and checking governmental activity are essentially the modern purpose of an ombudsperson. Contemporary Africa has forty-six offices of ombudsmen.

A few years after independence, Tanzania became the first African country to create such an office—the Permanent Commission of Enquiry—in 1965. Within a year it was dealing with 3,000 complaints annually. Ghana and Mauritius followed Tanzania. In 1973, so did Zambia, with 550 cases a year, Sudan, and various states in Nigeria. Except for Sudan and the Nigerian states, the early model consisted of the ombudsperson being appointed by the executive, but many African countries in more recent times tied the ombuds office to Parliament, from which it derives its funding and to which it reports at least annually. From the beginning, too, ombudspersons had no enforcement powers; they could recommend only—either to a president in the early years or to a parliament.[27]

In South Africa, Thuli Madonsela, the public protector (ombudsperson), in 2014 labeled President Jacob Zuma as a fraudster, with instructions that he should repay the nation $21 million for corrupt expenditures on his private villa at Nkandla in the hills of KwaZulu-Natal. That was an impressive decision even if it led neither to apology nor remorse (nor initially to any other action) on the part of the president.[28] Instead, more than a year later, the minister of police absolved President Zuma of any obligation to repay the state. A cattle kraal, a chicken run, and an amphitheater were all erected as "security measures," he decided, being intrinsic to the Nkandla edifice, along with a swimming pool. The ruling African National Congress (ANC) also continued its lengthy attacks on the public protector, who finally protested without effect to the speaker of Parliament. One parliamentary opposition leader, supporting the Office of the Public Protector, said that her reports showed that the ANC was "completely foolish and incompetent."[29]

It took until 2016 for Madonsela's criticisms to make their way through the South African court system, for the Constitutional Court to chastise Zuma severely, and for Zuma to agree—finally—to reimburse the state for some relatively minor expenditures at Nkandla, as the public protector had demanded. Moreover, speaking on behalf of a unanimous court, the chief justice described the Office of the Public Protector as a "vital" part of South Africa's democracy and as a "gift" to the nation.[30] In this case, backed by public opinion, an ombuds office's investigation and her final "State Capture" report had a significant post hoc anticorruption effect. Most other ombudspersons in Africa have been less successful, having been less courageous and more apt to have had their official critical reports responded to politely, but without remedial action.

Beyond South Africa, nearly all other ombuds investigations and pronouncements have been less dramatic. For the most part, ombuds offices are woefully underfunded and understaffed. By design, their offices are often intended by ruling parties to be cosmetic. Those appointed to be the national ombudsperson know how little is expected of them. In many instances, their reporting lines are to parliaments, where their annual reports may languish for want of a sponsor. In too many cases, ombudsmen attend to petty (if individually important) concerns. Only rarely, as in South Africa, do they take on heads of state or matters that rivet the eyes of the nation. Another exception is that in Rwanda, the office of ombudsman functions as a de facto anticorruption commission (see chapter 6).

All of these legal and regulatory mechanisms may, and sometimes are, employed and deployed to uncover questionable use of government monies, abuses of official positions, failures of commission, and instances of omission. In theory, each of these legislative and regulatory instruments can be utilized to expose and then to control corruption. Brazil's Corregedoria Geral da União (federal inspector general) audited the accounts of 130 of 5,560 randomly selected municipalities between 2000 and 2011 to uncover fraud and the misuse of central government monies, reducing the opportunities for corruption.[31] By publicizing these kinds of efforts and doing their own investigations, the media, if free and financially secure, can name and shame corrupt citizens and corrupt multinational corporations. But the existence of an independent domestic judicial system is also fundamental to any and all activity against corruption.

The Courts

Judges free of political or executive direction are essential to the effective employment of legal means to curb corruption. The existence of a truly independent and fair judiciary provides the checks and balances and separations of power that are essential to democratic practice and the rule of law. That kind of court system exists (as Chief Justice John Marshall made clear in *Marbury v. Madison* in 1803) to check the powers of the executive and the legislative branches. A strong association exists between the control and diminution of corruption and court systems that operate free of executive and party interference.[32]

With effective legislation, careful investigations by anticorruption commissions or auditors general, and diligent prosecution by commissions, attorneys general, or public prosecutors, timely trials by independent judges should in theory reduce the ranks of the corrupt in those many African countries (as in Singapore, Hong Kong, and Indonesia) where the legal settings are robust and strong dossiers have been prepared. That has not always been the case, however, as acquittals of key individuals in Botswana and Kenya, for example, have reflected poor prosecutorial preparation, weakly developed dossiers, or politically attuned jurists.

Having an independent judiciary capable of deciding cases of corruption solely on their merits means, at a minimum, "the insulation of judges and the judicial process from partisan pressure to influence the outcomes of individual cases."[33] Judges who are thus appropriately insulated are not asked by national executives (or their intermediaries) to go easy or hard on offenders or to acquit or convict defendants with little evidence. They also turn a deaf ear to importuning entreaties from legislators and to special pleading from relatives or business associates of the accused, and make it perfectly clear by attitude and action that no one dares to try to sway their decisions with offers of money or other emoluments. Nor do such judges ideally worry that their promotions or salary increases depend on pleasing a president and a parliament, or on pandering to ruling parties or ruling cliques.

In the developing world, however, judicial independence is mostly honored in the breach. A handful of countries employ judges primarily for cosmetic purposes, and many judges labor under despots such as President Robert Mugabe of Zimbabwe, who famously said, "The law is what I say it is," and routinely instructs judges how to conclude their cases.[34] Wherever the judicial institution is weak, outcomes are more often than not greatly influenced by political considerations. In many settings, bribery is not unknown and judges are easily corrupted. (For the recent Ghanaian imbroglio involving manifest bribery of judges, see below.) Indeed, where corruption has greatly infected a state, where corrupt dealings are normal and expected, judges often see little reason to refrain from "bending" or "profiting." If everyone in government from the top down is corrupt, why not members of the third branch?

Kenya's experience with crooked judges and court personnel illustrates the depth of the problem. Upon assuming office as chief judge in 2011, Willy Mutunga described the Kenyan judiciary as "deficient in integrity." Forty-three percent of Kenyans in 2010 reported bribing a judge. "Why hire a lawyer when you can buy a judge?" was a popular humorous refrain. "Litigants often bribed staff to get earlier court dates or to 'lose' case files and prevent hearings altogether."[35]

In this case, fortunately, after Kenya's vicious postelection violence in 2007–2008 revealed how politicized, inefficient, and shoddy its courts were, a new constitution in 2010 contained provisions for a major judicial overhaul. The constitution restructured the entire court system and separated the Judicial Service Commission from the presidency, thus making its selection of judges more transparent and much less overtly political. Equally important, Mutunga, a civil society leader and lawyer who was jailed by an earlier authoritarian regime, was chosen to lead the reform effort. By 2012, after laborious consultative processes, Mutunga and his team launched a Judiciary Transformation Framework. It simplified court procedures and created a case management system to improve accountability. Next, it tried to change the judiciary's institutional culture both by retraining and re-energizing holdover judges and dismissing those who were believed to be corrupt. Finally, it computerized the courts (reliable electricity was a problem) to make information more accessible to judges.

The 2013 Kenyan election greatly tested the reform efforts with its cases concerning the validity of the electoral process and the official count. The International Commission of Jurists severely criticized the Supreme Court's handling of an opposition petition challenging the election's result. Subsequently, the entire judicial reform effort was jeopardized when the chief administrative official for the courts was dismissed for misappropriating $25 million and a supreme court justice retired after being accused of taking $2 million in bribes.

Nevertheless, Kenyans told pollsters that the judicial system's responses to their needs had improved. Mutunga's leadership was widely credited with changing the judicial culture, having instilled in many judges the notion that their responsibility was to serve the people, not the government. The new chief registrar said that Kenya's judges were now more conscious that their authority "derive[d] from the people."[36]

Beyond Kenya, judges are suspected of being less than judicial in their behavior and in their willingness to be swayed by particularly persuasive (and wealthy) defendants in a number of countries in Asia and Africa. Nigerian jurists have certainly been suspect, but as part of President Buhari's national house-cleaning, he urged (even commanded) Nigeria's judges to rise to higher levels of conduct: "May I most especially urge that the Nigerian judiciary must do all that is possible to fight against the perception and the reality of growing judicial corruption. . . . As an institution dedicated to the promotion and protection of human rights, the judiciary must go the extra mile to sanitise itself and improve its capacity to act independently, courageously and tirelessly."[37]

Judges are often swayed by political reality even if, individually, they believe strongly in the common law or the Napoleonic or Roman Dutch traditions and in the impartiality that are their foundations. Even outstanding chief justices find it difficult in practice to put legal canons, institutional reputations, and regime legacies before momentary exigencies or the predilections of a powerful executive. Indeed, the problem becomes even more acute at the base of a court system where magistrates and local judges may be considered and may even consider themselves civil servants obedient to whichever party or movement is in power. The budgets of their courts, their selection and re-election as magistrates and judges, and their promotions and emoluments, all too often depend entirely on the favor of the executive.

Yet, increasingly in the modern developing world, the growing middle class and a mobile-telephone carrying populace connected to the global village want and believe in judicial independence. They go to court to obtain fairness (as a well as redress), and abhor partisanship and partiality. "People must feel they can resolve disputes satisfactorily and in a reasonable amount of time."[38] Even in despotic states, people want to believe that judges will listen without prejudice to accusers and defendants and then rule wisely and judiciously to resolve disputes. Public opinion is decisively in favor of consummate judicial independence.

When corruption infects judicial practice, it almost immediately destroys the rule of law, inhibits the peaceful and impartial resolution of disputes, undermines respect for contracts and private property, discourages domestic and foreign investment, and undermines economic growth prospects with serious and lasting consequences.

Absent an affirmative judicial atmosphere, reducing corruption is almost impossible. Having excellent anticorruption legislation and strong regulations, appropriate penal codes, and zealous investigators and prosecutors, not to mention well-performing auditors and ombudsmen, is insufficient if the courts are corruptible, or at least susceptible to influence. Even in stable, well-governed places like Singapore and Rwanda, judges know what is expected when a major case of alleged corruption is brought before them. Even in Botswana, a thorough democracy, judges try not to offend the government to which they owe their appointment. In neighboring South Africa, which has a respected Constitutional Court and a long tradition of judicial freedom, the fact that key figures in the ruling African National Congress openly talk of curtailing judicial independence and of making judges obey legislative more than constitutional law must inevitably chill any lingering sense of judicial freedom.

An International Anticorruption Court

Because corrupt countries usually endure corrupt judiciaries (South Africa is an exception), and because prosecuting perpetrators of venal or grand corruption is often an exercise in futility within such jurisdictions, some loftier or transcending method of bringing high-level miscreants to justice could be salutary. The establishment of an International Anti-Corruption Court (IACC) to fulfill those needs thus makes eminently good sense. "It is an idea whose time has come."[39]

An IACC would, by arresting, trying, and punishing corrupt high-level offenders across the globe, help to reduce the kinds of impunity that prevail within corrupt nations, and correspondingly deter venal corruption. The existence of such a new international institution would bring increased attention and notoriety to the excesses of corrupt endeavors and to kleptocracy more generally. It would also confer international legitimacy (presumably via support from the UN General Assembly) on anticorruption efforts that many national court systems often lack. Furthermore, an IACC could receive confidential reports from NGOs, individuals, whistleblowers, etc., within corrupt countries in a manner that is often unavailable or dangerous within jurisdictions awash with corrupt dealings.

As conceived, the IACC would focus its energies on venal or grand corruption—the large-scale theft or conversion of public riches to private gain (see chapter 1). It would not focus on the equally insidious and destructive petty corruption that bedevils citizens almost everywhere, especially in the polities of the developing world.

The new court would investigate and seek to prosecute, for example, heads of state who arrogantly preside over schemes to enrich themselves, their families and lineages, and their cronies. It would be less concerned about pursuing workers in motor vehicle offices, say, who provide fake licenses for a fee, or policemen who accept bribes at roadblocks.

The IACC would be composed of internationally approved and internationally experienced judges. They would not be beholden to national political elites for appointment or for their salaries. (Who would pay for the IACC is an open, and difficult, question.) They would draw on the expertise of the kinds and numbers of investigative and prosecutorial staff that most developing countries lack. Fragile and poorer places in Africa and Asia often find it difficult forensically to pursue the tortuous trails of corrupt politicians, especially those with highly placed friends. Most smaller countries also lack the means to track the shifting of ill-gotten funds across oceans and continents. The proposed court, to function well, would need its own regular leakers of information similar to that brought to light in the Panama Papers.

Mark L. Wolf, then chief judge of the Massachusetts District Court, first advanced the idea of an IACC in a talk in Russia in 2012.[40] His idea has since been embraced by jurists, scholars, human rights advocates, and UN officials internationally, as well as by prominent global NGOs, and by officials from such nations as Nigeria. But to launch the IACC, the notion will have to draw substantial support from a range of major and minor world powers—and ultimately from a groundswell of influential public opinion and from an authorizing body such as the UN General Assembly. That approach follows the successful establishment of such important normative-shifting initiatives as the International Campaign to Ban Landmines and the adoption of the Responsibility to Protect initiative by the UN General Assembly in 2005.

The International Criminal Court (ICC) is obviously an analogue. Many of its procedures might be embodied in the statutes or protocols that eventually establish an IACC. One, complementarity, seems just as fundamental to the IACC's function as it is to the ICC. That is, the IACC would attempt to assume jurisdiction only when and where the corrupt countries themselves refused or otherwise forfeited their rights as the original jurisdiction to investigate and then to prosecute malefactors. (The nations that never ratified the Rome Statute that created the ICC are immune from its attention except when specifically authorized by the UN Security Council.) The IACC would need some similar method of imposing itself on those countries failing to ratify the IACC's enabling statute and thus barring its investigations.

Exactly how all of these issues are addressed will help to determine the ultimate success of the IACC. There is no doubt, however, that an IACC is much needed, and that its existence and its ability to punish corrupt offenders, plus the threat of so doing, will help to chill corrupt activity worldwide.

Role of the Domestic Media

Transparency and accountability, essential in winning the battle against corruption everywhere, depend in significant part on an active, inquisitive, free, and untrammeled media. Press, radio, and television journalists keep politicians and bureaucrats honest by asking both naïve and searching questions, pursuing rumors, checking on procedures, scrutinizing contract awards, and being perpetually dissatisfied with bland answers and attempts to mislead and obfuscate. Even in a largely well-run place like Botswana, the existence in the 1990s of the nation's first private newspapers permitted "the intellectual class" to review government policy and the behavior of politicians.[41] (Although the national attorney general prosecuted journalists and editors, and prepared legislation to hamper the press, his cases failed in the courts and his bill had to be withdrawn, bolstering the legitimacy of media scrutiny the more. South Africa's 2013–2014 "Secrecy" bill also had to be modified because of public dismay.) Elsewhere in Africa and Asia, wherever the media is relatively free and relatively brave, potentially corrupt acts can at least be brought to public attention: "Journalists can turn corruption from a seemingly low risk, high profit activity . . . to one that is high risk and low profit."[42] Civil society or mass protests can take anticorruption pursuits farther, but absent the transparency provided by media attention and publicity and some method of sanctioning those who are exposed, the persons who plunder the state and its citizens often escape accountability. Simply making information available, thus being transparent, curbs corruption only when the revealed details are disseminated as broadly as possible and are causally connected to a loss of office or perquisites or to judicially mandated punishments.[43] Freedom of the press (print and online) is highly correlated with sustainable curbs on corruption.[44] Indeed, two authorities conclude that "greater freedom of the press in a country significantly reduces the likelihood of citizens paying bribes by 13 per cent."[45]

As Nelson Mandela said in a speech in Prague in 1992, "I cannot overemphasize the value we place on a free, independent and outspoken press. . . . Such a free press will temper the appetite of any government to amass power at the expense of the citizen."[46] But in large parts of the developing world, especially in Africa (and even since 2014–2016 in South Africa), Afghanistan, Pakistan, Yemen, and China, media freedom has been jeopardized. Politicians, especially corrupt ones, fear nosy journalists and what they might report.

Most sub-Saharan Africans obtain their news via the radio, although increasingly text-messaging services are growing in importance. In sub-Saharan Africa the majority of radio and television services are "official," i.e. government-owned and controlled. Many newspapers also are government-owned; some are subsidized by the ruling party or run by proprietors fronting for the ruling party. It is thus increasingly difficult to pursue independent journalistic endeavors in much of Africa (or China or the stans). Without the kinds of financial backing that still mostly exist only in the developed world, editors and writers often find themselves inhibited and forced to self-censor. Sometimes they are subject to arrest and torture, as in Cameroon, Eritrea, the Gambia, Sudan, and Zimbabwe, and censored officially. Only in a handful of African and Asian countries is the media fully free, and watchful of corruption.

Media freedom in Africa is heavily compromised. It is largely free in Botswana and Namibia; under attack, but still lively, in places such as Ghana, Kenya, Liberia, Malawi, Senegal, South Africa, and Tanzania; vibrant and often wild in Nigeria, where corruption flourishes regardless; heavily controlled at a minimum in Angola, Burundi, Djibouti, Ethiopia, Côte d'Ivoire, Gabon, Guinea, Rwanda, Sierra Leone, South Sudan, Sudan, Swaziland, Togo, and Zimbabwe; and nonexistent in Equatorial Guinea, Eritrea, and the Gambia. President Isaias Afewerki of Eritrea admits that he has no interest in allowing his people to express themselves. Democracy is less important than building up his country. In the Gambia, death threats and middle-of-the-night arrests were the lot of any would-be reporters who refused to sing the government's praises, until the very end of 2016, after a surprising election result.[47]

The media's powerful investigative capabilities are hampered in many jurisdictions when ruling parties or political leaders gain financial control over press and television outlets and curb scrutiny of official actions or offer only unstinting praise for ruling elites. Another constraint, practiced particularly acutely in Singapore, is the threat of punitively expensive libel and defamation suits against the press and others who report adversely on governmental activities. The laws themselves, including those that bar criticism of monarchs or other rulers, may be less restrictive than the ways in which judges have learned to interpret them. Certainly, all of these judicially enforced methods deter transparency and enhance corrupt impunity. Performing the role of

watchdog—being the upholder of integrity—is extremely difficult, even perilous—under such circumstances.

According to Freedom House and the Committee to Protect Journalists,
only a few African countries possess a free media. "Many governments are
intent on suppressing in-depth journalism,"[48] Even in a peaceful and stable
country such as Senegal, journalists often have been harassed, with the police
raiding printing establishments and confiscating issues. Rwanda has imprisoned journalists for "invasions of privacy," and in Côte d'Ivoire and Ethiopia,
writers have been incarcerated for questioning governmental spending priorities. In 2012, a Swazi editor was fired for exposing the prime minister's notably
corrupt land deals. In the new nation of South Sudan, a fledgling newspaper
was shuttered for suggesting that the president's daughter showed a lack of
patriotism by marrying an Ethiopian.[49]

In Africa, especially where corruption runs rampant, the media is muzzled
or neutered. Even online news aggregators, or the Internet, may be monitored
and sometimes blocked. Without the eyes and ears of the media being openly
engaged, news outlets can only with great difficulty act as tribunes of the
people. They can hardly enhance transparency, call attention to abuses of public power for private gain, or hold corrupt governments accountable if—nationally—there is little rule of law and hardly any good governance. Effective
transparency, after all, depends on publicizing the results as widely as possible. Shining a light into the Augean Stables is the first step in cleansing them.
Illuminating corruption makes it that much more difficult for public servants
to steal, take kickbacks, give favors to friends, and so on.

One of the great triumphs of investigative uncovering of corruption occurred in Ghana in 2015. Anas Aremeyaw Anas, an enterprising journalist
from a locally based investigative company called Tiger Eye PI, captured
nearly 500 hours of video implicating thirty-four judges, including twelve
high-court justices, in a broad bribery scandal. Twenty-two of the thirty-four
were videoed asking for bribes, extorting cash from litigants, and negotiating
the release of persons standing trial. The attorney general granted the journalist whistleblower status, conveying immunity, as the video evidence was
shown to the accused judges and magistrates themselves. The entire video
trove was given to the chief justice of Ghana for action. She held hearings
behind closed doors in the Supreme Court before deciding to suspend all 34
and an additional 150 court personnel who were alleged to have contributed
to the abuse of justice in Ghana over many years.[50]

That recent positive experience was exceptional and salutary. Most African
countries are less hospitable than Ghana to investigative journalism, and the
efforts of hard-charging reporters are often less effective. Reporters without
Borders' Press Freedom Index for 2016 rated 180 countries, including nearly
all of those in Africa. Eritrea finished dead last, a place it had held previously,

just below North Korea, Turkmenistan, Syria, China, Vietnam, and Sudan, in ascending order. Equatorial Guinea, Djibouti, and Somalia were also well down on the list, with very little press freedom. In sub-Saharan Africa, only Namibia (17th), Ghana (26th), Cape Verde (32nd), South Africa (39th), and Niger (48th) ranked among the best forty countries. (The United States was 41st, the United Kingdom 38th, and Finland, the Netherlands, and Norway, 1st, 2nd, and 3rd, respectively.)[51]

These low African rankings suggest that preventing corruption is still a very great work in progress in Africa. No matter how effective a nation's legal framework might be, no matter how energetic are auditors general and ombudsmen, and no matter the dedication of members of anticorruption commissions, a vigorous and active media is an essential bulwark against the natural tendency of corrupt waters to seek their lowest levels.

Transparency and Freedom of Information

Nation-states that have effective freedom of information laws give citizens and the media access (even after delays) to governmental records. Consequently, such belated transparency accentuates the vulnerability of politicians and officials who abuse their positions. Even if no explicit trail remains that could lead to or hint at past influence peddling, graft, nepotism, receipt of bribes, and the like, sufficient incriminating material may be contained in the records at least to suggest malfeasance and private gains. This result is easiest to imagine in investigating the process of tenders, where bidders may have won contracts illegitimately. Likewise, other forms of favoritism may be revealed. Overconfident or unwitting public servants may leave evidence, mostly implicit, of how they falsified accounts, did the shady bidding of superiors, or made decisions against the public interest.

Bringing such transparency to budgeting processes also allows the media and the public to scrutinize governmental actions and to ensure that the machinery of government is acting in the public interest rather than as a collection of private interests. In most democracies, budgetary and official expenditure information is readily available, and auditing outcomes are also open to inspection. But in corrupt countries, most of these kinds of data are masked. Where venal corrupt behavior prevails, as in so many despotic states, revealing such information, and whistleblowing, is treasonous and excessively dangerous. Many Zimbabweans have lost their lives in suspicious circumstances for prying or exposing shady dealings by the ruling regime. Kenyans have suffered in the same manner, as have Nigerians.

In the 1990s, the World Bank discovered that in some countries monies budgeted for schooling never seemed to arrive at individual learning centers. In Uganda, for example, the bank realized that only 20 percent of allocated funds were actually making their way to individual primary schools. The bank persuaded Uganda's ministry of finance to inform school headmasters and the national media whenever budgeted funds were dispatched, and to what uses those funds were directed. In 1999, a survey revealed that 90 percent of the allocated amounts were finally reaching local schools. Making the necessary information public and transparent greatly reduced the diversion of transmitted funds.[52]

By 2012, Uganda became one of the few sub-Saharan countries where citizens could track official spending by going to a budget website and accessing both historical and current data. The website even included budgets of local governments, and information in several local languages.

When Afrobarometer surveyed information availability in twenty-nine African countries between 2010 and 2012, 77 percent of those who responded said that it was "difficult" or "very difficult" to learn how tax revenues were employed by their nation-states. Transparency, in other words, is routinely honored in the breach despite an African Platform on Access to Information that admonishes all African governments to respect every citizen's right to government-held materials and information.[53] Many developing world, especially sub-Saharan, nations either do not know that they should be open to their citizens or simply decide that withholding information is safer and less compromising.

South Korea, in contrast, significantly reduced corrupt behavior, at least in local governments, when it created an electronic platform called the Online Procedures Enhancement for Civil Application (OPEN), which provided abundant information for citizens requesting government services and removed individual bureaucratic discretion from dealings between civil authorities and citizens. One study showed that e-government measures were "a powerful predictor of anticorruption" effectiveness, second only to strong rules of law.[54] E-government reduces secrecy, offers timely access to governmental measures, and improves all aspects of transparency. Digital government also reduces the ability of officials to act arbitrarily. (See also chapter 2, the discussion of access to e-government as measured by the IPI.)

Transparency, and greater access to more and more relevant information, obviously makes the duplicity and shadiness of corrupt practices more difficult to sustain. It helps a public and a civil society to be able fully to look into or inside something, to see if it is indeed fishy or possibly improper. Otherwise, observers and citizens cannot easily form opinions or, in the case of corruption, declaim it. Better-educated citizenries can also process such information more readily than can others. But, as several authors suggest, transparency improves the chance of curbing corruption when material open to inspection actually is publicized, the more routinely and the more fully the better, and where and when the public beneficiaries of transparency are actually able to impose sanctions and accountability to end any sleaze revealed. Those sanctions may be formal or informal, but the effectiveness of formal sanctions depends on the strength of national rules of law and the existence of independent and disinterested prosecutors and judges. Only when both conditions—publicity and accountability—are satisfied will more transparency produce less corruption.[55] Furthermore, having more access to information (even in those states with formal freedom of information acts) correlates poorly with increased control of corruption *unless* the society in question has a high degree of social openness.[56] More transparency is better than less transparency, but is not a panacea on its own.

International Measures against Corruption

These many domestic legal and ancillary methods of helping to eradicate corrupt practices in the developing world are buttressed, assisted, amplified, and advanced by relatively recent signal improvements in the ways individual developed nations and organizations of those nations have adopted international legislation and conventions that make it illegal for corporations to corrupt overseas governments, officials, or businesses, to provide inducements, to give special favors, to launder money, or to engage in any of a range of activities that are corrupt. In Europe until the end of the twentieth century and in the United States until 1977, expenditures overseas, including paying bribes to secure contracts, were expected, legal, and tax deductible as a cost of doing business.

No longer. The U.S. Foreign Corrupt Practices Act of 1977, with later amendments in 1988 and 1998, made it unlawful for any publicly traded companies, their agents, their officers, their employees, and even their stockholders to pay, induce, or influence foreign government officials to obtain or retain business. Its provisions apply to all U.S. persons, certain foreign issuers of securities listed in the United States, and, since 1998, to foreign firms or persons who make or advance similar corrupt payment schemes in the United States to foreign officials to secure "any improper advantage." The act prohibits bribing foreign political parties, political party officials, and candidates for future political office. It is illegal for American banks and other financial institutions to handle the proceeds of overseas corruption. Additionally, companies whose securities are listed in the United States must keep their books and records so that they accurately and faithfully reflect the relevant corporation's foreign transactions and maintain a proper system of internal accounting controls so that overseas briberies will not be obscured. Because bribing is usually carried out behind closed doors, and because much of it is done across the globe in possibly inaccessible venues, this act compels transparent accounting; corporations that omit or falsely describe material payments are in violation of the act.

For its first several decades, this act inhibited American corporations and their overseas agents and subsidiaries with substantial activities in foreign lands from setting inducements and other kinds of payments to distant officials against their taxes. But neither the U.S. Department of Justice nor the Securities and Exchange Commission made investigations and prosecutions under the act a major priority. Only late in the last century, at the end of the first Clinton administration, and in the present century, especially under the Obama administration, has more stringent attention been paid to the provisions of the act. On Sept. 30, 2016, seventy-five multinational corporations were involved in ongoing and unresolved investigations by the U.S. Department of Justice or the U.S. Securities and Exchange Commission, or both. A further sixty-three firms were probably also being probed by those enforcement bodies.[57] (See further discussion in chapter 9.)

The 1998 amendments to the 1977 act consciously were coordinated with the writing of the OECD Convention on Combating Bribery of Foreign Officials in International Business Transactions, adopted in 1997 and ratified in succeeding years. President Clinton acknowledged the closeness of both anticorruption instruments and the role of American negotiators in developing the convention. Bribery, he said, was contrary to "basic principles of fair competition and harmful to . . . economic development." Hence, the convention obligated European and other major industrial powers to criminalize bribery and monitor the international battle against corruption.[58] It asked participating and ratifying countries to pass their own laws against paying bribes in foreign lands so that international efforts to prosecute both the supply and demand sides of corruption could be successful. The convention (with further amendments in 2006 and 2009) did not, however, require the disbarment of offending corporations from procurement opportunities.

Signatories to the convention and other states which voluntarily accede to its provisions must criminalize bribing of foreign public officials even when those bribes are forcefully solicited, abrogate existing statutes of limitation to allow additional time to find and prosecute perpetrators, require transparent accounting and halt the creation of false documentation, reduce bank secrecy, and alter extradition regulations to permit transnational prosecutions. The thirty-four members of the OECD, plus seven nonmembers—Argentina, Brazil, Bulgaria, Colombia, Latvia, Russia, and South Africa—all ratified the convention. (Those nation-states account for two-thirds of world exports and about 90 percent of all global investment outflows.) But, despite monitoring by an OECD working group of peers, not all members of the OECD have in fact prepared new laws against bribery. In 2015, only four (the United States, the United Kingdom, Germany, and Switzerland) were active enforcers. Six (Australia, Austria, Canada, Finland, Norway, and Italy) were moderate enforcers. Nine (France, Greece, Hungary, Netherlands, New Zealand, Portugal, South Korea, Sweden, and South Africa) are regarded by Transparency International as having "limited" enforcement capabilities under the act; twenty are rated as producing little or no enforcement, and caring too little. That last group includes Argentina, Brazil, Denmark, Estonia, Japan, Russia, Spain, and Turkey.[59] These fine U.S. and OECD restrictions against corrupt behavior on the demand side have only gradually begun (twenty years after the convention's promulgation) to influence the extent to which bribes are paid to secure lucrative African, Asian, Middle Eastern, and Latin American opportunities. Further, it is impossible to estimate the effect of such national and regional prohibitory initiatives on the number and size of illicit transactions, but both the act and the convention did help to strengthen global efforts to marginalize corrupt behavior by corporations in the developing world. Arguably, too, the existence of the act and the convention made possible the investigation and prosecution of many major offenders in the first decade of the twenty-first century and, as a result, led to the passage of important national laws against overseas purchases of influence. One researcher contends that the central role of the U.S. Foreign Corrupt Practices Act of 1977 (FCPA) in establishing "a convergence of law, public policy and best practices" cannot be overemphasized, particularly with regard to the global criminalization of corruption but also with regard to the positive attention now given to every kind of business transaction that affects or takes place in the developing world. The existence of the FCPA has also helped to shift how corruption is best addressed—from punishment primarily to punishment, prevention, and compliance.[60] But there is little evidence that the receiving countries are any less corrupt than they were because of the prohibitions in the FCPA and the OECD convention (or any of the other restrictions on external bribe payers).

The British Bribery Act of 2010 is the foremost among post-convention legal codes. (Australia, Austria, Canada, Finland, Israel, Italy, the Netherlands, and South Korea have since enacted relevant laws, and France was poised to do so in 2016. Canada's is called the Corruption of Foreign Public Officials Act.) Not limited to foreign bribery, the British act is similar in intent and language to the convention and the U.S. act, but its reach overseas is a little less broad and it permits bribes to be paid by military commands and spies. The major difference from its predecessors, however, is the need for prosecutors under the British act to prove criminal intent: bribers must have "intended to obtain or retain" a business advantage. Unlike the American act, the British law makes no exception for minor facilitation payments—for payments to lubricate customs checks, visas, and other "minor" licenses. The British act and Italian and Portuguese legislation (but not the Foreign Corrupt Practices

Act) also permit a corporation accused of overseas bribing to defend itself by showing that it had already put into place adequate procedures to prevent such corrupt activities, i.e., that an employee of the firm was acting in violation of express instructions. This means that companies must always enact such regulations or risk running afoul of the law—companies are responsible for preventing bribes being paid. The British legislation obviously applies to British-domiciled firms, but also to non-British companies based in the United Kingdom and to all foreign subsidiaries of British and non-British concerns.

The United Kingdom's 2016 Criminal Finances Bill further permitted law enforcement agencies to compel suspected criminals, money launderers, and other corrupt persons to explain the sources of any wealth. Under so-called unexplained wealth orders, those unable to verify new assets and earnings would risk having their properties seized—a reasonable deterrent.

France's law would update stringent 1993 legislation, introduce a new anticorruption agency, advocate preventive as well as punitive action, and reiterate the illegality of active and passive corruption at home and abroad. It also prohibits domestic and international influence peddling, facilitation payments, and provides for strict bookkeeping requirements.

The Netherlands amended its criminal code in 2015 to simplify and streamline what constituted bribery beyond its borders. It also increased penalties. Transparency International's Bribe Payers Index ranked the Netherlands highly, as did the latest versions of the CPI. But, according to a leading Dutch researcher, large Dutch firms were still heavily engaged in helping to corrupt such countries as Angola, Brazil, Equatorial Guinea, Nigeria, and Uzbekistan. Royal Dutch Shell was among the large companies being investigated.[61]

South Korea's new Improper Solicitation and Graft Act took effect at the end of September 2016. It bars public servants, journalists, and teachers from accepting gifts, even curtailing meals worth more than 39,000 won, or $27, if there is a potential conflict of interest. If there is a likely conflict of interest, moreover, lawyers, among other professionals, are not permitted to accept any gift worth more than $45, or $90 if a wedding or funeral is involved. Parents are no longer allowed to bring gifts to teachers.[62] What the new legislation, with its stringent bans on even small purchases of influence, signifies is an attempt to replace South Korea's established norm of purchasing favor with lavish expenditures on meals and presents. The South Korean National Police Agency even trained senior police officials and prepared intensive 500-page investigation manuals to its officers to help them to enforce the act.

In 2015, the British secretary of international development (finally) created a central International Corruption Unit to investigate cases of cross-border and foreign corruption. The unit brought together existing criminal operations within that department, the Metropolitan Police Service, the City of London Police, and the National Crime Agency, the last of which runs the unit. The head of the new unit said that "the work we're doing is absolutely vital for helping countries get back what is rightfully theirs."[63]

There are no specific all-European bars to corruption analogous to national legislation or the OECD convention. The European Anti-Fraud Office investigates and prevents fraud within the European Union and its institutions and advises the European Commission on anticorruption policies, especially with regard to invitations to join Europe. The European Council's Group of States against Corruption (GRECO) monitors member states' compliance with the anticorruption standards of the council and identifies deficiencies in national anticorruption policies.

Strengthening the moral hand of administrators, legislators, prosecutors, judges, and diplomats in all of these legal endeavors has been the lofty and well-articulated sentiment of the very ambitious United Nations Convention against Corruption (UNCAC), adopted in 2003 and fully ratified in 2005, when the thirtieth nation officially acceded to it. (At the end of 2015, it had 140 member signatories and 178 states that were parties to it. Chad, Djibouti, Somalia, and North Korea had neither signed nor ratified the convention.[64])

The UNCAC seeks no less than the extirpation of all manner of corrupt behavior, not just that caused by corporate bribery. Indeed, UNCAC offers a road map guiding signatory nations toward both legislation and determined action against corruption in all of its pernicious forms. UN Secretary General Kofi Annan termed corruption an "insidious plague" capable of corroding societies, undermining democracy, eroding the quality of human life, and allowing threats to human society to flourish. Corruption, he said, was an "evil phenomenon" particularly destructive to the developing world and hurtful to the poor. UNCAC required member states legally to repress corruption and to return ill-gotten gains to the countries relieved of such "stolen" goods.

UNCAC, suggests one authority, "has clearly increased [the] international commitment to fight corruption," even though it provides regulatory guidance to member states rather than real changes to their legal processes.[65] Together with the OECD convention and tough legislative examples, there is an emerging global norm against corruption and various rhetorical and directly punitive methods of reducing its scope and impact. Nevertheless, it would be hard in 2016 to conclude that the combination of global commitment and national prosecution has, in fact, significantly reduced the value or volume of corrupt transactions across the developing world or even from North to South or West to East.

In 2015, the Association of Southeast Asian Nations (ASEAN) and its ASEAN Economic Community, with a combined GDP of $2.3 trillion, decided to consider following the lead of the Asia Pacific Economic Cooperation Forum's Anti-Corruption Principles for the Public and Private Sectors and discuss implementing an ASEAN Integrity Community to battle corruption.

If adopted, such a community declaration would outlaw bribery by multinational enterprises and local corporations, mandate transparent financial reporting and corporate auditing, train corporate and governmental compliance officers, and enact protection for whistleblowers.

In gross terms, we know that bribes by foreigners continue to be delivered to Africans, Asians, Middle Easterners, and Latin Americans. Two-thirds of them occur in the extractive, construction, transportation, and information sectors of the demand-side economies, in that order. More than half of all bribes between 1997 and 2014 were paid by corporate or management chief executive officers, more from very large firms than smaller ones. State-owned enterprise heads took 27 percent of the bribes by number of incidents but 80 percent of the total by value; customs officials received 11 percent of all the bribes reported but barely over 1 percent of the value. Cabinet ministers, by contrast, pocketed 4 percent by value but featured in only 3 percent of the reports.[66]

More telling in some respects are the major fines paid by a number of major multinational corporations for attempting to corrupt and effectively corrupting overseas governments and their political leaders. Siemens paid $800 million, Halliburton $579 million, BAE Systems $400 million, and such other defense contractors and large businesses as Analogic, JGC, Daimler, Alcatel-Lucent, Boeing, Embraer SA, Lockheed Martin, General Dynamics, General Electric, Raytheon, L-3, ENI, the Och-Ziff Capital Management Group, Snamprogetti, Bridgestone, Diageo, Walmart, Las Vegas Sands, Pfizer, AstraZeneca, and Johnson & Johnson collectively from 1998 to 2016 remitted a total of at least $3.4 billion in criminal fines and negotiated penalties. They were all implicated in foreign bribery schemes designed to secure large contracts and were later compelled to settle with their home country legal authorities.

Very few of these larger cases go to a domestic court. Moreover, prosecutors have not had the right or the desire (unlike the World Bank) to bar such corporate miscreants from continuing to tender for defense and other procurement benefits in their home nations. Nor have they wanted to reduce the ability of these concerns to continue to employ large numbers of workers, especially during and after the post-2008 global recession. Thus, major court convictions largely have been of individuals or relatively specialized firms that, in several cases, have egregiously violated American, British, Australian, and other rules. A leading authority on international anticorruption legislation suggests that both the U.S. Department of Justice and the SEC engage too much in selective enforcement practices, preferring to allow a privileged class of seemingly critical business entities to remain significant contributors to global trade.[67] Investigators and prosecutors elsewhere in the developed world may have made similar decisions. Nonetheless, it is evident that bribing greedy African, Asian, Middle Eastern, and Latin American heads of state, ministers of energy, and ministers, say, of education, is now more dangerous for outsiders or their agents; that some major Western corporations shun particularly corrupt developing countries to avoid becoming enmeshed in bribery scandals; and that the whole business of inducing an action through the exchange of favors or cash has become more clandestine than ever thanks to UNCAC, the OECD, and individual national initiatives. But it is equally hard to conclude that the total amounts involved have been reduced.[68]

As a result, across the developing world, in country after country, bar the likes of Botswana, construction and other projects still may not be completed by the best qualified firms, textbooks may be supplied to legions of children by unqualified providers, endless costs to consumers may be inflated to cover the wages of corruption, national treasuries receive fewer inflows than their operations require and deserve because corrupt operators have avoided paying taxes, and environmental regulations are breached, to the detriment of everyone. The scourge of corruption affects not only the daily lives of the poorest of the poor and their middle class brethren and has direct political ramifications, but it also lowers a society's moral tone irreparably. Neither domestic nor international legislation has so far vitiated such a stark conclusion, despite these strong efforts on the supply side. Equally tough international action, by an IACC, may be needed on the demand side to complement newly strengthened ordinances and enforcement by individual nations and several regional bodies.

IV

The Virtue of Anticorruption Investigative Commissions

HONG KONG, SINGAPORE, INDONESIA

Many countries in the developing world have attempted to reduce corruption by establishing commissions or other kinds of investigative agencies to uncover corrupt practices. These bodies, called by various names at different times, have been established and developed for a multiplicity of country-specific reasons, the guiding principle of which has been to eliminate (or at least to curb) corrupt practices by exposing those who give and take bribes, who do favors for consideration, who procure positions for relatives, and who embezzle. The commission approach has always promised to curb corruption by investigating and prosecuting allegations of misfeasance by individuals, bureaucracies, and corporations; by identifying those persons who are worthy of prosecution; and by educating and socializing publics against corruption.

These commissions take many forms. All grew out of or reflect a diffuse or particular national will to manage or contain corruption—or to pretend to do so. Sometimes, as in Hong Kong, specific egregious corrupt incidents sparked countervailing responses. Sometimes donors (as in the case of many African countries) have spurred the impulse to battle corruption by helping to establish new governmental or quasi-governmental entities or by threatening to withdraw financial assistance unless such entities were created. Often, especially when and where police and prosecutors are suspected of cooperating with corrupt politicians, drug and gun traffickers, and other dark characters, or of facilitating the spread of corruption or of being themselves deeply enmeshed in the national web of corruption, national parliaments and executives (encouraged by civil society) opted to put entirely new and idiosyncratic organizations in charge of immensely important and challenging campaigns against corruption.

The investigative anticorruption commission model has been explored and implemented in South America, the provinces of Australia, forty-five of the fifty-four members of the African Union, and several of the key nation-states of East Asia and Southeast Asia. These commissions have varied titles and varied mandates, but all, at least at their inception, were charged with the extirpation of corruption within their national borders. It may be that some regimes established commissions merely to please donors, never intending them to be more than cosmetic. Others may have hoped, but not expected, that their commissions would work relentlessly to curb corruption. A few may not have realized that anticorruption commissions function well only where they are strongly supported by a national political will and by committed leadership from the national executive and the national legislature. Indeed, no matter how well-intended the commission instrument may be, it succeeds as an investigatory and prosecutorial body only when it has overwhelming community and political support.

According to one World Bank commentator, anticorruption commissions (however they are named) "fail to reduce public sector venality" in all but a few special circumstances. They often manifest attempts by policy-makers to appease scandalized citizens, but not necessarily to undertake meaningful reform. Some efforts are token. Serious attempts to revamp public-sector management are few, especially when leaders are more concerned about retaining personal power than changing the ways in which citizens interact with their governments. After all, prosecuting corrupt politicians and high officials interferes with the primary object of patrimonial rule. Effective clientelism depends on providing access to wealth or at least access to opportunities to purloin from the public purse or to take advantage of a public position to gain personally. "Entrenched interests" push back against the activities of any commission, more often than not rendering it impotent or capturing it to oppress opponents.[1]

Given such an exemplary analysis, for which there is much evidence (see especially chapter 5), the exceptional and salutary cases of the Singapore and Hong Kong anticorruption commissions and the mixed but significant experience of Indonesia's example are important to explore. They are among the few anticorruption endeavors that have demonstrated how, under the right conditions and with determined national leadership, the commission model can in fact decrease levels of corruption and markedly reduce public sector venality. These successful bundles of investigation and prosecution, gradually gaining credibility and slowly commanding grudging public support, have within their own jurisdictions demonstrated how stern assaults on even entrenched corrupt interests can, together with earnest educational and preventive efforts, transform wildly open and brazenly crooked places into paragons of probity. Indeed, preventing corruption from occurring is always more productive than punishing corruption after the fact.

Singapore's Initiative

Under Britain, the Singapore colony (as discussed briefly in chapter 3) was riddled with corruption. Police detectives doubled as thieves and opium smugglers, protection rackets were run collaboratively by Chinese gangs and senior police officers, and graft and extortion were common. Few citizens were unaffected by such criminal pursuits. In 1952, after a major scandal and internal investigations, the British governor created the Corrupt Practices Investigation Bureau (CPIB) independent of the police. But, by the time that Singapore became self-governing in 1959, the CPIB had reduced the impress of domestic corruption very little. Public officials were still consistently soliciting bribes; the poorly educated public hardly knew its rights and was in any event accustomed to paying bribes to obtain permits, certificates, and so on. The Chinese Triads had extended their reach. Moreover, local laws were weak, making obtaining evidence difficult. Anyway, the CPIB investigators had only limited powers of arrest and property confiscation and little motivation to pursue corrupt crimes energetically.[2]

Lee Kuan Yew and the other leaders first of self-governing and then of independent Singapore in 1960 promulgated the tough Prevention of Corruption Act (see chapter 3) and reinvigorated the CPIB. That meant (as later in Hong Kong and Indonesia) replacing seconded police officers with full-time civilian investigators, streamlining administrative procedures, educating the public regarding its rights and civil servants about how to behave in order to avoid suspicion and serve citizens effectively. Massive instructional manuals were prepared and distributed.

Subsequently, the CPIB began to take its preventive mission deep into the ministries and departments to reform regulations and procedures so as to reduce misconduct. It also played a significant role in screening candidates for appointment to high-level official positions. But its main function, especially in the early years of the Republic, was to receive tips and complaints from the public (and from the government itself) and to convert them into efficient investigations of persons suspected of abusing their official posts for private gain. When it had prepared a sufficient case, the CPIB turned its dossiers over to the attorney general's office for prosecution.

The technical competence of the heads of the CPIB and the diligent forensic work of its investigators might have on their own reduced corruption levels in Singapore in the 1960s and 1970s. But the driving force behind the commission, and the main reason why the CPIB developed a sharp competence and credibility in the eyes of the public, was Prime Minister Lee. He and his government provided the resources (from S$1 million in 1978 to S$34 million in 2011) and personnel required; the commission's own investigative actions prepared the way for signal exposures and convictions of major corrupt culprits.[3] With Lee demonstrating abundant political will, the government of Singapore acted competently and effectively.

By 2003, the CPIB was completing 99 percent of its investigations, usually within 90 days of inception. Prosecutions took place in 85 percent of those cases, resulting in an almost perfect record of convictions.[4] The courts, obviously, were compliant. By the end of the twentieth century each part of the finely tuned Singaporean governmental apparatus knew what its roles were and what it had to do to enforce the rules and, by then, to maintain the prevailing ethos against corrupt behavior. Whereas in its earlier years the CPIB had a pioneering function and was relied upon by Lee and others to raise standards and be the vanguard of the city-state's war against corruption, by the end of the twentieth century a culture of corruption had been transformed into an expectation of integrity. The CPIB could operate more modestly and technocratically.

Political will, in this case especially but in other instances as well, was decisive. Lee's personal and official crusade against corruption was fundamental to his legitimacy as head of the Singaporean government and to his survival as a leader. It undergirded his drive to transform a little city-state with no resources into a powerful first-world oasis. The CPIB became one of his instruments, incapable as it was of accomplishing all that it did without the nononsense support of the prime minister's office. (Lee's all-encompassing role in relieving Singapore of corruption is discussed at length in chapter 8). The CPIB reported directly to Lee and, after Lee left office, the CPIB's independence from politics and political influence was enshrined in the constitution. Hence, the battle against corruption waged by the CPIB, one of the earliest of the developing world's best anticorruption institutions, cannot be understood apart from Lee and the message that he conveyed forcibly to, and inculcated in, the body politic of Singapore.

The Hong Kong Model

Hong Kong's Independent Commission against Corruption is the exemplar, the model for all similar serious efforts, and a testament to what can be achieved by a quasi-governmental body determined to reduce widespread corruption and sleaze *if* the conditions are ripe and political circumstances endorse radical behavioral shifts.

From the founding of the Hong Kong Colony in 1842, gift-giving had been traditional; officials were accustomed to receiving tribute and to benefiting in at least minor ways from their positions—from their ability to influence decisions and outcomes. Illicit gambling flourished in colonial Hong Kong, as it did throughout the bicultural cities of Asia. There were illegal brothels, shady pawnshops, and many other questionable activities. A then not very prosperous colony, Hong Kong harbored criminal pursuits and criminal gangs that contributed to corrupt practices and to opportunities to receive and pay bribes. At the end of the nineteenth century, in one notable episode of cleansing, fully half of the colony's police establishment—British, Indian, and Chinese—was dismissed and convicted of accepting bribes. Many, even including British sanitary inspectors, had been paid to look away or stay silent. A 1902 governmental inquiry concluded that the colony's public works department was riddled with corrupt practices; no construction project, given the possibility of profiting from the use of imaginative building methods or improper materials, was immune from payoffs and payouts.

Hong Kong attempted in 1898 to legislate corruption out of existence by imposing stiff fines and imprisonment with hard labor for offenders. But, as was common elsewhere, the Hong Kong Colony left investigations and prosecutions to the regular police, who were themselves steeped in corruption throughout the first decades of the twentieth century. Floods of immigrants from China after the Japanese invasion, and a burst of impressive engineering and tunneling activity before Japanese forces overran the colony in 1941, provided ample openings for permit-granting, protection rackets, extortion, kickbacks, and paying for convenience and for speedy bureaucratic action.[5] All flourished. The rich bribed, the poor—laborers, artisans, and shopkeepers—in Hong Kong as elsewhere, paid such unofficial "taxes" and were surrounded by shoddy results and poor governance.

Hong Kong's venality, before and after World War II, mirrored that of many of the pre-Communist cities of China. All manner of illegal pursuits flourished, much of them controlled by triads or gangs based in Shanghai. As early as 1946, a British commissioner of police privately noted that he had "never seen such widespread corruption." One of his men had received $50 per head for recommending recruits; an assistant superintendent was trafficking in contracts for uniforms. Every transaction demanded a lubricating gift. Rackets abounded.[6] Nevertheless, Hong Kong's colonial overlords tolerated corrupt practices because they believed them to be deeply embedded in traditional Chinese culture.[7]

There were abundant openings (and possibly great needs) for the spread and intensification of corruption, and the Prevention of Corruption Act of 1948 and the establishment of a Police Anti-Corruption Bureau in 1952 did little to moderate its proliferation. Riots that engulfed the colony in 1966 were partially about and opposed to corruption, as were the intensifying struggles between Maoist and Kuomintang supporters within Hong Kong. But, before 1970, the dangers of corruption infecting the colony were rarely discussed in public; "Corruption was deeply rooted, widespread, generally tolerated [and] every part of the public service was infected."[8] The local press was muted before an article in the influential *Far Eastern Economic Review* exposed "squeeze" in both the public and private sectors. The *Review* called corruption a dominant way of life in the colony.[9]

The flight from the colony in 1973 of a British police senior superintendent suspected of having been greatly and illicitly enriched by his service to the colony over many years (he accepted lavish payments from subordinates and took payoffs from criminal gangs) made coping with corruption and "squeeze" an imperative for a recently arrived British governor whose predecessors and their administrations had largely operated in denial. After all, corrupt practices in Hong Kong and elsewhere were long entrenched and (mistakenly) believed fundamental to the continued prosperity of the colony.[10]

Political Will in Hong Kong

Fortunately, Britain's vigorous new governor was a committed, strong leader who less on moral and more on practical and credibility grounds decided that he had to crush, or at least attempt to reduce, corruption in the colony. Beyond the colony, of course, postrevolutionary fervor and deprivation had been succeeded by disaster—the Cultural Revolution. Governor Sir Murray MacLehose may have been influenced by Hong Kong's position as a supposed and to-be-strengthened outpost adjacent to a communist autocracy. He may have understood the improvements that the indigenous administration of another British-inspired city state—Singapore—had accomplished. He may have appreciated that capitalist examples on the edge of a communist behemoth had to be impeccably upright if they were to succeed as imperial or ex-imperial outposts in the modern era. Certainly MacLehose was "keen to re-establish legitimacy and repair the 'gap' between Government and people."[11] Whatever the motive, he knew that he had to act.

Sir Murray imposed his will, as governors could. He understood that public confidence in the legitimacy of the colony's government was very much at stake and, regrettably, that the police could no longer be permitted to investigate themselves. The temptations were too great; negative incentives were hard otherwise to remove. It made good administrative and political sense to create some completely independent new body—a special commission—with strong and certain powers to investigate, educate, and prevent corruption in Hong Kong. Sir Murray had the significant advantage that he did not need to consult with, or ask permission of, the local legislature or other persons within the colony. He could act magisterially, if wisely, and with a broad popular backing (as did a prime minister in Singapore and presidents in Botswana and Rwanda), but without needing to bargain with interest groups or other power centers. As far as can be ascertained, he drew on no pre-existing models.

Hong Kong's Independent Commission against Corruption (ICAC) opened for business in early 1974. It reported only to the governor himself, an innovative and important safeguard in a situation where that senior office (owing allegiance as it did to the distant Crown) was widely regarded as incorruptible. Elsewhere, in more fully democratic contexts, such a commission's links to an elected or a national person might have been suspect. In this case, the nature of colonial rule made it possible to establish the commission's true independence. Attempts to emulate the ICAC elsewhere have proven difficult precisely because of the constitutional, actual, or perceived absences of real independence.

The ordinance that created the commission and the governor's charge to it were also salient. Importantly, not only was the commission enjoined to ferret out corrupt practices within the colony, but it was also tasked with preventing any practices or behavior that led to or approximated corruption. And it was further fatefully asked to educate the public (under the rubric "community relations") about the dangers and intrinsic harms of corrupt practices.

Moreover, the ICAC's powers, as indicated earlier, rested on sure legal foundations, with deep and broad definitions of corruption and, notably, the (iniquitous) placing on the accused of the burden of proof to explain away any unusual or unexpected increments of wealth. The commission could detain and interrogate suspects. It could take their passports. It could gain access to bank statements and other relevant documents. It possessed the power of subpoena. The commission and its officers possessed broad authority to arrest persons suspected of corruption, broadly defined, and including dishonesty, false accounting, and deception. Criminality of any kind invited investigation.

Despite all of its abilities to bulldoze aside objections and ignore protestations of innocence, the commission had to transfer its cases to the public prosecutor's office for further action. "It is an important safeguard against oppressive prosecution," declared one commissioner, that investigation and prosecution should be separate responsibilities. Moreover, the corruption commission should not be permitted to hold hearings; courts should be the proper place for trials.[12] (In Hong Kong such separation of powers worked well. In Africa, handing dossiers to prosecuting authorities has been much more subject to inaction, interminable delay, and compromising political abuse. See chapter 5.)

After some aggressive early years, the ICAC decided that it would investigate *all* complaints—"no picking and choosing"—brought to its attention, but that it would only rarely initiate investigations itself. "If the confidence of the community was to be won, the ordinary man had to feel that his suspicion would be taken seriously. . . . Furthermore . . . public awareness of the policy of investigating every allegation provided strong protection from allegations" that the agency itself was contaminated with political influence.[13] Additionally, investigating every complaint, no matter how minor, fostered a community-wide understanding that no aspect of corrupt activity would be tolerated. The commission opened telephone hotlines and special complaint centers. Several of the commission's later leaders asserted that being a reactive body with a citizens' review board was essential to the public legitimacy that it obtained and for much of the favorable press that ICAC operations received.

Citizenry and civil society oversight of the ICAC was channeled through four advisory committees of prominent local citizens and one of local legislators. To give added transparency to the workings of the ICAC, they reviewed all complaints that were not pursued, and all other ICAC actions. Three advisory committees separately followed the three functional divisions of the commission—operations, prevention, and education—and a fourth advised the commissioner on policy and staffing. A fifth committee, composed of members of the legislative and executive councils of the territory, considered complaints against the commission and, if necessary, recommended disciplinary action.

Crucially, and conceivably the most significant reason for the ICAC's success, it was funded directly by a single annual appropriation from the local treasury. Its various internal financial allocations were not subject to scrutiny by anyone except the governor. It received what it needed. Its funding was also sufficient from the outset to employ hundreds, not handfuls, of experienced police and other investigators, all free of civil service restrictions and political interference. It recruited experienced police officers from the UK. Moreover, the commissioner of the ICAC had the power to hire and fire at will, thus giving the commission's leadership the ability to enforce internal codes against corruption within the ICAC.[14]

Human Resources

The ICAC, from its inception, was the largest anticorruption commission in existence, with much more numerous personnel than its counterpart in Singapore and the many less-capable organizations in Africa. In 2003, the ICAC employed 1,239 persons (1,393 in 2011), equivalent to more than 7 percent of the entire civil service roster of the territory. The operating costs of the ICAC amounted to $14 million in 1982, comprised 0.3 percent of the entire Hong Kong budgeted outflows in 2003, and grew to $105 million in 2011.[15]

Sir Murray chose an experienced Hong Kong British administrator to be the first head of the ICAC and to set the tone of probity and energy that was important in battling corruption effectively. He also recruited a British deputy, then serving in Malta, with vast investigative experience. The governor further separated employees of the ICAC from the civil service. They were rewarded at a pay scale higher than police and other civil servants and, managerially, were employed by the commission on renewable contracts, not by the Hong Kong government. These innovations further contributed to the ICAC's independence and to its ability unblinkingly to proceed against corrupt local officials and corrupt businessmen, journalists, and even the local police. As in all reform efforts, the character of the initial leadership cadre, and its morale, proved decisive.

In 1976 and 1977, after a year building operations and recruiting staff and gaining an awareness of the range of corruption that the ICAC could face, it moved smartly against local syndicates—first, a drug trafficking gang that had been paying police $10,000 per day for protection. Such police-organized licenses for vice extended to most gambling and prostitution endeavors within the colony. Police station leaders were consorting with triad bosses. By 1977, the ICAC was investigating twenty-three large syndicates, eighteen of which were police-run.

Hundreds of police officers (out of an establishment of 18,000) were initially charged with corruption. Later, after massive police protests and a partial amnesty, the number of those indicted, prosecuted successfully, and cashiered, was reduced. But, by 1980 the ICAC had succeeded in permanently reducing the pursuit of illicit gain by the police and was beginning to move against the triads and commercial private sector culprits. It had substantially limited profits from corrupt dealings, especially crooked monies pocketed by policemen, and—presumably—the troublesome tolls paid unwittingly and unwillingly by ordinary citizens of the colony.

By 1980, too, the ICAC had begun to employ its preventive arsenal, an instrument that it gradually perfected but that many subsequent commissions neglected. Its methods, later extended (and rarely embraced extensively beyond Hong Kong and Singapore) were to visit every department of government—especially public works, urban services, and housing—to make sure that its members (particularly those who exercised discretion, giving permits and the like) knew that the ICAC was now closely observing their operations. Its officers also eventually acquainted all of Hong Kong's questionable businesses (including the publicly owned telephone company) with the new rules to make sure that everyone knew what was and what was not permitted.

Hong Kong law penalized corrupt transactions between middlemen and agents of a firm. As a result, the number of gambling casinos and brothels within the colony declined, as did what were termed "lubricious amusement and recreation centres."[16] License fraud diminished and false bids were reduced. As the first ICAC commissioner declared in 1976, "Underhand dealings with an employee of a private sector business are not . . . less reprehensible than underhand dealings with a civil servant."[17]

Prevention and Education

The prevention bureau did more, too. It analyzed the operations of crucial departments, such as public works, and the ordinances under which they operated. Doing so permitted that part of the ICAC to recommend simplified legal changes that reduced the existing jurisdictional ambivalence that had allowed alternative decision-making by inspectors and other permitting authorities. One early, lengthy report scrutinized supervisory accountability within the entire civil service. Preventive efforts were intended to render corruption much more difficult.[18] The more limited the discretion of a bureaucrat or an inspector, the easier it is to administer regulations and requirements and the less likely decisions can be purchased.

In Hong Kong, the prevention section of the ICAC operated in ways that overlapped with official audit operations, in some countries the purview of the office of the auditor general. Auditors, if they are bent on performing well, can uncover fraud and contract-fixing by looking intensely at the entire bid and tender process, at departmental excess spending, and at schemes which are more costly than common sense might have predicted.[19]

The ICAC's community relations department was also central to the battle against corruption. Its main function was to build trust and social capital regarding the functioning of the ICAC and the reach of its powers. The department publicized the actions of the ICAC and attempted to ensure that all residents in the colony, especially the governmental and corporate communities (and small shopkeepers), knew how effective the ICAC could be and what was licit and what illicit. It also took its campaign into the colony's schools, working particularly with teachers to encourage them to insert anticorruption explanatory activities into their lesson plans. As one of the ICAC's commissioners rightly concluded, only permanent alterations in the attitude of the public regarding the perniciousness of corruption "could make a lasting difference" in curing it as an illness.[20]

By 1986, 72 percent Hong Kong's citizens knew that public servants need not be "tipped" or paid "tea money" to do their jobs, up from 32 percent nine years earlier. The community relations workers had begun to alter attitudes within the colony, especially among the sections of the community that had been most affected by corrupt predations, such as taxi drivers and restaurant owners, who had faced extortion requests by police officers and gangs. That ICAC department, by this time, had also begun to work effectively with the business community and to inform them of the colony's new behavioral expectations. By 1988, reports of corruption in the private sector began consistently to exceed those referring to the public sector.[21] In those years, and later, the community relations department's outreach extended across the banking and industrial arenas, as far as it could among youth organizations, and to new migrants from mainland China.

During the first ten years of the ICAC's existence, it investigated about 3,000 individual cases and passed them along to prosecutors for action. Seventy percent of those cases resulted in successful punishments. Many involved corrupt policemen of all ranks. But others, especially during the commission's second decade, involved inspectors who—for consideration—had approved devious construction methods and the use of inferior materials in buildings that later collapsed. (About 32,000 inhabitants were removed from dangerous apartment blocks in 1988 alone. One Chinese construction tycoon had bribed various clerks of works with millions of Hong Kong dollars.[22]) According to a regression analysis of the ICAC anticorruption enforcement efforts (the likelihood that an individual would be found guilty after being investigated and prosecuted) from 1974 to 2007, the Hong Kong model had proved very effective.[23]

During its second decade, the ICAC also brought about reforms in the running of the Hong Kong Stock Exchange and the local legal profession, where touting and illegal commissions had long constituted common, if illicit, practices. Senior lawyers in the government's own legal department and the British head of the police department's commercial crime unit were together charged with accepting hefty bribes to influence the conduct of major commercial legal investigations. Those interventions involved serious sums connected to narcotics trafficking, arms smuggling, triad gangsterism, and major instances of extortion. The ICAC in the 1980s also investigated big time commercial frauds involving investment banks that had falsified accounts in order to mislead shareholders and financiers. It stopped the fixing of races at the Royal Hong Kong Jockey Club.

During its first decade, the prevention section of ICAC completed 804 studies of potentially corrupting deficiencies in governmental departments, and the community relations (educational) division initiated more than 100,000 anticorruption proselytizing meetings.[24] From 1974 to 2013, the prevention bureau completed nearly 3,600 studies, and the community relations department annually attracted nearly 3 million visits to its website.[25] The message that Sir Murray, his successors, and the ICAC wished Hong Kongers to hear had been disseminated widely. Hardly anyone in the territory, as it came to be called, could have been unaware of the wrongs and dangers of corrupt dealings. (After 1997, Hong Kong became a special administrative region within the People's Republic of China.)

By 1989, according to two limited public opinion surveys, 85 percent of politically active respondents agreed that corruption was no longer a serious problem in Hong Kong. As compared to traffic, environmental pollution, housing, education, and hygiene issues, corruption was a major articulated concern for only 1 percent of the adult population.[26] The ICAC had achieved major changes, at least in the perception of corruption. Survey respondents also affirmed the ICAC's independence, and thought that its strong coercive powers were justified. Even in 2008, the ICAC continued to earn high local public opinion ratings; 98 percent of the citizens of Hong Kong affirmed the value of the commission model.[27]

After the Chinese takeover in 1997, the ICAC's then former commissioner asserted that "the public service [in the territory] is fundamentally cleaner." Likewise, the attitude of the Hong Kong public had changed dramatically. It regarded corruption as "evil and destructive." Citizens were much more willing than before to expose and report corrupt dealings and, remarkably, to do so openly instead of anonymously, as in the 1970s. A business ethics campaign launched the 1990s by the ICAC had borne fruit, if responses to surveys could be believed. Within a few years, more than 1,200 firms had adopted strict codes of corporate conduct.[28] Inside the government, "no department wants an ICAC investigation with the . . . potentially adverse effects for the public image of the department and the future careers of its senior members."[29]

Results for Hong Kong

The ICAC's success in combating corruption can also be seen in the annual releases of Transparency International's Corruption Perceptions Index (CPI). From 1995 to 2015, Hong Kong has been rated as high as the 12th least corrupt country or city-state (2008 and 2009) and as low as the 18th most corrupt entity (1996, 1997, and 2015). CPI's scores for Hong Kong (originally on a 10-point scale and now on a 100-point scale) have hardly varied, from the equivalent of 71 in 1995 to 75 in 2015; during the years from 2002 to 2011 Hong Kong's scores were consistently over 80 and as high as 84. Statistically, the changes in scores and ranks are hardly significant.[30] But what is at least impressionistically noticeable is Hong Kong's rise over more than twenty years, from 1974 to 1997, as a financial and commercial center, in large part as a result of its ability to reduce the impress and perception of corruption. "Clean business is good for profits."[31]

Hong Kong's comparatively stellar rankings have been maintained since the territory was transferred from British to Chinese control. In 2009, the ICAC forwarded for prosecution only twenty-one government official cases. In 2013, despite a minor meals allowance overexpenditure by the Chinese head of the ICAC, local politicians and professors told the BBC that they remained confident that the ICAC was an independent and staunch instrument, still effective in combating corruption. "Beijing is very concerned, and they don't want to see the downfall of the ICAC."[32]

The commission received 2,652 complaints in 2013, 1,649 concerning the private sector, 808 regarding government departments, and 195 for public bodies. Seventy percent of the complainants used their own names. Additionally, the ICAC investigated 557 election-related complaints. Overall, a total of 220 persons were prosecuted and 158 (about 72 percent) convicted.[33]

In 2014, the power of Hong Kong's anticorruption machinery—and of the continuing relevance of political will—was demonstrated anew, if sordidly and surprisingly, when the former chief secretary of the territory's administration was convicted of five charges of misconduct in public office. He was sentenced to a seven-year term in prison. After 2000, he had accepted $3.2 million in payments, unsecured loans, and free apartment rentals from Thomas Kwok, a prominent Hong Kong and Shanghai property magnate. (Rafael Hui Si-yan, the chief secretary, also received $1.42 million from Beijing, secretly.) Kwok and several associates were also found guilty. Hui, the former chief secretary, had been Kwok's "eyes and ears" in government. Hui admitted to expensive tastes, a preference for luxury, and the need to keep a mistress in Shanghai.[34]

After a lengthy investigation, the ICAC also struck in 2015 against Sir Donald Tsang Yam-kuen, Hong Kong's second chief executive after the Chinese takeover in 1997. Sir Donald, said the ICAC, had failed to declare the rental of a flat in nearby Shenzhen from a businessman who had applied for broadcasting licenses in Hong Kong. He had also recommended an architect for a public honor in Hong Kong who had worked on the flat's design. Earlier Sir Donald had admitted using the jet aircraft and yachts of wealthy tycoons for personal trips.[35]

In 2014, before Hui's trial, Hong Kong scored 74 (out of 100) on the Corruption Perceptions Index, below Denmark's top score of 92. Hong Kong had fallen a mere three points in the rankings since 2012. That 74 score tied Hong Kong with Barbados and Ireland for 17th place on the list, slightly below the United Kingdom, Belgium, and Japan, and below Singapore's 7th place ranking (score 84), but above all other Asian and African jurisdictions. (Bhutan and Botswana were ranked 30th and 31st in 2014, with scores of 65 and 63, respectively.)[36]

These largely salutary results for Hong Kong continued well through 2015, and probably into 2017. Arguably, the 18 percent increase in corruption complaints in 2015 over 2014 suggests not that Hong Kong has necessarily become more corrupt under Chinese oversight but that the ICAC, under a tough investigative head, greatly encouraged intensified "civic vigilance."[37] (She was later dismissed, possibly because of her zeal in investigating corrupt dealings by Hong Kong's Chinese-backed chief executive.[38]) The ICAC believed that more complaints were registered as a result of an increasing trust among the citizenry of its operations. But there was also an increase in prosecutions, year after year, albeit more for theft and deception than for bribery. Since 2010, according to the CPI, Hong Kong's rankings slipped from 12th to 18th, but given the shifts in the way the CPI is now constructed, that downgrading might mean less than it appears. However, the ICAC's internal morale has plummeted since the enforced resignation of its tough investigative leader, and that factor could begin to threaten the ICAC's ability to sustain its vigilance against corruption in the territory.[39]

Sir Murray's intervention in Hong Kong in 1974 seems to have worked well and sustainably. Because of the ICAC, and because of its ability to reframe and retrain the way in which British, Indian, and increasingly Chinese civil servants, customs and building inspectors, and police approached their duties, Hong Kong became and has remained an oasis of comparative probity on the edge of East Asia—a sentinel of anticorruption and an example for its neighbors and for any and all developing nations. It battled private and public sector corruption equally, thus gaining legitimacy and efficacy by attacking both varieties of offense. No other commission has proven so disruptive in the struggle against corrupt practices. No other commission is as responsible for thoroughly reforming how citizens approach the vicissitudes of everyday sleaze as well as the enormities of venal corruption. (Yet, it has recently become clear that the ICAC mandate and local legislation includes a major loophole; Hong Kongers are free to bribe liberally beyond the territory's borders. The ICAC cannot pursue corruption by citizens of Hong Kong if their offenses are committed elsewhere.)

Unfortunately, both Heilbrunn and de Speville suggest that the Hong Kong model cannot easily be replicated. Other polities (bar Singapore and Botswana) lack "a relatively sound administrative and legal infrastructure," especially an uncorrupted criminal justice system.[40] Too many spend too little on their anticorruption activities and commissions. Too few prevent and educate, and too many fail to pursue the corrupt. Hardly any are truly independent of the executive and the legislature. Hong Kong's commission was gestated by benign and strong leadership, nurtured in favorable times, and guided by persons of integrity. Its legitimacy was rapidly established as its anticorruption actions gained momentum. Most of all, by quickly breaking the back of corrupt gangs and syndicates and, not least, by re-educating the citizens of Hong Kong, the ICAC altered the political culture of Hong Kong dramatically and quickly. Only in Singapore and possibly in Rwanda have political cultures been transformed so tellingly. China, using much more draconian methods, may be doing the same now. Conceivably, the Philippines may be following China, using similar harsh, vigilante methods.

Indonesia's Mixed Initiatives

Efforts in Indonesia to create an effective political culture opposed to corruption have been less dramatic and less sustainable despite energetic attempts for more than a decade by a decisive and well-motivated anticorruption commission. Its battle has always been uphill, difficult, and often openly and tenaciously opposed by the many elite Indonesians who greatly profited from decades of state theft under President Haji Mohammad Suharto (1967–1998), a consummate enabler of corruption and opportunity.[41] It is a struggle that is not yet won and is long from over.

In 2015, despite many vicissitudes, the forcefully named Corruption Eradication Commission (Komisi Pemberantasan Korupsi—KPK), the Indonesian archipelago's most respected institution, had become deeply embroiled in a major envy battle with the national police, the security forces, and the national attorney general—and not for the first time. Since the wildly corrupt days at the end of the twentieth century under Suharto, the KPK (founded 2002) had managed to imprison hundreds of officials, politicians, and businessmen for corrupt acts. Although possibly only brushing the surface of Indonesian bribery and fraud, the KPK had established a healthy reputation for pushing back against the prevailing national culture of permissiveness. "There are few institutions . . . that are not riddled with corruption from top to bottom," a senior diplomat told reporters. Further, "corruption in Indonesia is from womb to tomb."[42]

Joko Widodo, a reformist and "clean" president elected in late 2014, was presumed to want to strengthen the KPK. But his surprise appointment in 2015 of a three-star police general as the new national police chief astonished many Indonesians; the KPK revealed that the proposed police chief was a key suspect in a massive bribery investigation. In retaliation, the police (as they had done in 2009) arrested a KPK deputy chairman and threatened to detain its chairman. "It's the KPK versus everyone," said a former KPK deputy chair. The attorney general and the police were jealous, he said, "and they create hatred" among political parties, politicians, businessmen, and so on.[43] Essentially, because the KPK tried to derail the top police appointment, the police marshaled several old accusations against leaders of the KPK, leaving legitimacy everywhere in tatters and Widodo with a political mess of his own making to clean up. (He eventually withdrew the attempted appointment, but replaced his nominee with an equally tainted replacement, the then interim national police chief.)

Widodo's unwise patronage-determined appointment of both police chiefs undermined the standing of the KPK and greatly weakened the vast nation's always tenuous assault on corruption. The police have long wanted to destroy their rival and enemy, an agency that had previously managed to block some profiteering in the police and security establishments and across the country. In a Gallup Poll, 91 percent (nearly thirty points higher than the rest of Southeast Asia) of Indonesians asserted that corruption was indeed "widespread" in the government of Indonesia. In 2015, Transparency International's Corruption Perceptions Index rated Indonesia 88th of 168 countries, equal with Egypt and Algeria, just below Sri Lanka, and just above Armenia, with a low score of 36.[44]

Before the troubles of 2014, the actions and presence of the KPK had managed demonstrably to reduce bribery, graft, peculation, and other corrupt ills in post-Suharto Indonesia, a country that had become a somewhat democratic assembly of 250 million people of many ethnicities and backgrounds. Consciously modeled on Hong Kong's Independent Commission against Corruption (ICAC), the KPK in its first five years proudly convicted all of the alleged perpetrators that it brought to trial before a special anticorruption court. That number included governors, parliamentarians, cabinet ministers, a few judges, a prosecutor, and an entire election commission. It also seized about $39 million in stolen state assets.[45]

From 2007, under new, bold leadership, the KPK continued to investigate and jail senior politicians, including a close relative of President Susilo Bambang Yudhoyono. It seemed set to attack corruption across the archipelago with a vigor even more pronounced than the first (2002–2007) KPK. It did so, moreover, with legitimacy derived from its actions and from strong popular support. By then, too, the KPK had maintained a strict internal code of ethics. Its image was clean. In 2008, the well-trusted Indonesian Survey Institute learned that 48 percent of the Indonesians polled believed the KPK to be a "very good" institution pursuing corruption effectively.[46] The media, which was given excellent access to the commission, and which wrote juicy stories, crowed about the work of the KPK, and civil society was supportive.

But as the KPK came to be perceived by the Indonesian political and military elites as a permanent institution capable of interfering massively with their pursuit of the many available low- and high-hanging fruits of corruption, so those many affluent and would-be affluent members of the Indonesian establishment began to mobilize against the KPK. The commission's success and the ambition of its new (2007) chair (appointed by Parliament along with four fully qualified vice chairs, one of whom was a state auditor, another a university rector, and a third a police inspector general) threatened in a serious manner permanently to disrupt the ease with which politicians, soldiers, and bureaucrats traditionally had abused their public positions for private gain.

The KPK indeed set out to destroy Indonesia's prevalent system of corruption and to galvanize national reforms.[47] By 2011, it had a trained cadre of more than 750 technocrats, good intelligence networks, and abundant experience.

It also cooperated and collaborated with anticorruption agencies across the globe; its reach extended beyond Southeast Asia. To its advantage, the KPK could monitor telephone and other communication methods without the need of a court order. It developed an anonymous online complaint system, very useful for tips. Improved in-house software allowed KPK auditors to identify bureaucrats who were likely living above their means. A civil society organization called Indonesia Corruption Watch funneled evidence to the KPK. So did many whistleblowers. Its Rapid Movement Unit caught suspects red-handed, with evidence hard to refute in court. And one dramatic arrest after another—of a judge taking a bribe in a public park, of a parliamentarian laundering money—gave the KPK further credibility. A raid on the main customs office discovered millions of rupiah in bribes. The KPK even arrested the father of the president's daughter-in-law.

The KPK, in the manner of Hong Kong's ICAC, also educated the public and attempted equally to train ministers and their high-level public officials to ferret out and cease corrupt practices within their immediate jurisdictions. It sent teaching teams into the schools and ran business ethics workshops. It produced films and television programs and used billboard displays and opportunities provided by music festivals to retail its anticorruption message. It was not reluctant to embarrass those establishments that were slow to reform. The KPK further focused on the bosses, not the lower-paid civil servants, winning their cooperation. The KPK also tried to go out into the nation's vast hinterland to encourage anticorruption efforts in bigger cities.

Although Yudhoyono was publicly supportive of the KPK, and neither he nor Parliament cut its operating budget, Parliament refused to allocate funds properly to house the KPK's growing staff. But after the 2009 elections, following the KPK's investigation of thirty politicians for bribes totaling $2.7 million and its detailed examination of a $524 million bailout of a major bank that had identified the corrupt involvement of a senior police general, the president and leading members of the legislature began to attempt to check the commission's power. By first decentralizing the special anticorruption court, where the KPK had won so many of its victories, it greatly weakened the commission and made prosecutions much less likely to succeed. The KPK and its local and international allies were able initially to beat back additional legislative maneuvers to harm whistleblowers, to grant amnesty to those who surrendered their bribes, to end the ability of the KPK to eavesdrop electronically, and to curtail the commission's substantial powers more generally.

But not entirely. The KPK truly annoyed the police. The nation's least-loved institution attacked its most respected one. The police launched an investigation against the KPK's chair for murder. He was subsequently tried, convicted, and sentenced to eighteen years in prison—a verdict that seemed highly questionable, at least to some external experts. Two of the commission's vice chairs were also accused by the police of abusing their office and of extortion; the first charge was later revealed to be a fabrication and the second was based on a forged document.[48] For a time, the KPK's momentum obviously stalled, but impressive levels of public and civil society support and backing from outside Indonesia kept the KPK's mission intact and restored its ability to continue the crusade against corruption.

From the beginning of 2008 to the end of 2011, the KPK prosecuted 139 cases, more than half the number for which investigations had been started. It convicted a host of parliamentarians, ministers, governors, mayors, ambassadors, central bankers, judges, prosecutors, and the head of a state-owned enterprise. It recovered $93 million in state assets. During the same period, the office of the attorney general and the police indicted many more culprits, but obtained fewer convictions and much lighter sentences. A law professor reviewing the importance of the KPK's efforts in 2011—as compared to the work of the attorney general's office and the police—said that the KPK, most significantly, had ended the culture of impunity that hitherto had prevailed for high-status politicians and security officials: "If you do corruption, we are going to prosecute you."[49]

Building up to the 2015 crisis, Widodo's seeming lack of concerned leadership and his overriding interest in appeasing the police and his and their Golkar political party backers left the KPK (fortunately with abundant public support) as the main bulwark against the onrushing, never moderated, tide of corruption that has always threatened to inundate Indonesia. In early 2016, for example, the KPK arrested a Supreme Court administrative official (the head of a subdivision for civil lawsuits) for taking bribes, in one instance about $30,000, plus a suitcase filled with even more cash.[50] Yet, unlike much smaller Singapore and Hong Kong, where commission efforts and the exercise of abundant political will had drastically curbed corrupt practices and dramatically altered the prevailing political culture, Indonesia in 2016 remained Janus-faced: corruption was still rampant; its valiant anticorruption commission remained energetic but lonely.

The European Union bemoans Indonesia's widespread political corruption, its corrupt judiciary, and the extensive bribery that still seems a way of life. In one celebrated recent case, an influential and long-serving parliamentarian and speaker of Indonesia's House of Representatives offered to cut a deal with the Indonesian head of a major American mining concern that sought to lengthen its lease on a number of vital properties in order to invest $17 billion to extend the world's largest gold mine and the world's third largest copper digging. President Widodo was known to be opposed to any lease extensions. The speaker asked for 20 percent of the company's mining stakes to change the president's mind. Unfortunately for the speaker, the company executive surreptitiously recorded the request and gave the recording to the minister of energy, who in turn presented it to the ethics council of the House of Representatives. The speaker resigned but kept his parliamentary seat.[51]

As this example hints, corruption continues at the highest levels in Indonesia despite an active and experienced investigative commission. Handicapped as it has been by inconsistent backing from the presidency and by hostility from the police, the KPK is still unable on its own to dampen the venal and petty corruption that continues to bedevil Indonesia. President Widodo has focused more on improving the archipelago's weak infrastructure and championing manufacturing than he has on supporting the KPK and other efforts to battle corruption. (In mid-2016, he also surprised critics by breaking with his party and appointing a well-respected head of the national counterterrorism agency to lead the country's police force. "Articulate and intelligent," the new police chief was said to be "committed to cleaning up" that corrupt institution.[52]) Indonesia is admittedly much more populous than Singapore and Hong Kong, much more complicated, and with many more competing internal interests. But absent strong exertions of political will and determined leadership at the highest level, Indonesia will never easily moderate corruption in the manner of Hong Kong and Singapore (or even Croatia, below).

Croatia's Commission

Croatia is a small Balkan state, once part of Yugoslavia and, until 1999, ruled by a Soviet-style autocrat. But by 2010, copying Hong Kong, it had established the Bureau for the Suppression of Corruption and Organized Crime (USKOK), which became among the most effective such units anywhere. From 2005 to 2015, it prosecuted for corruption and accepting kickbacks more than 2,000 suspects, convicting a phenomenal 95 percent. Those tried and jailed included a prime minister (imprisoned for more than eight years for profiting from the sale of a state-owned oil company), a deputy prime minister, three former cabinet ministers, a top general, an ambassador to the UN, tax officials, the mayor of Zagreb (the nation's capital), and ten high officials of the notoriously corrupt Croatian Privatization Fund. The USKOK also indicted those who took bribes in exchange for better grades in local universities and doctors who accepted cash in exchange for false injury reports.

Driving the USKOK's attempt to shift Croatia from a state of plunder to a state with but modest levels of corruption was a new national political leadership and a national consciousness that was intent on being accepted (as Macedonia and Montenegro, examined in chapter 6) into the European Community. An efficient assault on corruption and organized crime was a precondition for that accession. In the twenty-first century, Croatian civil society also focused on initiatives that could help to reduce corruption in the young state.

The USKOK was established in 2001, but it was not until 2005 that the bureau gained the kinds of political support (ironically from a prime minister who was later jailed) and the institutional leadership that it needed to grow and act against impunity. The ratification of the UN Convention against Corruption (UNCAC) in that last year by the Croatian Parliament was critical; it conferred new powers to freeze assets, employ wiretaps, and conduct undercover operations, all of which proved essential in the battle against organized crime and corruption. A new team of special judges was also enlisted to hear cases of corruption.

The USKOK, unlike most of the African commissions examined in the next chapter, resisted political retaliation despite its merciless investigations of members of the nation's ruling class. The realization that the European Union was scrutinizing every move within Croatia, and was suspicious of potential apostasy, helped to provide powerful support for the USKOK. Also crucial was the impeccable integrity of the leaders of the USKOK. Without the legitimacy that they had developed between 2005 and 2010 by prosecuting fairly, fearlessly, and relentlessly, the USKOK would have been defenseless against the maneuverings of those whom they were bringing to justice. Thanks to the media attention that the USKOK had cultivated and received, the public was behind the USKOK, as was the EU. In 2010, 33 percent of Croatians trusted the judiciary and 58 percent trusted the police. By about 2013, a former speaker of the Croatian Parliament asserted that anticorrupt policies were "deeply rooted in our society. . . . There [was] no way back to the old bad habits." Even so, a Eurobarometer poll in 2013 revealed that Croatians believed corruption in their country to be "widespread," a possible reflection of a spate of successful prosecutions.[53] The Corruptions Perceptions Index in 2015 ranked Croatia 50th (up 11 places from 2014) and below Saudi Arabia and Bahrain, but tied with Hungary and Slovakia and above Italy. It was the least corrupt Balkan state after Slovenia, ranked 35th, according to the CPI.

Mostly Winning the War

Well-run, well-motivated, energetic, and accomplished anticorruption commissions cannot single-handedly transform a corrupt polity into one where soliciting and giving bribes, inflating contracts, trading on influence, and pursuing similar nefarious opportunities is shunned. Commissions cannot institute a new ethos to complement strict rules and regulations. They can, together with the courts, expose, investigate, prosecute, and punish perpetrators and, overall, cleanse the proverbial Augean Stables. They can and do educate public servants and citizens and in that manner create a climate of and an expectation of integrity. But they can only do so, and be effective as commissions, if they are supported, even boosted, by national political leadership.

This factor provides the political will that is fundamental in the Asian (and Croatian) cases and elsewhere to the success or failure of anticorruption efforts and of anticorruption commission actions everywhere.

Governors in Hong Kong and prime ministers in Singapore motivated and protected the early phases of their anticorruption commissions. Indonesia's KPK, in contrast, has usually received lukewarm support from its governmental masters. Leaders in Hong Kong and Singapore powerfully articulated both the rationale and the mandate of their commission examples. They brought the citizens of their small city-states to appreciate how much was at stake and how beneficial reforms and major reform processes would be for the two polities and for every citizen. It then became necessary for the Hong Kong and Singapore commissions not just to identify and deal with culprits, but also to prevent and educate—to offer new ways in which public servants could appreciate their roles and responsibilities and assimilate the value of integrity. The Indonesians, in much larger settings, tried very hard to do the same, but without the kind of unwavering political support that was required.

As of late 2016, with a renewed drive by Widodo to cleanse Indonesia of *pungli*, or corruption, those who seek to reduce sleaze and graft in Indonesia may be receiving renewed support from the presidency. Personally helping to raid the Transport Ministry headquarters, to seize 1 billion rupiah in illicit cash from bribes, and to discharge several officials, Widodo warned all Indonesian officials to "stop . . . or face the sack." He also admitted having failed as president to create a "state of justice" within the country. At the same time, he introduced a special online site where whistleblowers and others could report corrupt actions.[54]

Indonesia is still corrupt; the other two Asian city-states are not. That Indonesia has improved, but hardly been transformed, is less the fault of the KPK than it is the inevitable result of size, complexity, and the lack of a leadership willing and able to alter the national incentive structure. The lessons of Hong Kong and Singapore (and of Croatia) are that attitudes and behaviors can be changed rapidly and markedly if corrupt practices become too costly (jobs are forfeited, ill-won gains are confiscated, perpetrators are found out) and if other ways are found to reward citizens and public servants psychologically and economically. Hong Kong and Singapore did so. Croatia, backed by the European Community, gave its people the pride and esteem that flowed from pronounced integrity. Indonesia may ultimately follow, whether Widodo is or is not the man that we thought he was.

V

African Investigative Commissions

FROM INTEGRITY TO INTERFERENCE

The Hong Kong model has not transferred well, if at all. According to one study, in West Africa country-level commissions were ineffective, unable to overcome corruption.[1] They lacked resources, to be sure, but, most of all, none were backed by executive or legislative political will. None were created as part of a comprehensive national anticorruption strategy. None ever enjoyed Hong Kong's enviable sustained organizational development. Another, more comprehensive, study concluded that African anticorruption commissions had been "consigned to a form of existence that not only constrains, but almost guarantees their inability to attain achievable levels of success."[2]

Nearly all of the post–Hong Kong models in Africa were and are donor-funded. Even so, most were insufficiently financed, short of experienced staff, and in one case devoid of dedicated facilities. Most damaging, these African commissions suffered from a lack of independence, from weak mandates, from insufficiently trained investigators, from an inability to prosecute without interference (attorneys general and public prosecutors nearly always decided whom to try), and from a lack of esprit de corps (which Hong Kong's ICAC developed and still expresses).

Hong Kong and Singapore were able deeply to alter their prevailing national political cultures; they established incentives in favor of honesty and probity instead of those hitherto prevailing of greed and acquisitiveness. Few African countries (bar Botswana, Mauritius, and now Rwanda) ever tried to struggle against corrupt behavior as a given. Thus, most of the African commissions operated with little public support, or at least without developing a consensus that corrupt practices were eradicable. Where civil society (as in most of Africa) is inexperienced or relatively powerless, where national political leadership is uninterested or unfocused on reducing corruption, and where the existence of corrupt behavior is considered normal (even if illegal), it may still be Herculean to expect anticorruption commissions to succeed simply by attempting to go about their investigative, prosecutorial, preventive, and educational business in the customary manner.

That a nation-state (especially in Africa) legislates an anticorruption commission and gives it broad responsibilities and broad statutory authority need not mean that it will or can operate effectively or successfully. Yet commissions themselves, overall, have managed to point their official fingers at corruption and to bring attention to a variety of astonishing abuses of the public purse and official positions. Even so, in too few cases did the existing national levels of corruption recede. Politicians and officials still want "to eat."

A More Effective African Model

Two members of the African Union, Botswana and Mauritius, both already ranking low in corruption compared to nearly all other sub-Saharan African countries according to the Corruption Perceptions Index, established anticorruption commissions that were modeled on Hong Kong's ICAC. But they both did so well after establishing themselves as noncorrupt paragons; their first leaders successfully propelled their nascent nation-states down an unusual path predicated on antagonism to anything irregular. In Botswana's singular case, its first president gradually but firmly established norms against corruption (see chapter 8) and produced mainland Africa's most robust societal expectations of governmental integrity. Mauritius' first prime minister, Sir Seewoosagur Ramgoolam, tried to do the same, and shifted the island-state's political culture considerably. Mauritius has maintained to this writing an ultimate judicial appeal procedure to Britain's Privy Council, thus giving its legal processes a significant extra safeguard and, hence, a further assurance of probity.

There were unexpected breaches of Botswana's anticorruption ethos in the early 1990s, however, when the general manager of a state corporation was discovered to have received massive bribes from construction companies for mostly unneeded or wasteful projects (mentioned already in chapter 2). A contract to supply textbooks for primary schools included major kickbacks to the officials involved. The vice president and two ministers acquired land through shadowy means on the outskirts of the capital. The president and sitting cabinet ministers failed to repay loans to the National Development Bank. After decades of public integrity, Botswana had slipped into familiar African pursuits. All of the usual crimes had been committed: abuse of office, preferential treatment for influential firms and relatives, tender fraud, the acceptance of bribes, and graft.

In the midst of these sudden scandals, Botswana decided to take advice from Hong Kong. It hired the ICAC's deputy commissioner to start what soon became the Botswana Directorate on Corruption and Economic Crime (DCEC) and to advise Parliament on the passage of a new legal framework (described in chapter 3). But Botswana refused to make the DCEC as fully independent as the ICAC; Botswana's version reported to the president, who made all appointments. Its budget, and for a time its operational control, came from the Ministry of Justice. Its 270-plus employees (as of 2011) were civil servants, not independent contractors as in Hong Kong. It was given a broader mandate than the ICAC so that it could pursue fraud and tax evasion as well as corruption, but doing so stretched the institution too far given the country's shortage of trained personnel. In contrast to the ICAC, it further lacked the citizen oversight mechanisms that had enhanced public accountability and support in Hong Kong. However, as in Hong Kong, the DCEC could execute searches and seizures, trace and freeze assets, prevent travel, and make arrests. But it was not permitted to intercept telecommunications, and the president's office could bar the commission from seeing documents prejudicial to state security.

Mauritius established its commission almost a decade after Botswana's came into existence. But there had been an anticorruption tribunal from 1993 to 1995 and an even more short-lived Economic Crime Office in 2000. The latter had investigated several cabinet ministers for fraud, prompting resignations and a national election that resulted in a change of government. Afterwards, following financial missteps involving Air Mauritius and theft from a national pension fund by many politicians and businessmen, and to some extent because of Mauritius' ratification of the United Nations Convention against Corruption (UNCAC; see chapter 3) and the Southern African Development Community (SADC) Protocol against Corruption, in 2002 Mauritius passed its own Prevention of Corruption Act and established its Independent Commission against Corruption, a direct copy of Hong Kong's ICAC.

Mauritius' MICAC was authorized to investigate corruption, money laundering, procurement fraud, and similar crimes and, with the permission of the Directorate of Public Prosecution, to try culprits in court. It explicitly could go undercover, but without tapping telephones; it could examine contracts and demand financial disclosures. It possessed powers of arrest and could seize evidence and assets. As in Hong Kong, it was additionally responsible for educating the public about the dangers of corruption and for preventing corrupt activity, especially in governmental operations. The MICAC's director general owed his appointment to Mauritius' ceremonial president (not to the prime minister—the head of government), which might have given the MICAC full independence in the Hong Kong manner. But the MICAC was also accountable to a parliamentary committee composed of members from both ruling and opposition parties, thus somewhat limiting the commission's autonomy.

The DCEC and the MICAC followed Hong Kong's lead as far as attempting to prevent corruption and educate against it. They sought to strengthen ministerial service delivery capacities, eliminate bureaucratic bottlenecks and delays, and shrink official discretion—all so as to reduce opportunities (and temptations) to perform corruptly. Both anticorruption commissions also persuaded cabinet officials to establish special anticorruption units or integrity committees within their ministries and state-owned enterprises. Both the DCEC and the MICAC also entered ministries, engaged in detailed studies, and produced major critiques of each ministry with recommendations for how the operations of those ministries and their divisions should be improved to prevent corruption. In Botswana, the commission helped in this manner to reform the motor vehicle insurance fund and a small business grant operation. It managed to alter the manner in which tenders were prepared for major building construction maintenance projects. Later, in Botswana, each ministry had to submit quarterly reports on its own anticorruption efforts.

Botswana and Mauritius both tried to reach students in their primary and secondary schools to forestall any propensities toward corruption. The DCEC offered curriculum materials, sponsored anticorruption clubs, sent a "Mr. Integrity" mascot to tour schools, visited rural villages to talk about the dangers of corruption, and even opened a few distance branch offices. It wrote a weekly column on corruption prevention in a state-run newspaper and eventually learned how to woo the independent press. It went on the radio, too, for most Africans receive their news over that medium. The DCEC established a hotline to receive complaints and was happy to let the press send tips. The MICAC even more aggressively courted its lively local press, which helped the MICAC to publicize its efforts against corrupt practices. It prepared thirty thorough studies of individual ministries and state-owned enterprises so that their internal anticorruption efforts could be upgraded.

Both the MICAC and the DCEC moved against major and minor culprits. Over time, their conviction and general success rates improved. From 2007 to 2013, the DCEC completed investigations of a very senior official who was suspected of illegal transfers of public land; of a managing director of Debswana, the state-controlled dominant diamond mining and selling concern and the fount of virtually all national prosperity; of the head of the state's public procurement agency (he had allegedly awarded contracts to his relatives); and of three cabinet ministers who had given state equipment and other kinds of contracts essentially to themselves via their relatives. The

MICAC indicted such high political persons as a minister of health, the head of a major political party, the mayors of the capital and other big cities, the chief commissioner of a semiautonomous offshore island, and the heads of several quasigovernmental bodies.

But whereas the MICAC and the DCEC could claim high conviction rates (80 and 75 percent) in the latter years of their operations, many of those jailed were small-time offenders. Bigger "fish" were much harder to incarcerate. The DCEC lost several high-profile cases in the courts, even after appeals to the High Court. But the cause may have been poor preparation by the public prosecutors and not failures of commission by the DCEC. Or those acquittals may have resulted in Botswana from political interference and illicit deal making. One local close observer of corruption wondered if the "will" really existed to manage such sharp blows to the ruling political party.[3] Mauritius could not investigate cases of conspiracy by corrupt officials because its legal authority to do so was limited. But that stricture did not impede Botswana. Later, the chief justice of Botswana's High Court created a specialized tribunal exclusively for corruption cases.

Despite these failures or omissions, 62 percent of Botswanans polled by Afrobarometer in 2012 were positive about the commission. Even hostile critics praised the DCEC's efforts to prevent corruption and educate officials and students about its evils.[4] Mauritius' work was equally well received, especially its Public Sector Anti-Corruption Framework in 2010 and a number of best-practices guidelines for different governmental areas, such as contract management and licensing.

Given these strict legal provisions and the bright-lined national political culture established and enforced by founding President Seretse Khama, it might be expected that Botswana in 2016 would exhibit low levels of corruption. And so it does—by African and global measures. According to the Transparency International's Corruption Perceptions Index, in 2015 Botswana was Africa's least corrupt country, as it had been for twenty consecutive years. It ranked 28th of 168 countries. Its closest African competitors were Cape Verde and the Seychelles (both 40th), Rwanda (44th), and Mauritius and Namibia (both 45th). Botswana's raw scores are also high, at 63, behind Denmark's first-place ranking with a score (out of 100) of 91.[5]

Without in any way impugning the CPI or Botswana's active Transparency International chapter, some local experts and observers believe that their country is less perfect than it was—that in recent years the ugly beast of corruption has reared up and shown itself in more and more instances of questionable contracting (tendering), in revived cases of alleged favoritism and nepotism, and in a general suspicion that an informal coterie is benefiting more than it should from its ties to state house.

In 2013, nearly all of the national contracts to supply bread to schools and prisons were won, suspiciously, by a bakery owned by the mayor of Lobatse, a prominent member of the ruling Botswana Democratic Party (BDP). The head of the Public Procurement and Asset Disposal Board (which oversees tendering) presided over a meeting that awarded a contract to his nephew. The former director of the Public Service Management Directorate was also charged with nepotism. Several public officials fabricated ghost positions in which they installed relatives and claimed their wages. To cap it all, the BDP's secretary general brazenly claimed (without being rebuked) that "I always hear people complaining of how . . . BDP members win tenders but they seem to forget that we are . . . the ruling party. How do you expect us to rule when we don't have money?"[6]

By 2013, certainly, many Tswana believed that corruption had burst its old bounds—"the state . . . has been captured for some narrow interests." Botswana, according to local journalists and academics, was gradually regressing to the sub-Saharan African mean of corrupt practice. However, as of 2016 at least, corruption was not yet a way of life in Botswana. There was still a strong presumption against pilfering from the state and abusing a public position; those who use a public office to influence decisions in their favor are severely criticized. Moreover, unlike in nearby South Africa, "it is uncommon for officials to use public funds" to cover private expenses.[7] There are still strong societal sanctions against corrupt behavior, and Botswana's fundamental early political decision to confront the malady still produces positive results. In other words, Botswana has probably crossed the normative boundary into an appreciation of ethical universalism.

Of equal, and reinforcing, value, Botswana is sub-Saharan Africa's leading democracy. The parliamentary opposition is smaller and less powerful than the ruling BDP, but in and out of Parliament members of opposition parties harry the government and draw attention to what appear to be corrupt lapses. Their critiques have occasioned important resignations from major governmental boards and parastatal organizations. Questions in Parliament further have led to the sacking of the head of the Botswana Examination Council for failing to oversee the marking and release of school results in 2012.[8] Indeed, it appears that parliamentary questioning, even in or, possibly, particularly in Botswana, has been more effective in curbing corruption than has the official anticorruption agency.

As African commissions go, as tentative and (as compared to Singapore, Hong Kong, and Indonesia) as resource-constrained as the Botswanan and Mauritian anticorruption bodies were, and are, they operate within contexts favorable to curbing corruption. In both countries, public opinion supports the work of the commissions and praises their accomplishments, however incomplete. Better still, the Botswanan and Mauritian commissions are creatures of a positive executive political will; their presidents and prime ministers have wanted effective commissions and supported what the commissions have been doing. Elsewhere in Africa, where thirty-eight other states have anticorruption commissions intended to function as effectively as those in Botswana and Mauritius, several have tried hard to curtail corrupt practices with but limited support from political leaders and political elites. A few have fought energetically to fulfill their difficult mandates. Others have been purposely hamstrung from inception.

Nigeria and Ghana had two commissions that enjoyed brief periods of great achievement under serious and determined organizational leaders. But, despite (or because of) their successful prosecutions of corrupt offenders, both commission's trajectories were soon deflected.

Three Steps Forward, Four Backward

Because of its many-centuries-old tradition of "the dash" and consideration for services, Nigeria is a special, tough, and complicated case. As Jordan Smith writes, corruption is "woven into the fabric of political and economic life." Nigeria is rife with corruption, and "no one is more aware of this reality than ordinary Nigerians."[9] British Prime Minister David Cameron was unwittingly candid at an anticorruption summit in London. Nigeria, he said, was "fantastically corrupt"—and along with Afghanistan was one of the two "most corrupt countries in the world."[10] But being cognizant of, and being concerned about how corrupt practices and their grip on the national body politic greatly hinder the country's growth, distort the trajectory of its development, and permit insurgents such as the Niger Delta Avengers, the Movement to Emancipate the Niger Delta (MEND), and Boko Haram to flourish, did not before late 2015 motivate more than spasmodic anticorruption actions. When incoming Nigerian President Muhammadu Buhari delivered an unsmiling acceptance speech, one of his two main pledges was to end the "evil of corruption" that scourged his massive nation. He promised a war against corruption, emphasizing "accountability, integrity, and transparency." Corruption "will not be tolerated," he declared. The previous national administration had allegedly "lost" an amazing N11 trillion ($50 billion) in revenue, including about $15 billion in crude oil and crude oil earnings and $6 billion in monies stolen by cabinet ministers.

President Muhammadu Buhari's administration may be the first genuinely to battle corruption in Nigeria. At least that is his promise. He gained legitimacy in the anticorruption struggle by cutting his annual presidential salary in half, by declaring his assets, and by sacking a raft of officials who had been pilfering from the national oil pot.

Buhari also decided to take charge of oil affairs himself. He said that he did not trust anyone else to check on oil receipts, be transparent, and recover billions of dollars in stolen funds. (In 2014, the head of the Central Bank of Nigeria claimed that the Nigerian National Petroleum Corporation, Nigeria's largest employer, had lost, mislaid, or corruptly distributed $20 billion in revenues.) Much of the gross mismanagement of payments from multinational petroleum drillers and exploiters occurred when Diezani Alison-Madueke was minister of mines and petroleum in President Goodluck Jonathan's administration. She was arrested in October 2015 in London on charges of bribery and money laundering. "Nigeria has surely been short-changed by Nigerians who were trusted with public offices in the oil sector," said Osadolor Etiosa, a prominent Nigerian journalist and commentator. Buhari, himself a minister in charge of oil in the 1970s, promised to break up the company to improve oversight.[11]

As in so many developing countries, Nigeria in the late twentieth and early twenty-first centuries has centered its politics on spoils, especially on the redistribution of abundant state petroleum revenues and associated state resources. For decades those spoils have been appropriated by officeholders and others in positions to aggregate rents and rewards, and sometimes to provide further ongoing patronage. This neopatrimonialism or, as others label it, prebendalism, has been a feature of Nigerian political life since independence in 1960, if not decades before in traditionally ruled domains.[12] It has long been assumed that persons occupying Nigerian public office of any kind will use their positions to accumulate lucrative resources for themselves and for members of their families, lineages, and ethnic groups. That is their supposed responsibility to their kin—as well as to themselves. Fulfilling the obligations to the nation that come with holding state office is thus secondary to the ingathering of riches, and to their onward dissemination to favored groups. In the local vernacular, Nigerian political and bureaucratic figures have long craved opportunities (at all levels), to "chop"—to feast at the public table.

Precolonial, colonial, and postcolonial Nigeria, like Ghana, exhibited and exhibits very high levels of corruption. There is no section or region of Nigeria that was or is free from corruption. According to a persuasive 2006 estimate, Nigerian leaders had by that year stolen or mismanaged about $412 billion since independence in 1960—the equivalent of six Marshall Plans. By at least the 1980s, astute commentators noted that corruption in Nigeria had long ceased to be an aberration; it was merely how the system worked.[13] Members of the National Assembly have knowingly been called a "consortium of certified crooks." Nobel Prize winning author and social critic Wole Soyinka says that Nigeria by 2008 had become "a byword for the most breathtaking scams in high places, for endemic corruption, a contempt for accountability and transparency, and the abuse of national resources in the pursuit of personal and party power."[14] Baker, a businessman with a deep appreciation for everything Nigerian, calls it "the most corrupt country in the world!!"[15]

Nor are there institutions within pre-Buhari Nigeria that functioned with appreciably low levels of corruption. About two of Nigeria's thirty-six states managed in recent years, under estimable governors, to reduce corrupt practices. But the other thirty-four, including a handful of wide-open violators, took corrupt behavior to extremes, as did the federal government. Between 1999 and 2007, governors from thirty-one of the nation's thirty-six states had been indicted by one or more anticorruption commissions for all manner of fraud and abuse of public office. One, Diepreye Alamieyeseigha, sometime governor of Bayelsa State (1999–2005), embezzled as much as $55 million in oil revenues. He owned properties in Cape Town and London and bank accounts and other assets in the Bahamas, the British Virgin Islands, Cyprus, Denmark, and the Seychelles.[16]

The late twentieth century decades of military rule, essentially from 1979 to 1999, were marked by extreme episodes of greed, serial looting, and the pillaging of the national treasury, not least under the heavy-handed regime of General Sani Abacha (1993–1998). There were fake public contracts for phantom projects, such as the $7 billion mill that never rolled any steel, a vastly overpriced $3 billion aluminum smelter, and the theft of at least $5 billion from the national treasury.[17] Some of Abacha's ill-gotten gains were stashed in Switzerland (and millions of dollars were still being repatriated in 2016), where he had 120 bank accounts and at least $670 million. A large proportion of Abacha's loot was spent on debauchery and the deflowering of the Nigerian nation-state. After Abacha's sudden death in 1998, his purloined wealth, some eventually recovered from secret accounts overseas, was estimated at $4.3 billion.[18] Earlier, General Ibrahim Babangida, president from 1985 to 1993, had run off with $12 billion in oil revenues.[19]

With the return of civilian rule under President (and former general) Olusegun Obasanjo in 1999, the newly elected democratic government obviously had a mandate to attempt to restore Nigeria's moral atmosphere and the legitimacy of those who ruled. Doing so meant attacking corruption as energetically as Obasanjo and his associates could imagine ways to do so. Clauses in the country's new (1999) constitution—such as "the state shall abolish all corrupt practices and abuse of power"—the passage of Nigeria's Corrupt Practices and Other Related Offences Act of 2000, the Economic and Financial Crimes Commission Act of 2002 (replaced by a 2004 act of the same name), and a widespread awareness throughout the nation that norms of behavior had drastically to improve, led to the creation of the Independent Corrupt Practices and Other Related Offences Commission (ICPC) in 2000, the Economic and Financial Crimes Commission (EFCC) in 2003, and the revitalization of the Code of Conduct Bureau and Tribunal, dating from 1979.[20]

The last two bodies were meant to oversee the declaration of assets by all public officials, bans on politicians and others holding foreign bank accounts, and the policing of conflicts of interest. But, in large part because the National Assembly never enacted enabling legislation, the Code of Conduct Bureau's enforcement efforts have been limited; the public was prevented (pre-Buhari) from seeing the asset revelations that the bureau had received.

The ICPC had the prime responsibility to ferret out corrupt acts and prosecute them. On paper, it had broad authority to examine how public bodies operated, to supervise reforms to their procedures, and to endeavor to educate Nigeria's many millions of people about the dangers and waste of corruption. Accepting "gratifications"—anything promised with intent to influence the performance or nonperformance of official duties—was outlawed. So were a vast range of associated illegal acts and behaviors.

In the first five years of its existence, the ICPC received a total of 942 petitions alleging wrongdoing on the part of leading political and official persons. In August 2003, about 400 of the petitions were under investigation and about 60 were at various stages of prosecution. By 2003, the ICPC had begun investigating the speaker of the National Assembly, the president of the Senate, other prominent federal politicians, the operators of a national pension fund, and ministry of education officials who had allegedly mismanaged finances associated with the country's educational reform efforts. The ICPC failed, however, to secure any major convictions, mostly because of backroom political maneuvering, judicial delays, severe underfunding, and Obasanjo's indifference (despite his strong anticorruption rhetoric). Additionally, the ICPC interpreted its mandate as excluding corrupt activity prior to 2003 and the corrupt practices of governors, which it referred to the federal chief justice. Two critics suggest that although Obasanjo initially preferred to fight corruption through the judicial actions of the ICPC, it was a largely ineffective body. Another student of the ICPC calls it a puppet of the executive and excoriates its dismal performance.[21]

The EFCC, created to supplement and replace the weak and internationally criticized ICPC, was supposed to attack a plethora of advance fee abuses and to enforce Nigeria's many existing banking laws. Its empowering act authorized the EFCC to "prevent, investigate, prosecute and penalize economic and financial crimes." It was further charged with enforcing the Money Laundering (Prohibition) Act of 2004. The EFCC was encouraged to ferret out and confiscate ill-gotten wealth and to join the global war against financial duplicity. Under these provisions the EFCC gained a mandate to manage the main direct battle in Nigeria against all manner of what was termed the "menace" of corrupt behavior. The appointing authority in this case was much the same as for the ICPC; the president was at any time allowed to remove its chairman without notable cause. In many ways, too, the national attorney general also had a statutory right to interfere in the day-to-day workings of the commission.

Leadership at this level, especially where corrupt behavior prevails, obviously matters. For the EFCC's first head, Obasanjo reluctantly appointed Nuhu Ribadu, a lawyer and assistant commissioner of police in charge of legal and prosecution matters. But neither Obasanjo nor Parliament initially provided office accommodations or, until 2004, included the EFCC in the national budget. The EFCC began as but a token response to the inherited crisis of corruption and to the country's condemnation internationally for its notable failure to address those major lapses.[22]

Ribadu, possibly without any early enthusiastic backing from a president personally accused of massive graft and electoral chicanery, proceeded to pursue corrupt practices in Nigeria with a zeal that startled and thrilled the long-suffering citizens of Africa's most populous (and most crooked) land. First, Ribadu jailed prominent fraudsters who had bilked unsuspecting overseas persons with promises of great fortunes in exchange for "advance fees"—the so-called "419" email and Internet scams. About 250 convictions were soon secured and more than $250 million was returned to those who had fallen for the Nigerian enticements.[23]

Second, Ribadu investigated and prosecuted high officials (including many friends of Obasanjo); the president's daughter, a senator; key figures in the police and the ruling party; and governors of influential states. Ribadu charged the inspector general of the Federal Police with 149 counts of money laundering, embezzlement of 10 billion naira (approximately $50 million) of police funds, and hiding more than $50 million in secret accounts. He prosecuted the governor of the oil-rich state who had properties all over the world and had been caught in Britain carrying £1 million. (The same governor had constructed a massive stadium and a large airfield in his home state.) After being found guilty, the governor forfeited $7.9 million and was impeached by his state legislature.[24]

The EFCC also reported that Obasanjo's first-term vice president had corruptly enriched himself by gaining control over petroleum revenues. By 2006, the EFCC had investigated and arrested more than 2,000 allegedly corrupt persons, prosecuted 300 cases, obtained 88 convictions, and recovered $5 billion in stolen assets.[25] But there were many more miscreants to prosecute. Corruption still flourished.

When Obasanjo left office after two terms in 2007 (and having had his ambition for a third term thwarted), Ribadu became vulnerable despite his accomplishments having been well reported and applauded in Nigeria's fearless media. Having convicted so many corrupt individuals and having recovered sizable amounts of cash and property, having successfully prosecuted key members of the political establishment, and having disrupted the comfortable purpose of winning and holding elected posts, Ribadu was soon forced out of office by incoming President Umaru Yar'Adua and a cabal orchestrated by the new federal attorney general and minister of justice. Ribadu's key associates within the EFCC were purged. The Yar'Adua administration also decreed that the EFCC, going forward, could only initiate proceedings with the approval of the minister of justice, thus effectively emasculating what was left of Nigeria's only independent anticorruption effort. The promising battle against corruption in Nigeria was effectively paused.

Ribadu, for the first time in Nigeria's history, had stripped away the veils of corrupt behavior among politicians, officials, and ordinary criminals. But, despite courageously establishing a strong EFCC, putting people in jail, and confiscating many illicit profits, Ribadu in four years could hardly have even begun to reform the prevailing operational norms of Nigerian political life, much less upend a deep-seated political culture. Greedy goats still liked to eat where they were tethered.[26] Even support from Obasanjo had been compromised and perceived that way nationally. The president had refused to declare his own assets and had permitted his brother-in-law to profit from a massive diversion of monies from local government statutory funds.

Under Yar'Adua's abbreviated presidency and during the two presidential terms of Goodluck Jonathan, the EFCC was less active than during Ribadu's era. His fate cautioned successors to be gentle. Yet, despite a lack of determined political will at the highest levels, the rump EFCC continued to take the Federal Government and some of the states to task over corruption excesses. The commission process at least brought attention to continuing examples of corrupt behavior, successfully prosecuted a selection of the many potential culprits, and acted as a sometime trumpet of conscience. But without the genuine support of President Jonathan (2010–2015) or more than one or two of his cabinet ministers, the EFCC could hardly sweep Nigeria's Augean Stables clean in the post-Ribadu era. Indeed, billions of additional petrodollars went missing from the federal treasury during the Jonathan era (see paragraph on Alison-Madueke, above).

Pending the salutary effect of potential Buhari-driven reforms, Nigeria was still awash with corruption in late 2016. For example, a Canadian-related hydroelectric generating company was accused of violating procurement regulations by billing a federal agency N$14 billion ($47 million) for nonexistent transmission facilities.[27] Everywhere one looks or probes, the evidence of ill-gotten earnings, stolen proceeds, and abuse of public office for private gain appears. In Nigeria, "you're more likely to get into trouble with the police authorities if you don't pay a bribe than if you do."[28] Despite a civil society anxious for change and a lively, investigative, public media intent on uncovering scandals, the ICPC and the EECC—no matter how well led—hardly stood a chance. Absent serious exercises of favorable political will that, pre-Buhari, were anathema to Nigeria's rulers and most of their associates, absent a leader capable of introducing a new political ethos, and absent the kinds of political culture shifts that took a decade or so in Singapore, Botswana, and Hong Kong, the EFCC, unlike Canute, could hardly hold back the relentless waters of plunder.

Nevertheless, as one notable sign that Buhari's threats to crack down hard on Nigerian corruption were beginning to have a cautionary effect, in late 2015, almost every purveyor of luxury goods from very expensive Range Rovers and Jaguars to villas in gated communities was bereft of clients. Sales had dried up. One member of a commission appointed by Buhari to investigate graft even reported that former ministers were offering to return massive millions of stolen naira.

One prominent Nigerian who failed to report dangerously fraudulent behavior was President Jonathan's national security advisor. According to the results of a forensic audit ordered by Buhari that was completed in late 2015, the advisor, a military officer, had helped to misappropriate more than $2 billion in arms and equipment purchases meant to strengthen Nigeria's armed forces. Apparently, Colonel Mohammed Sambo Dasuki, the advisor, had awarded fictitious and phantom contracts for the purchase of jet fighters, helicopters, bombs, and ammunition. But the contracts were never executed and the aircraft and associated equipment were never supplied to the Nigerian Air Force. Likewise, supplies and materiel for the Nigerian army were supposedly ordered, but nothing ever arrived, despite the increasingly difficult battles against the Boko Haram insurgency. Dasuki managed instead to transfer large sums in naira, euros, and dollars to nonexistent external companies, presumably to the benefit of Dasuki and his superiors and cronies. "It is worrisome and disappointing," said the auditor's report, "that those entrusted with the security of this great nation were busy using proxies to siphon the national treasury, while innocent lives were wasted daily." Dasuki's riposte was immediate: "There was no contract awarded or equipment bought without approval from the then President and Commander-In-Chief. I am not a thief or treasury looter as being portrayed."[29]

By late 2015 and through 2016, Buhari's many initiatives had given hope to those Nigerians who had long fought corrupt practices but too often failed. "We now have at the federal government level," said the head of an anticorruption academy, "a government that actually appreciates the work of the anticorruption agencies."[30] Nevertheless, when Buhari attended Cameron's anticorruption summit in London in 2016 and overheard the British prime minister trashing Nigeria, he expressed shock and said that he was embarrassed. But Buhari issued no rebuttals. He, and everyone else at the summit, understood that Nigeria's anticorruption crusade was still nascent, a work in progress that would take years, if not decades, to undo deeply ingrained corrupt practices. No matter how tough Buhari behaved, no matter how much he cracked down on alleged highly placed political thieves, no matter the swelling political will that his actions represented, Nigerian official life had long existed to gain spoils, not necessarily to provide good governance. In late 2016 Buhari was still seeking through the existing commissions and by fiat to transform a political culture that regarded ethical universalism as a bizarre foreign implant worth rejecting.

GHANA

Ghana has a tradition of corrupt dealings (recall Minister of Finance Krobo Edusei's golden bed?) almost as hoary as Nigeria's. Whether reprised by modern novelistic interpretations of both countries or the recorded experiences of early administrators and travelers, it is hardly surprising that West Africa's reputation for bribery, graft, procurement fraud, and general sleaze should be more enduring and more calamitous than that for eastern and southern Africa.[31] The regimes of President Kwame Nkrumah (1960–1966, and earlier as chief minister), General Joseph Ankrah (1966–1969), Brig. Akwasi Afrifra (1969–1970), Edward Akuffo-Addo (1970–1972), General Ignatius Acheampong (1972–1978), and General Fred Akuffo (1978–1979) only piled corruption on corruption. The short-lived prime ministerial reign of Oxford-educated Kofi Busia (1969–1972) did little to arrest the illicit dispersal of public funds to private accounts. The mercurial national leadership of Flight Lieutenant Jerry Rawlings (1979, 1981–2001), first as chairman of a military junta and then as president, shifted the destination of many of those illegal accumulations, but it took the decidedly differently oriented presidency of John Kufuor (2001–2009) to begin to modernize Ghana's prevailing political culture which, until his day, had accepted the misappropriation of public resources as a respectable occupation.

It was under the elected Rawlings presidency that Ghana opted to establish its own anticorruption exercise. In 1993, Rawlings decided that he wanted Ghana to have not one but two anticorruption agencies. The Ghanaian Commission for Human Rights and Administrative Justice (CHRAJ) performed a kind of ombudsman's role in the areas of employment abuses (the Office of Ombudsman was abolished), human and family rights, and prison inspections. But the CHRAJ specifically was tasked with monitoring "injustice and corruption, abuse of power and unfair treatment of persons by public officers." Meanwhile, the country's Serious Frauds Office (SFO) was established in 1998 to investigate procurement and tendering abuses, plus "serious financial" harm to the state.[32]

In many respects the two bodies possessed overlapping responsibilities and functions. The CHRAJ, for example, oversaw compliance with the Code of Conduct for Public Officers and all allegations that officials were misappropriating public monies, while the SFO, sharing some of the same terrain, investigated cases when the offenses were more costly and more injurious to the state. Ultimately, the CHRAJ limited its purview to public cases while the SFO focused on private sector forgery, money laundering, and other instances of fraud. In 2010, the SFO became the Economic and Organized Crime Office, with a license to prevent drug, gun, and people smuggling.

The CHRAJ was empowered to investigate allegations of administrative injustice and all kinds of corruption in the public service, including the police and prison services. Additionally, based on the Hong Kong model, the CHRAJ was responsible for educating the public against corruption. It could question any Ghanaian on any subject, issue subpoenas, compel attendance of suspects, and prosecute offenders. But only the Supreme Court could order documents to be produced, which limited the commission's capacity. It reported annually to Parliament and periodically to the attorney general and the auditor general.

Emile Short, the first leader of the CHRAJ and an experienced lawyer from Cape Coast who had practiced there, in the United States, and in Britain, was appointed by Rawlings with life tenure. After hiring 738 staff and establishing 110 district offices to receive complaints from the public—the typical trigger of investigations in Ghana and many other African countries with anticorruption commissions—Short wrestled with his limited government-allocated budget and, to function properly, obtained substantial additional funds from Danida, the Danish aid agency, and from its British and American counterparts.

Short, unlike Ribadu in Nigeria, did not want to engage in a "witch-hunting" exercise. He believed that the CHRAJ had to "strike a balance between holding public officials accountable and . . . not being unduly intrusive." Summoning suspected miscreants on the "slightest allegation of corruption or illegal acquisition of wealth" would have been wrong and impolitic.[33] For that reason, and because the CHRAJ had been tasked with returning citizen properties that had been seized by the pre-1993 military rulers of Ghana, it was only in 1996 that the commission investigated its first major case of alleged abuse of office and theft of public funds, by two cabinet ministers and two senior presidential advisors.

Rather than a private examination of witnesses, the CHRAJ held public hearings in a courtlike atmosphere. One adviser was acquitted, the other compelled to pay back taxes and be discharged from government service. The CHRAJ asked one minister to refund more than the profits he had made by illicit transactions. It recommended that the other minister be reprimanded for "negligent behavior." But the Rawlings regime pushed back, rejecting the

CHRAJ conclusions. Short, in turn, condemned the rejection, and the public loudly backed him and the commission, forcing Rawlings to recant and retire the three men who had been tried by the CHRAJ.[34]

The CHRAJ gained credibility and proceeded to investigate allegations of corruption that reached it from the media and the public. By 2003, despite national budget allocations that were still less than the commission required ($1.7 million in 2004), it was investigating more than 13,000 complaints of improper behavior annually, not all involving corruption. By this time, Rawlings, who had often clashed with Short, had retired and been replaced (positively for the CHRAJ) by Kufuor. By then the CHRAJ's approval rating was over 90 percent.[35]

Nevertheless, despite that high standing in the eyes of the public, the CHRAJ, like so many other African anticorruption commissions, had to pass its developed cases along to the attorney general and minister of justice. Too often, the incumbents in those posts refused to prosecute their colleagues and friends and simply ignored the findings of the CHRAJ. Even more debilitating, the democratic governments of Ghana refused from 2003 to 2011 to confirm Short's replacement permanently. Lauretta Lamptey remained an interim head of the CHRAJ all of those years, limiting her ability to investigate high-level corruption. Finally, in 2011, President John Atta Mills appointed Lamptey, a lawyer and investment banker, to be the CHRAJ's lead commissioner.

This African anticorruption commission, like so many others, raised citizens' consciousness about the evils of corruption and investigated sufficient major politicians to give legitimacy to its work and the process of hunting down alleged peculators and peddlers of abuse. But, as with so many similar operations, Ghanaian governments purposely limited the reach of the CHRAJ by refusing to provide financial autonomy and adequate resources, by chipping away at its mandate, and by failing to give it prosecutorial authority. Thus, Ghanaian corruption still persists, if somewhat less flagrantly than before. (But see how Ghanaian judges were caught accepting bribes, chapter 3.)

Nigeria and Ghana, like the other former British colonial nation-states in West Africa, followed similar trajectories in attempting to corral corruption by establishing investigatorial and prosecutorial commissions. During their democratic periods both also enjoyed a free and vibrant press, radio, and television, and many journalists who tried—in some celebrated cases relentlessly—to draw healthy attention to possible instances of abuse of public office and other forms of corruption. But, beginning with the latter Rawlings regime and Kufuor and his successors, Ghana was more and more perceived as better governed and less corrupt than Nigeria. In 2015, according to the Corruption Perceptions Index, Ghana ranked 56th, Nigeria 136th (of 168). Fifteen years earlier, ranking only ninety nations, the same index placed Ghana 52nd and Nigeria 90th. The 2015 Index of African Governance placed Ghana 7th and Nigeria 39th out of fifty-four nations.

Just for Show: Halfhearted Innovators

Many of the remaining thirty-six sub-Saharan African anticorruption commissions were established to satisfy foreign assistance organizations and with funds supplied from abroad. Several employed numerous personnel and established branch offices to receive complaints and allegations from the public. Some were as positively led as the Nigerian and Ghanaian examples. But nearly all were restricted in their anticorruption accomplishments by political interference, were held on short leashes by executives, had critical cases turned back by prosecutors and attorneys general, were purposely starved (in at least several cases) of financial resources and talent, and were only in rare instances able to fulfill the mandates of their respective missions. Political will was lacking in nearly every case. Political considerations almost always prevailed over the pursuit of integrity.

TANZANIA, KENYA, ETHIOPIA, MADAGASCAR

Ethiopia, Kenya, and Tanzania represent three important contiguous populous-state examples of the structural inability of many African countries to replicate, or even come very close to emulating, the Hong Kong, Singapore, and Botswanan examples. Madagascar is a fourth, Francophone, case that resembles the first three. Devoid of demonstrated political will and a number of other desirable institutional attributes that contribute to effective curbs on corruption, all four countries were punctilious in writing strong laws against corruption and in following Hong Kong's lead to establish supposedly robust anticorruption commissions. But in each of those cases, the commission instrument failed dramatically to disturb prevailing political cultures, with their relative receptivity to the continued corrupt behavior practiced by politicians, public servants, police officers, and, indeed, almost everyone who interacted with citizens.

Tanzania

Tanzania's continued high levels of corruption (witness the 2014–2015 scandals discussed in chapter 3) testify prominently to the difficulty most weakly governed countries have in coping successfully with corrupt behavior. Unless the prevailing political culture is altered, no amount of legal or procedural reform can change incentive structures for the better. Tanzanian regimes tried, one decade after another, more in response to donors than to electorates, to promulgate better laws and develop agencies that would pursue corrupt persons. But, in the end, the results have been more cosmetic than salutary.

In 1996, the Tanzanian Presidential Commission on Corruption, led by Justice Joseph Sinde Warioba, found that corruption at all levels was widespread, particularly harming the delivery of police enforcement services, effective judicial independence, honest revenue collection efforts, and the allocation of agricultural and commercial lands. His report detailed a major absence of administrative transparency and accountability, the appointment of all manner of public servants made without proper procedures, massive tax evasions connived at by officials, illicit trading of commodities and fuels, false contracts, and fraudulent land deals. Warioba particularly noted the total lack of political will to demand different behaviors or to bring about serious reforms.

A National Anticorruption Strategy and Action Plan of 1999 set forth a number of priorities, including better legal frameworks, protection of whistleblowers and witnesses, and public education (based on the Hong Kong model). Yet that plan failed to clarify the responsibilities and authority of the existing Prevention of Corruption Bureau (created in 1991) and of the cabinet minister who had been put in charge of change—of manufacturing "good governance."

Nevertheless, by 2003, the Tanzanian Bureau boasted a large staff of 714 employees, only 100 of whom were headquartered in Dar es Salaam, the commercial capital, while the others were in twenty-one regional offices. About 200 of the staff were investigators, but of the approximately 1,200 individual dockets opened between 2003 and 2004, only about 10 percent made it to court. Thirteen individuals were convicted, 25 acquitted, and 1,027 of the cases were closed without prosecution.[36]

Following this demonstrated inability to make much of a dent in the fabric of national and local corruption, Tanzania issued a new National Framework on Good Governance and established a Parastatal Sector Reform Programme, a Judiciary Reform Programme, a Civil Service Reform Programme, and a Human Rights Commission. President Benjamin Mkapa (1995–2005), reelected in 2000, pledged once and for all to end corrupt practices in his country. The 1971 act was also strengthened in 2002.

But little changed. Indeed, largely because of a continued lack of demonstrated political will, corrupt behavior continued as it had for decades. None of these fine anticorruption arrangements worked in Tanzania (or in other similarly situated countries) to control corruption or its allied abuses. According to one careful report, all of Tanzania's ostensible anticorruption programs and good governance initiatives focused on the collection of information—without putting it to use. Upper-level Tanzanians maintained "a bureaucratic camouflage which ensured that access to [the] information [was] circumscribed and any application of the information collected [was] rendered useless." Within all of the agencies charged with reporting or halting corruption, the report also detected low levels of morale and high levels of inertia.[37] As one result, Tanzania failed in 2004 to satisfy the Millennium Challenge Corporation's criteria for "good governance," a requirement for official U.S. grants from that source. In other words, Tanzania was unable at that time to "govern justly . . . and encourage economic freedom." The country was deemed thoroughly corrupt, a central failure of governance.[38]

In yet another response, Tanzania's president and Parliament developed instruments that were intended to be stronger and more effective than all previous efforts. In 2007, Parliament passed the Prevention and Combating of Corruption Act that created yet a new and renamed Prevention and Combat of Corruption Bureau. The bureau's mandate this time was to "raise awareness and guide government on anticorruption issues as well as arrest, instigate, initiate proceedings and prosecute cases of corruption," the last admittedly with permission of the director of public prosecutions.[39] Tanzania also promulgated a Public Leadership Code of Ethics that superseded a similar but weaker code from the 1970s and created an Ethics Inspectorate and a Commission on Ethics. Soon, too, Tanzania had another newly appointed minister of good governance.

These were ostensibly strong public reform moves against corruption and the appearance of corruption. But the 2007 Prevention of Corruption Bureau has manifestly been unable to curb corruption in the country any more than could its predecessors. It has lacked a crucial independence from the Tanzanian executive, without which no anticorruption agency can be effective when all around it politicians and officials are bent on stealing and misusing their positions for personal or family gain. Moreover, the bureau still has no guaranteed budget of its own—a critical consideration—and its leaders and other personnel are still appointed from within the nation's existing dominant political party system. As individuals, their professional and pecuniary advancement thus has depended on their political betters (and their political competitors)—a fatal flaw common to many African anticorruption efforts.

Those who have closely examined the Tanzanian case report that political interference is rife. The director general of the bureau and his deputy are appointed by the country's president, and are political operatives and members of the ruling Chama Cha Mapinduzi (CCM) party. Moreover, the bureau is reliant on Parliament for its funding, has too few resources and too few personnel to investigate cases easily, and lacks subpoena authority. Civil society in Tanzania and outside observers accuse the bureau of avoiding high-profile potential cases of corruption and of focusing its efforts only on petty corruption and "small fry" offenders.[40] Moreover, the director of public prosecutions has too often refused to take forward even those few cases presented to his office by the bureau.

All of these weaknesses may have been lessened as a result of the election in late 2015 of the ruling CCM Party's technocratic new president, John Magufuli. He scrapped expensive Independence Day celebrations to save millions of schillings (it was "shameful," he said, to spend money on lavish state events when Tanzanians were dying of cholera), reduced presidential convoys, prohibited expensive air transport by almost all senior politicians and officials, banned pay perquisites (such as extra sitting emoluments) for legislators and hotel arrangements for civil servants, cut down severely on overseas travel, and went on a series of unannounced walkabouts in Dar es Salaam to hospitals and other governmental establishments. When he found managers away from their jobs, he sacked them on the spot and set in motion procedures (at least in governmental establishments and parastatal bodies) that might curb bribe asking and bribe taking. Again, as in Nigeria (above) and Kenya (below), Magufuli's clean broom sweep is a hopeful work in progress. Positive leadership exemplifying determined political will is always critical and salutary.[41] (See also chapter 8.)

Kenya

Neighboring Kenya, where a series of large-scale corruption scandals has embroiled the nation since the 1980s, enacted the Anti-corruption and Economic Crimes Act in 2003 and the Public Officers Ethics Act of 2003 after the regime of President Mwai Kibaki had replaced the notoriously corrupt autocratic rule of President Daniel arap Moi (1978–2002). Donors had earlier withheld aid disbursements until Moi in 1997 created the short-lived, badly led, and wildly compromised Kenyan Anti-Corruption Authority. The High Court, under Moi's control, finally declared that authority unconstitutional in 2000.

The 2003 act established the Kenyan Anti-Corruption Commission (KACC) to examine any matter that raised suspicions of corrupt practice. It was also able to act preemptively if it suspected that a corrupt act was about to occur. Further, it was empowered to discover the corrupt acts of public bodies by scrutinizing their practices and procedures and recommending improvements. It could act on its own initiative, rather than waiting for complaints or instructions from cabinet officials. Like Hong Kong's ICAC, it too was charged with educating the public against corruption and enlisting public support.

An Anti-Corruption Advisory Board of civilians nominated and Parliament approved the director of the agency. But no tenure was specified. Moreover, the Ministry of Finance ratified and disbursed the KACC's budget, limiting its freedom. Even though the controlling act stipulated the full independence of the KACC, it also indicated that Parliament was ultimately in charge. Since

Parliament was controlled by the ruling party, the director of the commission could not reasonably escape his or her ties to the party and its leaders in the legislature and the executive. The KACC, in other words, was fatally compromised from the start, but less so because of its organizational and institutional framework than because of Kenya's abiding political realities.

Corruption in Kenya since independence from Britain has included one wildly irruptive scandal after another. Few parliamentarians, few police commanders, and no ministers or the president had any desire or incentive to upset the prevailing national understanding that public services and public operations could be procured only by cash. Police officers and magistrates told investigators that most people, especially matatu drivers, offered bribes even before policemen stuck out their hands or otherwise made it clear that passing road blocks or receiving other "services" required a gift. Furthermore, the KACC reported that 80 percent of new police recruits had paid bribes to get their jobs. Corruption was so stubbornly ingrained in Kenya's political culture that young men begin raising money very early in their villages, "usually around $2000," to "bribe recruitment officials" to get a police job.[42] The prevailing ethos, said John Githongo, was looting. "It is looting and grand corruption."[43] As in Suharto's Indonesia, "there was a price for everything and everyone knew the price."[44]

Githongo, the head of Transparency International's Nairobi office, was known as a rare Kenyan of integrity. President Kibaki, newly elected in 2002 after the long, plundering years of President Moi and his cronies, appointed Githongo permanent secretary for ethics and governance in the office of the president. In theory, he was to be the president's right-hand man, capable of alerting Kibaki to incipient corrupt behavior and thus supporting Kibaki's efforts to stanch such practices. His effort was intended to be more direct and more conclusive than the ongoing work of the KACC. Reform was in the air. But cabinet ministers and other associates of Kibaki, having largely been excluded from good deals during the long Moi era, could not wait to "eat." One of their more ingenious and nefarious schemes was to create a nonexistent company, Anglo-Leasing, to receive $1 billion-plus contracts to print new high-technology passports, to construct ships for the navy, and to create special forensic laboratories. The Anglo-Leasing scheme involved overpriced and fake contracts and a total siphoning of state revenues equivalent to about 16 percent of the national budget. Githongo warned the president, who seemed to know about the Anglo-Leasing charade. Githongo told Kibaki about a number of other clever ways in which the public purse was being abused for private gain. But the president refused to do anything. Githongo was told to "go easy" on investigations.[45] Githongo soon fled to Oxford and wrote a damning report, naming names.

After the Githongo imbroglio, after Anglo-Leasing, and following more and more revelations of corruption, the postelection violence of 2007 and 2008, and the installation of a new government, Kenyans wrote and ratified a brand-new constitution, in 2010. Following provisions in that document, Kenya also created yet another new institution to combat corruption. The Ethics and Anti-Corruption Commission (EACC), established in 2011 to replace its predecessors, develops and promotes standards and best practices in integrity and anticorruption, articulates codes of ethics, oversees the national ethics code for public officers, receives complaints of ethical breaches, investigates and recommends prosecutions of violators of the code of ethics, conducts investigations on its own initiative or, after receiving complaints, educates against corruption, attempts to halt corrupt practices, and mediates and negotiates to prevent corruption.

The EACC credits itself with substantial asset recovery from corrupt officials, with helping to create the strong legal framework that guides the commission, with implementing the National Anti-Corruption Plan of 2006, and with drafting a strong Leadership and Integrity Act in 2012, albeit an act that was subsequently eviscerated by Parliament. The EACC also facilitated the prosecution of seven individuals by the director of public prosecutions. One salient case involved the jailing of a managing director of the Kenya Tourist Board for theft and fraud. The EACC developed the incriminating dossier and delivered it to the public prosecutor, but it and many other indictments by the EACC were ignored by prosecutors, sometimes on the orders of the executive. Ogalo and Marsden report that the EACC had a zero success rate for prosecuting police officers for taking bribes. Indeed, in 2013, a national Global Corruption Barometer survey showed that 53 percent of all Kenyans had paid bribes to policemen and that 30 percent had bribed judges. Service providers, according to another survey, demanded bribes 65 percent of the time; 15 percent asked for cash a second time, after the first request was refused; 10 percent a third time; 4 percent a fourth time, and on and on.[46] Some service providers were at least persistent in that one area.

That same survey in 2013 indicated that none of the much-vaunted reform efforts of the EACC and other empowered interventions (the Public Officer Ethics Act, the Public Procurement and Disposal Act, the Proceeds of Crime and Anti–Money Laundering Act, the Public Audit Act, the Leadership and Integrity Act, and the Public Finance Management Act) had dented the Kenyan climate of corruption. A full 61 percent of all Kenyans still felt that corruption was a "serious problem" in their country. Forty-six percent felt that the efforts of the government at battling corruption were "ineffective." The EACC's own 2012 survey showed that 70 percent of Kenyans totally agreed that Kenyan political leaders were involved in corruption, and 29 percent believed that the Kenyan government had "no sincere desire and will to fight corruption."[47]

Kenya even established the Public Complaints Standing Committee in 2007 to receive and document all manner of complaints against public officers in ministries, statutory bodies, and other institutions of the state. This forwarding-looking instrument was directed to investigate allegations of corruption, abuses of public positions, unethical conduct, lapses of integrity, maladministration, injustice, inattention, discourtesy, and "ineptitude."[48] The committee was supposed to become Kenya's Office of Ombudsman and be modeled, in its accomplishments, on South Africa's Office of Public Protector. In 2011, it was restyled the Committee on Administrative Justice; it has produced few visible results.

Kenya's biggest problem, however, is that the EACC was and is viewed by the general public as toothless. Despite its staff of 4,540 and a $22 million annual budget, like nearly all other African commissions, it is subject to political interference and has been unable for those and other reasons to prevent Kenyan society's moral decay.[49] It also operates within an atmosphere where the ruling political party's two top leaders were indicted by the International Criminal Court (with both trials discontinued after massive witness tampering). Commissions only succeed, in other words, when the dominant political leadership wants them to succeed and when a commission (as in Hong Kong) manages decisively to reconfigure a society's political culture—its core operating value system.

Such reconfiguring had not happened in Kenya by the end of 2016, but pressure by the IMF and a realization by President Uhuru Kenyatta that Kenya's ability to attract foreign capital was at risk led to the prosecution in 2015 of two former finance ministers, one of whom was a sitting Kenyan senator, and senior politicians responsible for the long-ago Anglo-Leasing fraud. The receipt of new information from Britain's Serious Fraud Office and the Swiss government probably helped to reactivate their cases.

At the end of 2015, the EACC indicated that its failure to stamp out corruption was the fault of Kenya's judges. With about 300 major cases pending, the judges needed to work harder to deliver convictions. "If we get one single conviction, it will definitely transform the public perception and it will transform the activities and attitudes of public servants," said Halakhe Waqo, the head of the EACC. But Githongo, along with many other Kenyans, believes that the problem is still political, with graft and greed remaining the dominant pursuits of the country's leadership class. "What we don't have here is that sense of shame," he said. "People remain in office even though they have manifestly lost public confidence."[50]

Echoing Waqo, and under pressure from Kenyan civil society and Kenyans generally (marathon athletes were besieging the headquarters of Athletics

Kenya, claiming that the heads of the federation had stolen their prize monies, while Kenyan generals were accused of smuggling sugar profitably through Somalia into Kenya), President Kenyatta near the end of 2015 made a lengthy speech promising complete reforms and the type of Buhari-like actions that Githongo had called for years earlier. Corruption, he said, was a paramount security threat. He asked religious leaders to declare corruption a "sin against God and humanity."

He himself was "determined to bring back the spirit of Selfless Service. Senior officials must exhibit the highest standard of ethical behaviour and lead by example as is required of them under Chapter 6 of the Constitution. I direct the Inspector General to enforce this requirement without fear or favour." Further, he promised a coordinated effort to "reverse perverse incentives that lead to corruption, to close the loop-holes that dishonest officials use to steal and to tighten our legislation work, to improve our investigations and prosecutions." The chief justice agreed to "fast track" cases of corruption.[51]

Given Kenya's long history of corrupt dealings, President Kenyatta may have been whistling piously in the dark. Alternatively, he may seriously still attempt to turn Kenya around by coaxing or coercing the machinery of government to be less corrupt. But, by late 2016, observers could not point to any perceptible reductions in Kenyan corruption.

Ethiopia

The late Prime Minister Meles Zenawi (1995–2012) ruled Ethiopia as an astute authoritarian modernizer. He brooked little interference from opponents or associates, and he was keenly aware of the ways in which his poor country could be improved. The Revised Federal Ethics and Anti-Corruption Proclamation of 2005, which re-established the Federal Ethics and Anti-Corruption Commission (FEACC) begun in 2001, was issued with his approval and on his instigation. The FEACC was supposed to expose, investigate, and prosecute corrupt acts and improprieties. In particular, this new initiative was focused on serious cases of grand corruption—corruption involving huge sums committed by high officials in government and parastatal corporations, corrupt acts by public officials, corrupt offenses which caused "grave danger to the national sovereignty, economy, security or social life"—i.e., anything and everything, even behavior that occurred between private persons and corporations. Subsequently, seven of the nine states in Ethiopia also established their own Ethics and Anti-Corruption Commissions (EAC).[52]

Meles purposely gave the FEACC strong powers. Indeed, on paper, the FEACC was among the best-endowed post–Hong Kong commission instruments on the African continent. It had a far and purposeful reach. Ostensibly, it had its own funding, albeit as allocated by the government. Furthermore, unlike some other African anticorruption efforts, the FEACC could prosecute directly, without having to refer cases to the attorney general or to some other government official. On "reasonable suspicion" of chicanery, it was empowered to examine bank accounts and obtain court orders to freeze assets. If an offender were convicted, it could order the sequestration of such assets. (The proclamation gave the FEACC the right to demand the declaration of all holdings by public officers.) The 2005 law further approved rewards for persons who reported and worked against corrupt practices and for whistleblowers. On the Hong Kong model, the FEACC also could recommend changes to the procedures of ministries and other governmental bodies and, unusually, preside over the direct implementation of such recommendations.

In addition to such ostensible perquisites and the ability to bring to bear the full zeal of a presumably ambitious and active commission against the taint of corrupt behavior, the prime minister nominated the head and deputy head of the FEACC, whose six-year appointments (theoretically long and stable terms) were approved by the legislature. The original proclamation also made it clear that no one—except Meles—was permitted to interfere with the commission, with how it investigated or prosecuted cases.[53] The commissioner and deputy commissioner were Meles' appointees. Possibly in order to keep the FEACC weak and obedient, Meles and Parliament also limited the FEACC's funding. In 2011, it was receiving only $1 million a year for its operations, an amount that in subsequent years did not keep up with the pace of local inflation.[54]

Despite sparse resources, the FEACC attempted to follow a Hong Kong–like course. It pursued many of the usual commission methods. It established a toll-free anticorruption hotline and distributed thousands of fliers, posters, and brochures against corruption. In 2010, the FEACC persuaded Parliament to pass a Disclosure and Registration of Assets Proclamation that compelled politicians and officials to declare their assets to the FEACC. But by 2011, with 500 officials registered and limited capacity to examine their declarations, one estimate suggested that the agency would require twenty-two years to ascertain whether every enrollee was behaving with integrity in her or his public capacity.[55]

In the manner of Hong Kong's ICAC, also, the FEACC encompassed both an Ethics and Education Directorate and a Prevention Directorate. The latter examined public offices and public enterprises to expose potentially corrupt procedures and practices and to recommend and then to implement necessary improvements. Unlike the ICAC, however, the FEACC was able to move quickly when it learned about, say, a large government contract that seemed questionable. The staff of the Prevention Directorate could intervene to forestall corrupt acts.

The Ethics and Education Directorate attempted to rouse the people of Ethiopia against corrupt practices—to alter the prevailing social and political climate. Toward that end, it provided face to face ethics training for government employees and private businessmen, offered periodic workshops, and produced materials excoriating corruption. It also broadcast to Ethiopia's less literate peoples and put its offerings on local television, where an urban audience could be informed.

How much good all of this earnest activity did is unclear. Meles ran Ethiopia. The pursuit of malefactors was permitted so long as they were his enemies or were supposedly loyal followers who—as in the case of the head of the Ethiopian Telecommunications Corporation and his staff—stepped out of line and attempted to cut good deals only for themselves. (They apparently benefited from improper and underhand arrangements with a Swedish provider.) Indeed, the FEACC may have been predominantly an ornamental exercise developed by Meles to help him to demonstrate internally and externally that Ethiopia was a modernist country with a modern ruler. As in many African polities, overseas donors wanted Ethiopia to possess the instruments necessary to root out corrupt practices, and so the FEACC came to be. But without political will and the firm support of the key power in the country, it remained a paper tiger.

Indeed, all of these commission efforts apparently did little to stem corruption under Meles and (post-2012) his successor. The UN Economic Commission for Africa, based in Addis Ababa, classified the Ethiopian executive as being "largely or completely corrupt." Global Integrity in 2006 reported that corruption was "a norm of social, economic and political intercourse. Ten percent was the 'official' kick-back expected on all projects." In 2008, Transparency Ethiopia's Corruption Diagnostic Baseline Survey discovered that of twenty-nine Ethiopian institutions rated by citizens for inspiring public confidence and trust, the FEACC only ranked 21st of 29. It labored under serious resource constraints. The courts, obedient to the executive, were also regarded as weak.[56] In 2015, Ethiopia's CPI rating was 103rd (of 168), higher than the prior year. "Corrupt practices among senior and lower-level government officials remain[ed] very high," said the CPI in 2014.[57] Furthermore, when Meles died suddenly in 2012, he was said to have been worth at least $3 billion, a not inconsiderable sum in deeply impoverished Ethiopia.[58]

Madagascar

Madagascar is another telling African case because it is one of the few Francophone African polities to have taken direct lessons from Hong Kong and to have attempted to emulate the success of the ICAC. Madagascar's anticorruption efforts were also initiated by a charismatic, strong-willed, dominant leader dedicated (or so he said) to the eradication of corruption. Yet even with the Hong Kong inspiration and support from the top of the domestic political tree, Madagascar's success was limited. It thus becomes but another significant failure among the many sub-Saharan African attempts to learn how to lessen corruption's impact.

Before crusading and charismatic Marc Ravalomanana, a wealthy businessman, succeeded several authoritarian presidents of Madagascar in 2001, corrupt practices permeated every corner of the world's fourth largest island. Military men had ruled Madagascar for many years since independence in 1960; they and their French postcolonial allies had made little pretense of curbing corruption. In 2002, Transparency International's Corruption Perceptions Index rated Madagascar 98th of the 102 countries covered that year, just above Nigeria and Bangladesh.[59]

Ravalomanana was determined, rhetorically, to stamp out corruption. His party in Parliament passed an anticorruption law in 2004 and simultaneously created the Independent Anti-Corruption Bureau (BIANCO). One of the heads of the ICAC in Hong Kong cited BIANCO as a successful spin-off of the Hong Kong model.[60] But, even though the 2004 act criminalized active and passive bribery, listed prosecutable abuses of official power, decried the embezzlement of public funds, prohibited trading on influence, and forbade favoritism, BIANCO was unable to create an anticorruption climate similar to that of Hong Kong. It was nominally independent, with operational autonomy, sufficient financial resources, and staff tenure outside the national civil service. As in Hong Kong, BIANCO was also charged with educating Malagasy speakers about corruption and reforming the nation's prevailing ethos.

According to studies arranged by Transparency International and the Bertelsmann Foundation, BIANCO managed to slow the spread of small-scale corruption. But its approach to grand (venal) corruption was hampered by its inability (according to the law) to initiate its own investigations or to prosecute offenders directly. It was effectively prohibited from questioning cabinet ministers. Despite Ravalomanana's early backing, BIANCO operated without a reinforced national political will, and without the ability or the inspiration to begin altering Madagascar's prevailing political culture of corruption.[61]

The military coup of 2009 ended Ravalomanana's rule and, effectively, BIANCO. Given the chaos that followed the coup and the battles between Ravalomanana and Andry Rajoelina until 2014, the nation had many other priorities. In 2014, the CPI rated Madagascar 133rd of 174, just below Pakistan and Togo and just above Nicaragua, Iran, and Nigeria. In 2015, Madagascar rose ten places, to 123rd place.[62] Hery Rajaonarimampianina, Madagascar's new president, named the fight against corruption a key priority, possibly through the resuscitation of BIANCO.

But a late 2014 report agreed that Madagascar was perceived by investors as "one of the most corrupt countries in the world." "Corruption is so widespread," it continued, "that the shortfall it brings about for the state coffers is enormous." Wealth "cannot be created" because of the "prevalence of corruption." This report also quotes the general manager of BIANCO as saying that his bureau lacked "grit" in the performance of its mission. There existed, he and the report concluded, a profound lack of political will to counter corruption. Prime Minister Roger Kolo said that corruption had taken root in Malagasy society. As a prime example, cited by Kolo, gold mined in Madagascar appeared on the world market despite the absence of officially recorded gold exports from his country.[63]

Political Interference from on High

Zambia and Malawi are two side-by-side countries with similar colonial historical and missionary experiences and comparable population sizes. They were both components of the ill-conceived Federation of Rhodesia and Nyasaland, and both gained independence in 1964. One had copper and grew wealthy; the other contained few mineral resources, grows tobacco for China and maize for itself, and remains poor. One had a humanistic, well-intentioned head of a single-party state for its first twenty-seven years, the other an American-trained full-bore autocrat for its initial twenty-nine postcolonial years.

A nation-state of 15 million people, much larger than any of the other "much improved" cases (chapter 6) except for Rwanda, Zambia contains 70 different language groups, of which four are large and two, the Cibemba and Cinyanja speakers, vie for primacy. Zambia's annual GDP per capita is $1,810; its export earnings in 2017 depended entirely on the global price of copper, 86 percent of its exports. Zambia, because of mining, is sub-Saharan Africa's most urbanized country, with about 60 percent of the population living in cities and towns.

Zambia was a largely corruption-free country before independence in 1964. Under President Kenneth D. Kaunda (1964–1991), however, corruption grew apace but external measurement indexes had not yet been created. Responding to the first rumblings of corrupt behavior, Zambia promulgated the Corrupt Practices Act in 1980 and established the Anti-Corruption Commission (AAC) in 1982. From then on it had a well-run, if sometimes frustrated, Anti-Corruption Commission. Moreover, its operation was, unusually and intriguingly, run by a nonindigenous individual who organized the commission and later moved to Malawi to assist that country's new government in organizing its own anticorruption endeavor. Subsequently, Paul Russell, a Briton who had arrived in Northern Rhodesia in 1962 as a police cadet, advised Lesotho and Sierra Leone when they, too, decided to attack corrupt practices by creating commissions.

Russell's many successes as an organizer of and advisor to African anticorruption endeavors, as well as his failures, varied not according to how rich or poor, copper-based or tobacco-based each country was, but directly as to the clear preferences of the political leaders to whom he reported and their individual determinations either to curb corrupt practices or to let them flourish. The outcomes of the Zambian and Malawian struggles against corruption once again emphasize the overriding importance of political will and, in turn, how difficult altering national norms of behavior can be in the absence of sustainable top-down backing for the investigators who attempt to operate in the trenches, opposing and corralling corrupt behavior.

Zambia's President Kaunda was serious about turning back corruption when he asked Russell, a Zambian police superintendent whom he knew from state house guard duties and from his work with the Police Mobile Unit, to take charge of domestic anticorruption efforts. In 1965, after the unilateral declaration of independence in neighboring Rhodesia (after 1980, Zimbabwe), Kaunda had declared a national state of emergency. It remained in place throughout his entire remaining single-party government—until 1991. Under state-of-emergency regulations it was relatively straightforward for cases of corruption to be declared economic crimes against the state. Many involved illegal currency movements and emerald smuggling. Russell, as a member of the police Special Investigation Team on Economy and Trade from 1974 to 1982, was closely involved in apprehending and collecting fines from those culprits, some of whom, ironically, became cabinet ministers in post-Kaunda administrations.

Russell visited Hong Kong and other places and then modeled the Zambian AAC on the ICAC. "It was my deliberate policy," Russell writes, "to expose as much corruption as possible. I also began seriously to get the people of Zambia educated and better informed on corruption." As a direct result, citizens were much more likely than before to report instances of corrupt behavior. "This had a knock-on effect."[64] The ACC was "seen as a place where if you made a report someone would help . . . one way or the other." The ACC came to be trusted.

The AAC investigated the country's state-owned mining corporation, the state-owned iron and steel manufacturer, the state-owned supermarket chain's general manager, the managing director of the Zambia National Building Society, the head of the National Insurance Company, the shady activities of a governor of the Bank of Zambia, the chief immigration officer, the governor of the Lusaka Urban District, and many illicit smugglers of ivory and emeralds—some of whom were Nigerian and Ghanaian.

The ACC and Russell tried a minister of mines (also vice president of the Prescribed Minerals and Materials Commission) in the Supreme Court, accusing him of corruptly soliciting gratification (an expensive Mercedes Benz sedan) from a German company in exchange for a mining concession. His acquittal may have resulted from the length of the mandatory minimum sentences specified for convictions under the Corrupt Practices Act, because of the minister's elevated age, or because of the faulty procedural construction of the state's case.[65]

A managing director of the state-owned Zambia Airways was sacked after Russell stormed into its London headquarters on Kaunda's orders and, flourishing a large pair of scissors, cut the Zambian-issued official credit cards of all of its employees.[66]

Several cabinet ministers were also relieved of their positions, usually after Russell and his team had done due diligence and provided Kaunda with the necessary evidence. Russell had Kaunda's strong support, even when Russell pursued ministerial malefactors (in one case even setting up a road block to ensnare a cabinet minister who had mistakenly thought that he was immune from the law). Another was removed from office by Kaunda for behaving arrogantly and crossing Russell.

The president's backing also helped Russell's attempt to curtail animal poaching in the early 1990s, when killing rhinoceroses for their keratin-composed "horns" and elephants for their ivory tusks first became big business internationally. In 1992, more than 1,500 Zambians were arrested for poaching or trafficking animal products. Nearly 1,200 weapons of all kinds were confiscated.

Between 1984 and 1990, the AAC investigated 1,011 cases. Of that number, 460 resulted in prosecutions, with 128 convictions and 47 acquittals, a reasonable record for an African anticorruption commission in those early times.[67] According to Russell, all received complaints were processed daily by a committee within the AAC and either approved for investigation, sent to the prevention and educational divisions within the AAC for noncriminal but instructive use, referred directly to the police, or rejected. After an investigation was completed, the dossier and other materials were given to the director of public prosecutions, who would agree to prosecute, or not. If the DPP refused to prosecute, because doing so was "against the public interest," or on any other grounds, that would end the case.

Of the above 385 prosecutions that resulted in neither convictions nor acquittals, apparently the court system in Zambia in the 1980s was sufficiently shambolic that defendants either died before verdicts were issued or the courts' record systems lost the cases. There was always a major logjam, and Russell said that "the Courts were manifestly incompetent and inefficient and each year the numbers rolling over mounted up." The "clear-up" rate in the courts "was horrible."[68] Battling corruption was accordingly hampered in these pioneering years, and since, by inefficiency and underfunding, as well as by political hesitancy.

The Zambian Anti-Corruption Commission's actions under Russell's leadership—but critically because of Kaunda's determination and political leadership—nevertheless certainly helped to moderate the spread of corruption within the country and within the ruling United National Independence Party (UNIP). Admittedly, the ACC may not have uncovered or been allowed to investigate very large-scale, if less obvious, corrupt dealings—for example, the maneuvering that helped the shady but powerful Lonrho Corporation accumulate assets and curry economic favor from Kaunda.

Russell's efficacy became greatly marginalized when UNIP's single-party rule and Kaunda's leadership gave way to donor-motivated multi-party elections and democracy. As a result, Frederick Chiluba was elected president in 1991 and, despite this new president's evangelical background, Russell soon realized that Chiluba wanted desperately to "chop." He believed that it was his own time to "eat"—to gain riches and have a "free-for-all."

Chiluba looted state resources in several ways. One was to pilfer a secret Zambian official bank account held in London by the Zambian National Commercial Bank. That account was purportedly employed for national security purposes and was controlled by the director general of the Zambian Security Intelligence Services. A woman in the Ministry of Finance was the only person authorized to make transfers to the Intelligence Services through the London account, and she was paid very well by Zambian standards for doing what she was told, and keeping quiet about it. She shifted money into the London account and Chiluba managed to use most of it to procure fancy suits and other clothing in Switzerland and to purchase property in Belgium and South Africa. The director general kept quiet as well, and the Zambian auditor general "failed to exercise his duties." Furthermore, the auditor general was unwilling to challenge the director general and Chiluba.[69]

Chiluba fired the top police, special branch, and military chiefs inherited from Kaunda and gradually marginalized the AAC's anticorruption activities. Drug trafficking and facilitated poaching also accelerated during Chiluba's time. The Species Protection Department within the ACC, for example, continued to operate with salutary effect until Chiluba became implicated by the ACC in "some highly dubious dealings."[70]

ACC investigations and attempted prosecutions (which after 1991 had to clear the desk of the newly appointed director of public prosecutions) were compromised by political expediency. Cases of the kind that formerly had moved smoothly from the ACC to the courts were blocked, usually on presidential orders. With the withdrawal of executive and therefore political backing, the ACC became more and more powerless. Corruption flourished to a degree that Zambia had never before experienced.

Chiluba directly obstructed his country's AAC and reorganized it under new laws in 1996. According to some estimates, during Chiluba's presidency, corruption levels rose 40 percent, along with attacks on the press and civil society. From 1997 to 2001, of about 4,800 suspected infractions by individuals, only 1,500 were investigated. Convictions over that period numbered ninety-one.[71]

One infamous example of presidential interference occurred in Zambia when Russell was still in office. The ACC decided after lengthy investigations that the minister of local government was very much "on the take." When a detailed indictment was presented to the DPP, however, a period of lengthy delay ensued. Eventually, the commission was informed that, "on presidential orders," no prosecution would occur and that the investigation was quashed. Ironically, the minister of local government at the time was Michael Sata, a long-time political operative (originally a UNIP supporter) who later became president of Zambia.[72]

Levy Mwanawasa (2002–2008), successor to Chiluba, was genuinely determined to eliminate corrupt behavior. He established a special task force to uncover all of his predecessor's misdeeds and to work alongside the inherited AAC. The task force combined donor support with strong (but shifting) political will. Nevertheless, in its first five years it secured only three convictions and recovered a mere $36 million in assets, about 10 percent of the total amount illegally transferred out of Zambia during the Chiluba years. The task force's efforts to pursue presumed offenders and repatriate their ill-gotten gains was hampered by a lack of transparency and by the task force's own temporary institutional nature, and also by Mwanawasa's untimely death in 2008.

Far more action against Chiluba and those who stole during his presidency took place elsewhere. In a London court, in civil proceedings brought by Zambia's attorney general, Chiluba was convicted of stealing the equivalent of $58 million; his wife was subsequently jailed in Zambia for more than three years for taking at least than $300,000 worth of goods from State House.[73] But, in Zambia, after Chiluba's return home and after Rupiah Banda had succeeded to the presidency, a principal resident magistrate in Lusaka decreed that the prosecution had failed to prove its case, and, in 2009, acquitted Chiluba of theft; Chiluba claimed that the monies in question were "political donations."[74] When Chiluba died in 2011, he was given a state funeral.

Under Mwanawasa the ACC regrouped, and with significant donor backing and the firm support of the president, it began again to chase corrupt politicians and bureaucrats. From 2004 to 2008, the AAC received more than 4,000 corruption-related complaints. About 2,000 were investigated and 53 convictions obtained despite the AAC being underfunded and understaffed (it had a mere 217 employees in 2007). The percentage of local corporations ranking corruption as a major obstacle to success dropped from 46 percent in 2002 to 12 percent in 2007. The percentage of businessmen who expected to have to make informal payments to public officials to obtain decisions or permits dropped from 44 to 14 in the same years, and those who expected to be compelled to give "gifts" to gain government contracts fell from 36 percent to 27 percent over that period. To the extent that these declines in anticipated corruption and the efforts of the revived ACC signaled success, "the fight against grand corruption ultimately hinge[d] on the President's will." Mwanawasa was sincere in his attempt to overcome Chiluba's malign influence and to eliminate any stains on his own legacy.[75]

Corruption nevertheless continued. Under President Rupiah Banda (2008–2011), the ACC discovered that senior officials were retaining per diem payments for training workshops that never took place or never existed. Thirty-two civil servants were implicated and about $6 million lost to embezzlement.[76] A long-time minister of the Southern Province later admitted to a Zambian scholar, "There is nobody who is not using my philosophy of politics of benefits. There is nobody who goes into Parliament naked; we go into Parliament because of allowances. There is no more patriotism. Patriotism was only there when we were fighting colonialists. . . . I know people will say Munkombwe has gone into government because he wants to eat but who does not want to eat?"[77] (Sir Robert Walpole, the influential British statesman, said as much, and in similar words, to the British House of Commons in 1730: "Was [it] a crime to get great estates by great office?" What else could "anyone expect?"[78])

The ACC could not keep up with the different kinds of corrupt behavior that persisted in Zambia in the post-Mwanawasa years. Donors were particularly leery of monies allocated to the national health system; significant portions simply disappeared, making the externally financed battles against HIV-AIDS that much more trying.

President Banda disbanded the national anticorruption commission, but it was reinstated by President Sata (2011–2014). (In 2011, Sata nevertheless discharged the director general of the ACC because of his ties to outgoing President Banda. At his own inauguration as president in 2011, Sata lavishly promised to tackle corruption—the "scourge" of Zambia and Africa.[79])

In 2014, the ACC received 2,245 complaints, investigated 469, indicted 64, and convicted 10. Among the prosecutions were those of parliamentarians and ministers from the ruling Patriotic Front party. Nine arrests were subsequently made from among that group, and only one conviction recorded. According to the local Transparency International chapter, the slow pace of the ACC and its limited successes testified to its ineffectuality and the futility of its operations.[80]

Nevertheless, from 2004 to 2013, Zambia improved its anticorruption scores overall, according to the World Bank's Control of Corruption Indicator, from 27 to 44, a total of 17. Zambia thus ranked seventh for that period, just after Liberia, Belarus, and Montenegro, and above Swaziland, Niger, and

Indonesia. In contrast, according to the Corruption Perceptions Index, 2004–2014, Zambia improved by just twelve points, from 26 to 38, behind Montenegro (15), Romania, Serbia, and Indonesia (all 14). On the CPI overall rankings, in 2015 Zambia was only the 76th least corrupt nation, along with Bosnia, Brazil, Burkina Faso, India, and Tunisia. In Africa, Botswana, Cape Verde, the Seychelles, Mauritius, Lesotho, Namibia, Rwanda, Ghana, and others all exhibited better scores and higher rankings. Zambia ranked seven places above Liberia (discussed in the next chapter).

The Zambian Bribe Payers Index, run by the local Anti-Corruption Commission and Transparency International, also indicates that Zambia made progress between 2009 and 2012, reducing the incidence of corruption in the public sector from 14 percent to 10 percent. That meant that an average adult Zambian faced bribe requests from a public official in a public institution about 10 percent of the time. About 36 percent of local firms expected to be asked for bribes to secure contracts in 2002. By 2013, that number was down to 14 percent.[81] An Afrobarometer survey in 2013 suggested that 10 percent of Zambians had a personal direct experience with corruption in the prior twelve months. That was a lower figure than Transparency International found in 2011, when its Global Corruption Barometer survey revealed that 45 percent of Zambians had paid bribes and 67 percent believed that corruption had increased since 2008. By 2013, the Global Corruption Barometer survey in Zambia reported that only 47 percent of those interviewed said that corruption had increased since 2011, a salutary gain.[82]

In 2011, Zambia's auditor general, reporting to Parliament, found $98 million worth of financial irregularities—unauthorized expenditures, pilfering of petty cash, unaccounted for revenues, and so on—in governmental ministries. But the revelations of the auditor general appear regularly to have been ignored, except by the Zambian ACC (see below).[83]

The following initiatives made a difference from 2004 to 2014 and largely explain why the perception of Zambia's comparative anticorruption efficacy increased:

1. Under President Mwanawasa, Zambia established a Task Force against Corruption (which Banda later dismantled).
2. Mwanawasa placed new integrity committees in each ministry and in the police and tax administrations.
3. President Banda promoted a National Anti-Corruption policy in 2009.
4. Banda ordered comprehensive audits of all major ministries and public agencies.
5. The Public Procurement Act of 2008 required open bidding and improved transparency for contract awards.

6. Parliament passed the Public Interest Disclosure Act of 2010 to protect whistleblowers (but not to provide access to official information).

7. During President Sata's time, the Anti-Corruption Commission opened investigations against several cabinet ministers from Sata's own ruling political party.

8. Sata reintroduced the "abuse of office" clause of the Anti-Corruption Act. It had been dropped by Banda.

9. Sata's administration created several commissions of inquiry to examine the potentially corrupt affairs of the Banda regime. There were investigations of the Zambia Revenue Authority, the Oil Procurement Commission, and the Land Commission—all revealing substantial abuse of office.

10. Under Sata, Zambia complied with the provisions of the Extractive Industries Transparency Initiative and joined the Construction Sector Transparency Initiative.

11. Under Sata, the Anti-Corruption Act of 2012 criminalized active and passive corruption, extortion, bribery of foreign officials, money laundering, and abuse of office. The act required all public institutions and ministries to establish integrity committees.

12. During the Sata era, cabinet ministers were required to declare their assets, but members of Parliament and civil servants were not.

13. Sata introduced a bill of rights and increased press freedom.

14. Sata simplified and improved bureaucratic practices, making it much easier to open new businesses, thus reducing discretion.

15. Sata transformed the Office of Public Prosecutions in 2014 into the National Prosecution Authority, which led to improved efforts against corruption.

All of these initiatives proved significant in strengthening Zambia's ability to curtail corruption and to improve the perception of its success. But of equal importance were the actions of the ACC and of the Anti–Money Laundering Unit of the national Drug Enforcement Commission. In 2014, the ACC received more than 2,200 complaints of corruption from the public and authorized 469 of that number for further examination. The ACC also took up twenty-two new cases of alleged financial misappropriation discovered by the auditor general, in addition to forty-nine already being processed. It examined several tender irregularities brought to its attention by the Zambian Public Procurement Authority. The ACC had also begun in 2014 to investigate serving cabinet ministers and members of Parliament belonging to the then ruling Patriotic Front. Even though its conviction rate in 2014 was very low, the ACC was at least helping to expose corruption in Zambia.

The ACC itself noted in 2014 that Zambia's ethical standards were still lax, and that all of its own efforts both to investigate and to educate public officials about the ills of corruption had achieved but limited success. But it was still trying to "promote a culture of honesty and integrity in the discharge of public duties."[84]

Judicial independence was also a work in progress as late as 2014. The courts were regarded by local and external observers as being "not immune to political interference." (Sata had replaced many top judges.) According to a Global Corruption Barometer survey, Zambians believed that their judges were corrupt; 13 percent of respondents had bribed magistrates and judges.[85]

Zambia's improvements in its anticorruption scores on the two major indexes clearly resulted from the political will demonstrated by Mwanawasa, by his unexpected attention to the problem after the rampantly corrupt Chiluba years, by the legislative and procedural improvements introduced by him and, in some cases, carried forward by his successors, and by the boost in morale and legitimacy thereby experienced by indigenous civil society and foreign donors.

Starting from the low base of the Chiluba presidency, Zambia is now less corrupt than it was. Its anticorruption institutions operate less effectively than they might, but exposure and prosecution are more likely than before. If President Edgar Lungu (elected in 2015) interferes with the ACC or the National Prosecution Authority and ignores the findings of the Office of the Auditor General, Zambia will slide backward. Effective presidential leadership in this and all of the other cases is the determining variable.

Perverse Results: Malawi

Because Chiluba had quickly eviscerated the Zambian ACC, Russell welcomed an invitation in 1997 to move to Malawi, where a postauthoritarian multi-party democracy had also been promoted by donors (they were much more influential in Malawi than elsewhere in southern Africa) and where the United Democratic Front (UDF) had won a decisive election in 1993. President Bakili Muluzi's new government decided to set up the Anti-Corruption Bureau (ACB) in 1995 and recruited Russell to advise (but not to run) its Malawian exercise. The new ACB (drawing on Zambian legislation) focused as did the Zambian ACC and other anticorruption endeavors in sub-Saharan Africa on bribery, fraud, misappropriation of funds, and the abuse of authority and public office.[86] But its jurisdiction never extended, as had the ICAC's, to the private sector. Nonetheless, the ACB, especially in its later years, was mandated to prevent corruption and to educate against it in the manner of Hong Kong, but with distinctively fewer resources.

The actions and success of Africa's anticorruption commissions were compromised and well-meaning enforcement endeavors frustrated. Malawi's ACB during the Muluzi era, and under President Bingu wa Mutharika after 2004, failed to indict more than a handful of miscreants despite the rampant purchasing of politicians and other instances of suspected corruption. The ACB was compelled to open cases only after the registering of a complaint. In 2002, it was dealing with about 1,700 complaints but had investigated and concluded only 118 cases. In 2009, Malawi's ACB received more than 500 complaints, investigated about 100, and recommended for prosecution about 20.[87] It was during this period that Global Integrity investigated Malawi and accused the ACB of not targeting "the big fish." It also indicated that nearly all investigations were stalled because key personnel were absent.

Muluzi's ten years in office were characterized by endemic corruption, with the president and many of his cabinet ministers using their offices as springboards to great wealth. Muluzi's family controlled 60 percent of all national sugar sales and ran most of the nation's buses. Others had their own scams. In one case, the minister of education took kickbacks from a British printer in connection with the supply of school exercise books worth more than $2 million. (The exercise books arrived months late, well after schools had opened.) Another cabinet minister paid a motor vehicle firm large sums for repairs to government vehicles that were never completed, or perhaps to vehicles that were never even conveyed to the shop. The National Audit Office in 2003 discovered thousands of improper government accounts invented to hide peculation.

Petty corruption also flourished. Given a particularly "inefficient and ineffective public service delivery [system] and rigidity in the bureaucracy, [a] lack of automation in most government departments in Malawi, and the fact that almost every transaction [had] to be supported by official stamps, signatures and copious documentation,'" busy clients were ready to bribe officials to obtain faster action. Moreover, public officials were known to develop "rules and norms different from those that were expected by the public" and intentionally to slow down the process so as to encourage speed payments. "This has given rise to opportunities for public officials to apply rules and regulations selectively and discriminatorily, thus perpetuating corruption."[88]

Under Muluzi (and even with Russell's intervention), the Anti-Corruption Bureau that had been established in 1995 was severely hampered in its activities since it could initiate no prosecutions without permission from the director of public prosecutions (DPP), a Muluzi crony. Despite the ACB investigation of a number of serious cases, no prosecutions of cabinet ministers were approved by the DPP during Muluzi's entire reign. The ACB developed incriminating dossiers about the nefarious actions of an attorney general and a minister of local government. But the DPP would not take those cases and others to court. Even so, the ACB tried to do what it could to uncover and develop prosecutable cases.

The ACB revealed a number of brazen fraudulent schemes. In early 1998, to discuss but one example from the bureau's early years, a complaint arrived alleging that the general manager of the state Petroleum Control Commission (PCC) had purchased an expensive motor car worth more than K1 million, far in excess of his stated income. The general manager and the minister of energy and mining, it became apparent, had corruptly awarded a contract to supply imported petrol at inflated prices to the PCC. The contractor was a Tanzanian who had been barred from operating in Malawi, but he apparently knew how to pay well. As per new regulations, all of Malawi's petrol had to be trucked in, overland, from Tanzania and the contractor's depot and allocated to local filling stations by the state-owned body. As a result of the inflated contract, local prices to the consumers rose.

The fuel supplier had meanwhile opened bank accounts for the general manager and the minister in Guernsey and Europe. More than $1.7 million was paid to the general manager, who was prosecuted by the ACB in 2001. The minister, a close associate of Muluzi, was implicated but never prosecuted.[89]

In another common case, the minister of finance in 1999 prevailed upon his staff and the chair of an official tender evaluation body to throw its support illegally to an untried new firm and away from the incumbent Swiss holder of a contract to inspect imports to Malawi. The ACB declared in 2000 that the minister of finance had "acted in a manner conducive or connected to corrupt practices" and that his principal official had done the same. "The tender process . . . was tainted with bad practice and strong suspicion of corruption." The ACB recommended that the false award be rescinded and that the president of Malawi be asked to take appropriate action against the minister and his key official.[90] But nothing was ever done, and the minister of finance later became vice president of the nation.

In the midst of a developing national food crisis, with poor maize harvests in 2001 and poor rains in the succeeding 2001–2002 planting season, Malawi relied on its previously created National Food Reserve Agency and a Strategic Grain Reserve (SGR), the latter managed by officials of the state's Agricultural Development and Marketing Corporation (ADMARC), which stored maize purchased for and donated into the SGR. The ACB subsequently discovered that ADMARC, without authority, had sold most of its accumulated supplies of maize instead of holding them in reserve, thus harming the public; when great shortages of maize in 2001 occasioned hunger and hundreds of deaths throughout the nation, ADMARC and others had to purchase new supplies of maize from South Africa. The government consequently lost many millions of kwacha as a result of these maladroit maneuvers. Many well-connected traders and politicians, given preferential access to stored supplies of the staple grain, profited considerably by selling inexpensive precrisis maize expensively to the public once shortages became apparent. One of those buyers of SGR maize was Joyce Banda, later president, who sold 841 tons of SGR maize to great personal gain. (Banda, an ADMARC board member, was subsequently also accused of benefiting from a contract awarded to her by ADMARC to construct a transit depot.) Nationwide, the swindle was enormous. The ACB discovered that maize stored to alleviate famine had in fact been sold illegally to favored clients; the manager of the marketing board and presumed prime culprit had apparently used his $15 million profits to purchase a five-star hotel (and much else), but he promised to reimburse the state, and eventually became minister of finance.[91]

In 2003, Muluzi's campaign for a constitution-breaking third presidential term included operation "Moving with a Bag of Money" that led to the bribing of forty opposition members of Parliament. During the ten-year Muluzi administration, a local critic wrote, clientelist practices prevailed. The bureaucracy was characterized by "patronage through appointment, offers of lucrative contracts, and enticement of party loyalists and opposition MPs with cash."[92]

It was about this time that Transparency International reviewed Malawi's anticorruption efforts: It declared that the ACB was "ineffective in both prevention and prosecution of corruption in the country." It also commented that there was no strong political will to fight corruption. The country's political leadership merely wanted to "save face."[93] Public opinion polls revealed that 65 percent of Malawians queried believed that politicians and officials were not to be trusted. They were uniformly corrupt.[94]

When Bingu wa Mutharika (originally Brightson Webster Ryson Thom) became president of Malawi in 2004, he had served as governor of the nation's Reserve Bank, as secretary general of the Common Market for East and Central Africa (COMESA), and as an economist with the African Development Bank. He was dismissed from COMESA for "abuse of office." He claimed a Ph.D. in development economics that had in fact been purchased from a for-profit online diploma mill—Pacific Western University—in Encino, California. He was the nominee of and heir to President Muluzi and would not have been elected president without Muluzi's strong support and the backing of Muluzi's UDF party. During his swearing-in ceremony as president, Mutharika declared that under his administration there would be "zero tolerance of corruption." He promised "swift investigation, prosecution, and punishment" of all public officials who stole and abused their positions.[95]

Mutharika broke with Muluzi shortly after being inaugurated and spent the next several years pursuing miscreants from his predecessor's period in office. His new Democratic People's Party (DPP) claimed in early 2004 to be investigating the finances of ten former senior ministers; a new era in anticorruption effort seemed about to begin. The ACB was involved, working closely with the responsive public prosecutor and following up on the many reports of official malfeasance that it received (a total of more than 3,000 from 1997 to 2006).[96] The prosecutor, the ACB, and the attorney general together paraded suspects before the media, but the few cases that eventually made it into court were badly prepared, and many acquittals followed. Local observers believed that the 2004–2006 anticorruption blitz was essentially an exercise in political persecution. Mutharika was never secure in office; looking active on the anticorruption front pleased the donors on which Malawi had long been dependent for project and budgetary support.

Even so, the ACB and public prosecutor could claim success when they jailed the mayor of the nation's most populous city, a political ally of Muluzi, for two years for stealing from his administration's road maintenance fund. Two members of Mutharika's own cabinet were accused of illicitly retaining funds for cancelled overseas journeys but were excused when they promised to reimburse the nation.

The ACB tried to investigate Muluzi's shady involvement with a business park that had been constructed on prime land in Blantyre and then leased to the government. Subsequently, the ACB learned that more than $7 million had been paid into various accounts controlled by Muluzi from sources in Libya, Morocco, Rwanda, and Taiwan. The ACB believed that it had discovered major diversions of foreign assistance into Muluzi's pocket. Libyan-supplied tractors were but one item. Muluzi claimed that he was simply receiving funds for the UDF.

Nevertheless, when the ACB tried to arrest Muluzi in 2006, Mutharika suspended the director of the ACB, completely vitiating its independence. The prosecutor, presumably on orders, dropped all forty-two counts of theft and abuse of office against Muluzi. Mutharika needed the support in Parliament, where he lacked a majority, of UDF politicians still close to Muluzi. Mutharika also may have wondered if prosecuting Muluzi provided a proper precedent. He, too, would eventually become an ex-president.

Mutharika was by this time deciding that it was his moment to benefit from the proverbial fatted calf. He decided to move out of the official presidential palace in Blantyre and to remove members of Parliament from the opulent new state house in Lilongwe, Malawi's legislative headquarters, so that he could move in. He then ordered a new official automobile—a Mercedes Maybach limousine with a price tag of more than $400,000, part of the cost of which was intended to be drawn from funds in an official Emergency Drought Recovery Programme (with grants supplied by foreign donors). He also purchased an expensive $13.6 million jet aircraft for presidential use. But, much more by way of venal scale peculation was occurring during this period, cleverly concealed.

Mutharika, advised by his brother Peter (subsequently elected in 2014 as president of Malawi), was systematically misappropriating or stealing large amounts from the national treasury and depositing it in banks in Southeast Asia for his and his brother's own personal use, or to contest future elections. The total amount discovered in 2015 by a German-sponsored audit conducted by a major global accounting firm was about $47 million. Peter, on behalf of his brother, apparently made frequent visits to Singapore and Malaysia to deposit substantial kwacha in their names.[97]

President Joyce Banda, who ruled for two years in between the two Mutharika regimes, also endured a large-scale corruption and money-laundering scandal, called "Cashgate," that culminated in 2013 but had been going on for several years under her predecessor's as well as her own administration. Twenty-five cabinet ministers lost their positions for taking part in fraudulent overinvoicing schemes and the falsification of payrolls worth at least $54 million. The looting of the national treasury reached "a fever pitch" in late 2013 when a third of the total amount was pilfered, much of it on a single day. The managers of eight local commercial banks and senior officials in the office of the accountant general were in league with the rogue politicians and profited from rubber-stamping suspicious payment vouchers. The nation's budget director was killed during these investigations, presumably to keep him from exposing the scheme.[98]

Given the massive corruption that punctuated the Mutharika and Banda eras, whatever the ACB had been doing, the "biggest fish" had been acting with impunity. "Ordinary Malawians," explained one commentator, "look at abuse of state resources by those in power as acceptable." Anyway, he continued, "people join politics in Malawi mainly to make money."[99] Hindered by Muluzi and Bingu wa Mutharika and at least the first public prosecutor, the understaffed, underfinanced, and largely powerless Malawian ACB was hardly able to contain corruption, much less curtail its sustainable growth throughout the first twenty years of its existence. (Russell had departed in 2005.)

After Peter Mutharika became president in 2014, he installed a new director of the ACB and urged him to engage in an all-out attack on Malawian corruption. As he told the Council on Foreign Relations in New York, "We can get rid of [corruption] . . . we are fighting corruption, no question about it. But you know, there will always be corruption, I suppose, in every society, in the sense that there will be some people who are always going to—you know, to have shortcuts to get riches. But I think there are serious penalties if you are caught, and I assure you that, and they know that I will not abide—that my government will not abide corruption."[100] The second President Mutharika spoke as vigorously and assuredly as his predecessors about how corruption would be curtailed. But, as of late 2016, there was no evidence that his regime was moving any more strongly against corrupt politicians and other public servants than its predecessors.

Logistics, Funding, and Capacity Building

Compared to Tanzania, Kenya, and Indonesia, Malawi and Zambia were always short-staffed. In 2008, Malawi's roster was only 124, and its Prevention Division consisted of a mere four employees. Zambia's ACC, in the same year, had more than double the ACB's number of workers, but the number of trained examiners was too small to do justice to every complaint. Since investigators usually comprise about 10 percent of an anticorruption commission's roster, both Zambia and Malawi, especially in contrast to Tanzania, were severely short-staffed and underfunded, which meant that they had difficulty hiring competent staff. In contrast to that of Hong Kong, the infrastructure of these two commissions (and nearly every other African commission as well) has been woefully weak. Accounting standards have been honored in the breach, modern software and other technical capabilities were lacking through at least 2010, and human resource management functions have been wanting.

Despite laudable provisions in the legislative acts to which they owed their birth and gestation, neither of these last two of Africa's anti-corruption agencies in Malawi and Zambia could never free themselves from executive, ministerial, and party interference. Zambia's commission reported to its president, as did Tanzania's, but like Ghana's SFO, Malawi's anticorruption commission operated under the aegis of its country's minister of justice (an uncomfortable arrangement). In other cases, as in Uganda and Ghana, the reporting line was to Parliament (that is, to a cabinet minister), an equally insecure linkage. In each case, as in Ethiopia and Tanzania, guarantees on paper of independence for the commissions were, in practice, meaningless. Every effective head of state or of government exercised undue influence on the anticorruption efforts of his or her nation's commissions, as well as the successful operations of auditors general.

Financial independence is also essential if an anticorruption commission is to function well. Even if its operating funds come largely from donors (40 percent in Malawi in 2008), the budgets of nearly all of the sub-Saharan African agencies are subject to approval first by ministries of finance and then by the appropriation of national legislatures. Withholding or slowing the disbursement of funds is an easy way for bureaucrats or parliamentarians to hamstring the work of agencies hard on their avaricious heels. In Ghana, however, salaries and allowances of the commissioners were charged directly to the state's consolidated fund, giving its two anticorruption agencies more protection than those in other countries.

Constitutionally, all heads of anticorruption commissions were protected from dismissal except for "infirmity of body or mind." They were, on paper, thus encouraged to act fearlessly and boldly. But, again in practice, nearly all of the heads of such agencies danced to the tunes of the national ruling political parties and national executives to which they owed both their appointments and their continued exercise of office. Ethiopia gave its anticorruption leaders a seemingly secure six-year term, Nigeria four years, and Zambia a term only three years long. In practice, however, the length of a director general's term meant very little.

Equally important constraints on the ability of most African anticorruption efforts, as in Tanzania, resulted from their need to beg attorneys general or directors of public prosecutions to take cases prepared by the commissions to court. Only Ethiopia's agency could do so directly, but probably only with the permission of the prime minister. Hong Kong's anticorruption leaders believed that their ICAC was better off being compelled to receive complaints, to investigate them well, and to hand fully developed cases over to separate prosecutors for action. In Africa, however, where the positions of attorneys general and prosecutors general are much more politicized, that recipe has led to many cases ready for court being dropped or shunted sideways.

Zambia's agency was explicitly permitted to initiate investigations, not just wait for complaints, but Ghana's Supreme Court decreed that its CHRAJ could not, and a number of other African commissions were prevented by law or procedure from following up on leads without complaints. If a commission in Africa is reactive rather than proactive, too much that is questionable may escape its examination. Furthermore, such a commission always has a ready excuse to avoid surveying questionable procedures and media-reported instances of improper behavior.

In several cases, too, the authority of the anticorruption commission overlapped confusingly with or conflicted with that of the national auditor general, in some cases also with an official ombudsman. The mandates of the Zambian, Ugandan, and Malawian anticorruption commissions included both prevention and education, based on the Hong Kong model. Neither of the Ghanaian commissions was asked to educate or prevent.

In Uganda during the same period, the attorney general refused to bring charges against suspects even after their dismissal from statutory bodies and punishment by Parliament. The Ethics Commission could investigate infractions of the Leadership Code (at one point in 2003, 17,000 Ugandans were subject to the code and had to complete a 19-page form) only after receiving a "justified and relevant" complaint from a citizen who had paid a sizable fee to register the complaint. In several prominent cases, senior politicians had refused to file required declarations of assets (a violation of the state's Leadership Code) but the government had declined to support the anticorruption commission's determination to act. The high court in fact ruled that the president's powers trumped any rulings of the anticorruption commission.

In Uganda, too, a solicitor general refused to give the anticorruption commission files relating to the commission's own actions. The official consortium of donors, meeting in 2003, perceived that there was a culture of impunity with respect to corruption in Uganda. Prosecutions were rare and major offenders were neither called to account nor prosecuted.[101] A year later, Uganda's anticorruption commission underwent a self-assessment and found much room for improvement, especially with regard to capacity building—i.e., skills development—so that it could chase corruption more energetically and effectively.

Emasculating Anticorruption Efforts

All African endeavors (except those of Nigeria) against corruption were funded by Western bilateral donors or the United Nations Development Programme (UNDP), their modes of operations and strategic design thus naturally reflecting the interests and primary concerns of those well-meaning outsiders. Often, when the priorities of distant donors changed because of political shifts in their own countries, so fledgling anticorruption commissions had to alter course or refocus their activities.

As in Tanzania, the operations of all of these pre-2004 commissions were severely compromised by their lack of financial and political independence. Even in relatively democratic Ghana, the powers of the president (then John Kufuor) were so extensive that the two integrity commissions were clearly unable to operate independently. Additionally, only the attorney general could authorize prosecutions. In Ghana, at the time, the attorney general was partisan and operated "with a keen eye on political profit." Indeed, in 2003–2004, the government was accused of being lackadaisical in its pursuit of corruption; despite the attention of energetic civil society anticorruption awareness initiatives, a lively free press, and the two statutory anticorruption bodies, no key regime operatives were prosecuted between 1994 and 2004.[102]

Even if the commissions in most of sub-Saharan Africa had been professionally proficient and populated by skilled personnel, almost every attempt to investigate and indict persons of political prominence would have been (as indeed they were) thwarted by presidents, prime ministers, and other ruling party bigwigs. Even after competitive elections in countries like Malawi and Zambia, incoming executives wielded such supreme power that anticorruption and integrity operations were in almost every case overwhelmed. The lack of independence of the commissions was palpable. So was their legal subordination to the executive and the legislature. Above all, in no case did political will favor them or what they were mandated to do.

Altering Value Systems

It is striking that the supposed charge to the African commissions that they follow Hong Kong and educate their citizenries against corruption and act boldly to prevent the commitment of corrupt acts was either ignored or at least bungled in much of Africa. The legal codes were just as strong, but without a commitment to anticorruption efforts on the part of rulers and ruling classes, most of the African commissions were unable to change the prevailing political cultures of corruption that disfigured their countries. Consummate political leadership was lacking, and ruling elites resisted all serious anticorruption endeavors.

Some critics might argue that Hong Kong succeeded in large part because the exercisers of political will and the leaders of the anticorruption effort were outsiders, seconded from a country and a culture where most of the battles against corruption had been won (and where rule of law had long been established). Zambia's and Malawi's commissions also had the same kind of professional oversight. But Singapore never did, and Botswana only did so at the very beginning of its commission's existence. Mauritius relied on its own personnel, as Rwanda does now.

If there had been or if there is political commitment, dedicated resources were and are important. Dependent for the most part on donors, Africa's anticorruption efforts were most often wholly inadequate. Despite legal provisions giving the commissions the right to invigilate bank statements and other accounts, and to seize critical information, a wall of political, judicial, and executive resistance usually reduced the powers of the African commissions to nugatory levels. Consequently, they were and are unable to corroborate complaints easily, or to investigate likely sources of chicanery. More telling, major expenditures that have benefited political parties or particular cohorts of leaders—in the area, for example, of arms procurement or energy purchases—have been and are deemed "too sensitive" or "too security sensitive" to be examined.

The test for the African commission process is straightforward: to what extent has the existence of commissions, weak as they were and subject as they were to political and executive interference, proven even minimally successful in mitigating the impact of corruption or modifying corrosive behavior by public officials and private entrepreneurs? Success should be seen in reduced levels of corruption, whether registered by the Corruption Perceptions Index or by some other internationally validated method. But there is no significant evidence that the tides of corruption have receded anywhere outside of Botswana, Mauritius, Rwanda, and Liberia,—among the "most improved" country examples discussed in the next chapter. Corruption in 2016 in sub-

Saharan Africa and in all of our country cases is at least as prevalent as it was in 2004, 1994, and 1984, if not more so.

Individual instances of peculation and bribe taking can be pursued through standard police and court procedures. Venal crookedness can also be caught, and anticorruption commissions can pursue such outrages usefully. Likewise, complaints about abuses of authority can be investigated and bureaucrats punished. But, to cure corruption in Africa means transforming societal responses, a major overhaul that can only be accomplished by committed, canny, and resolute national leadership.

VI

The Most Improved
RESULTS

Another way of examining what works best in the anticorruption tool kit comes from a careful review of the globe's most improved nation-states in terms of their scores over the decade 2004–2014 according to both the Corruption Perceptions Index (CPI) and the World Bank's Control of Corruption Indicator (WBCC). The five winners in these arbitrary and time-bound anticorruption sweepstakes are hardly the obvious high performers. But how and why these five countries transformed themselves from being perceived as extremely corrupt to much less corrupt over ten years is instructive and telling. There are major lessons across the cases, and within each case, for those who seek to strengthen the manner in which their own countries can battle corruption effectively.

The five countries are Georgia, Rwanda, Liberia, Macedonia, and Montenegro in order of "most improved." Over that particular study decade, Poland, Qatar, and Belarus are three additional nation-states that were also perceived as raising their scores significantly, but not by both measuring methods.

Of the top five countries, only Georgia, Liberia, Macedonia, and Montenegro were judged "most improved" by both the CPI and the WBCC. Rwanda, a country with especially forceful leadership, ranked second according to the WBCC and is therefore included in this chapter. Dominica, a tiny and anomalous Caribbean island case, was second on the CPI but is excluded from this discussion of how improvements came about because of its unrepresentative size—only 70,000 people—and because of well-founded and well-sourced suspicions that the perceived improvements in Dominica over 2004–2014 were mostly mirages. Indeed, in 2016, the administration of Prime Minister Roosevelt Skerrit that had presided over the supposed improvements was mired in scandal: Skerrit had personally profited by selling citizenships and passports to questionable Nigerians (including a defrocked petroleum industries minister) and other fugitives, had built himself a large villa at government expense, had awarded no-bid contracts to cronies and relatives, and so on.[1] In 2015, the CPI failed to rate Dominica, presumably because of too few reliable sources of perception.

Several other countries could be added to the list on the basis of CPI rankings alone, or WBCC ratings alone. But the above five nation-states were selected for study because they scored highly and because they represent different geographical regions and governmental styles. Three are solid democracies, two are guided democracies, and one is a smuggling state with a democratic overlay. Several are small in terms of population, but Rwanda is medium-sized. (The size variable is discussed in chapter 8; clearly corruption is easier to extirpate in a smallish country.) The individual case studies that follow elaborate upon those designations and explain how each country improved its anticorruption responses so demonstrably over the ten-year period. Another set of country cases could be substituted for this group of five, but the better performers would have improved for reasons similar to the set discussed in this chapter.

An expanded list of countries that have achieved anticorruption advances and rank highly in their regions and reasonably high on both the CPI and the WBCC includes Chile, Estonia, Slovenia, South Korea, Taiwan, and Uruguay. In 2014, according to the CPI, Chile and Uruguay were the 21st least corrupt global countries, with tied scores of 73 out of 100. But, in each of those worthy cases, they showed less dramatic improvement in their index scores across the decade than did the five cases singled out for closer examination in this chapter. Only Estonia showed significant change, but over an earlier fifteen year period, according to the WBCC. On the CPI, Estonia gained nine scoring points to 69 between 2004 and 2014 to rank 26th along with France and Qatar. In 2004, it had shared the scores and a ranking of 31st along with Botswana and Slovenia (39th with a CPI score of 58 in 2014, 1 point ahead of Cape Verde). The others, all high performers from the start, improved their scores only marginally from 1996 to 2011.[2] Uruguay was still 21st in the 2015 CPI rankings with a score of 74, but Chile and Estonia (along with France and the United Arab Emirates) had both slipped two places, ranking 23rd, with 70 points. Slovenia was 35th, with 60 points.

(Because the CPI scoring methods were altered in 2012, essentially changing from employing relative scores—country to country, "normalized" and "matched"—to using raw scores on a 1–100 scale, the CPI ratings from 2004 to 2014 technically are not comparable. Nevertheless, the ten-year time frame provides a rough way of analyzing which countries rid themselves of corruption most effectively over a recent decade, and how.)

As indicated in the earlier discussion of the Corruption Perceptions Index (CPI), being designated "most improved" depends largely on perceptions of corruption. Recall that the CPI measures how observers inside and outside a country, usually only a limited number, view that country's performance on the corruption scale. Because perceptions change slowly, the "most improved" on the CPI list have indeed over a decade clearly impressed those observers (separate ones for each country) who provide the scores to Transparency International and who have increased their particular country ratings dramatically. But, because those scores reflect impressions rather than any objective reality, they have suggestive rather than scientific validity.

Likewise, since the World Bank corruption measure is a composite that builds its results by aggregating the scores of about twenty separate indicators and indexes (see chapter 2), its findings are both more inclusive and much less precise than the CPI. What constitutes "corruption" may differ markedly among its twenty sources. Moreover, although the World Bank's Control of Corruption Indicator (WBCC) scores are rendered elaborately and precisely to the fifth decimal place, they are no more meaningful, valid, or scientific than the results provided by the CPI.

We use both of those measures in this chapter (and throughout this book), however, because there are none better (see chapter 2) and because the CPI and the WBCC have perfected their methodologies over two decades, giving their results some authority. Furthermore, the CPI and a precursor version of the WBCC are highly correlated and "yield substantially the same results."[3]

Even so, given the cases discussed below, it is possible that rising scores over the decade resulted from a false optic—that the introduction of new legal and procedural curbs on corruption boosted the perception (mostly externally) that nefarious practices were being curtailed even while abuse of authority and peculation continued clandestinely to infect the state—especially in the Balkans. Macedonia and Montenegro may only have won the "most improved" perception sweepstakes because of the particular decade being measured or because both countries were innovating and making substantial legal and procedural changes without fundamentally moving very far along the ethically universalist continuum. Indeed, Macedonia and Montenegro exhibit great "implementation gaps" between promise and performance.[4] Their improvements over the decade also say too little about the sustainability of any relevant gains. Backsliding is too easy once admission to the European Union has been achieved.

Georgia

In the decade under review, Georgia ranked as the most improved country in terms of corruption. Between 2004 and 2014, according the Corruption Perceptions Index, Georgia's scores improved from 20 to 52, a 32 point gain. According to the World Bank's Control of Corruption indicator, between 2004 and 2013 Georgia gained 38 points, from 29 to 67. In 2014, Georgia's population was about 5 million and its annual per capita GDP $3,600.

As those large shifts in "perception" and "control" indicate, Georgia as a Soviet and post-Soviet state was "notorious for its levels of graft, corruption, and bribery." In 2001, state officials received between $75 and $101 million in bribes. Officials in the Ministry of Fuel and Energy embezzled $380 million, half of the foreign assistance received to reconstruct Georgia's energy sector.[5] Esadze estimates that 50 to 60 percent of all aid was stolen by corrupt officials in the 1990s. "Policemen, judges, tax and customs officials [paid] huge amounts to acquire their official positions [to] enable them to extract bribes."[6] In the universities, applicants paid as much as $30,000 to secure admission and obtain top grades.[7] It was "one of the most corrupt Soviet republics," a reputation that it continued to merit until 2003, when the Rose Revolution ended the long post-Soviet, heavy-handed reign of Eduard Shevardnadze. Until then, Georgia had the largest shadow, or underground, economy in the post-Soviet space, exceeding even the excesses in Uzbekistan, Kyrgyzstan, Turkmenistan, and Azerbaijan. It specialized in siphoning off raw materials from the official economy.[8]

Mikheil Saakashvili, the American-trained leader of the Rose Revolution and soon-to-be new president of Georgia, led the charge against Shevardnadze and Moscow's corrupt ways. "It is impossible to remain in this government," he said when resigning as minister of justice from Shevardnadze's last cabinet. The leadership is sinking in the morass of corruption and . . . the state apparatus is merging with international criminal bodies and . . . the country is turning into a criminal enclave."[9] After the Rose Revolution, Saakashvili fought corruption for the same reason that Lee Kuan Yew attacked corrupt practices in Singapore—to legitimize his rule, to impress foreigners in general and the democratic West in particular, and in order to position Georgia for entry into the European Union and NATO. Saakashvili, like Lee, knew that he could only win the battle against corruption if he wrestled organized crime, endemic in Georgia and the entire post-Soviet space, to a standstill.

There was much to be said for Saakashvili's rhetoric and for the earnest manner in which he motivated his aroused followers, his associates and close supporters, and his governing team to cleanse Georgia of the stain of corruption. It forcefully expressed political will. But he and his government also implemented critical reforms, albeit with scant regard for democratic principles and citizen input:

1. The new Georgian state greatly simplified the regulatory framework for all businesses and made it much easier for new businesses to open.
2. It introduced major tax reforms, reducing the array of taxes from twenty-one to six. It also changed how taxes were to be collected, preferably fairly.
3. It created a single treasury account for the central government, making theft and fraud more difficult.
4. It adopted a medium-term expenditure framework to manage public finances.
5. It strengthened the state's oversight of all financial practices by establishing new institutions to limit graft. Public officials were required to declare their assets and incomes.
6. The state criminalized money laundering and measurably increased the types of financial transactions that had to be monitored for improprieties.
7. It cut "unnecessary" bureaucracy by 50 percent; it eliminated five ministries.[10]
8. The new reformers discharged the entire staff of the ministry of education and recruited new employees by competitive examination. The final roster reduced the ministry's staff from 289 to 155, and they were each paid more than before.
9. To cure corruption in universities, admission decisions after 2004 became the responsibility of a new National Assessment and Examinations Center. It administered a Unified National Examination; those who took it were identified by bar codes, not names, and separately evaluated by two assessors.
10. The new National Center for Education Accreditation examined university credentials, helped to close a number of diploma mills, and ended up reducing the number of approved higher educational institutions from 237 to 43.[11]
11. Mostly by jawboning and threatening drastic retrenchment in the lecturer ranks, the Ministry of Education managed to reduce corrupt dealings within the remaining forty-three universities.
12. Georgia abolished the post-Soviet traffic police force, overhauled the regular police (discharging 15,000 police personnel), and recruited an entirely new cadre of police officers and policemen, thus theoretically removing those who had been accustomed to receiving bribes and replacing them with professionals imbued with a new motivational spirit. Police salaries were increased, too.[12]

13. It raised salaries for state employees fifteen-fold.
14. It eliminated bureaucratic obstacles, including removing 750 (of 900) unnecessary licenses and permits, and thus discretion from bureaucrats. Property registration became easier.[13]
15. It simplified customs procedures, again limiting discretion.
16. It forbade nepotism and tightened regulations on conflicts of interest.
17. The state severely limited the ability of civil servants to move from government positions into private businesses, especially those previously under their surveillance and supervision.[14]
18. It introduced a strong freedom of information act.
19. In a signal way, Saakashvili's regime arrested a number of corrupt officials (2004–2005) so as to demonstrate (in the manner of Lee in Singapore) that the new Georgia was serious about reducing corruption and being intolerant of bribery, extortion, fraud, and the like.

All of these alterations in conventional pre–Rose Revolution practice abruptly jolted the old political culture and created a new one—a new paradigm of behavior between citizens and the state. Most salient was number 19: the arrests of the head of the railways, the head of the football federation, a former minister of transport, and a former minister of fuel and energy—all for corrupt dealings. Those arrests helped to make the point that graft and theft were no longer permitted. They also instilled fear of discovery in the ranks of public officials.[15] In 2004 alone, $50 million was confiscated from imprisoned Shevardnadze acolytes and property valued at €40 million was repossessed. Mansions were taken from disgraced former ministers. Under number 2, Shevardnadze's son-in-law was arrested for evading taxes. So were other "big fish."

Between 2003 and 2010, nearly 1,000 public officials were charged with corruption, including fifteen deputy ministers, thirty-one deputy chairpersons of city councils, a provincial governor, and six members of Parliament. Saakashvili and his prosecutor general enunciated a zero-tolerance policy and stuck to it. Suspects could be shot if they resisted arrest.

Reforming the police, the actions of the ministry of finance, and the assiduous workings of the office of the prosecutor general were also important anticorruption initiatives. A new financial monitoring service reduced money laundering. Auditing services were improved and the old Chamber of Control was reconfigured and given new powers to inspect the books of all governmental establishments. An ombudsman was appointed. By 2008, many fewer companies than before reported that they had been asked for bribes in the ordinary course of acquiring permits to do business. In 2009, 97 percent of citizens said that they did not have to pay a bribe in the preceding twelve months. Citizens also responded positively to a Transparency International poll; 57 percent indicated that governmental efforts to battle corruption had been "effective."[16]

As Global Integrity concluded in 2011, "Georgia has largely fulfilled the recommendations of international anticorruption organizations, such as the Group of States Against Corruption under the Council of Europe and the Anti-Corruption Network for Eastern Europe and Central Asia under the Organization for Economic Cooperation and Development. A significant part of the anticorruption legislation has been amended and refined in compliance with international standards." But Global Integrity reminded Georgia that executive authority still remained too dominant and too unaccountable. It also noted undue interference with the nascent private sector.[17] It could have added that the judiciary was still not fully independent.

Saakashvili showed political will in the curbing of corruption. By demonstrating personal integrity and pursuing corrupt politicians and officials, he persuaded younger bureaucrats and politicians to follow his lead and to commit themselves in their official capacities to honest behavior. He thus altered the prevailing political culture, as do all strong leaders who hope to reduce corrupt practices. He consequently persuaded increasing numbers of followers, and citizens more broadly, to appreciate how beating back the juggernaut of corruption could benefit the new Georgia, elevate people's everyday lives, invite new foreign direct investment, and remove the stain of moral decay that had long infected Georgia, as it had so many other post-Soviet republics.

When positive, visionary leadership combines with a series of very practical and redesigned control measures, it is possible rapidly to curb corruption, and to reduce its impact on national well-being. Saakashvili and his team did exactly that, and Georgia benefited—as upward changes to its CPI and WBCC scores demonstrated over the decade.

Rwanda

Ten years after the Rwandan genocide, Rwanda was regarded by casual observers as no less corrupt than its neighbors, but its CPI score in 2004 placed its perceptions score higher than Ghana, Senegal, Macedonia, Montenegro, Zambia, Indonesia, Tanzania, Nigeria, Uganda, and Kenya, in that order. In 2004, in Africa, only Botswana, the Seychelles, Cape Verde, Mauritius, Namibia, and South Africa had higher CPI scores. Starting from a relatively high base, therefore, according to the CPI, Rwanda gained only 10 points by 2014. But the WBCC ranks Rwanda as the second "most improved" country from 2004 to 2013, with an upward change of 33 points, only 5 points behind Georgia. (The big jump in Rwanda's scores took place between 2005 and 2006, when Rwanda gained 26 points.) According to the WBCC, Rwanda improved much more than Liberia (20 points) and Zambia (17 points). No other African country came close, although Niger and Swaziland gained 16 points over the period, São Tomé and Principe 14, Lesotho 13, Gabon and Ethiopia 12, and Cape Verde 11.

Whatever the different index methods employed, Rwanda has shown remarkable improvement in governance as well as in anticorruption performance since 2004 or so—since President Paul Kagame decided in about that year to transform postgenocidal Rwanda into "the Singapore of Africa." (Kagame officially became head of state only in 2000.) For the first ten years of his forceful reign in Rwanda (1994–2004), Kagame focused on consolidating his hold on power, on rebuilding the state, on winning a major interethnic war against Hutu anti-Rwandan genocidaire forces based in the Democratic Republic of Congo, and on installing new Congolese governments in Kinshasa.

Once Kagame had accomplished those important missions and had established himself within the African Union and with donors as a person capable of bringing about major governmental changes and producing stability in eastern Africa, he turned to the task of increasing national productivity and prosperity. Just as Lee Kuan Yew transformed Singapore from a ramshackle British-run harbor into one of the great entrepôts and financial centers of the developing world, so Kagame began to envisage capital flowing into his isolated, landlocked mini-country; it has the highest population densities on the land anywhere on the African continent. Given that Rwanda produces little more than coffee, a crop dependent on a fluctuating world market, to create a Singapore-like result in Rwanda, and to attract foreign investors, meant radical shifts in Rwanda's prevailing political and social culture. In 2014, Rwanda's population was 12 million and its annual per capita GDP only $698.

Kagame, following Lee, determined to rid Rwanda of corruption. "Corruption," he said, "is clearly, very largely, behind the problems [that] African countries face. It is very bad in African or Third World countries." Moreover, eliminating corruption is hard because "it has become a way of life in some places."[18] But Kagame did the hard things. He exhorted his people to reject corrupt practices and report corrupt individuals to the police, who were given expanded powers. He erected big billboards all over Kigali, the capital, warning against corruption: "He Who Practices Corruption Destroys His Country." He sacked a few cabinet ministers and associates for theft and graft. He also used the imprimatur of his office to enforce existing legislation against corruption.

New laws and constitutional changes were put in place to criminalize corrupt acts, outlaw extortion, forbid bribery both active and passive, and prohibit money laundering. Kagame promulgated a strict code of conduct for his officials and, as in Liberia, made mandatory the annual disclosure of their assets by all officials—in this case more than 4,000 persons. Kagame further introduced an office of auditor general and appointed an ombudsman. That last official was responsible for checking the net worth filings of officials; in so many Asian and African countries (such as Tanzania) those statements would pile up in an obscure office. Not so in Rwanda, where the ombudsman carefully examines them for signs of ill-gotten profits and the misuse of public office.

The office of the ombudsman operates as if it were an anticorruption agency, although shorn of prosecutorial powers. A public procurement agency makes sure that tenders and all contract bids are proper and that no officials are receiving kickbacks. The police were professionalized after 2004. Crime rates fell and, following Singapore again, the police even began nabbing citizens for littering. Rwanda, reported the *Economist*, has become "the cleanest country in Africa."[19]

Of equal significance, Rwanda downsized its civil service cadre (as in Georgia), dismissing two-thirds of the entire bureaucratic establishment. Ghost workers, as many as 6,500 in one sweep, were also removed from the rolls. Competitive tests were introduced to accentuate the need for competency in the civil service. Since 2005, too, government salaries have been raised regularly.

Like Georgia, Rwanda under Kagame also reduced bureaucratic controls and permits, made striking improvements in the speed by which businesses could be opened, streamlined a broad range of administrative procedures, reduced the regulatory burden, cut red tape, and by about 2010 produced one of the better motivated, better rewarded, and more effective African public services. In the process, naturally, discretion became more limited than before and opportunities for chicanery, bribery, and all kinds of influence peddling were reduced.

But these important legal and procedural improvements were less salutary in altering the political culture of Rwanda than was the emphasis from 2004 on of zero tolerance for infractions. It became obvious to all that Kagame, and therefore the government, were serious about ending corruption. In 2004, all 503 members of the Rwandan judiciary, from top to bottom, were dismissed because of corruption.[20] The president of a state-owned bank was prosecuted for giving friends unsecured loans. Three years later, sixty-two police officers were sacked for soliciting bribes. According to the chair of the ombudsman's office, Rwanda became less corrupt as "we . . . removed corrupt leaders [and] added additional training and supervision."[21] In 2013, TI's Global Corruption Barometer reported that only 13 percent of Rwandese polled had paid a bribe within the previous two years (compared to 53 percent in Kenya, 57 percent in South Africa, 62 percent in Zimbabwe, and 7 percent in Switzerland and the United States).[22]

Most of all, once Kagame made his authoritarian will known, made humiliating examples of corrupt politicians, and began mercilessly to limit personal freedom throughout the entire public service, being "on the take" became highly dangerous for those both high and low. Positions and privileges could be forfeited, and were. Given the autocratic nature of the Kagame regime, altering the prevailing political culture was comparatively easy, especially over time. Even in a society three times the population of Singapore, determined leadership action against corruption could make a difference in comparatively short order.

When visiting Kigali some years ago, I asked one of my former Kennedy School students—a native Rwandan but someone who had grown up in Kinshasa—why there was so little evidence of crime. "He doesn't allow it," was her prompt answer.

As in Singapore, Kagame could and did explain that all Rwandans would be better off absent corrupt behavior. A poor country, Rwanda without corruption would become more hospitable and attractive to foreign investment. There would be no drag on GDP per capita. Better health care, enhanced educational opportunities, and improved infrastructure would be possible for all Rwandans if corrupt enrichment ceased to skew priorities.

Kagame understood that "you can't fight corruption from the bottom. You have to fight it from the top."[23] He therefore even banned his own relatives and kin of ministers from governmental employment. He showed no favor to longtime associates who appeared to be acting dishonestly and abusing his trust. As in our other cases, but more easily and clearly demonstrated in the cases of Rwanda and Singapore, visionary leaders are capable of reducing corrupt practices if they enunciate a clear and thorough program against corruption (always popular with citizens) and carry it out with determination and integrity, sparing no one.

Liberia

In terms of anticorruption perceptions, Liberia from 2004 had nowhere to go but up. In 2003, at the conclusion of fourteen years of brutal civil war, Liberia's main focus, first under an interim transitional government, was to restore order and to attempt to begin to revive Liberia economically, politically, and morally. For the preceding decade, mayhem, theft, and destruction had been Liberia's lot. Everybody who had a gun, or other ways of extorting revenue, was corrupt. Charles Taylor, who had come to power by force and then by a coerced election, acted autocratically. Integrity was hardly expected; being wildly corrupt and zero-sum was normal and expected. Under dire conditions, survival was the goal of most citizens. Elites close to Taylor and his enforcers grabbed what they could, and shared only with Taylor and "the system."

Ellen Johnson-Sirleaf, an American-educated former Liberian treasury and UNDP official, was elected president of Liberia in 2006. Her inaugural address spelled out a clear commitment to tolerate no corruption under her administration. Among her first acts were the discharging of virtually all hold-over civil servants in the ministry of finance; she promised a thorough investigation of allegations of embezzlement and graft within the ministry. Across the entire government, she dismissed 17,000 holdover civil servants.

Early on she enunciated an anticorruption strategy by:

1. Declaring her own assets;
2. Requiring her new appointees and all cabinet ministers to follow suit and publish lists of their own financial holdings and assets in the local press;
3. Issuing a tough code of conduct for all public servants;
4. Strengthening the independence of the General Auditing Commission;
5. Establishing the Liberian Anti-Corruption Commission;
6. Reforming the national public financial management system and promulgating the Public Finance Management Act;
7. Formulating a new, transparent, national budget process;
8. Agreeing to comply with the tough provisions of the Extractive Industries Transparency Initiative (EITI) and strictures contained in the regulation of diamond mining and transport according to the protocols of the Kimberley Initiative;
9. Bolstering the Public Procurement Commission to make bidding processes transparent and to erect new barriers against kickbacks;
10. Paying Liberia's civil servants their wages, something that had not happened for months or years;
11. Turning the lights on. In order to gain credibility and build confidence nationally, she strove mightily to bring electric power availability back first to Monrovia and later to other cities and towns;
12. Turning to external advisors and donors for assistance in building the capacity of the Liberian government to manage assets, scrutinize expenditures, minimize waste, and curtail fraud.

Innovative during Johnson-Sirleaf's first presidency was a special oversight system that shared authority for financial management among local officials and external advisors. Within each ministry and state-owned enterprise were local officials and foreign overseers, all of whom had jointly to sign expenditure permits and contract approvals. Because that unusual derogation of national sovereignty succeeded in limiting peculation and mismanagement, it was no longer needed in 2010, and the system was dismantled.

This dual control mechanism included:

1. The centralization of revenue collection and expenditure disbursement within the ministry of finance and the Liberian Central

Bank. The IMF selected the head of the Central Bank, ensuring that transparency and fiscal accountability standards were maintained. The bank was further staffed with outside technocrats recruited by the IMF.

2. All national budgeting and expenditure management practices were revamped, strengthened, and made public.
3. Competitive bidding practices were overhauled and upgraded.
4. The Anti-Corruption Commission (ACC) was charged with preventing corruption in the private as well as the official public arenas, and with devising new control mechanisms.
5. Outside assistance was given to the General Auditing Commission and the reformed Contracts and Monopolies Commission.
6. An overall effort was begun to build capacity within the public service for more effective and knowledgeable administration, including an ethics component.[24]

All of these initiatives markedly increased the positive perceptions locally and externally of Johnson-Sirleaf's gradual victory, on behalf of all Liberians, against the scourge of corruption. As Liberia slowly became less corrupt, so too did outside investors (including China) begin to exploit Liberia's mineral resources, harvest its timber, and revive what had been a moribund economy (potentially bringing corrupt temptations in their train). National revenues increased enormously, from a very low base. National debts were paid or reduced. As prosperity increased, so Johnson-Sirleaf's anticorruption efforts became more widely appreciated and more necessary.

Donor-funded efforts made a major difference in strengthening Liberia's anticorruption performance from 2004 to 2014. According to the CPI, Liberia's score grew from a very low 8 to a respectable 37, a 29-point improvement. But in 2014 that still left Liberia only 94th in rank (along with Egypt, Gabon, Colombia, Armenia, and Panama), behind Benin, Burkina Faso, and Zambia, and ahead of Algeria, China, and Mexico. In 2015, it had vaulted upward to 83rd place, with a score, still, of 37. According to the World Bank Control of Corruption measurement scheme, Liberia also started with a raw score of 8 but grew to 34 in 2012 and then slipped to 28 in 2013, putting it well behind African performers such as Botswana (80), Cape Verde (75), Mauritius (66), Namibia (65), Lesotho (64), and Zambia (44), but ahead of many others and being similar in score to a several of the middle-ranking African countries.

As with Georgia and several of the other cases in this chapter, manifest political will and uncompromising leadership were major factors in improving Liberia's anticorruption performance over the 2004–2014 period. Even though Johnson-Sirleaf's personal integrity has been questioned and issues have arisen over possible nepotism involving her sons, Liberia (pre-Ebola) was perceived as a less and less corrupt African country because of strong and committed leadership, an abundance of demonstrated political will, and Johnson-Sirleaf's manifest willingness to ride herd on those in her government who would have preferred to act corruptly and "take a little." The actions of the Anti-Corruption Commission also helped demonstrably, but that body could not have proceeded very far without supportive backing from the president.

Johnson-Sirleaf's presidency has not produced a perfect Liberia or a Liberia without corruption. The police were still regarded as wildly corrupt in 2016. Caused partially by low wages, traffic policemen still solicit bribes at randomly erected checkpoints. Crime victims have to pay to summon investigative personnel or even to register a case. Suspected criminals often have been suspected of being able to bribe their way out of custody or of being in close cahoots with the police themselves.[25]

Global Witness (a London-based NGO) further highlighted a major case of Liberian grand corruption in 2016 that implicated a well-connected local lawyer and chair of the country's ruling party. Arrested by Liberian authorities, he is accused of paying bribes on behalf of a British-based mining company. Said one observer, "When the law got in their way in Liberia, they paid bribes to change it."[26] These bribes to Liberian officials responsible for approving permits to prospect and to mine iron ore in lucrative concessions amounted to at least $125,000, and probably much more. According to emails and cables seen by Global Witness, there was clear "evidence of serial bribery in Liberia." Moreover, the mining company "was able to bribe many of Liberia's top politicians" with ease.[27] Johnson-Sirleaf's government said that it would investigate and prosecute the case with vigor.

Absent Johnson-Sirleaf's determined leadership since 2003, and the restored pride and sense of renewed political culture that she gave to post-Taylor Liberia, corruption would have continued at much higher levels, been more widely accepted as inevitable across the postconflict country, and would have proven much more difficult to temper and reform.

Macedonia

According to the CPI, Macedonia's scores improved by 18 points, from 27 to 45, between 2004 and 2014 (well before the riots and attacks on the government in 2015). In the WBCC compilation, Macedonia advanced from 38 to 59 between 2004 and 2013, a 21 point gain. Globally, however, Macedonia was only the 64th best country in the CPI rankings, after Ghana, Cuba, and Oman and just before Turkey and Kuwait. In the Balkans, it sat well behind Slovenia, Slovakia, and Croatia, but ahead of Montenegro and Serbia. It was also judged less corrupt than Greece. Macedonia's population numbers about 2 million, 25 percent of whom are Albanian by language and 64 percent of whom are Slavic-speaking Macedonians. Its annual GDP per capita is about $11,000.

Recent Transparency International examinations of corruption in Macedonia belie the undeniable numerical improvements reported by both of the major corruption measurement methodologies. Public opinion surveys in 2013 indicated a high degree of pessimism: 41 percent of those surveyed said that corruption had increased over previous years while 29 percent believed that it had remained the same.[28] Many Macedonians complained in 2013 that the country's well-crafted laws against corruption had not been enforced and that too few cases of corruption had been prosecuted.[29] (The protestors of 2015 echoed those concerns.) There was a widespread feeling, too, that the judiciary was tainted and took orders from the executive. Public trust of national institutions was low. The Group of States against Corruption (GRECO) suggests that too many members of the government and Parliament enjoy immunity from criminal prosecution, which permits corruption.

Given civil society and citizen concerns about Macedonian levels of corruption, explaining the country's numerical improvement on both indexes must reflect Macedonia's relatively high level of perceived corruption in 2004, when it ranked 97th of 145 (CPI), well below both Bosnia and Serbia.[30] Subsequently, Macedonia:

1. Created a Supreme Audit Office to supervise all electoral spending.
2. Created the State Commission for the Prevention of Corruption to monitor political party expenditures and state enterprises and to report on illicit dealings and expenditures.
3. Empowered the State Election Commission and the Broadcasting Council to oversee election procedures and party advertising during elections.
4. Enacted a strong Law on the Prevention of Corruption in 2004. Inter alia, that law permits the arrest of members of Parliament who are caught "in the act."
5. Amended that law in 2011 to strengthen it and to introduce new sections sanctioning passive and active bribery, with stiff penalties for both. Passive bribery was defined as the request or receipt of a gift or benefit in order to perform or not perform an official act. Active bribery, according to statute, is the promising, giving, and offering of a gift or benefit to an official for the performance or failure to perform an official duty. A provision prohibiting the bribing of foreign officials was strengthened, irrespective of whether the offenses occurred at home or abroad. Bribery in the private sector was criminalized, as well.

6. Revoked parliamentary immunity in notable cases in 2007 for parliamentarians and a former prime minister accused of abuse of power and corruption.

7. Reinforced constitutional conflict of interest guidelines and produced a new law on conflict of interest in 2007 that prohibits bribery and inappropriate receiving of gifts. It further mandates the declaration by all public officials of their assets, income, liabilities, and potential conflicts of interest. It defines the last offense as a conflict between public duties and the "private interests of the official, where the official has a private interest which impacts or can impact on the performance of his/her public authorisations and duties."[31] This is the fundamental legislation against corruption.

8. Beginning in 2012, the State Commission for Prevention of Corruption systematically verified all statements of conflict of interest and declarations of personal wealth and pursued those public officials and parliamentarians who have been slow to declare or report. It also began to investigate allegedly corrupt public officials upon receiving complaints from whistleblowers and other citizens.

9. Imposed special extra 70 percent taxes to penalize "unexplained enrichment" by public officials. (That was an unusually innovative proposal.) The national Public Revenue Office examines all declarations of assets and questions that self-reporting, when necessary.

10. Enacted in 2010 a Code of Ethics for Members of the Government and the Public Office Holders. Public officers include those in positions of public trust at the local authority and municipal government level (eighty-four cities and towns) as well as those active nationally. One mayor of a major town extolled this effort because it involved municipal councilors, associations of citizens, business representatives, and media personnel.[32]

11. Broke major people-smuggling rings, arresting migrant traffickers and their police accomplices. A key migrant smuggling route goes from Greece across Macedonia to the rest of Europe, in recent years transporting hundreds of thousands of Syrians, Sudanese, Afghans, and Pakistanis.

12. Suppressed police corruption through action by the Ministry of Internal Affairs, especially its Sector for Internal Control and Professional Standards. That sector pursues complaints made by citizens against the police. It also prevents corruption by training police and builds upon the Code of Police Ethics of 2004. Reported corrupt acts by police personnel decreased between 2009 and 2012.[33]

13. Stepped up anticorruption training for public servants, public prosecutors, and judges.[34]

Despite all of this worthy effort and legislation, Transparency International's Corruption Barometer Survey in 2013 captured dissatisfaction with Macedonia's progress against corruption. So have other opinion polls and reports by European bodies. Global Integrity criticized Macedonia for shutting down its free press.[35] But a desire on the part of the Macedonian populace for faster and stronger action against corrupt practices need not vitiate the CPI and WBCC scoring methods. Macedonia has in fact introduced major initiatives, enunciated above, to curb corruption. Those initiatives have strengthened the perception of improvement in the battle against corruption without necessarily demonstrating that Macedonia has conquered widespread tendencies to benefit from graft, bribery, and influence peddling.

Nothing in the process of coping with corruption was as important for both Macedonia and Montenegro, however, as the possibility of being admitted into the European Union and joining NATO. Reducing corruption is one of the key criteria for admission into the EU and NATO and the driving force for all major policy initiatives in both countries, as was the case in such still notoriously corrupt countries as Bulgaria and Romania. Without the pull of Europe, neither Macedonia nor Montenegro (see the following section) would have battled corruption so intensely nor improved so dramatically through 2014.

As a Norwegian NGO concluded in 2015, "The issue of anticorruption reform can be characterised as the strategy for Europeanisation of the country. With the adoption of the State Programme, the country has fulfilled a part of the political criteria required by the EU, but it largely remains at the declarative level only." Further, wrote the Norwegians, "The anti-corruption legal framework is relatively good. However, the high number of legislative acts has led to a fragmented legal system that makes implementation and monitoring difficult. Loopholes in the legislation have hampered the fight against corruption. A regulatory framework laying down the ethical principles applicable to public officials other than civil servants is absent . . . [and] security sector personnel are not governed by civil service rules but by general public service rules in which ethical standards are weakly regulated. In fact, prevention is better organised and perceived as more important than prosecuting and repressing corruption in the country. The weak independence of the judiciary remains a matter of serious concern affecting the fight against corruption."[36]

Macedonia managed to improve some external perceptions of corrupt behavior by creating strong, new institutions on paper, and by permitting a well-functioning office of ombudsman to receive complaints, act energetically to resolve them, and to pursue allegedly corrupt politicians and officials. But, as much as it improved in terms of perceptions (to satisfy Europe), Macedonia obviously failed to alter the opinions of its own skeptical and aggrieved citizens.

In 2015, the CPI ranked Macedonia 66th, a slight slippage, with a score of 42. That ranked Macedonia below Montenegro and South Africa, but ahead of Bulgaria and Turkey. A European Commission investigation suggested that Macedonia was not yet ready to accede to the European Union. It questioned the independence of the police and the courts from the executive, and the government's effective control over the supposedly independent State Commission for the Prevention of Corruption.

Intercepted (and leaked) covert wireless transmissions implicated sixteen officials and politicians in abuses of power and of corruption in public procurement, urban planning, political party financing, and public employment. These same sixteen also interfered with the independence of the judiciary, the media, and elections. The nation's press had lost its freedom, as well.[37] Thus, as much as Macedonia had improved in perceptions between 2004 and 2014, the fundamental character of the Balkan regime was, in 2016, still more corrupt than not.

Montenegro

Montenegro was the unlikely 5th "most improved" country on the CPI list, 2004–2014, with a rise in scores from 27 to 42, a total of 15. It increased 18 points on the WBCC list, from 33 to 51, where it also had the 6th best improvement ranking, just ahead of Zambia. Yet, in 2014, Montenegro only ranked 76th of 174 countries on the CPI, below Romania, Senegal, and Swaziland, and above Sâo Tomé, Serbia, and Tunisia. By 2015, it was rated more highly than Macedonia, achieving 61st place in the rankings with a score of 44. It was scored the same as Italy and South Africa. It was also invited to join NATO in 2016.

Despite these scores and ranks, Montenegro remains heavily dependent economically (and to some extent politically) on smuggling, money laundering, drug and people trafficking, the financing of terrorism, and other well-organized criminal pursuits. As the European Commission reported in 2012, "Drug trafficking remains a major concern since the country is a transit area on the smuggling route to and from the EU."[38]

Montenegro has been ruled heavy-handedly from before the breakup of the Socialist Yugoslav Federation and before and after Montenegro's split from Serbia, of which it was a mostly autonomous section from 1992 to 2006. Its population is now about 703,000, of whom 45 percent are Montenegrins and the remainder Serbs, Bosniaks, and Albanians. In 2013, its annual GDP per capita was $15,000.

As indicated in the previous section, Montenegro's remarkable numerical decrease in the perception of national corruption reflects strenuous efforts to improve its candidacy for admission someday to the European Union. Success for its candidacy depends heavily on reducing organized crime and corruption and increasing the prosecution of war offenses.[39]

As in Macedonia and Georgia, Montenegro tried to strengthen its chances of EU and NATO accession by:

1. Adopting a new (2013) Action Plan for the Fight against Corruption and Organized Crime. In 2011, the Directorate for Anti-Corruption Initiatives (DCAI) was placed under the Ministry of Justice. In its first year, it received seventy complaints and acted on twenty-seven of them, sending the investigation reports to the police for prosecution. It also began a program to raise awareness about corruption among citizens. Four public property administrators went to prison because they abused their official positions. A customs official was jailed for bribery. Sixteen municipal officials, managers of public companies, policemen, and a judge were incarcerated for bribery. Even so, said a European Commission report, the number of final convictions, with the confiscation of assets, remained "too low."[40]

2. Amending its national election law in 2011 and 2014 to strengthen electoral procedures and safeguards to meet European Union and Organization of Security and Cooperation in Europe requirements for fairness and transparency. The integrity and accuracy of voter lists still remain a work in progress, however, as does the effectiveness and probity of the State Election Commission.

3. Enacting a Law on Financing Political Parties in 2011 that is supposed to regulate funding and end corruption in this critical area. That law forbids material and financial assistance from foreign entities, trade unions, state-owned enterprises, public institutions, religious bodies, nongovernmental organizations, casinos, gambling houses, persons or bodies being investigated for corruption, and more. The State Audit Office is required to scrutinize all political party financing, as in Macedonia, with stiff penalties for infractions. Major irregularities continue to be noted, however.[41]

4. Making "abuse of state resources" a criminal offense.

5. Reforming the entire national public administration, in accord with EU mandates. New methods of recruiting civil servants were initiated, as were controls over the management of the public service.

6. Introducing new laws to strengthen judicial impartiality and independence and to meet European expectations. In particular, new safeguards were enacted in 2012 to safeguard against political influence and to require written competency tests for all new judges. Renowned lawyers replaced legislators on the Judicial Council, which approves judicial appointments. Transparency and accountability for

all legal procedures were enhanced. A judicial training center was established. A European-led upgrading of judicial statistical efforts was also introduced to improve reliability and to strengthen transparency. Trial backlogs were reduced. Labor laws were also introduced to protect whistleblowers in 2011. In this key area, the impact, expectations, and role of the European Commission were paramount.[42] However, nothing very much happened fundamentally to alter Montenegro's high-level political corruption.

7. Improving access to information via amended legislation in 2012, thus bolstering transparency.

8. Introducing a code of conduct in 2012 for civil servants, state administrators, the president of the country, all parliamentarians, judges on the state constitutional and supreme courts, and all prosecutors. The code prohibits public servants from using official documents and state resources while pursuing private matters and requires those same officials to report infractions by others. (This code strikes at the heart of corruption, but is only enforceable with consummate political will.)

9. Amending the existing law on Prevention of Conflict of Interests in 2011 to cover all public officials, elected or appointed, adding severe penalties. Public officials are forbidden from simultaneously holding both public offices and positions in business corporations or nongovernmental entities. All public officials and their families must also declare their incomes and property holdings. They are not allowed to receive significant gifts. The Commission for Prevention of Conflict of Interests supervises the implementation of this law and is supposedly independent. Its members are elected by Parliament. They can decide on violations of the law, give opinions on perceived conflicts, determine the value of gifts, and comment on draft laws.

10. Creating a Public Procurement Commission in 2012 to oversee all tenders and contracts and to reduce graft. This area had been lightly regulated prior to 2012, and the Montenegrin public had no understanding of how easy it was to violate the rules in this important, but shadowy, sector. Massive potential for abuse obviously existed, so these reforms constituted at least a beginning in the battle for integrity in procurement.[43]

All of these new legal and regulatory reforms clearly enhanced Montenegro's ability to reduce corruption nationally. Some may have been responsive to indigenously derived democratic impulses (Montenegro has but a rudimentary civil society), but the driving force was Europe. Without the pull of accession to the EU, incentives for anticorruption efforts would have been less urgent, less compelling, and less effective. As in Macedonia, external standards, external review processes, and the magnetic pull of joining Europe palpably helped to begin the long climb of Montenegro and Macedonia from the corrupt doldrums to more elevated perceptions of progress. Being limited in population, too, made leadership a dominant factor in both cases and in the survival of anticorruption efforts of all kinds.

Equally important, Montenegro is an autocratically administered state. Thus, whatever the Montenegrin prime minister advocated in order to smooth a path into Europe usually occurred. (Most of the time since the early 1990s the prime minister or president has been Milo Djukanovic.) The pull of Europe and NATO and the push of political will helped to create the perception of improvement that was reflected in Montenegro's raised scores.

Nonetheless, the same Norwegian NGO, also investigating Montenegro, concluded pessimistically that "decision-making powers [were] concentrated at the apex of the administration where the minister [was] the only person responsible for approving and authorising any expenditure, with no real scheme for delegation or for managing delegated powers. Under these circumstances it is very unlikely that a culture of financial management and responsibility will emerge. Therefore the internal financial control tends to be formulaic, with little effect on the control of corruption."[44]

How Best to Improve

A review of the five cases discussed in this chapter, together with an analysis of the well-known and well-examined premier cases of Singapore, Hong Kong, and Croatia, suggests that anticorruption efforts rarely succeed without exemplary efforts on the part of state leaderships and political elites. The exertion of political will is critical.

To lower perceived levels of corruption, it is necessary to cut off the head of the snake—to exercise political will in demonstrable ways, especially against those near the very top of public life. As President Kagame of Rwanda said, "You have to go for the people at the top and make sure people know that life can equally be good without corruption."[45] Grand rhetoric, as in Georgia and Liberia, is helpful, but more significant is the kind of public actions against corrupt personnel that Lee Kuan Yew undertook and that the ICAC and a comparable Singaporean commission demonstrated. Citizens notice when their leaders begin to operate on behalf of national rather than private interests. When there are educational campaigns, as in Hong Kong and, in a different manner in Liberia and Georgia, they can be effective too.

The five "most improved" nation-states and places such as Chile, Estonia, and Uruguay have streamlined their regulatory and bureaucratic procedures, simplified "doing business" in World Bank terms, put procurement on e-platforms (enhancing transparency), greatly narrowed opportunities for personal discretion (and thus corruption), imposed asset disclosure requirements and monitored the returns closely, restricted political donations, moved from patronage- to merit-based appointment systems, supported free media operations, reduced or abolished (Estonia) tariffs, and strengthened political institutions capable of curtailing corruption more generally.

The dismissal of an entire police force or a raft of judges provides a further kind of demonstration effect. Important as well is the introduction or reconfiguration of existing or innovative new institutions, as in Montenegro and Macedonia. (The pull of Europe, and EU requirements—especially its Cooperation and Verification Mechanism—were powerful in producing upward and sustainable change in Georgia and perhaps Croatia, but only initially motivated Bulgaria, Macedonia, and Montenegro. Bulgaria still shows little lasting control of corruption.) Transforming legal frameworks and empowering anticorruption entities, auditors general, and the judiciary are critical, too. But domestic agency—indigenous leadership action—is much more instructive and transformative.

All of these actions altered prevailing political cultures for the good, in Georgia and Estonia's post-Soviet cases dramatically, and shifted all of the cases from particularism toward true ethical universalism. But in no instance were these necessary innovations sufficient. The exercise of political will in every case, even in Uruguay's, was essential. Nothing succeeds so well or so sustainably as determined and tough-minded leadership, guiding and pushing all of the instruments and personalities of a state to operate on behalf of the people—entirely in and for the public interest.

VII

Nordic, Antipodean, and Other Exceptionalism

HOW DID ANTICORRUPTION TAKE ROOT?

Ever since the Corruption Perceptions Index (CPI) was introduced in 1995, the list of the perceived least corrupt ten nation-states has almost always been led by the Nordic nations, New Zealand, Switzerland, and Singapore. In 2015, as in most recent years going back to 1995, Denmark was anointed the globe's most noncorrupt state, followed by Finland, Sweden, New Zealand, the Netherlands, Norway, Switzerland, Singapore, Canada, and tied for tenth spot, Germany, Luxembourg, and the United Kingdom. All of the top ten had scores in the 80s and low 90s. That is, Denmark, with a top score of 91 in 2015 and a single point more in 2014, and Finland, one point lower in 2015, do not score a perfect 100, but in 2015 and 2014 both countries had high scores and (perceptibly) slightly less corruption than Sweden and New Zealand—and the rest of the top ten.[1] Earlier, Finland and New Zealand had often led the anticorruption brigade. The World Bank's Control of Corruption Indicator (WBCC) tracks Denmark, the other Nordics, and the others essentially in the same manner from 1996, always at or very close to the top. So do the much newer World Justice and Open Budget indexes. The 2015 Legatum Prosperity Index also highly ranks most of the same countries: Norway, Switzerland, Denmark, New Zealand, Sweden, Canada, Australia, the Netherlands, Finland, Ireland (a surprise), the United States, and Iceland, in order from number one to number twelve.[2] It is evident that in terms of winning the battle against corruption (and much else, such as providing higher standards of living), there is something exceptional about these top-ranking noncorrupt countries. President

Obama showers praises on the Nordics: "If only everyone could be like the Scandinavians, this would all be easy."[3]

Since these scores and rankings are based on opinions (see chapter 2) of practiced observers, they follow or accord well with popular views of the lack of corruption in the Nordic nations, New Zealand, and the other top ten countries. (Australia and Iceland ranked 13th in 2015 on the CPI.) But those high rankings over many years should not be taken as suggesting that the top ten or top twelve countries harbor no corrupt cabinet ministers, customs officers, police inspectors, postal employees, or corporate executives. (Even Finland had a major corruption scandal in 2016.) Nor should the positive scores indicate that each of the countries has banished greed and all impetus to maximize self-interest. Instead, the national top rankings, especially those which have been sustained over two decades, show that in those special countries corrupt dealings are more suspect than they routinely are elsewhere, that the public anticipates few, if any, daily confrontations with bribery, extortion, and graft, and—conclusively—that corruption is far less an approved societal norm in such polities than it is in the bottom 100 countries on the CPI.[4] In the top ten and possibly the top fifty nation-states scored by the CPI, being caught committing a corrupt offense is not only criminal. It is shameful and embarrassing in ways that are less well internalized in countries perceived internationally and locally to be much more corrupt. A visitor to Nigeria expects to be asked routinely for a bribe. Not so in Denmark or Canada.

The globe's less corrupt countries have embraced "ethical universalism." Citizens of such favored places are surprised (but not astonished) when they encounter instances of sharp dealing, or when the media reports that a public official has taken unfair advantage of his or her position. The plague of corruption occasions few outbreaks within these favored countries compared to constant irruptions of scandal in those many benighted nations where corruption is normal, expected, persistent, and seemingly untouchable.

The Danes need not be better persons than Nigerians. Indeed, the Danes, the New Zealanders, the Finns, the Swedes, and so on during the eighteenth and nineteenth centuries were as wildly corrupt and corrupted for their time as are today's Nigerians. What brought about improved anticorruption performance in those nations before and during the first decades of the twentieth century?

Today, the Nordics display very high levels of trust, are thoroughly Protestant, wealthy with comparatively low levels of inequality, well-educated, and relatively homogeneous.[5] Learning whether any or all of these criteria were important over time is relevant. So is discovering how and why the Nordics and others gradually transformed themselves from corrupt outposts to nations of probity and minimal corruption.[6] Answering such questions will assist our quest for best practices and offer lessons to be learned by today's corrupt countries. Although there are no magic bullets, and the paths from corruption to noncorruption in the (now) better places are disparate and diverse, we can learn from their formative experiences. Likewise, the causes of the conversion of political entities devoted in earlier times to corrupt pursuits into places that came eventually to eschew such behavior are telling.

The Danish Saga

Unlike all of the other successful cases, Denmark's transition to an anticorrupt society resulted strikingly from the replacement of "protodemocratic" tendencies in the seventeenth century with an absolute monarchy that could, and did, insist on loyalty and obedience to the Crown—and no diversion of resources that by right belonged to the king. Although it took two full centuries to reduce corruption among the king's bureaucrats from a common to a rare occurrence, a series of gradual reforms over the decades inculcated the antibribery, antigraft norms that are now fundamental to the Danish community and to Danish political life.

From the late fourteenth to the early sixteenth centuries, what are now Denmark, Finland, Iceland, Norway, and Sweden were united in succession to the Vikings and other plunderers as the Kalmar Union, dominated by the Danes. At the time, it was the largest political jurisdiction in Europe, its borders extending from Greenland to Russia to Germany. Central and Northern Sweden (including Finland) then seceded in 1523 and Denmark henceforth ruled a domain that extended from north of Hamburg to the farthest reaches of Greenland, including Iceland, Norway, and southern Sweden.

The Danish king during the sixteenth century was also the secular leader of the Lutheran state church after 1536. As the monarch of Denmark, henceforth, he was responsible for the well-being of his subjects and parishioners. This top-down model of governance and formative institution-building introduced new components of statecraft and incipient bureaucratic creativity that both made possible and were required to win Denmark's many military escapades.[7]

Because Denmark and Sweden, global powers of the day, were often at pike's end from the sixteenth through the eighteenth centuries, it was essential in both cases to collect taxes and other revenues efficiently to pay for their military ambitions. Civil administrators were required, especially collectors of taxes. As earlier in England, the nobles, landowners, and common people of both jurisdictions, particularly those in Denmark, were prepared to provide payments willingly to the state only in exchange for stability, the rule of law, the provision of infrastructure, and a share in the glories of monarchical success. Citizens had to pay to maintain a government and to assure military victories, but the rulers in return were obliged to govern well, provide security (though military might), and remain legitimate by refraining as much as possible from abusing their leadership privileges.

It was after 1660 in Denmark that these varied early-modern European experiences were organized into a distinct method of governance. Until that point, the Danish king had ruled his vast realm with the consent and cooperation of a wealthy land-holding nobility and what for the time was a nascent urban middle class. The nobles until 1660 held the majority of the kingdom's offices, collected taxes, imposed a personal rule on their own districts, and largely interfered as best they could with the prerogatives of the Crown. But, after a resounding national military loss to Sweden in 1658 (Denmark was compelled to give up what is now much of southern Sweden) and a serious economic crisis, King Frederick III became the first hereditary sovereign of the reconfigured Denmark, the better to resist further losses to Sweden and to revive the power of the Danish state. This chain of absolute leadership, possibly the most complete at that time in Europe, lasted until 1848–1849.

From 1658 onward, the exercise of enlightened political will was critical to Denmark's eventual emergence as a modern, well-governed state. It was an absolutist political will of a Hobbesian kind that embodied a social contract between ruler and ruled. The king derived his authority ultimately from the people and was thus required to promote "the common good," as derived from listening to the wishes of his subjects. "The autocrat is expected to work for the general good as formulated in free public debate."[8]

Frederick III and his lineal successors sought from the start of absolutism to reduce the remaining power of the nobles and, increasingly, to boost the authority and extend the reach of the monarchy. To do so—which took at least a century—kings came to rely upon an administrative service that was directly paid by the monarchy and was made loyal to it and not, as previously, to the decentralized aristocracy. Possibly for the first time in Europe, a Danish public service (parallel developments were occurring in Sweden) was created that was directly run by and for the kings of the day. The king hired and fired, demanded professional attitudes and performance (an innovation), and introduced what became a meritocracy during the eighteenth century. In time, this meant that Denmark was run by "bourgeois bureaucrats," not aristocrats or persons who owed their positions to their lineage or their class. "Civil servants of non-noble origin would be more likely to be loyal to the king" and do his bidding rather than that of some regional lord.[9] Most of all, these bureaucrats were dependent upon income from the king's employ and therefore more easily monitored and kept in line. But to ensure administrative loyalty and positive performance, the king established an office of chief prosecutor to ferret out and investigate any bureaucrats who abused their offices or withheld tax payments.

The professional and merit-based qualifications for the new bureaucracy were enhanced in the eighteenth century when all judges for the first time had to be law graduates of the University of Copenhagen, a requirement that was formally codified in 1821. Increasingly, after the middle of the eighteenth century, law graduates began to assume most civil service positions, and by the beginning of the nineteenth century, the Danish public service had become thoroughly merit-based.

There were rough periods along the way. Corruption may have been already ingrained in Denmark as in other European states (especially in well-documented England) by 1660.[10] A chancellor to the monarch busily profited during the late seventeenth century from the sale of clerical and secular positions, from accepting bribes, and from peculation. (He was imprisoned for life.) One of his eighteenth century successors solicited bribes, and was banished. King Frederick IV sold offices in the realm for cash in order to finance wars with Sweden from 1700 to 1720 and the construction of central administrative facilities in Copenhagen. But only a minority of public positions was ever purchased; the king still demanded competence from the buyers, offices sold were only transferred to that person and not to his heirs, and incompetent buyers could still be dismissed by the king or his chief administrative head. These procedures, and the prosecution of miscreants, such as the two chancellors, helped, over time, to lower expectations of corruption and to develop an ethos within which corruption did not become a norm. So did the oaths of fealty to the monarch that each bureaucrat was required to swear, many in person. They constituted a form of contract, long in use. Each oath-taker understood, moreover, that he had to follow the king's laws and guidelines, behave honestly, and work diligently. Avoiding corruption was not specified, but was implied. According to a leading authority on these developments, "The intentional moves . . . after 1660 to create a corps of bureaucrats loyal to the king and with formal qualifications . . . over the years contributed to a state governed by law."[11]

Denmark's development of a political culture that barred corrupt activity was also greatly assisted by its early codification of, and then adherence to, a framework of laws. As early as 1683, Denmark became a legal entity, that is, a polity governed by laws rather than by mere kingly fiat. A decade later, several laws were promulgated that severely punished civil servants tempted by disloyalty and the rewards of corrupt practice. For public servants, acceptance of bribes and "gifts" was explicitly banned in 1676; that prohibition was made more extensive in 1700. Forgery became a criminal offense and embezzlements were considered thefts from the Crown, with a life prison sentence for offenders. Later, more officials were included under these restrictions, especially customs personnel.

Under King Christian V at the end of the seventeenth century, new guidelines for the conduct of bureaucrats and judges were promulgated. Several kinds of public servants, and all judges, had to deposit sureties or find guarantors to repay the Crown in case of misbehavior, which included succumbing to corruption. Christian V specified that judges would be appointed on the basis of their high qualifications, not in accord with their class, and that they should strictly follow the law at all times.

These innovations presumably contributed to the legitimacy of the absolute monarchy. Tyranny appears to have been tempered with monarchical modesty, an insistence on what passed for good governance in that era, and a certain amount of compassion for citizens. The kings of eighteenth century Denmark also encouraged a reasonable level of participation on the part of their subjects. Citizens' voices were enabled when Denmark's king, following other European regimes, began to receive petitions of complaint, or supplications, from his constituents. By 1799, the civil administration, on behalf of the king, was receiving 12,000 petitions annually, many more than at the beginning of the next century. Some of those petitions complained about the conduct of civil servants, some about tax collectors and customs officials, and some about governance deficiencies. By so giving their subjects a chance to express opinions on many critical subjects, kings began to be responsive to public opinion.[12] Doing so presumably increased social trust as well as monarchical legitimacy throughout the kingdom.

These important advances did not mean that eighteenth and nineteenth century Denmark was free from corrupt behavior. Nevertheless, the foremost researcher of corruption in these Danish eras found relatively few offenders (a mere 203 cases) between 1740 and 1936, when public servants were dismissed for offenses that could be construed as corrupt.[13] Yet, there was what for Denmark was an epidemic of embezzlement (borrowings from public trust funds) and corruption (a little bribe taking) after the disastrous Napoleonic wars (Denmark was on the losing side, became insolvent, and ceded Norway to Sweden), which the monarchy took seriously and prosecuted assertively. This awareness of and concerted attack on corruption followed many petitions or complaints from citizens, the dispatch of representatives of the chancellery and the judiciary to outlying cities and provinces to discover irregularities, audits of official books everywhere (very telling), and an overall scrutiny of affairs of state that had not been possible to maintain during the continental wars.[14]

Corruption, as it had been for two centuries, was a threat to kingly rule, and no amnesties or special dispensations were granted, even to previously loyal bureaucrats. This strong line against embezzlement and other forms of corruption secured the monarchy's legitimacy, restored the integrity of the public service, reassured citizens, and reinforced the evolving Danish norm of integrity and honesty. New laws were enacted that centralized the state's fiscal administration and led to the publishing, for the first time, of the state budget and thus increased financial transparency. In 1840 (improved and extended in 1866), a new penal code contained provisions specifying misconduct in office and relevant penalties. By 1861, civil servants were receiving fixed salaries and the promise of a pension. From that time forward, public officials had even greater incentives than before to behave well and not to abuse their positions. Thus, after about 1830, by which time Denmark had righted itself and re-established the norm that corrupt practices were wrong, and from roughly 1860 onwards, the country experienced a refreshing absence of corruption (or corruption discovered) that has continued to the present day.

Political will and determined leadership were important ingredients in this multi-century successful endeavor to delegitimize corruption in one of the key Scandinavian states. Without a succession of strongly principled monarchs to demand adherence to service standards on the part of their bureaucratic establishment, and without a sense (as in modern Singapore) that the very authority of the state (and the monarchy) would be undermined if the king's servants abused the public for personal gain, a sense that enhanced public trust (and a public's willingness to supply taxes and warrior power) were essential even to run an absolute kingdom and be successful, and a sense that corruption was disloyal, Denmark might have experienced much more graft and embezzlement across many more decades than it did. Moreover, the kings of Denmark listened to their people more than other monarchs elsewhere, thus building even more trust and credibility.

By the nineteenth century, Danes had begun an important shift away from thinking of themselves as belonging to one or another "estate," such as the nobles or the peasants, and had begun to conceive of themselves as a "people" or a "nation" of like-minded speakers of the Danish tongue. Along with this national feeling came a highly developed sense of social cohesion that helped to inhibit corrupt practices. Protestantism probably influenced outcomes as well, as did high levels of literacy, comparatively high income levels, ethnic and linguistic homogeneity, and the smallish (and reduced) size of the kingdom. But what is striking is that Danish rulers and Danish citizens alike early came to embrace a preference for probity in public office. This preference seems to stem from attitudes toward the responsibilities of office holders that were inculcated from above in the centuries after 1660, and which were bolstered during a crackdown in the post-Napoleonic era. A robust, long-evolved, political culture and incipient embrace of ethical universalism came to infuse Danes even before they fully enjoyed democracy, which arrived on the backs of widespread civic protests and a liberal constitution in 1849, well after an abhorrence of corrupt practice had become an emerging civic norm.[15]

This abhorrence deepened throughout the remainder of the nineteenth century as democratic practices evolved and the small country became smaller (after the loss in battle to Prussia of the Duchies of Schleswig and Holstein in 1864) and more homogeneous and Nordic (having forfeited its

German speakers). Schooling, free and universal at the elementary level from 1814, shifted at upper levels by mid-century from being in German and Latin to education in the Danish vernacular. The state church also began running itself democratically. Revivalism, an assertion of folk or individual humanistic forms of Protestantism, also arose in opposition to the state Lutheran establishment in Denmark before 1850 (and in Sweden even later). This deepening and extending of a Danish identity and an emphasis on the nation's cultural heritage was in part propelled by the creation of populist folk high schools with their emphasis on civic virtues rather than state organization, funding, and control. (Danes also feared Prussian imperialism, the destruction of the Danish state, and potential Germanization emanating from the newly consolidated power on the Continent.)[16]

Denmark's greatest contemporary exponent of the Danish "cause" sought to replace state paternalism with "the hegemony of the people's spirit."[17] The consequent growth in the nineteenth century of an agricultural cooperative movement stemmed in part from this new populism and from populist assertions of a nascent social democratic nationalism that led to parliamentary dominance by a political party representative of the country's peasants—the "folk" of Denmark. All of these popular expressions of a modernizing Danish identity helped to grow social trust and fortify a suspicion of any practices (such as bribe taking) that undermined the emerging democratic political culture. It left less room than earlier for pursuits that were associated with privilege and advantage-taking by elites and that undermined the embryonic Danish embrace of a corruption-free political environment.

The Swedes, the Norse

The Swedish route to the same societal result occurred, and over essentially the same time period, in a very different manner. Since either Denmark or Sweden governed Norway until 1920, and since Sweden controlled Finland until 1809, the gradual development of anticorrupt norms in both of those modern countries may be explained by their nurturing early experiences under one or both dispensations. Iceland's effective anticorruption political culture may also be attributed to its long centuries under first Norwegian and then Danish rule (effectively until 1885, with full independence in 1918); Iceland has been rated highly by both of the main corruption perception scoring methods since their respective inceptions. Thus, explaining the causes of Danish and Swedish normative disdain for corruption indicates why the Nordic nations as a group have scored so highly on all existing twenty-first century anticorruption measures.

Whereas the Danes gradually developed or were constrained to develop an antipathy to both venal and petty corruption under the Crown, the Swedes under their kings embraced a form of limited representative democracy for much of the eighteenth century, with some democratic parliamentary procedures and the inauguration of a rule of law. The constitution of 1719–1720 transferred substantial power from a hitherto absolutist monarchy to the Diet of Estates. The diet—representing nobles, clerics, townsmen, and peasants—set taxation rates, promulgated laws, and controlled declarations of war. It also influenced the Council of the Realm, a ruling directorate that also functioned as a court of appeal.

From 1771 until 1792, however, King Gustavus III, supported by military leaders and some nobles, resumed a largely monarchical rule. He greatly circumscribed representative democracy during the age of European and American revolutions, replaced the Council of the Realm with a High Court under his control and attempted to transform Sweden into a kingdom along modified Danish lines. But his successors in the Napoleonic era had the misfortune to lose a major war against Russia while managing in very difficult circumstances—and thanks to British assistance—to hold off a simultaneous Danish attack from the south. Succumbing to Russian might meant the loss of Finland as part of Sweden in 1809, the consequent shrinking by one-third of the Swedish kingdom, and a successful putsch on the part of military officers and high-level officials to remove King Gustavus IV Adolphus. They wrote a new, liberal, constitution and installed as monarch of Sweden Field Marshall Jean Bernadotte (King Carl XIV Johan), a close ally of Napoleon and a French citizen.

The restored Diet of Estates and the new king subsequently ruled in concert, together with a strengthened High Court. Although Bernadotte's powers were substantial, Sweden had now entered an era of experimental and emerging governance during which Parliament and the people could gradually increase their own political influence under a developing rule of law ultimately delivered by judges of inferior courts and the High Court. Meanwhile, in 1814 Norway, briefly independent, enacted the most liberal constitution in Europe before succumbing to Swedish military prowess and suzerainty.

As in Denmark, this period after the Napoleonic wars brought a great upsurge in corruption-related crime. Eighteenth-century Sweden was not devoid of corrupt behavior, but the number of incidents of bribery and embezzlement were relatively low (except about 1790) compared to the great spike upwards of such reported infractions after 1810.[18] Unsettled conditions after the wars, post-wartime inflation, the country's reduced economic circumstances, and lapses in auditing and other controls contributed to this corruption-linked crime wave. Whatever the reasons, the cases that were appealed to the High Court encompassed embezzlement (including the theft of monies by postal clerks from letters); abuse of public office for private gain (including forging documents in order to purloin funds from the intended recipients); extortion, or the compelled payment of excessive fees or taxes; and soliciting bribes.[19]

Innovative research in the Swedish archives shows that forgery, fraud, and "misconduct" (breaches of duty or legal infractions) by officials were the major corruption-related offenses from 1820 to 1840, along with embezzlement, and that most were perpetrated by local administrators in townships, not by upper level bureaucrats in Stockholm. Those local persons were much more directly engaged in tax collection and the supervision of other fiscal matters than were officers of the state. City officials and country judges were frequent culprits, although, earlier, high-court judges had been implicated. As a result, "tidying up the Swedish state [in the early nineteenth century] mostly was a matter of tidying up the rural administration."[20]

To reduce peculation and abuse and accelerate the "tidying up" of state affairs, Swedish lawmakers introduced significant legal and procedural changes. A newly passed regulation stipulated that civil servants were to cease "borrowing" funds at will from the treasury; henceforth, they could not simply pay back what they had borrowed and be exonerated. The Riksdag, formerly the Diet, furthermore prohibited the continued purchasing of military, clerical, and secular positions and promotions, thus leading the way to making merit a criterion for entrance into and later advancement within the bureaucracy. Once the custom of purchasing positions and promotions had been abolished, it became possible to transform the incipient Swedish bureaucracy into a meritocratic enterprise. Indeed, already there were fewer cases in the courts of malfeasance, or abuse of office, which suggests to the leading researchers of corruption in this period that the Swedish administrative system was already in the process of being transformed from a nonmeritocratic, patronage-dominated, patrimonial institution into a more professionalized entity serving the full nation.[21] By 1834, as debates in the Riksdag substantiate, there was a deepening national sense that public servants owed their best efforts to the interests of the full nation, not to themselves, and were expected to perform impartially.

In shifting toward a more competence-recruited bureaucracy, Sweden was possibly learning or adapting from Denmark. Equally likely, as several scholars argue, Sweden was drawing on the ideas of the European Enlightenment as transmitted by the liberal thinkers who were steeped in British and French thought and who dominated opposition to the nation's overbearing monarchy in the late eighteenth century and to conservative nobles in the early nineteenth century. Some of those more modern thinkers were also capitalists from Sweden's growing industrial class. Even some nobles were advancing new and less-conservative ideas, and the peasant estate in parliament had become more independent of the king. By this time, too, Sweden had a much freer press than most European countries; liberal notions percolated through the media into Swedish society. They entered Sweden's main universities, where standards were slowly being elevated and from which a new generation of civil servants was being recruited. The country's courts were also, possibly because of their eighteenth century tradition, much less corrupt and much less under executive influence than those of other contemporary polities. The prosecution of corruption could therefore check illegal tendencies of public servants because, by the middle of the nineteenth century, the Swedish state could project its credible commitment—its ability to enforce the emerging new rules of bureaucratic (and other) behavior. Sweden could also collect taxes from a broad base well before, and more thoroughly than, its peers.

All of these new factors, including the power of positive ideas from outside of Sweden, dramatically shifted the manner in which the nation would be run, administered, and mobilized behind values that in retrospect seem obvious and destined, but which in the early nineteenth century profoundly altered the manner in which Sweden would henceforth be governed and respond to its public—and regard corruption. Because a meritocracy was viewed as more professional, because "absolute impartiality in the implementation of the laws" became a goal, because accountability became highly valued, and because all of these attributes contributed to competent efficiency, a Swedish understanding of how governmental services were best delivered produced intolerance for the endurance of practices that were corrupt (and interfered with a well-functioning state).[22] The norm of ethical universalism took hold.

But it was not until at least the 1840s and 1850s, and in some matters not until the 1860s, that this new norm and the other reforms to Swedish administrative practice took full root. It was only in the latter period that civil servants were fully salaried and expected to hold but one full-time position rather than several part-time public and private ones. Around this time, "the old view of an administrative office as [personal] property" slowly disappeared.[23] Moreover, public schooling became free and literacy naturally spread, standards for university degrees improved, nobles lost their remaining rights to public posts, local and regional governments gained greater autonomy, and taxes were monetized instead of often being proffered in kind as grain or animals. Between 1855 and 1860, the manner in which civil servants were paid was strengthened. In 1866, a modern bicameral parliament was established, abolishing the estates. Two years later, Parliament decreed that civil servants would no longer be remunerated directly for services to individual citizens but that citizens would instead remit fees to the government. Together, these and other reforms created the modern Swedish state. In it there was less room for corruption than there had been a century before. Indeed, the new Parliament found many ingenious ways to prevent civil servants from being tempted by corruption; it strengthened legal sanctions (1862), including a specification of "misconduct" in public office.

Before the 1870s, Sweden was still thoroughly rural. Ten percent of the nation's people lived in cities; Stockholm numbered only 100,000 residents. About 75 percent of economically active Swedes were engaged in farm-related pursuits.[24] Yet, despite the decentralized nature of the country, civil society in the guise of abundant voluntary associations was very forward looking. Many associations were temperance-focused, some church and Bible-study related, some engaged in relief efforts for the poor, some cared for abandoned children, some sought to improve workhouses, and a number were concerned with additional aspects of philanthropy. Others, significantly, were motivated by mass education; they attempted to further "useful knowledge"—"to elevate the mind" of the working classes. With rapid industrialization toward the end of the nineteenth century, these associations were joined by what became a large labor movement; its influence, the simultaneous growth of the various temperance societies, and the very large groupings of followers of assorted evangelical churches all testified to the social power of civil society in the early twentieth century. This civil activity was largely led by persons from the emerging middle-class both in cities and towns, and also in the countryside. It brought together a novel sense of Swedes belonging to Sweden, and engendered broad swaths of newly strengthened social trust. In turn, that sense of trust contributed to a swelling norm of anticorruption.

These reforms and the new norm presumably reflected societal shifts in attitudes, the spread of education, the aspirations of a rising middle class, and the acculturation of Swedes and Swedish officialdom to impatience with corrupt dealings. From the early nineteenth century to the second half, Swedes came to believe in the importance of what we now can label ethical universalism. Uslaner concludes reasonably that Swedes and other Nordic citizens believed in an "egalitarian social order" that mitigated against dishonest dealings. Civil servants (who were paid very well relative to private positions by the beginning of the twentieth century) would have been immediately suspect if "they became rich." Rothstein suggests that the indirect approach helped to reduce and then effectively to outlaw corruption in the Swedish case.[25] Equally likely, as Sweden became more liberal and democratic, as its civil service became more autonomous, and as laws against corruption became stricter and more heavily enforced by investigators and in the courts, a strong norm against corruption took root in both Sweden and Norway (still ruled by Sweden).

The Finns

In Finland, many of these same societal developments were taking place during the nineteenth century, when Swedish-inspired bureaucratic rule, carried out mostly by Swedish-speaking Finns, endured under Russian suzerainty.

Finland was an autonomously ruled duchy under the czar, largely governing itself in the domestic sphere until 1894, when Czar Nicholas II tried to impose direct Russian rule. Finland, like Sweden, was rural and agricultural, poor, and as yet not very literate. Industrialization had not yet occurred. Corruption was not a prominent feature, mostly because of the Swedish example and Swedish-inherited rules. Additionally, because peasants, merchants, and nobles all benefited economically from their separation from Sweden and because all sections of society felt equally privileged, corruption was usually confined to the shipping trade. In that sphere, decisions made by the new rulers of the Duchy could be helpful and determine profits. Ship owners hence sought influence at court.[26]

Democracy arrived after the middle of the century, influenced by Nordic and European intellectual currents, and propelled by the rise of Finnish nationalism. (Finns constituted 80 percent of the total population by about 1870.) Universal free primary education was introduced in 1866 along with secondary schooling in Finnish (not Swedish), but the major spread of mass education in Finland only occurred in the 1920s and 1930s, to some extent because of the gradual manner in which the Finnish language gained equal status with Swedish after 1892.

The Parliament Law of 1869 marked another major advance. It inaugurated regular parliamentary sessions and gave ordinary Finns the voice in national affairs that they had long lacked. By 1906, all Finns could vote. Even so, the old governing elites retained their sway within the Duchy at least until the end of the nineteenth century. Some took advantage of the rewards available from the increasing influence of Russia in Finland after about 1860, many of which were obtained corruptly from Russian-speaking bureaucrats. The extent to which the emerging Finnish postmercantile and proto-industrial state was riddled with more than office-seeking and questionable influence peddling is not clear. Emerging democratic practices and inherited Swedish rules of law dueled with opportunities for self-enrichment among civil servants.

A firmly Finnish responsibility for all of these issues began only after the Russian Revolution. Finland discarded the Russian yoke in 1917, endured a year-long, very violent, civil war during 1918 and continued turmoil in 1919 before finally achieving peace and writing a new constitution late in that year. The constitution was based on Swedish law and principles and reflected a desire for a strictly regulated public service. From that post–World War period, Finns chose to rule themselves "collegially," so that decision-making power was spread (inhibiting corrupt acts by a sole actor). Independent Finland also became a consensus-driven welfare state with a powerful bureaucracy, but its inherited administrative culture frowned on anything that resembled corruption or infringed upon a norm of fair public service.

By the late nineteenth century, the Finns had been sufficiently concerned with the problem of corruption that they decided to codify existing strong social mores against such practices. In 1889, possibly also because Finnish society was ready and literacy was rapidly spreading, the newly enacted penal code outlawed giving and taking bribes, "aggravated" bribery, bribery of members of Parliament, bribery in a business or corporate setting, buying votes during elections, and the "negligent" abuse of public office. Subsequently, civil servants became subject to a set of laws that penalized malfeasance and other offenses committed while in state employment.[27]

But, as in the other Nordic nations, the determining variable was less the tough rules and their enforcement that made the difference than it was the growing sense of social trust and civic order that infused embryonic Finnish society. One authority contends that institutional design was not essential to Finnish anticorruption. Its judiciary, for example, lacked the power of complete constitutional oversight. Nor was comparative wealth (which may have contributed to Danish, Swedish, and Norwegian resistance to corruption) the decisive condition that gave rise in early twentieth century Finland to a shunning of corruption. Until after World War II, Finns were much poorer and less well-fed than other Nordics; Finnish prosperity occurred later than in the neighboring countries. Instead, as in the other high ranking CPI and WBCC polities, Finnish democracy and governance were sufficiently direct, transparent, and accountable so that Finns were able "to monitor what their politicians [were] doing and to take effective action when something [seemed] amiss." The press was free, and it was active in chasing corruption. Additionally, confirming the embrace by Finland and other high-ranking countries of ethical universalism was "its citizens' complete lack of tolerance for corruption." Because of its comparatively small population, in Finland "if one loses respect . . . then one has lost a lot. So the risk of being accused, and left out . . . has been exceptionally big."[28] The power of shame and shaming has helped to curb corruption in Finland.

Finnish aversion to corruption builds upon long instilled democratic values such as "openness, fairness, transparency, and responsibility."[29] Those are learned responses that again testify to the importance of nurturing norms over decades. Prevailing political cultures must be altered or reconfigured before corruption may be banished from any political jurisdiction, as in Finland.

New Zealand and Australia

Superficially, at least, New Zealand's movement from frontier forms of wild corruption in the nineteenth century to a much greater adherence to noncorrupt norms resembles the Swedish story. Responsibility for a substantial shift in attitudes toward corruption falls on indirect actions and decisions more than on conscious, substantial, attacks against corrupt behavior. Again, institutional design is less critical than norm development.

New Zealand was settled by Europeans beginning in the 1840s and, with a mere 40,000 British inhabitants, established a self-governing representative government in 1856. This very early embrace of democracy, a scant few years after Canada, and the tiny size of the initial electorate, exerted a critical influence on the gradual emergence of societal norms. The first settlers were carefully selected in Britain. Many were middle class; most were educated. Nearly all were churchly. The majority enshrined Victorian respectability.[30] Furthermore, the two main islands of the colony were for many decades harshly separated from each other by geography. In many of these isolated settlements, as well as in the cities, individualism tempered by a necessary set of reciprocal alliances led gradually to the creation of abundant social capital. Corruption, as an informal behavior, was not condoned readily across a range of strongly Presbyterian (Church of Scotland)–influenced groupings during the early years of self-rule. New Zealand also enjoyed a free press from the start.

It is important that such anticorrupt norms existed before the great rise in immigration during the 1860s, when the discovery of gold led to an influx of chancers poorer than the earlier immigrants. Another wave of state-assisted indigent Britons arrived in the 1870s. By the end of that decade, New Zealand's population numbered 464,000. But because the franchise was only permitted to be exercised by persons of property, and because those with property in many places could vote in several constituencies, New Zealand was a very unrepresentative democracy (only 18 percent of the white population could vote) until the franchise was widened in 1879. But in 1887, still no more than 29 percent of the total white population exercised the franchise, and plural ballot-casting continued. The right to vote was finally acquired by all New Zealanders (including women) in 1893, well ahead of many large democracies, and this widening of the franchise may have helped to strengthen democratic instincts within the country. But, for at least two more decades, political life and the public service was still directed by men of standing. The efforts of prominent males, most of whom knew each other, may have initially constrained corrupt behavior nationally as well as within what was still a tiny public service. But those conditions also meant that the exercise of influence was in limited hands, and could have been easily abused.

From the beginnings of self-government, "the condition . . . of the Civil Service [was] very unsatisfactory." Clerks were barely paid, the public service lacked zealous attention to duty, and its members were "eager to follow . . . more profitable pursuits."[31] The passage of the Civil Service Act in 1866, the making of appointments to the service dependent on competitive examinations, and the provision of pensions all helped to regularize what had been a chaotic system. But politicians largely ignored the act, and an informal system of patronage appointments continued. In 1882, "this Service [was] not conducted in the manner in which it ought to be conducted." Even new legislation in 1890 did little to rationalize the appointments to, and the conduct of, New Zealand's bureaucratic establishment. A few years later, members of the House of Assembly were filling many positions with their own relatives, and the period of Liberal Party rule that lasted into the twentieth century was marked by lip-service only being paid to the rules. "Every member of the House . . . had a relative or a friend in a government job."[32] Indeed, "The back door stood so wide open that anyone with influence could find his way into a departmental job." [33]

Nevertheless, when Sidney and Beatrice Webb visited New Zealand in 1898, they observed that although the Liberal Party administration had behaved "unscrupulously" in its conduct of public business, and in some cases had been "partisan and corrupt," they had expected to find even more "jobbery" than appeared evident. Indeed, Sidney Webb, having just come from the "Augean Stables of America," viewed customary local favoritism as mere "peccadilloes." Beatrice Webb wrote that despite general charges of corruption, she could not discover "anything that approaches to American spoils systems or the taking of bribes."[34]

New Zealand may already have been only lightly corrupt, but it was not until the passage of the Public Service Act of 1912 that it began to benefit from a nascent, well-ordered, bureaucratic establishment. The shift away from direct payments for favors and services, and thus from at least some levels of corruption, began with the 1912 reforms.

What the Webbs may have been unaware of, or prevented from discovering, was the large-scale corruption in the 1890s and before regarding the taking of land from the Maori. After the New Zealand Settlements Act of 1863 was promulgated, the second wave of overseas colonists proceeded to confiscate more than 3 million acres of land belonging to Maori tribes, despite the 1840 Treaty of Waitangi's promise to respect Maori rights to land. Under two other acts in the early 1860s, whites were permitted to purchase land directly from Maori owners; soon the greater part of the North Island had passed from indigenous to settler control. This "free trade" was carried out in an "often unscrupulous manner" that left much bitterness in its wake.[35]

By that time, New Zealand had become a former colony, later a dominion, with a distinctive democratic personality and political culture. It had begun to prize equalitarianism more than individualism and libertarianism. It believed in social justice, ignoring what its whites had done to the Maori. Rewards "must be evenly spread," with no one settler taking undue advantage (of another settler). It had a laboring poor but no deep wells of poverty, and few slums. Its central government and hundreds of local governments were "exceptionally close" to the nonindigenous people.[36] Participation in government was plentiful. There was an acceptance of, if not a desire for, an active state, possibly a utilitarian, socializing state. The press was free, and watchful.

Somehow their ties to the land, their reliance on sheep and dairy farming, their relative homogeneity (94 percent of the population—still slightly less than 1 million—was descended by 1912 from Scottish or English stock, 6 percent were Maori), the limited size of their cities and towns, or all four factors together seem to have engendered high levels of social trust and social capital. Two authors suggest that the choice of sleepy and protected Wellington as a national capital, succeeding industrial and entrepreneurial Auckland, helped to prevent the emergence of government and governance within a financially aggressive environment. Wellington became a quintessential government town, to the benefit of a growing hostility to corruption within civil service ranks.[37] New Zealanders conformed, too, to social codes and social strictures that regarded too much greed or abuse of position as inappropriate.

The country's political institutions from at least the beginning of the twentieth century were motivated by a need to serve the will of the people—to deliver high orders of governance. In turn, good governance left little room for the kinds of priority shifting that comes with corruption. An insular but educated community with Protestant values and high amounts of social capital, developed in adversity and isolation, rejected the violations of public office that were apparent in the late 1890s and proceeded to embrace the ethical universalism that keeps societal corruption at bay. Possibly from 1912, but certainly from the 1920s, civil servants possessed an "inner check" that embodied their professional devotion "to the ideal of the public interest."[38]

This attention to serving the public well was also reinforced by self-interest. The New Zealand public servant from the early twentieth century was "subject to more extensive controls than most private citizens; he is more likely to be caught if he commits an indiscretion; his career may suffer even if there is only a suspicion of unsatisfactory conduct."[39] Exactly when these controls were imposed is unclear, but even in the 1890s there was awareness by politicians and civil servants of the value of strict audits. The Secret Commissions Act of 1910 banned the receipt of "valuable considerations," especially in the negotiation of public contracts; it also penalized bribery and other corrupt acts. (The Crimes Act of 1961 updated many of its provisions and stipulated precise sentence lengths for offenders.) At some point in the 1920s or 1930s, audits and other methods of strengthening public servant conscientiousness, and of intensifying an embryonic esprit de corps within the country's surprisingly large bureaucratic establishment, became routine. By that time the anticorruption norm had become accepted widely.

Government service was eventually generously paid and secure. That helped to reduce the incentive to take advantage of state positions for private gain. Gregory reports that so long as a public official "remained totally non-corrupt . . . even if [he or she was] only adequately competent," he or she kept what in local terms was a very good job and career because security of tenure in New Zealand (unlike contemporary Africa) did not require accepting lower wages than in private sector employment.[40] Even in the Ministry of Works, possibly from the late nineteenth century, there developed an aura of ethical probity which made tendering (and therefore much venal corruption) more transparent than in most other countries, and even more than in most dominions.

Conceivably, too, political and bureaucratic leadership in and after World War II built upon and strengthened prevailing norms of impartiality, service delivery, and adherence to the rule of law. A British-type loyalty to civil service rather than political service was emphasized by a series of remarkable officials and accepted by dominant politicians.

All of these elements helped to build an effective ethos opposed to corruption in New Zealand. But why does New Zealand rank significantly higher than Australia, its much larger Antipodean neighbor with which it shares a robust British heritage, a similar chronology, and approximately similar political aspirations? Australia did begin as a penal colony and New Zealand as a settler outpost, and that difference may (but is unlikely to have) disposed the young Australia to criminality and an openness to corruption. Or, possibly, New Zealand's long cultural attachment to the mother country, its embrace of welfare-state values, and its small size may have denied corruption as firm a toe hold as in its neighbor. Australia was always more individualistic than New Zealand. It was much more populous, and it was a federal entity, with separate states and many more opportunities to be acquisitive and avaricious. New Zealand's small size may have enabled positive norms to be instilled more easily; Australia was much larger in area, much more disparate, and until 1901 a set of separate colonies following different political trajectories.

New Zealanders originally may have been better educated, more middle class, and wealthier than Australians, but the latter soon caught up. Conceivably the Scots influences in New Zealand (many Irish came to Australia and brought Roman Catholicism) helped tilt Calvinist New Zealanders against corruption, but even such suggestive and likely notions are insufficient to explain New Zealand's slightly higher, and more sustained, anticorruption evaluations. New Zealand has always ranked above Australia on the CPI list and the WBCC indicator even if the actual scoring differences are comparatively minor (nine points in 2015, eleven points in 2014, but only five in 2012 on the CPI). But their respective nineteenth century levels of corruption are distinct, with much more corruption in Australia than in New Zealand through the early twentieth century.[41] Additionally, New Zealand had a distinct governmental class before one was developed in Australia and a capital city devoted to good government well before Canberra was established in Australia.

Norms are nurtured in different settings. New Zealand had an interest during and after the nineteenth century to govern well and fairly. Those goals militated for transparency and against corruption. Strong sanctions helped to buttress this emerging anticorruption ethos, much later reinforced by a national political will.

In Australia, where even as late as the 1930s the public service was much larger and more corrupt than in New Zealand, a shift away from tolerance to disapproval followed the appointment of a new head of the Public Service Board. He insisted on a level of probity that was new, and personally supervised disciplinary proceedings against offenders. In the manner of Lee Kuan Yew much later, he favored the dismissal of anyone found guilty of abusing a position of trust, even in very minor ways. He also strengthened procedures for appointment and promotion on merit, purging the public service of any persons who appeared to be serving themselves instead of citizens, their clients. This cleansing and reorienting of the Australian public service took place both before and after World War II and testifies to the importance of political will (as in Hong Kong), even if exercised by a nonpolitician allied to and serving at the behest of supportive elected premiers.

The Netherlands

Another high-performing, low corruption, nation is the Netherlands. Before 1795, despite the earlier anti-Hapsburg charters that had prohibited the sale of state offices and other forms of extortion, the public service in the Dutch Republic was as riddled with the purchase of positions, blatant nepotism, and (unspecified) financial improprieties as other contemporary European states. Most public servants paid the government for their offices and thus felt justified in recouping their investments from the general public. "The hunt for lucrative positions dominated the political process in the Dutch Republic."[42] Fraud and theft were not uncommon, and kickbacks from private contractors were expected. In 1787, there were exposés of plundering by public servants. By 1797, with reform sentiments having swept Europe along with revolution, the National Meeting (Parliament) issued decrees meant to regulate the conduct of bureaucrats. In the next year, all civil servants were discharged and invited to reapply for their posts.

From 1805, public personnel could no longer accept gifts from the public with impunity. What had hitherto been administrative fees charged to citizens individually by office holders were banned. All bureaucrats now had to swear an oath of purification upon assuming their posts and promise never to accept bribes. They also had to affirm that they had no personal or family conflicts of interest that would interfere with their ability faithfully to serve the public impartially. More and more, these officials were appointed with less reference to family background than before.

In 1848, influenced by radical and modernist ideas elsewhere in Europe and with a Liberal Party leader in control for the first time, decisions and appointments came to be made with greater transparency than ever before in the Dutch Republic. Rational criteria were employed, including educational attainments and knowledge of bureaucratic processes. Talent became more significant for new appointments than relationships or other forms of patronage. Satisfying the "general interest" became more important—at least in theory and at least in the open declarations of Liberal politicians—than satisfying private interests. Although civil servants, mayors, and provincial commissioners still continued for many years to be selected because of their political sympathies as much as because of their intrinsic abilities, from the middle of the nineteenth century the people and the press of the Netherlands agreed in a new and more modern manner that public servants were obliged to work for the public, not themselves, that the national interest superseded provincial interest, and that no municipality or set of persons could be favored over others.

Despite these advances, until 1890 most officials were able to continue seeking special payments for their services from the public, the better to supplement their meager state wages. In that year, a salary structure was introduced that provided for regular pay increases. Earlier, in 1870, appointments to the public service were made (at least in theory) on the basis of competitive examinations. Yet, Dutch bureaucrats were still fiddling their expenses throughout much of the century and many of them held regular outside jobs while in state employ. There were several serious cases of embezzlement in the early years of the century, too.[43]

Only in the twentieth century, for the most part from the 1920s, could the Dutch public service be counted as less corrupt than its counterparts in nearby European nations. Stricter regulations, greater scrutiny, and an enhanced professionalization of the bureaucracy, coupled with an awareness by citizens of their rights, shifted the Netherlands more toward a Nordic sense of ethical universalism and away from the comparatively lax standards of the previous century.

Canada

Despite the massive municipal scandals of 2013 and the parliamentary and corporate misdeeds of 2015 and 2016, Canada also ranks highly on the CPI and other rating schemes, having overcome a long early record of corrupt dealings. Even before the passage of the British North America Act, and the creation of the Canadian confederation in 1867, the affairs of the provinces of Upper and Lower Canada were controlled by patronage. "Dishonest" public servants were "intent on personal plunder rather than public service . . . to the detriment of the colonists' vital interests."[44] After 1867, when the Canadian federal bureaucracy was tiny, patronage continued to detract from impartial performance; many conflicts of interest arose and, more damagingly, a Royal Commission on the Civil Service in 1891–1892 noted that "certain officials" had falsified accounts, accepted bribes, received payments for fraudulently altering customs declarations, put ghost workers on the payroll, and engaged in many other nefarious and illicit activities.

Canadian corrupt behavior was more venal than petty in those early days, as it has largely remained. Politicians accepted kickbacks from avaricious industrialists and railway magnates. In 1872, for example, Prime Minister John Macdonald demanded first C$10,000 and then another C$10,000 to approve railway construction contracts. His minister of public works was forced to resign in 1891 after he gave preferential treatment to a Quebeçois building firm.[45] In the early 1890s, many members of Parliament took hefty bribes to influence the award of subsidies for new railways and to maintain existing stretches of rail all across Canada. Even as late as the administration of Sir Wilfred Laurier, prime minister from 1896 to 1911, various kinds of bribery and electoral manipulation were common. A number of such scandals embroiled the several Laurier administrations.

The provinces were also riddled with costly patronage, electoral vote buying, and other serious forms of corruption well past the middle of the twentieth century. Before World War I, Canada abounded in "stuffed envelopes quietly passed on street corners, nervous winks, and even telephone taps."[46] Alberta, Manitoba, and Saskatchewan, often known as the most right-dealing of Canada's federal entities, were engulfed with graft from 1910 until the 1950s. In Manitoba in 1915–1916, a contractor paid nearly C$1 million to the president of the Provincial Conservative Association in exchange for road-building and other valuable government construction contracts. In 1932, British Columbia's grasping patronage was termed "the coarsest that ever existed in any state." It "disgusted" the people.[47] In Newfoundland in the 1920s, politicians systematically pocketed monies meant for the Department of Liquor Control. Steel and coal companies were caught paying off the premier of the same province. The neighboring maritime provinces of Nova Scotia and New Brunswick were equally afflicted with corrupt dealings at the venal level; corruption played a major role in local political life. So it did for many decades in Quebec, where "amoral familism" (see chapter 1) was alive and well at least until the 1960s. Ontario, too, experienced frequent public outbreaks of shady dealing by politicians and other public servants.

In 1959, the mayor of Edmonton was forced to resign after he was found guilty of gross misconduct. In 1963, when W.A.C. Bennett, leader of the Social Credit Party in British Columbia, was re-elected premier for the fifth straight term, graft was widely assumed to have helped to assure victory. Earlier, a critic accused Bennett's administration of being riddled with "moral dishonesty and moral corruption." One of his key ministers had been jailed in 1958 for accepting bribes.[48] As late as 1983, prominent Nova Scotians, one a senator, were convicted of illegally assisting a liquor distributor who wanted to place his products favorably in provincially owned stores.

At the federal level, major electoral reforms in the 1870s were designed to reduce the wholesale purchasing of votes and the gaining of other poll advantages. A position of auditor general was established in 1878 to oversee the potentially sleazy practices of parliamentarians and officials. A multiple constituency system, which encouraged corruption among prospective members of Parliament, was only removed by legislated reforms in the 1920s. But major alterations in the manner in which political parties financed themselves at the national and provincial levels occurred as late as the 1960s, when limitations were imposed for the first time.

Canadians became markedly less tolerant of venal corruption by their politicians in the years after World War I. Various legislative acts curbed practices, such as holding second jobs, which had been accepted in the nineteenth century. Except for two major scandals, one concerning fraudulent customs payment schemes in 1926 and another in 1930 involving the diversion of the waters of the St. Lawrence River for private profit, prime ministers at the national level largely refrained from enriching themselves. Their administrations were mostly clean, and public servants, as in Australia and New Zealand, gradually demonstrated improved standards of official behavior. But even the most abstemious prime ministers were not above condoning arrangements that favored their political parties in ways that were later seen to be corrupt.[49] In 1964, Prime Minister Lester Pearson, an upright leader, felt obliged to remind his cabinet colleagues that they had "an obligation not simply to observe the law, but to act in a manner so scrupulous that it will bear the closest possible scrutiny. The conduct of public business," he continued, "must be beyond question in terms of moral standards." No one was permitted to place themselves "under obligation to any person who might profit from special consideration or favour."[50] Nevertheless, conflicts of interest persisted at both the federal and provincial levels, with an Ontario cabinet official being compelled to resign along with several senior bureaucrats who had given economic incentives to a company in which they held substantial interests. By the end of the 1970s, finally, a decade of infractions led to popular disgust and the enactment in the provinces of various laws intended to improve the conduct of federal and provincial officials.

In the 1980s and the early 1990s, Canadians hardly tolerated the various ways in which their political masters continued to abuse the Pearsonian rules. Prime Ministers Pierre Trudeau and John Turner gave more than 200 high-level patronage positions to supporters, knowing that an incoming administration would prefer to appoint very different people. The succeeding administration of Prime Minister Brian Mulroney lost six cabinet ministers under questionable circumstances. Once again a minister of public works could not resist temptation; an associate, a member of Parliament responsible for a riding near Ottawa where a major museum was being built with federal funds, was charged with ten counts of bribery, thirty-two counts of defrauding the government, and eight counts of breach of trust. The MP in question eventually pleaded guilty and served two years in jail.[51]

Corrupt malpractices have occurred as recently as 2015 with revelations of abuses of office by senators, despite increasingly tightened official standards and a hesitant but emerging new public norm against corrupt practices from at least the mid-1980s. A critic asked in 1993 if Canada were "doomed to watch a collision between the demands of the Canadian public for a politics cleansed of patronage, and a deaf immobilism in political practices?"[52] In fact, that question could still have been asked in 2016 regarding the Quebec municipal bribery scandals or at the federal level in 2014 and 2015. Nevertheless, Canada is perceived as being less corrupt than Australia, the United Kingdom, and the United States, and the underlying ethical expectations of its citizens and public servants may in fact justify that high standing.

Canadians took a number of twentieth century decades to compel their politicians, bureaucrats, and corporate executives to default to integrity rather than to grasping greed. Although a norm of anticorruption emerged only gradually and is obeyed only hesitantly by senior politicians, it was founded as it was in Australia, and possibly in the Nordic lands, on what one thoughtful theorist has called "civic republicanism"—a society that counters "the desire for self-gain (corruption) with the desire [to achieve] the greater good (virtue)." Civic republicanism privileges the common good over the individual good.[53]

From before confederation, and throughout the remainder of the nineteenth and twentieth centuries, a principal concern of the Canadians who thought in the manner of civic republicans was to counter corruption and simultaneously to produce a community that "upheld the best traits" of Britishness.[54] Both Australia and Canada consequently developed with an unshakeable attachment to the mother country (their imagined community) and to its ideals. Those ideals, those "imagined" ideals, greatly influenced trans-Atlantic norms, especially the emergence of such norms as fair play and political probity (virtue). Presbyterianism crossed the oceans to Canada and Australia as well; Christian civic republicanism (akin to ethical universalism) reinforced Canadian political civic republicanism as it did in New Zealand and the Lutheran lands of the Nordic north.

One author dubiously associates greater corruption in the Latin lands of southern Europe with Catholicism: "The Puritan conscience is more demanding of good behavior in public matters than the Catholic conscience." He also suggests that the harsh climate and thin soils of northern Europe engendered cooperative behavior among inhabitants (and in time attitudes antithetical to corruption), whereas the more "benign" climate of the European South permitted "selfish" behavior. A sense of public duty, he contends, came earlier and more strongly in the North than the South.[55]

The high ranking of these prominent components of the British Commonwealth of Nations, and especially Canada, on the CPI and WBCC lists since 1996 is founded at least in part on a national partiality to the notion of a greater communal good—a notion that emerged slowly from inherited societal DNA and was then nurtured and shaped by a succession of civil society leaders, churchmen and intellectuals, politicians, and jurists. Thus, even if politicians and local office holders still misbehave, the norm persists and guides the nation.

Changing the Societal Mold

In each of these compressed explanations, whole nation-states gradually shifted away from accepting corrupt behavior as normal and moved toward an eventual appreciation of the harms brought by corrupt practices. Human greed doubtless remained a strong ingredient of individual and national character, but its expression in the form of corruption was reduced less by stronger laws, ruthless enforcement actions, manipulating institutional design, modifying regulations, or by new economic incentives than it was by reshaping and reframing national political cultures. More democracy was not the entire answer. Nor were economic growth and the accumulation of capital the key transformative causes of nation-states embracing ethical universalism and large amounts of social trust. Protestant confessionalism may have assisted in the transformation, but even more important in altering the prevailing ethos of these countries over time was their development of broad forms of universal education, including that of young women. Egalitarianism in the Nordic lands and elsewhere helped lead to investments in universal educational offerings and to more mean years of schooling. Canada's experience was similar.

Rothstein and Uslaner show that levels of mass education in the nineteenth century are a central indicator of twenty-first century corruption ratings. A nation's educational attainments "as far back as 1870, measured as the mean number of years of schooling, strongly predict levels of corruption 140 years later—more so than . . . education levels over time." Furthermore, major expressions of social and economic equality preceded and motivated the nature and kinds of broad-based education that these societies produced.[56]

A society that gives its citizens more years of schooling has higher quantities and qualities of literacy and access to information about governmental responsibilities and the like, generates more social trust, enables improper favoritism to be identified and opposed, makes citizens aware of and inclined to demand social justice, spreads a signal that governance should be about service delivery not exactions of tribute, and is a strong force that helps to empower citizens economically is the kind of society in which norms of integrity emerge. Uslaner and Rothstein also assert that universal free education produces a "strong positive correlation between gender equality and low levels of corruption" by boosting awareness of the importance of equitable dealings. Expanded educational opportunities, they say, "are a major reason why the universal welfare state" and redistributive policies led to greater equality and, over time, societal refusals to accept corruption as a norm. New kinds of citizens were needed for the new secular societies, and the new nations, that were evolving in Europe after the late nineteenth century.[57]

The nineteenth century Nordics, the New Zealanders and Australians, the Dutch, the Canadians and some additional modern noncorrupt nations schooled their inhabitants along with Prussians, Germans, French, Americans, and a few others. That widening of educational opportunity along with the gradual democratization of church and secular society helped to build nations that grew intolerant of corruption. They became socialized in that manner, in considerable part because of what they learned at school and took from their new awareness of the world. They came to know their rights and to "manage to institutionalize open and nondiscriminatory access" to government.[58]

In addition to enabling broader access to education, many of the more enlightened polities of Europe abandoned the sale of offices and moved (as did the Nordics) to professionalize their bureaucracies. The Prussians did so as early as the 1770s, and more profoundly after 1849. A few years later, British India, followed by Britain itself, began filling the ranks of their respective civil services with people who had been selected competitively, and not entirely according to their rank or family connection. (Giving up patronage was hard, but in Britain and British India the gradual shift toward appointment and promotion on ability presaged the spread of a helpful anticorruption ethos, as it had in Prussia and the Nordics.) The embracing of the notion of "public service" as a positive good, even as a calling, presaged a slow shift toward a more ethically universalist bureaucratic and political norm—away from the Walpolean (chapter 5) emphasis on accumulating the spoils of office toward the new belief in service. That happened in the Nordics and spread to the early English-speaking overseas dominions from British India and Britain, but over decades.

Those countries which today are corrupt, however, even wildly so, are often former indigenously controlled colonies where few persons were in school until very modern times. Little educational opportunity in the nineteenth and early twentieth centuries equates with high levels of corruption in the twenty-first century.

More schooling leads to less corruption, especially if that schooling established a firm late nineteenth century foundation under societal reforms that continued in the Nordic and other positive cases throughout much of the twentieth century. But that conclusion fails to explain Botswana, Africa's least corrupt country. It had some missionary schooling in the nineteenth century but hardly more or much better than its now very corrupt neighbors, all with similar kinds of schooling. Nor does their formulation account for Rwanda's shift toward noncorruption despite little universal schooling before this century. It might, on the other hand, imply that the peoples of both Hong Kong and Singapore were well-educated over decades even if their conversion from practicing to shunning corruption came only because of leadership actions, not long acculturation.

The Nordic and other cases also show how political leadership in and after monarchical times combined with liberalizing and modernizing schools, churches, and society to create new communal responses to corruption and abuses of governmental office. In each instance there were individuals who catalyzed and reconfigured their national ethos to favor good governance over old-line patronage and "fixing." The manner in which these nations thought of themselves, and understood a state's obligations to its citizens, changed drastically over time thanks to human agency, the rise of secularism, civic republicanism, and the spread of liberal ideas. The new social contract emphasized "reciprocal accountability and integrity."[59]

In suggesting how best to cure the cancer of corruption globally in the second decade of the twenty-first century, a task for chapter 10, the lessons of this chapter are suggestive and significant. As Hong Kong, Singapore, and Botswana in modern times persuaded their citizens relatively rapidly to convert from accepting corruption as common and normal to refusing to abide those behaviors any longer, so in past times the Nordics, the Antipodeans, the Prussians, the Britons, the Netherlands, and Canada all shifted slowly but profoundly toward an intolerance of anything that smacked of illegal influence peddling or corruption. It is the consuming task of leaders and successions of leaders in less abstemious lands to move their nations in the direction of the Nordic norm by battling graft, extortion, and bribe taking in public life.

VIII

The Gift of Political
Will and Leadership

Prior chapters assert that exertions of political will—the leadership factor—are necessary (but not always sufficient) to curb corruption within nation-states. Developing states (and the Nordic and Antipodean exceptions) that successfully destroyed the incubus of corruption within their borders are (or were) run by strong leaders determined to prevent their governmental colleagues from abusing political or bureaucratic power for private gain. They dramatically altered their countries' inherited political cultures so as to eliminate rent seeking, contract fiddling, and influence peddling. In every case, those leaders are acting (or did act) not because of moral scruples but primarily because they fully understand how corrupt behavior destroys developmental prospects, envelops their nascent nations in a moral haze antithetical to economic growth and social betterment, and undermines a regime's (and their own) legitimacy.

Those leaders also know, from studying their surroundings, their own national histories, and the experiences of their neighbors that corruption starts at the top and slowly works its way through arteries and veins and finally flows inexorably into the capillaries of lower level individual action. Reducing petty or lubricating corruption alone does not do enough. Nor will corruption erode, they appreciate, without attacking its venal manifestations and all manner of traditional practices that enable politicians and officials to distort national priorities for personal gain.

Exhortation accomplishes too little. Leaders may denounce corruption, as so many have, and promise crusades to root out those recalcitrant governmental operatives who fail to heed that message. But only in those few instances where leaders break decisively with past practices; demonstrate high orders of personal integrity and honesty; and make examples of political lieutenants, elected colleagues, and well-placed officials does the rampant retrogression of corruption halt, and such hoary practices begin to recede. As the better leaders know, to end corruption in a nation or a community it is necessary to cut off the head of the snake and to send ripples of dismay down its sinewy musculature to a distant tail.

Few among the leaders of the developing world in the last fifty years have either known how to cope with corruption in this manner or have wanted to so destroy their own or their political movement's advantageous cash flows and political momentum. Too few have been sufficiently courageous; too few have understood that only new orders of leadership—the exertion of exceptional political will—would be equal to the supremely difficult task of transforming a nation of advantage takers and savvy illicit entrepreneurs into sober citizens content to expect and benefit from honest dealings and the daily fulfillment of the citizen-state natural social contract.

Those heads of state and government who transformed (or are transforming) their polities into (comparative) paragons of rent-taking abstinence intuitively understood and understand a fundamental human paradigm: that greed is natural and rational, that avarice is deep-rooted in human DNA. So are envy and the desire not to be outsmarted or outmaneuvered by colleagues' and compatriots' essential human traits. Everyone in a domestic political or bureaucratic chain of command takes his or her behavioral cues from her or his official superiors, especially from the "big" people at the top of the domestic political pyramid.

Whenever a permissive ethos prevails, up and down the governing ranks everyone with positions and power knows or learns what to do and how to behave. That is why lesser officials and lower-level politicians steal from the state that they are meant to serve and cheat their fellow citizens with no particular qualms. If immediate superiors steal and cheat, so lower-ranked civil servants and security personnel believe that they, too, have licenses to enrich themselves. The man on the police beat says that he solicits bribes, pilfers, and cheats "because everyone else does" and that he (or she) does not want to be left out of a chance to supplement meager wages. Farther up the scale, middle-ranking bureaucrats of all kinds look to their betters to see with what they can get away. Once it becomes known that certain kinds or all kinds of corrupt behavior are acceptable (or at least tolerated), then virtually all self-interested maximizers (nearly all of the rest of us) will hardly want to miss good and available opportunities to secure and then to employ official positions for private gain. Corruption becomes a path-dependent phenomenon, a "continuation equilibrium."[1] A cabinet minister in charge of public works improvements reports that as the incumbent, he is expected to produce rents that can be shared with other ministers and with his party.[2] Whatever one thinks of human nature and human fallibility, if a domestic political culture embraces corruption, nearly every citizen will seek opportunities to gain advantage and thus be corrupt. After all, political cultures are greatly determined by leadership signals, leadership postures, and leadership sins of both omission and commission.

The policeman who "fines" drivers for nonexistent infractions, the customs official who "under-invoices" a shipment of tractor parts and splits the difference with an importer, the office-bound bureaucrat who gives permits for foreign currency to favored businessmen for a "consideration," and the highly placed cabinet minister who prefers one foreign supplier of tanks or fighter aircraft over another in exchange for serious kickbacks are each behaving rationally by cheating their governments and the citizens whom they are pledged to serve. All are corrupt and corrupted, but by adapting a conscious strategy of self-enrichment through corrupt behavior, they merely obey national permissive norms and act within the often zero-sum expectations of their class and their condition. "In developing countries corruption is [often] not a deviation, but rather the norm . . . a 'natural' default state."[3] (Singling out "developing" countries rather than "all" countries is probably unfair and unnecessary.)

Where abusing a public position for private gain is common and expected, reforms can only take place by determined leadership intervention. Those attempted disruptions of prevailing modes of operation admittedly might otherwise occur by legislation, and the consequent enforcing of new legal restrictions. A vibrant media or other civil means could expose such behavior and foment societal outrage. So could audits, the outcries of whistleblowers, and the protests of citizens. Positive change could be accelerated, too, by the energetic actions of governmentally sponsored investigative agencies and great upsurges of governmentally arranged educational efforts against corrupt doings. But, so far, none of these ancillary methods has alone led to significant reductions in domestic levels of corruption, globally. Nor have good leaders failed to halt corruption because their policies and their efforts were simply not ingenious or robust enough. Nor did these "good" leaders fail to reduce corruption because other internal political factors defeated them.

Advances in the struggle against corruption have always been propelled primarily by individual leaders breaking the prevalent national mold and by comparatively dramatic expectation shifting, setting in motion a gradual revolution in the way business and bureaucracy are practiced within national borders. Successful leaders are consciously disruptive (e.g., John Magufuli in Tanzania and Xi Jinping in China, not to mention the massive shifts promoted by the few Lee Kuan Yews of the world).

As will be described below, in those rare situations where leaders are decisively uncorrupted themselves and where their refusal to accept tainted political allies as colleagues becomes widely known, a governmental culture of discipline and probity can be established that positively rewards honesty and integrity among immediate subordinates and down a long chain of public servants from the police commissioner and the hospital director to the policeman on patrol or the nurse in a clinical corridor. There is at least circumstantial evidence that positive and responsible leadership examples can influence entire nations.[4] The converse is also true. Once a leader indicates (by omission or commission, and by personal carryings-on) that the rot of corruption reaches right into the presidential palace—that the entire nation is up for sale and everything has its price—all those in positions to benefit scramble to make the most of their golden opportunities to grab.

Africa and Asia's best led and least corrupt countries are among the wealthiest globally and per capita in their regions, having in every case risen from abject poverty to riches more quickly and sustainably than most others in the developing world. They are also among the best governed, as measured by indexes that assess corruption and transparency as well as according to a number of other attributes of good stewardship.[5] Economic studies show that corruption detracts substantially from a nation's growth and its growth prospects. It is almost impossible to sustain accelerated levels of economic growth if corruption is a national default norm and if governmental energies are devoted more to enriching personal coffers than to filling the public purse. Those findings suggest that the more corruption the less development; the most corrupt countries in Asia and Africa (and Central America and Oceania) are for the most part the most weakly governed, according to rating schemes; the poorest; and often the most conflicted. But although good leadership seems highly correlated with high governance marks and bad leadership with deficient governmental accomplishments and lackluster ratings, there could theoretically be structural or cultural differences that predispose countries to poverty or wealth, irrespective of who leads and how.

Do Size and Wealth Matter?

Size may play a determining role in a successful attack on corruption. Many of the better-governed countries across the globe, and a high proportion of the ones with positive Transparency International rankings, are manageably small. More populous countries in the developing world are mostly corrupt. Compare Singapore, Botswana, Mauritius, Cape Verde, Rwanda and the other "most improved" states in preceding chapters to the likes of Vietnam, Indonesia, Pakistan, Nigeria, Kenya, Tanzania, and South Africa. (Rwanda, with 12 million people, has many more inhabitants than places such as Singapore and Botswana.) For sure, it is easier to root out corruption if there are fewer total miscreants.[6]

Being an island also helps, possibly because of increased cultural homogeneity, reduced ethnic rivalries, greater economic equality, historic isolation, smallish size (Mauritius, not Madagascar), and implicitly tighter societal controls. Two-thirds of all island states are well-governed, according to the usual index criteria. About half of the globe's better-governed places are islands.[7] The exceptions, of course, include the oil-exporting islands, such as Equatorial Guinea (which also has a poorer mainland component).

Wealth could be a variable as well, since on a per capita basis places such as Singapore, Botswana, Denmark, Finland, Sweden, Norway, and New Zealand are all among the wealthiest countries per capita worldwide, and Nigeria, Pakistan, and Tanzania are among the poorest. The former group also exhibits low unemployment levels. By 2002, both Hong Kong and Singapore had surpassed Sweden in GDP per capita. But Rwanda and Liberia are also poor, and a number of the smaller countries of Africa and Asia are just as corrupt as their much larger neighbors. Furthermore, prosperity follows anticorruption successes rather than causes them.

Leaders may be able positively to influence a less populous place more easily than a vast one, especially if the vast one is more urban than rural, and less rather than more homogenous. Certainly, common sense says that it is easier to effect policy changes in a city-state than in a federalized entity like Nigeria with thirty-six disparate and heavily populated multi-ethnic jurisdictions called states. Singapore, although a mélange of various southern Chinese ethnic groups, plus Malays, Tamils, Indonesians, and more, in the 1970s had only 2 million inhabitants and was intrinsically more controllable than its much more populous neighbors. As Deng Xiaoping commented, "If I had only Shanghai, I too might be able to change Shanghai as quickly . . . but I have the whole of China!"[8] Today, if Xi Jinping's public assault on corruption in China (and on his enemies) succeeds in minimizing corrupt practices in that huge nation, determined and powerful leadership will be seen to be decisive, whatever the size of a polity.

Econometric research on this problem has been limited to United States federal and state jurisdictions and supports Huntington's early suggestion that there should be greater corruption (and opportunities to be corrupt) among the ranks of officials of subnational governments than among federal bureaucrats. The findings of sophisticated modeling using LOGIT Link show that "larger state-local governments . . . are positively and significantly linked with higher rates of corruption." Officials in U.S. states are more likely to abuse their positions than federal ones, and have greater opportunities, but there is also more corruption in larger states (with more temptations) than in smaller states.[9] Unfortunately, these conclusions can say little about whether the size of nation-states in the developing world is directly related to the ease of stanching corruption.

Economists argue, too, that the likelihood of corruption increases with polity size and that having a "big" government inhibits reducing societal sleaze. Smaller government means less corruption. But some of the least populous Nordic nations have relatively large governmental apparatuses, and low levels of corruption.[10]

We do now know that the least corrupt polities in the developing world were in almost every case wildly corrupt before independence or before a major period of transition—before a new leader assumed control and realized that corrupt practices jeopardized his or her goal of creating a modern, sustainable, political, and economic success; those young leaders sought to remain in power long enough to build a (new) nation from a diverse collection of peoples and destinies. Such leaders, as have so many other developing world heads of state, decried corruption from the onset of their electoral campaigns for high office and again shortly after their inaugurations. But unlike the vast majority of transactional rulers in the developing world, they turned fine words into systematic assaults on corruption, and produced results—as Xi Jinping may be doing now.[11] Instead of stealing from their citizens, they achieved accelerating GDPs per capita, more and higher quality educational opportunities, modernized health and social services, and greater personal and national security. These were and are considerable accomplishments that would have been impossible without successful attacks on corrupt behavior and efforts to persuade, coerce, or educate public servants (as in Hong Kong and Singapore) to cease soliciting bribes and citizens to stop offering under-the-table inducements.

Leaders More Than Institutions

Leaders make a major difference. "Outcomes for the citizens of the developing world depend greatly on the actions and determinations of [political] leaders and on critical political leadership decisions." Moreover, "In the developing world, the critical variable of leadership makes much more of a difference in every realm, particularly in the political realm, than it does in the developed world, where value systems of democracy are fully rooted, where political institutions such as legislatures and judiciaries are independent, where the reality of good governance is taken for granted, and where open economic practices are common."[12] The value added of responsible and enlightened leadership is much greater in those regions of the globe—especially Asia and Africa—where political cultures and political institutions are still decidedly embryonic. The North painfully created institutions that constrain executive power; much of the South still awaits the fashioning of such institutional instruments, the creation of which follows from leadership actions to establish abstemious and enlightened democratically inclined political cultures. It is out of this leadership-induced transformational broth of good or better governance that effective political instruments of democracy gradually emerge.[13]

Such propositions are applicable unreservedly to the struggle to reduce the societal drag of corruption. Compare outcomes within single nations such as Ghana during the presidencies of Jerry Rawlings and John Kufuor; South Africa under Nelson Mandela, Thabo Mbeki, and Jacob Zuma; Zambia led by Frederick Chiluba and Levy Mwanawasa; Indonesia under Suharto and Susilo Bambang Yudhoyonyo; the Democratic Republic of Congo before and after Mobutu Sese Seko; the Philippines under Ferdinand Marco and Corazon and Benigno Aquino; and China guided by Jiang Zemin and Xi Jinping. Such pairings are at least suggestive.

More directly quantitative work, including several seminal econometric studies, has verified the difference that political leaders make, although not specifically with regard to the reduction of corruption. On the basis of robust evidence, such studies show that human agency, irrespective of structure, context, and institutions, is capable of guiding whole populations in and out of poverty—of influencing economic growth attainments.[14] If leaders have had a discernible influence on the rise of GDP per capita (note the Singaporean and Botswanan experiences, and others), then it is at least reasonable to assert that the causal role of political leadership in combating corruption is plausible, and more than merely anecdotal.

Corruption begets more corruption. Just as political leaders can stimulate efforts to reduce the virulence of corruption, so leaders can open the floodgates of societal corruption by signaling a tolerance of personal enrichment or nodding and winking as behavioral norms are breached for the worse. In the developing world much more than the developed world, leaders cast large shadows; the acceptability and the growth of corruption within a nation depends on how leaders position themselves, how they deal with political party needs and the avarice of subordinates, and the extent to which they preside with integrity or not. When President Thabo Mbeki in South Africa refused in 2001 to rein in the acquisitive designs of one or more provincial leaders, and then followed those unfortunate post-Mandelan acts of omission with an uninformed stand on the origins of HIV/AIDS, his personal moral authority and his office's legitimacy both suffered. One consequence was an alarming rise in corrupt behavior throughout South Africa.

Reducing the Influence of Corruption

A handful of successful anticorruption political leaders can indeed "bring to bear a variety of powerful social sanctions and new loyalty patterns to reinforce new administrative norms" and the "legitimacy of effectiveness."[15] Singapore and Botswana, both ex–British possessions, are two disparate exemplars, Singapore before independence a veritable swamp of easygoing but criminalized gangs, Botswana a strait-laced desert land of pent-up ambitions during the same era of decolonization. Both were small, but the first was a storied entrepôt facing outward to the world, the other a desperately poor landlocked protectorate of vast territory with more cattle and sand than people—and few prospects. Singapore, without resources or even its own water supply, a Chinese-populated blip at the end of a Malay-dominated peninsula with antagonistic Indonesians practically at its doorstep, had only a British dockyard to substantiate its claim to nationhood.[16] Botswana, similarly water-dependent, had nothing at first aside from wild game and beef on the hoof to commend it to the world. Both were improbable outposts in which to nurture and develop inspiring and pace-setting leadership, and to initiate the kinds of anticorruption endeavors that would be respected, imitated, and feared well beyond their borders.

Alternative and perfectly plausible leaders could easily have emerged and taken either country down very different, and likely corrupt, paths. Nothing in the histories of the city-colony and the emerging protectorate implied that responsible leadership focused on anticorruption would or should have necessarily emerged. Both early leaders and their life histories were contingent; both could have converted their early political successes to malign autocracy, even kleptocracy. That neither did begs the big questions of how to nurture more leaders of their ilk and how growing middle classes can pressure electoral democracies to back positive-reinforcing rather than negative-reinforcing leaders. What happened in Botswana and Singapore, and several other polities discussed below, implies that nurturing and pressuring can effectively produce such exemplary results.

Neither nation was born noncorrupt. Singapore had long been penetrated by Chinese triads, Mafia-like operatives with ferocious appetites for illicit profiteering. It was acknowledged to be a permissive, wild, port city where corrupt dealings were customary and accepted by the British-run police force. Corruption had been made illegal in 1871, was nevertheless found to be rampant in 1879, highly prevalent in 1886, and still a dominant fact of life in 1937, with the police being deeply implicated. The Japanese occupation and the years after World War II only deepened expectations of graft and extortion. "Bribes and kickbacks were part of a way of life."[17] At independence, Botswana was a sleepier place, still lacking a modern capital, with sparse profits to be made corruptly. Yet, contemporaneous former British outposts in sub-Saharan Africa with spanking new governments and ruling elites rapidly discovered (and could have tutored Botswana) on how official positions could generate boundless opportunities for enrichment. Neither the city-state nor the new nation on the edge of the Kalahari desert needed necessarily to have shunned corruption as the way of new, indigenously run polities. Nearly every other ex-colony perpetuated the corrupt pursuits of its past incarnations (as did Hong Kong) or took full advantage of new opportunities thanks to Cold

War blandishments, foreign assistance revenues, or their own wishes to give their inhabitants first-world opportunities and attainments. But not Singapore and Botswana, led by singular young individuals who pioneered unique, but very distinctive, approaches to nation-building.

The difference was imposed from above and, in a sense, from without, by two determined and far-seeing men. Lee Kuan Yew, in Singapore, had scrambled his way to political prominence; Seretse Khama in Botswana possessed rational legitimacy and an ethnic preeminence that was unequalled locally and that he sagely converted into political capital. Neither was motivated exclusively by moral or religious scruples. But both, possibly because of their British academic training and their deep exposure to British mores, were intent on establishing substantial new transformative nations, not commonplace transactional states. Neither leader's first impulse was to benefit himself or his family. Given Lee's abundant personal self-confidence, he did not (nor did Khama) seek to govern grandly and omnipotently, in the manner of so many of their Asian and African peers. Rather, they both appreciated much more than their peers that only by fostering good governance could their nascent states survive and prosper. Unlike many of their neighbors, they genuinely enshrined the rule of law and other building blocks of well-run Scandinavian-style states. Beating back or preventing the rise of corruption was hence basic to both nation-building endeavors and fundamental to their mutual cases for taking charge of local leadership opportunities.

Lee and Khama, by force of political will, set about as first orders of business to impose full prohibitions against corruption. By instinct and calculation, they knew they had to demonstrate zero tolerance for corruption at all levels, and of all kinds. There could, they perceived, be no deviations permitted from an absolute jihad against the taint of corruption for fear that every minor mishap or trivial peculation would undermine both their overall crusade and the entire edifice of nation-building. They reckoned, in their very distinctly separate ways and styles, that they could be effective Canutes, holding back the onrushing tides of their colleagues' avarice. They guessed, without being certain that their slight new states would then stand a chance of surviving, even flourishing. And so they eventually did, thanks in large part to the separate decisions by two young leaders to inoculate their new enterprises against the maladies of corruption.

Lee's Prescription

Ten thousand members of 360 Chinese criminal gangs controlled Singapore during Britain's last days in the colony. These triads, as they were known, specialized in extortion, kidnapping for ransom, and a host of other illicit pursuits that depended on corruption being expected and normal—a routine part of the governance culture. Even in the final years of British rule, Singapore's police were notorious for scandal. The police mobile unit (a specialized kind of antiriot squad) took money as a matter of course from truck drivers to overlook infractions. Those who guarded the markets bilked everyday hawkers, the men and women who sold from stalls daily. Yet, so long as its naval outpost in Singapore were secure, Britain saw no need to impose external norms and thus to attempt to limit the spread of graft and influence peddling. It was not in its interest, as overlord, to bother.

But Lee, assuming power first as a local political leader in 1959 (during the era of "responsible" government, still under British rule), and then as the leader of one of the fourteen components of the Malaysian federation from 1963 to 1965, understood that continued corruption would vitiate any expectation of realizing his vision for the emerging city-state. When Singapore exited Malaysia under duress and Singapore and Lee were alone in the world from 1965, it became even more imperative for Lee to scrub the new nation clean of corruption. As a former legal advisor to the local Communist Party and as someone who fully knew the role of corruption and criminality in shabby Singapore, Lee well appreciated that only by taming the city and its shady pursuits would he and the city-state survive politically. The meritocratic, administrative state that he envisaged could not deliver appropriate measures of good governance and prosperity if it remained prey to inimical influences. Lee was motivated to endure politically and to build a Singapore that could prosper outside of the federation.

Governments, in his mind, were responsible for ensuring fundamental freedoms, including personal security and safety. Good governments established and maintained order, fairly and with the support of their constituents. Moreover, Lee—the ultimate pragmatist—believed in a nation of laws, a nation disciplined, and a nation decent.[18] All of these notions, derived from his brief and bitter Malaysian experience as well as his harrowing days under Japanese occupation, made corruption the enemy of the state—the metastasizing cancer from within.

Lee could not hope or pretend to grow a sparkling city-state without ending corrupt practices. Any lapses—any backing off from the battle against sleaze and fraud, no matter how minor—would undermine his attempt to transform a third-world port city into a glittering and enviable first-world oasis. From the start, Lee's task was difficult, even seemingly intractable, since his administration had to struggle against deeply engrained expectations of corrupt behavior locally and throughout surrounding Southeast Asia. In 1960 or 1965, few would have anticipated how successful Singapore would become under Lee, and how much the removal of corruption was fundamental to that success.

One key consideration for him in those early days was gaining political support—never a given—from Singapore's seething constituents. A wildly divided and linguistically fractured combination of various Chinese language groups, Malays, Tamils, Hindi-speaking Indians, and others, Singapore had no real identity or sense of cohesion. Corrupted, its enterprise would remain equally mixed and confused. Singapore, Lee feared and others expected, would wallow haphazardly, adrift amid the backwash of forward-thrusting Malaysia and Indonesia under Sukarno's corrupt despotism.

Lee's vision for Singapore's greatness was also threatened by a keen awareness of how easily his own and his political party's ability to create a modern city-state could be destroyed by perceptions of illegitimacy. In the city-state, idealistic students and others had become communists, disgusted as they were with the "venality, greed, and immorality" of many Asian leaders. Fighters for freedom, such as Sukarno, had become plunderers of their newly emancipated societies. In Singapore, at least, students and others viewed the local communists as dedicated, selfless, and noncorrupt.[19]

Lee deeply appreciated that insisting upon a principled, puritanical, approach to governance and to the temptations of accommodating abuse of office would be convenient, rhetorically, but taxing and tempestuous in practice. "It is easy," he admitted, "to start off with high moral standards, strong convictions, and a determination to beat down corruption. But it is difficult to live up to these good intentions unless the leaders are strong and determined enough to deal with all transgressors, and without exceptions."[20] The key to Lee's credibility as an anticorruption campaigner, and the main ingredient of his unqualified success, may be found in those last two quoted words. Unusually among virtually all other heads of state and heads of government of his era and since, Lee did more than just talk the talk. He acted decisively. Many others spoke piously, established anticorruption commissions (see chapter 5), and then proceeded to make the exceptions that Lee, clear-eyed and intent on cleaning up the pirate-infested swamp that he had inherited, refused to countenance. Hardly any leader except Seretse Khama in Botswana (and now Paul Kagame in Rwanda and Xi Jinping in China) was so obsessive, even ruthless, in cleansing a ruling cohort of anyone, even close and intimate political associates, who appeared to have succumbed to the temptations of corruption.

Lee followed this politically dangerous course because he had much earlier diagnosed exactly how corrupt practices could be eradicated: from the top down, never from the bottom up. "If the probity of the top leadership were exemplary, lower ranks would be less often tempted, and certainly rarely feel entitled, to cheat."[21] Lee's method from the start, and especially from the late 1960s when his purge of corrupt behavior was fully underway, was to confront and publicly to shame presumed malefactors as soon as they were suspected of indulging in illicit behavior or living above their means. He enunciated a zero-tolerance policy against elected or appointed officials who chose or seemed inclined to act inappropriately on behalf of friends, clients, kith or kin, or cliques by accepting or accommodating tainted favors.

Heads soon toppled. Tan Kia Gan, a close friend and sometime minister for national development, was serving as a director of the joint national airline in 1966 when Lee abruptly removed him from all of his appointed positions. Lee suspected Tan of taking payments from an aircraft supplier to favor that firm over another. Tan was ostracized despite the lack of evidence to convict him in court of accepting bribes.

Wee Toon Boon was minister of state in the Ministry of the Environment in 1975 when he accepted free air passage to nearby Indonesia, plus an expensive bungalow and loan guarantees. All of these emoluments came from a property developer who was angling for Singaporean government contracts. Lee discharged Wee on the spot, and this time the evidence was strong enough for the Singaporean courts to sentence Wee to four years in jail.

Four years later, Phey Yew Kok, head of the National Trade Union Congress and a member of Parliament for Lee's ruling People's Action Party (PAP), was believed to have stolen funds from the congress and invested them for himself. When accused and on bail pending a court appearance, Phey skipped to Thailand.

Teh Cheang Wan was minister of national development in 1986 when he took two large cash payments, the first from a land development company that sought to keep control of property that had been scheduled for compulsory acquisition by the state, the second from another developer who sought to acquire public land for private purposes. After his bribe taking was unearthed, Teh committed suicide rather than be disgraced.

The government's chief fire officer was peremptorily discharged when, at an official reception, Lee noticed the officer's "stunningly attractive wife" bedecked with expensive gold jewelry. Lee immediately suspected that her husband had to be living well beyond his means. "Her scintillating adornments," wrote one of Lee's critics, "caught the practiced eye of the prime minister."[22]

With these dismissals and prosecutions, and many more like them during the first three decades of Lee's rule, high-level Singaporeans rapidly learned that corruption, or even the most marginal suspicion of being corrupted, did not pay. Lee's zero-tolerance policy took some time to become fully acculturated, but, by the 1980s, breaches of trust had become remarkably rare. Lee had successfully shifted the incentive basis of corruption. His associates hardly became better people, but they soon understood how risky it was to dabble in anything that smelled even remotely of graft. The costs to their careers, their lifestyles, their families, and their reputations were—as Lee relentlessly showed—enormous.

Because Singaporeans began to appreciate that those who ruled and regulated them were not—as was so common in Asia—taking advantage of their official positions to enrich themselves, even the most jaundiced inhabitants of the island understood how dramatically Lee had lifted the burden of corruption from their daily lives. What was common before 1965 was no longer possible, even in Singapore's "Red-Light" district, even in the betting shops that were so much a part of overseas Chinese life, and even in daily encounters with the traffic police. Once Lee's administration began in the 1960s and 1970s to arrest those who fleeced dealers at the markets or who tried to fine innocent drivers for nonexistent infractions and pocket the proceeds—once it became perfectly clear that inspectors could no longer demand cash payments from subinspectors, and subinspectors from policemen on the beat— breaches of official trust became rare. Citizens noticed and, ever so dramatically, refused henceforth to pay bribes or to permit civil servants to cheat them out of their rights. Lee created a new, all-encompassing political culture in Singapore that privileged probity and both forbade indulging in corruption and made unseemly anyone who still chose to behave unethically and in a manner so deviant that his or her actions besmirched Singapore.

By dint of political will and some draconian initiatives, Lee truly transformed a rough and freewheeling Singapore into what he regarded as a decent and a clean society. He sought conformity in his people, for the greater social good. Greatly marginalizing corruption, and reducing that burden on his citizens and followers, was a part of a new social contract that virtually guaranteed security, safety, freedom from strife, high rates of economic growth, improved social standards, comfortable if somewhat regimented housing in blocks of apartments, and a sense of pride in the small nation's attainments for everyone who accepted Lee's prescription of good governance and accompanying curbs on freedom of expression and freedom of assembly. Central to Lee's crusade was the ongoing campaign against corruption.

In addition to the powerful demonstration and educationally preventive effect that flowed from his willingness to make examples when required of his friends, political associates, and all other public employees, Lee also strengthened the city-state's legal armaments (outlined in chapters 3 and 4). Singapore tightened regulations and loosened evidentiary restrictions. Very clear guidelines were spelled out for those who might still be tempted to take advantage of their official elected and appointed positions. Public servants and businessmen knew precisely what consequences they could suffer. Legislated written rules warned that persons suspected of "living beyond their means" or their nominal salaries, owning fancy homes or automobiles, wearing expensive watches and jewels, and displaying other accoutrements of wealth (as corroborating evidence) would be examined for presumed corruption.

Lee persuaded Singapore's Parliament to tighten the city-state's inherited laws as they pertained to corruption. Lee preferred to leave nothing to chance. Under the law, as discussed in chapter 3, an illicit gratuity was expanded to include the receipt of "anything" of value. The new legal framework also gave investigators from the police special branch and the inherited Corrupt Practices Investigation Bureau (CPIB) the authority to arrest and search presumed perpetrators and their families, scrutinize bank accounts, obtain income tax returns, and be as intrusive as necessary. The amended laws also permitted judges to accept the (hearsay) testimony of accomplices, to compel evidence even from unwilling witnesses, and to bar "misleading" testimony. The courts were able to impose large fines on corrupt individuals and to confiscate any benefits and property that were deemed the product of corrupt activity. Lee invited ordinary Singaporeans to implicate any and all persons suspected of giving and taking bribes.

From the 1960s, Lee took direct personal charge of the Corruption Protection Investigation Bureau, having it report directly to him. The CPIB became his and Singapore's watchdog, its surveillance arm, with vast informal power because it was backed by the prime minister and was known to be his favorite investigative instrument. Although comparatively thinly staffed and modestly resourced, and having to share some responsibilities with government prosecutors and the police, it played an increasingly strong and fundamental role in helping Lee cleanse Singapore of what more and more over time became minor cases of influence peddling and the abuse of public positions (see chapter 4).

Once Lee's way—his didactic and semi-authoritarian manner of governing, but with large doses of serious consultation and regular squeaky-clean elections—delivered large dollops of evenly distributed prosperity to nearly all Singaporeans, world-beating educational and health systems, a globally superior airline, and major quantities of esteem and a sense of being integral parts of a highly regarded new global nation, citizens easily traded former ways for the positive, durable results that Lee and his ruling colleagues had manufactured.[23] Corruption, because of such outstanding individual and national advances, easily became an old-fashioned, discarded, pursuit of the past. Generations grew to maturity that hardly knew what bribes were. Within the lifetime of one determined leader, and largely because of his insistence, very few Singaporeans condoned corruption. Lee had transformed a political culture.

Lee had not permitted his followers to continue to be corrupt. The demonstration effect of his leadership and his actions was powerful. But his example and his persistent tutelage also achieved, as the instrumental and expressive initiatives of a few great leaders are sometimes able to manage, a thorough reordering of citizen attitudes concerning the responsibilities owed to them by public representatives and officials. Lee rightly argued that a community's strong deterrent against corruption was crucial, "a public opinion which censures and condemns corrupt persons . . . in attitudes which make corruption so unacceptable that the stigma of corruption cannot be washed away by serving a prison sentence."[24] Lee, by the 1980s, had largely succeeded in socializing Singaporeans, whatever their family and ethnic backgrounds, to regard corrupt acts as shameful. As earlier in the Nordic nations, that implanting of a new norm helped and has continued to keep Singapore essentially free of what is usually regarded as corruption.

Lee, ever pragmatic, had a striking faith in his own ability—an ability to think straight and make a convincing case—to nudge or bully centuries of custom out of existence. His goal was never to create a utopian society but rather a prosperous one that worked, and worked exceptionally well, and one of which he and all constituents could be proud. Pragmatism, comments a leading Singaporean public intellectual, "can be an ethical principle if it improves people's lives."[25]

Lee had also created a quintessential administrative state that, by the 1980s and ever since, has been infused with a high level of managerial professionalism. The Singaporean state recruited and nurtured a meritocratic elite that it tracked carefully through secondary school and then trained and still trains locally and at overseas universities. Those carefully shepherded young people are subsequently streamed into the military, police, state corporations, and civil service. Merit applies, standards are strict, and the result is a cadre of public servants who are loyal to the state, generally effective, easy to control, conformist, and instinctively anticorrupt. Lee's Singapore eventually created an incentive structure for the public (and the private) sector which prized probity and accountability and—in a remarkable manner that has been hard elsewhere to duplicate—eschewed the dark dealings of corruption.

Lee put forward one additional policy nostrum to dampen corruption; by elevating public service salaries he eliminated the penalties of penury under which most civil servants and policemen, in early Singapore and now especially in Africa, typically toiled. Beginning in 1972, by which time Singapore had begun to grow robustly and Lee was more and more confident that he and his associates were successfully bringing both prosperity and integrity to the emerging city-state, he sponsored a drive to give Singaporeans the highest public service salaries in the world, as measured per capita and per underlying GDP. Lee believed in the telling aphorisms "Pay now or we pay later!" and "Feed them peanuts and they will behave like monkeys!"[26] In 1985, when Lee felt assured that he could indeed convert a Third World harbor into a First World oasis (the words are his), he boosted governmental salaries yet again. In 1994, culminating this drive for "appropriate" rewards, ministerial and public officer salaries were pegged at two-thirds the level of similar private sector wages, with automatic annual increases without parliamentary approval. Senior officers in the police, for example, saw their salaries fixed above the pay scales of senior officers in large American city systems. Given those healthy monetary returns, plus a political culture that had grown to inhibit the practice of anything that could remotely be construed as permitting corruption and a vigilant anticorruption investigating authority, it is no wonder that Singapore has for decades ranked among the least corrupt nation-states of all sizes on the Corruption Perceptions Index and the World Bank's Control of Corruption indicator. (Note, however, that there is no cross-national evidence that simply improving take-home pay can eliminate corruption.)[27]

Given the fact that Lee's eldest son serves as prime minister, his second son ran local businesses and chaired the city-state's Civil Aviation Authority, and his daughter runs Singapore's sovereign wealth fund, has nepotism replaced kleptocracy as Singapore's major corrupt methodology? Lee always reacted sharply to such accusations, asserting (with much evidence) that all of the positions and high places won by members of his family were achieved through talent. He strongly asserted, again with evidence, that Singapore above all else was a meritocracy. Nevertheless, in a small society such as Singapore, being closely related to the first prime minister (later the senior minister and the mentor minister) obviously enabled impressive talent to be nurtured, noticed, and rewarded. From Lee's point of view, his children had been exposed in his household to the kinds of standards that he wished Singapore to uphold. They were all imbued with his ideas and his regimen. (He was a strict parent, even though a longtime family retainer reported that he was also a kind and devoted father.)[28] Nevertheless, the fact that they were all Lees enabled them to enrich themselves even as they faithfully served Singapore and in no obvious way abused their many public positions. A leading academic critic of Lee admits that although there has been "a remarkable prevalence of family networks in Singapore Inc. and the public sphere more generally (especially Lee's family) . . . there is no active concept of [special] interest operating anywhere in the Singapore public sphere."[29]

In death and in life, Lee himself, and his family members, were never accused of accruing wealth beyond their means or of living ostentatiously. Compared to any number of ruling families and rulers, the Lees were as ascetic and as personally disciplined as the man himself. (Too much criticism, admittedly, of the Lees would have been dangerous and costly, for Lee frequently sued his attackers for libel in the local courts and always won the kinds of large judgments that bankrupted those who dared question his and his family's contributions to the emergence of Singapore as major city-state.[30])

Since the creation of the Berlin-based Corruption Perceptions Index in 1995, Singapore consistently has ranked among the globe's ten least corrupt nation-states. The World Bank's indicator has always agreed as well. In 2008, according to the CPI, Singapore was the fourth most free from corruption entity, after Denmark, Sweden, and New Zealand. (The United States ranked 20th.) Six years later, Singapore had slipped to seventh place after Denmark, New Zealand, Finland, Sweden, Norway, and Switzerland, but was a mere eight points below the top score and a single point below its own 2013 total. The U.S. had advanced to rank 17th, with a score eight points under Singapore's. In 2015, Singapore had fallen on the CPI to 8th place (of 168) with 85 points, below Switzerland and ahead of Canada.[31]

The fruits of anticorruption are even more demonstrable in terms of unadjusted annual GDP per capita—from $450 in 1965 to more than $60,500 in 2015—and in terms of the obsessively modern look and feel of the city-state itself. [32] By establishing a well-governed, stable, corruption-free Singapore, Lee was able to attract foreign (at first mostly American) multinational corporations to invest in the city-state and to establish their Asian outposts there. He transformed the old transshipment port and British naval base into a Southeast Asian and then a global center for profitable electronics manufacturing, petroleum refining, container assembling, and for banking and insurance. Tourism soon followed.

Job creation was of paramount concern. With corruption curbed and then banned, financial integrity boosted, and exchange controls abolished, by the end of his first ten years as prime minister, Lee was able to reduce unemployment from 14 percent to 5 percent and to boost growth rates to 5 and 6 percent yearly, a pace that continued for several decades. Under Lee, the city-state moved rapidly into skill-based pursuits; invested heavily in literate, numerative, and technical education; and converted its polyglot Chinese, Malay, Hindi, and Tamil speakers into citizens literate in written and conversational English. Lee also insisted on turning hot, humid, Equatorial Singapore into an air-conditioned mecca of trade. From the late 1970s, nearly all Singaporeans had jobs, were housed in multi-ethnic blocks of flats, and were growing wealthy and middle class in their aspirations.[33] He was succeeding in building a new nation. At his death in 2015, Singapore was far and away the First World, incorruptible, predictable, socially and politically thoroughly controlled oasis in a Third World setting that he had long planned to create. He had conveyed "grandeur and glory to all those united with him as they [sought] virtue together"—but not without acute curtailments of personal freedoms.[34]

Khama's Nostrum

A British governor set about controlling corruption in Hong Kong in 1974, but until Paul Kagame began an assault on Rwanda's corrupt dealings in the first decade of the twenty-first century and Chinese Communist Party chief Xi Jinping began defrocking corrupt party bigwigs, warlords, generals, and technocrats in the second decade of this century, Lee's effectiveness in the wars against corruption was unique—a pinnacle of accomplishment in a universe littered with failed attempts and more expressions of piety than genuine efforts. Including the many donor-sponsored and possibly well-meant attempts in Africa to deploy anticorruption agencies from the 1980s, hardly any political leaders genuinely sought to employ Lee's uncompromising methods, or anything similar, to squelch corruption.

Seretse Khama in Botswana was the exception. Unlike Lee, he wrote no memoirs and was fully explicit only in conversation about his antipathy to corruption, but those who resided in or visited Botswana in its early years either were told about or sensed his determination to prevent corruption from taking root. He decided from the first days of his presidency in 1966, if not well before, that corrupt practices were the ruin of Africa and had no place in his thinly populated, impoverished, former protectorate squeezed between South Africa and (then) South African–controlled Namibia.

Indigenous Botswana before independence had known little corruption. The English- and Afrikaans-speaking civil servants who had largely run the Bechuanaland Protectorate before independence had too few favors to offer, so unlike in neighboring South Africa, corrupt incidents were rare at the national governing level and little known at the indigenous, communal, level. Afrikaner-run South Africa was much more corrupted than the surrounding former British protectorates, and some of its petty corruption may have crossed the border along with white police or the staff of the transiting Rhodesia Railway. But at independence in 1966, it would have been hard for experienced observers to label the new Botswana corrupt.

But it was, as any newly created political jurisdiction, certainly corruptible. What Khama knew well from his acquaintance with the rest of newly enfranchised sub-Saharan Africa, especially Kwame Nkrumah's Ghana, Sékou Touré's Guinea, and Mobutu Sese Seko's Zaire, was how greedy were other leaders; the end of colonial rule had flung open the gates of avarice to the newly empowered. Tswanan civil servants and officials, whether foreign-born or local, were as likely to be tempted to pilfer as their counterparts elsewhere on the continent. Khama was anxious to prevent such races to richness through theft or misappropriation of state resources. He early instructed local politicians and public officials not to view their country's emancipation as a route to personal enrichment. He insisted from the start that cabinet ministers pay any debts promptly and cover their bank overdrafts. Khama preferred real national development efforts, honestly pursued.

This strong, vocal, principled stand against corruption was integral to Khama's profound sense of responsibility to his much less educated and experienced constituents, some of whom lacked land and worked herding the cattle of their better-off fellow Tswana. Khama sought to build a nation. That meant unifying Botswana's different peoples, eliminating what he termed "tribalism," and gradually instilling in his followers an innovative political culture, or bundle of values, to guide a young embryonic state as it took its place in Africa and in the world. Without Khama's vision and the efforts he undertook to mobilize the Ngwato, Kgatla, Kwena, Rolong, Ngwaketse, and Kalanga peoples behind his vision, Botswana under less farsighted leadership might have remained a collection of ethnic fiefdoms and a purely bovine economy controlled by wealthy barons like himself. Instead, Khama sought from the start to give Botswana and its peoples a central purpose. To do good, he said persistently, was his "real religion."[35]

Khama was almost alone among the African heads of state of that era in rejecting the panaceas and easy nostrums of governance. As a presumptive Ngwato paramount chief, he possessed unsurpassed rational legitimacy and easily could have ruled Botswana autocratically, permitting widespread corruption in the African manner. But he believed that the construction of a modern Botswanan state could only occur by refusing the convenient notions that other African presidents were advancing in their own and their party's self-interest. Those ideas seemed dangerous and wrong. He told Parliament at an early sitting that authoritarian rule was never to be tolerated, and he condemned North Korea and mainland China (where he had paid state visits) as tyrannical systems "hatched in the minds of men who appoint themselves philosophers, kings, and possessors of absolute truth."[36]

Khama bemoaned "the mess" that Africans elsewhere had made of their postindependence political choices. A state visit to Malawi, where American-trained Dr. Hastings K. Banda acted every inch the potentate, disturbed him. So did the coming to power in Uganda of Idi Amin, and even the humanistic but still one-man rules of Kenneth Kaunda in adjoining Zambia and Julius Nyerere in Tanzania. "The time has come," this intellectually honest leader said, "when we should sit down and look very closely at ourselves."[37] Corruption, spreading as it was in the rest of Africa, had no place in the young Botswana.

Khama preached the national need for enduring political behavioral platforms on which to construct a fully inclusive, united, nation-state that could hold its proverbial head high despite its small population, its limited resources, and its unfortunate proximity to apartheid-dominated South Africa. "Seretse was a democrat through and through," wrote his successor.[38] Khama determined to prevent corrupt practices from retarding Botswana's evolution from poverty to prosperity and from tribalism to modernity.

Khama set a personal example and insisted that his vice president, cabinet ministers, and top officials foster a humble tone and behave with impeccable integrity. According to Vice-President Quett Ketumile Masire, Khama's closest associate and successor in office, since corruption wrecked whole economies and benefited the few at the expense of the many, they "worked hard to avoid" corruption and to punish it severely if discovered. In the beginning, Masire wrote, Botswana was poor and it was very easy to operate fully transparently. It was expedient to continue the British practice of "properly accounting for things."[39] They also recruited to and promoted in the civil service on merit. They ensured that Botswana developed an autonomous judiciary. But, as Botswana became a nation-state and began (during Khama's last years before his untimely death) to receive abundant royalties from the exploitation of vast gem diamond deposits, it became necessary to quell corrupt tendencies within the public service.

Khama lived modestly as Botswana's first president and, as befitting a country with limited financial resources, kept his motorcades much shorter than those of other African presidents.[40] Cabinet ministers were forbidden to fly commercially anywhere in better than economy class. There were no costly presidential jet aircraft, the ostentatious mark of so many of Botswana's neighbors and rivals. Inside Botswana, too, cabinet ministers drove themselves in their own automobiles, a rare affectation in an Africa where heads of state and their subordinates from even puny countries insisted upon all of the perquisites enjoyed by leaders of much more wealthy nations.

Masire ruefully relates the story of his arrival by air in Addis Ababa for an important set of Organization of African Unity (OAU) meetings. Since he was traveling in the coach section, in the back of the airplane, by the time that he emerged to exit the aircraft his hosts had despaired of his arrival and rolled up the welcoming red carpet.[41]

After about 1972, when gem diamonds had been discovered and were starting to be exploited, Khama was alert to the dangers of rent seeking by anyone active in the new industry, and especially by the cabinet ministers responsible for shepherding this new national patrimony. He knew that some of his associates might try to invent special ways of profiting from the growing national largesse; they could arrange permits and employ other nonofficial methods of allowing some of the new wealth to stick to their own fingers. Once Botswana's minister of natural resources committed suicide in 1976, Khama redoubled his attack on the potentially corrupting influence of diamonds and on anything that could be construed as creeping "Dutch disease."

Of practical support for his anticorruption prevention campaign was Khama's unusual and very un-African decision to refuse to give too much autonomy to any of his political associates. Ministers could make no major moves on their own. Unwittingly echoing the nineteenth century Prussian preference for collegiate professional responsibility, Khama decreed that ministers had to involve or at least consult the heads of other departments, thus spreading and collectivizing authority.[42] For example, when Botswana chose to grant concessions or leases for the mining of diamonds and coal, several ministries had to be canvassed and the ultimate approval to be given by the entire cabinet, with President Khama in the chair. Khama specifically instructed an early minister of mines who had wanted to act on an important matter in his official capacity, according to the authority invested in him by the Mines and Minerals Act, that he simply could not. "No, this is not something for one man on his own; it is too important. Even if you think it is right, if anything goes wrong, you must share the responsibility with your colleagues . . . And if the people later think it is wrong, then you will have others defend why it was thought to be the right thing to do."[43] Given the immense opportunities for personal profit involved, Khama was not about to trust anyone, even those whom he had appointed. He also wisely insisted that his ministers should reveal the full implications of any official decisions taken by them, whether administrative or financial. He believed in full transparency, and practiced it himself.

Khama and Masire further behaved to their colleagues as Lee had done and was doing in contemporaneous times. They prosecuted the handful of Tswanan cabinet ministers and officials who misappropriated public funds or attempted illicitly to benefit from their high positions. One of those so indicted was Khama's cousin, a senior bureaucrat. Another was a ranking member of the ruling Botswana Democratic Party. A third was Masire's younger brother. In that last case, the report of a high-level commission that investigated the accusations against him was published for all Tswana to read. In a fourth significant case, Masire terminated an assistant minister and the permanent secretary of the Ministry of Local Government and Lands, although the minister's criminal conviction was eventually overturned on appeal.

What Khama and Masire, who was president from Khama's early death in 1980 until 1998, communicated so well to their citizens across the vast reaches of Botswana was that neither was in politics to gain wealth or power. They were in office to strengthen and construct a singular new nation more aboveboard than any other on the continent. Khama, who set the standard as Botswana's first liberation leader, cherished the unparalleled opportunity to implant the very best and most responsible of African values, to create an open and tolerant society, and to give his nation-state a political culture of democracy that was unique for its time and place in sub-Saharan Africa.[44]

As noted economists and political scientists have concluded, Botswana's spectacular progress, especially as compared to nearly all other mainland African nations, resulted from its establishment of solid political institutions, from strict respect for the rule of law and property rights, from a fair judiciary, and from the insightful manner in which Khama and Masire had governed their infant country and prevented any infection by corruption.[45]

Khama's refusal to condone corruption sets him apart from nearly every other first leader of mainland Africa. That unwillingness to abide corrupters or corruptees was fundamental in making Botswana the well-governed and minimally corrupt place that it became and that it is today. His successor presidents, emboldened by his leadership example in this and other areas, prevented corrupt practices from engulfing Botswana as they did most of its southern African neighbors. But most decisive was the lesson of personal leadership integrity that Khama exemplified and contributed to his country.

Legitimacy and integrity are core competencies of exemplary leadership. Without the first, effective leadership is impossible.[46] Followers decide whether elected political leaders retain or lose legitimacy—the respect and credibility that permit leaders to rule well and with popular support. Lee always understood how empowering legitimacy was and how essential it remained for him in his battle to transform Singapore into a First World oasis. Without legitimacy, all possibility of nation-building, or of the enactment of progressive measures, would be impossibly difficult. Khama's acute political sense, his evident modesty, and his moral rectitude buttressed his legitimacy among voters and among all Batswana, including and beyond his own Ngwato people.

Legitimacy ultimately depends less on competency than it does on authenticity, on "ethical probity, moral accountability, a refusal to abuse privilege and authority, a dampening of greed, a strengthening of trust, fairness and—in Africa—a playing down of the 'big man' themes of ostentation and pomposity."[47] The best leaders project integrity. They are never diverted by the prospect of financial gain or political ambition to sacrifice the public trust.[48] Additionally, like Khama, the best leaders are ethical and moral, but not moralistic. "Leaders exhibit ethical behavior when they demonstrate altruistic intent, empower rather than attempt to control followers, cultivate virtues, and avoid vices." To be ethical, in other words, is to be morally right, a characteristic which Khama embodied naturally and without any manipulation of his audiences.[49] It is the rare leader in the developing world who projects these values to his people in a consistent manner and who, moreover, shows self-mastery and demonstrates the important quality of intellectual honesty.[50] Khama was more punctilious than most in refusing to take policy or integrity shortcuts and to play politics according to rules that were more strict than his surroundings or traditional mores demanded.

Being fully legitimate and projecting unquestioned integrity helped Lee to grow Singapore and Khama to modernize Botswana. In both cases, magisterial administrative decisions as well as the banishment and prevention of corruption greatly enabled two poor and unpromising colonial outposts to emerge in the twentieth and twenty-first centuries as among the best governed and most economically and socially enriching entities in the developing world. In sub-Saharan Africa, Botswana has always been ranked among its top five countries since the Index of African Governance was invented in 2004 and first published in 2007.[51] Likewise, according to the CPI, Botswana has consistently been the highest scoring (least corrupt) country in the African Union. In 2015, the CPI put Botswana in 28th place (of 168) countries with a score of 63. The closest following African countries were Cape Verde (40th and 55 points), the Seychelles (40th and 55 points), Rwanda (44th and 54 points), and Mauritius and Namibia (both 45th and 53 points). Ghana was in 56th place, with 47 points.[52]

Thanks to diamonds (but not oil) and good management, Botswana grew in terms of GDP per capita at about 7 percent a year from the 1970s almost to 2014—an unprecedented steady rise by African and most developing world standards. Whereas most of the non–petroleum producing countries of Africa had GDPs per capita below $1,000, Botswana's in 2015 was $16,200 at purchasing power parity. Mauritius was sub-Saharan Africa's next wealthiest country, at $15,100. Only the Seychelles, a tiny island state, at $25,000, and equally sparsely populated and oil-rich Equatorial Guinea, at $19,000, were wealthier per capita.[53] Moreover, Botswana is one of the very few African nations that have known nothing but peace and stability since independence. Its schooling opportunities and provision of healthcare (despite a high incidence of HIV/ AIDS) are exceptional for Africa. Its university is among the better ones on the continent after the top South African institutions and one in Mauritius. In 2017, Botswana enjoys what too few of its fellow African nations can expect: a flourishing democracy, high standards of living, unquestioned rule of law, an absence of serious internal strife, effective government at several levels, and a sense of pride in the national model—in being citizens of Botswana.

Khama showed the way, especially with regard to policies that produced good governance and an antipathy to corruption. Masire coped with a surprising irruption of corrupt behavior in the early 1990s by creating a successful anticorruption commission (see chapter 5) and by giving it significant investigative and prosecutorial freedom, reiterating the regime's antagonism to corruption, and rapidly refurbishing the anticorruption ethic that Khama had enunciated. Masire believes that the fact that his administration pursued all serious allegations of corruption "and did not try to hide the fact [that] they occurred" strengthened Botswana's incipient democracy and its stance on corruption. Justice, he asserted, "must not only be done but must be seen to be done."[54]

Given Botswana's estimable CPI and WBCC performances, these reforms seems to have held corruption in check, building as they did on the ethical foundations laid by Khama. Opinion polls indicate that consistently since about 2005 the Tswanan public has lauded its government's anticorruption efforts, with an approval rate of more than 60 percent.[55]

Xi Jinping Purges the Corrupt

Xi Jinping, China's "most authoritarian leader since Chairman Mao," is vigorously waving high "the sword against corruption." He vowed to prosecute and persecute both fast-running "tigers" and lowly "flies."[56] If he succeeds over the next few years in curbing corrupt practices in Beijing, Shanghai, and other major Chinese cities, and if his anticorruption efforts begin to reduce the power of corrupt officials in the countryside, then Xi will have dramatically altered the entire political culture of post-Mao China, enriched the lives of more than 1.3 billion people, and demonstrated what committed leadership can produce in the globe's largest franchise. *If* he does perceptibly reduce corruption, and *if* Xi's reforms are sustained for the full years remaining in his presidential term or terms, and thereafter, then his efforts will have been the most supreme test of leadership as a decisive variable in overcoming corrupt values and corrupt inclinations.

Xi's task should not be underestimated. China has been corrupt and corrupted for centuries. Mao's rule permitted, if not encouraged, the permeation of corruption throughout the vast nation and deep into the most remote village settings. Deng Xiaoping and his successors turned a blind eye, for obvious political reasons, to the pillaging and graft that, by their times, had become a way of life in Communist China.[57] Deng's capitalistic opening of the Shenzhen economic opportunity zone, and his subsequent transformation of China into a major driver of global prosperity, fueled the enjoyment of corrupt rewards at the highest levels of Chinese rule and its movement downward through every hierarchical formation to the very lowest bureaucratic levels of society.

Xi's undertaking is immense. But because he has "effectively taken over the courts, the police, and the secret police," because he is "the center of everything," it is just possible that Xi can preside over a "great rejuvenation of the nation."[58] That is exactly what a significant slowing down of the spread of corruption nationally, or a possible diminution of corruption more generally, would mean in the planet's most populated polity. Xi watchers believe that his attack on the hoary institution of domestic corruption has three prime objectives: to save the nation and the ruling party before they are both completely swamped by corruption; to remove corruption as an impediment to continued rapid economic growth; and to use the corrupt failings of his enemies to eliminate them and consolidate his rule.

Nearly all of those arrested since Xi came to power have been allied to rival party factions; none of the military culprits have been his own appointees. Nor have there been any arrests for corruption of individuals currently serving at the very pinnacle of state and party power. Astute China watchers assert that Xi's crackdown on corruption is really all about loyalty to Xi and not about impermissible peculation and graft. It is also about deconstructing webs of patronage relationships within the ruling party.[59] But it may still have a profound effect on nefarious dealings by important Chinese officials who fear being ensnared in the takedown.

Xi's rule requires and depends upon a strong and resolute party; corruption poses an existential threat to the party and to its sustained rule.[60] Furthermore, an attack on especially corrupt elements within the party boosts his own power, could strengthen his legitimacy nationally and within the upper echelons of the party, and gives a canny tactician like himself greater room to maneuver as an all-powerful leader of a powerful state. It helps him to consolidate his rule and his own power and that of his closest associates.

Like Lee and others, Xi was aware of corruption within China's political system well before he reached the apex of the party, and took control. He apparently did nothing to curb corruption when he was party leader in Fujian, where corruption in industry was rife, where smuggling persisted, and where a local tycoon blatantly ran casinos and brothels without interference. Later, in Shanghai, after a major scandal involving corrupt dealings by associates of a prior president, he managed to begin a cleanup campaign that is still underway. But, even in Shanghai, he failed to show the zeal for battling corruption that he began demonstrating from the time that Wang Lijun tried to defect to the United States in 2012 and inadvertently exposed the extent of party corruption and crime in Chongqing, setting the stage for Xi, elevated to the presidency and party chairmanship later that year, to begin his purge of corrupt party leaders.

Between 2012 and 2017, Xi and Wang Qishan, head of the Chinese Central Commission on Discipline and Inspection and an old friend of Xi, arrested and punished more than 1 million alleged miscreants, many important. In 2015 alone, 336,000 party members were disciplined and prosecuted. The 2016 total almost reached that same high number.[61] Wang even threatened to pursue 150 allegedly corrupt Chinese officials who had fled to the United States and were in hiding. From 2014 through 2016, 2,442 similar suspects of economic crimes had been repatriated from seventy countries in an operation called "Fox Hunt." More than $1.24 billion was recovered from the suspects.[62]

Among Wang's big captures in China were Zhou Yongkang, seventy-two, China's once-feared chief of security and a former oil baron who was nabbed, expelled from the party, arrested in 2014 and then in 2015 imprisoned for life. His family held assets of at least $14 billion, and he was accused of being the ringmaster of five circles of corruption, particularly in Sichuan Province. (In 2015, Zhou's deputy in Sichuan, Li Chuncheng, also went on trial for taking $6.1 million in bribes. He was sentenced to thirteen years in jail and fined $158,000 along with Jiang Jiemin, former head of China's largest oil and gas company, who also received a thirteen-year prison sentence and the same fine.) Also in 2015, the Beijing No. 2 Intermediate Court declared a prominent businesswoman guilty of giving construction kickbacks to the minister of railways. She was jailed for twenty years and fined $408 million. General Gu Junshan's home disgorged four truckloads of wine, art, cash, and more, including a gold replica of a Chinese aircraft carrier. He was arrested, tried, and sentenced to death (commuted to life in prison).[63] General Xu Caihou, one of the two top members of the central military command and a member of the party's politburo, died of cancer in 2015 before he could answer charges of "taking particularly huge bribes."[64] Wang also arrested officials in the state planning and state assets commissions, and ultimately incarcerated forty-eight high officials who had long believed (pre-Xi) that they were sufficiently powerful to be immune from state-led retribution. Later, another twenty upper level party members were ensnared in the widening net of corruption.

In two months in early 2015, a blog devoted to Chinese anticorruption activities listed a dozen significant arrests and sentences of influential Chinese leaders. For example, the deputy head of the party in a part of Liaoning Province went to jail for thirteen years for receiving almost $1 million in bribes; he had helped a businessman obtain illegal payments for facilities being demolished. The deputy head of the China Foreign Languages Publishing Administration was jailed for life, and lost all of his property, for embezzling official funds and taking $1.6 million in bribes. A party chair in Yunnan Province went to prison for life for stealing jadeite products purchased with state funds. A neurosurgeon and official in Shanghai received a nineteen-year sentence for stealing property from a medical society, for embezzlement, for receiving bribes of nearly $500,000, and for holding property from unidentified sources.[65] Additionally, no fewer than fourteen generals and admirals were either being investigated or convicted of graft in 2015.[66]

These numbers escalated when the Communist Party announced that the governor of Fujian Province was being held on charges of corruption, the twenty-third provincial or ministerial level official to be targeted during 2015. That group included the party secretary of Guangshou, the party secretary of Taiyuan, the party secretary of Nanning, the vice governor of Inner Mongolia, the deputy secretary of Yunnan Province, and members of various standing committees and people's congresses.[67] Subsequently, anticorruption officials detained the president of the Agricultural Bank of China, the country's third largest. In 2016, one of the Communist Party's highest former officials, the one-time boss of the General Office (a kind of chief of staff), was charged with abuses of power and taking big bribes, at least $11.6 million. He was also linked to Zhou Yongkang and to Bo Xilai, the disgraced former commissar of Chongqing, and sentenced to a long prison term. Heads in every sector continued to roll throughout the year. By late 2016, Xi's campaign against corruption had ensnared 177 people of deputy-ministerial rank and above, and 50 generals. Forty-five legislators had been accused of buying votes to obtain their privileged positions.

A lower-level cadre explained how Xi's reforms had reduced his rewards. "For every $16 a high-level official embezzles, he can spit about $3 down to us lower-level officials. . . . The problem now is upper-level people can't embezzle the $16, so there are no [$3] for us." Upper officials had opened karaoke parlors and private clubs. Following Xi's crackdown, they had to close such special ventures and destroy documents betraying their questionable interests. "They've also sent their mistresses and illegitimate children overseas and moved assets out of the country."[68]

The party boss of Nanjing, a major city, ruefully remarked that it had been "easy to be a good official for a short period, but to remain a good official for a life-time is much harder." He was detained in 2015 for failing to be good for long enough.[69]

These are all significant moves by an increasingly authoritarian system to reduce corruption within the ruling party, within state-owned enterprises, within the security apparatus, and within the upper levels of the state bureaucracy. A particular effort is underway to weed out corrupt officers, since senior security positions have long been bought and sold. "Corruption in the military is so pervasive that it could undermine China's ability to wage war," say reformers.[70] In mid-2016, Xi's anticorruption juggernaut even sentenced Guo Boxiong, a prominent general and vice chair of the Central Military Commission, to prison for life for accepting massive bribes. He forfeited all of his assets and illicit gains.

China renewed Mao's attack on the game of golf, closing sixty-six illegal courses, banning future construction, and making sure that Communist Party members understood that all golfers were henceforth suspected of "deviant extravagance." Xi banned golfing—"green opium"—for eighty-eight million party members in late 2015. A newly distributed moral and ethical code further enjoined excessive eating and drinking and improper sexual relations.[71] President Xi also warned Chinese officials against using public funds to distribute "luxurious" mooncakes during the 2015 mid-autumn festival. Chasteness in giving must prevail, he indicated.

As a whole, this crackdown has had a powerful demonstration effect on an immense society, and particularly on all manner of functionaries who had long been accustomed to abusing their public positions for immense private gain. Whether previous levels of permissiveness will now recede, whether lower- and middle-ranking persons of authority will now recalculate their chances of getting caught and therefore refrain from soliciting bribes and dealing from within the system, can hardly be known. It is too soon to be sure. The Corruption Perceptions Index reports lowered ratings for anticorruption in China since 2012, but those results may reflect lagging opinions or the views of observers not yet seeing any direct results of Xi's assault on the citadel of corruption. In 2015, China ranked 83rd out of 168, just after Zambia and tied with Benin, Colombia, and Sri Lanka. Its raw score had dropped from 39 in 2012 and 40 in 2013 to 37 in 2014 and 2015.[72]

Xi's attack on corruption in China—if it ultimately transforms that vast world power into a paragon of at least somewhat greater virtue than now—is a consummate test of the limits of leadership. What Xi can accomplish may greatly strengthen the case that tough-minded, responsible leadership is essential (necessary but not sufficient) if corruption is to be diminished domestically and internationally. His initiatives also pertain to arguments about whether leaders can best make progress against corruption only in small states and whether authoritarianism is essential (see below) to win the struggle against long-entrenched patterns of corruption. In time, too, we will want to learn from villagers and city-dwellers in China whether Xi's campaign has made and is making their lives more manageable and less costly, and whether China runs more smoothly and efficiently because corruption has been capped, if not reversed.

Leadership and Corruption

Absent Lee and Khama, and absent the messages of integrity that they espoused and enforced, might Singapore and Botswana have anyway emerged in the twentieth century as noncorrupt nations? Would someone else have held the governmental mantle and, building upon an existing local ethos, prevented corruption? Were Lee and Khama simply historical accidents, leaders who adapted local circumstances to their nations' benefit? Or, without them and without the vision and principles that they espoused, would Singapore and Botswana have regressed, inevitably, to the Asian and African means?

Lee had the harder task. Without his unusually clear-headed leadership and his determination to free the young city-state from the permissive stain of criminalized corruption, it is convenient to argue that today's Singapore would be more like nearby Indonesia, Malaysia, and Thailand, where corruption flourishes, distorts priorities, robs citizens of social and economic opportunities, and encourages moral decay. Reducing corruption materially depends on the exercise of leadership, even in a British Crown colony such as Hong Kong was when Sir Murray MacLehose disrupted its prevailing corrupt political culture in 1974.

Khama's undertaking was easier. Corruption had not yet begun to dominate local pursuits when he assumed power in 1966. But nor had it in Tanzania when Julius Nyerere began to rule in 1962, in Kenya in 1963 when Jomo Kenyatta gained power, in Zambia when Kenneth Kaunda became president in

1964, in Malawi when Banda assumed power in 1964, and in Zimbabwe when Robert Mugabe emerged from a liberation war and was elected president in 1980. In all of those nation-states corruption has run wild, mostly since independence, but in a few places since a little later. But, not in Botswana.

In its case it is possible to argue that the Tswana people were less inclined toward corruption because of their inbuilt ethnic integrity, because they had been well-socialized by Congregationalist missionaries from before and after David Livingstone's time, and because they were intrinsically a more capitalistic society than most others. It can also be asserted that their cattle holdings made the Tswana elites, at least (and Khama was one of them), more wealthy and less avaricious than their urban counterparts in, say, Zambia. Perhaps. But the distinctive, even unique, nature of the Tswana (as opposed to all other Africans) is difficult to demonstrate. Given the quality of Khama's early political rivals, given the corrupt incidents of the 1990s, and given the performance of communities in the rest of sub-Saharan Africa that are similar if not congruent with the Tswana, it is at least plausible that without Khama's (and Masire's) leadership, Botswana would have ended up, particularly with diamond wealth, as just one more African kleptocracy.

Leadership does make a sustainable difference. Good leadership is essential for good governance, no less so in battling against corruption. Fortunately, in addition to the examples of Lee and Khama, we can also examine what Paul Kagame is doing in Rwanda (see chapter 6), what Xi Jinping is able to achieve by draconian means in China—a major work in progress, and what President Muhammadu Buhari is able to accomplish in immensely odious and onerous circumstances in Nigeria. On winning his 2015 election, Buhari said that corruption "distorts the economy" and "assaults our national character." Earlier, during the electoral campaign, he pledged to lead a war on corruption—the first step in remedying Nigeria's massive economic problems and its "embedded culture of corruption." Furthermore, he promised, "corruption would not be tolerated by [my] administration, and it shall no longer be allowed to stand as if it is a respected monument in this nation."[73] But, despite his good intentions and many salutary efforts (discussed in chapter 5), plus prosecutions, in late 2016, Nigeria remained mostly as corrupt as it had always been.

Xi and Kagame are authoritarians, disdaining dissent and capable of pursuing anticorruption initiatives without requiring democratic assent. They are able to compel subordinates to alter their behavior—or else. Dampening corrupt tendencies is obviously easier if leaders hold such unquestioned power and can change prevailing political cultures by fiat (Lee could qualify as well) and by ordering police to incarcerate designated offenders. A respectable argument, therefore, might be advanced that corrupt practices in the developing world may only be curbed by leaders wielding mailed fists—that the ability of a leader to act autocratically and coercively is necessary to rid societies of corruption. Xi and Kagame clearly qualify as that kind of strong leader, as would Lee even if his preemptory strikes against corrupt associates were always discharged well within the ambit of his prime ministerial prerogatives and consonant with democratic principles, if not strict practices. (And Singapore's court trials of allegedly corrupt politicians and officials were transparent and procedurally correct [if predictable], which China's are not.) Buhari, in the 1980s, attempted a very heavy-handed attack on Nigerian corruption, with many human rights abuses and some enforced successes, but those military-led assaults soon backfired and helped lead to the military coup that ended his first presidency—with Nigerian corruption still rampant. Buhari, then, had not demonstrated to Nigerians that he was acting only to advance a collective good. To embrace anticorruption campaigns, citizens need (as in the Nordic cases) to believe that their rulers are in fact pursuing such collective objectives and not personal vendettas.

That combating corruption requires authoritarianism is a plausible proposition. But such an argument cannot be substantiated by Hong Kong's experience, where a nonelected but accountable expatriate official initiated a bureaucratic and effectively consultative process that gradually resulted in the transformation of the Crown Colony from corrupt to noncorrupt. Nor does that argument hold regarding Botswana, where Khama made his preferences known, but never deviated from his tolerant and democratic instincts. Closet autocracy was not his preference, nor was such an approach necessary to prevent corruption from growing in the young Botswana, or during most of the long presidency of Masire.

Khama offered a persuasive vision and mobilized his followers behind that vision. He set standards without doing so arbitrarily. Some healthy combination of respectable ethical goals, together with transparent punishment for failures to live up to high requirements, is necessary to shift the calculus of reward and response, and to reconfigure the visceral and normal ambitions of avarice. Having a leader who is seen to be of sterling character is essential if attitudes are to be rearranged and high and low officials are to refrain from taking advantage of their public positions. Being an autocrat may help in modifying behavior rapidly, but a better method combines a velvet glove with a mailed fist.

Rhetoric is necessary, but never sufficient. Lee and Khama spoke well, and delivered results. They shifted the incentive structure of corruption considerably even if we have no way of knowing exactly what motivated their associates, subordinates, and bureaucrats to refrain from dipping hands into their respective national tills, bending the results of contract competitions, and favoring friends and relatives for jobs and other perquisites. Our evidence is suggestive, inferential, and developed from a long study of examples and counterexamples.

Along with Xi's, Buhari's next few years will test in a populous and difficult context the main propositions of this chapter. Buhari may be thwarted by the prevailing (corrupted) political culture of Nigeria. Or, no matter how much middle class Nigerians want to disable corruption, his positive ideas may simply be rejected by the local political class. If he comes to view the anticorruption project as too difficult politically or too dangerous in terms of his support base (and maybe his legitimacy among the Nigerian elite) then he may prove the argument of this chapter by leading essentially from behind. Most African leaders have done and are doing just that with regard to struggling against inherited levels of corruption. But not Lee. And not Khama and Masire. Circumstantially, their efforts and the Rwandan example make the case for responsible leadership's commanding role in reducing corruption. So may Xi and Buhari in a year or two.

One more example of the role of leadership, this time at the local level, stems from Bolivia in 1985–1991, when Ronald MacLean-Abaroa was a young, crusading mayor of La Paz, the capital. Inheriting a vastly corrupt, insolvent city, he worked with employees and citizens to increase transparency and improve efficiency so that the beleaguered municipality could again serve its constituents efficiently and well.

With support from the World Bank, he eliminated discretion (and therefore corrupt temptations) from the office of public works, contracted out major construction projects so as to limit workers' "ability to steal parts and gasoline," eliminated a number of licenses and permits (again, to inhibit discretion), streamlined application processes, and published a handbook of bureaucratic operations so that citizens would know their rights (as against public official denials and attempts to exercise impermissible favoritism). In a very innovative manner, MacLean-Abaroa decided to obtain revenue from property taxes. But instead of allowing city employees to value properties, as in the past, MacLean-Abaroa permitted homeowners to evaluate their own homes. But he also made clear that the city reserved the right to purchase all houses, after the self-assessment, for 1.5 times the homeowner's declared value.

During MacLean-Abaroa's three two-year terms as mayor, La Paz became decidedly less corrupt, tax revenues grew eighteen-fold, and new investments increased ten-fold. These successes certainly add an argument to the importance of leadership and political will as determinants of effective anticorruption strategies even though, after McLean-Abaroa left office, La Paz regressed to its corrupt norm. One-shot anticorruption campaigns have little lasting effect if the prevailing political culture is not permanently transformed, which takes time.

When MacLean-Abaroa was again elected mayor in 1995 he found that public officials were taking bribes of 10 to 15 percent for contract awards, and citizens had to pay routinely to obtain the permits and licenses that had once been free, and rightfully theirs. By 1996, a survey revealed that half of the residents of La Paz believed that corruption was worse than it had been before. The mayors who served from 1991 to 1995, when MacLean-Abaroa was out of office, were in jail or on the run.[74] A few years later MacLean-Abaroa ran unsuccessfully for president of Bolivia.

A clinching facet of this argument is what happens without a leadership finger in the dike of greed, as during the McLean-Abaroa interregnum. Societal corruption flows from the signals radiated by the political persons at their apex and is neither inherent nor inescapable in developing world communities. Where leaders such as Robert Mugabe of Zimbabwe, Jacob Zuma of South Africa, and Eduardo dos Santos in Angola openly self-aggrandize, distribute spoils to their families and acolytes, and allow only patrimonially blessed followers to benefit from increasing sleaze, then corruption flourishes. It seems likely, even if we cannot prove so conclusively, that Mobutu and Ne Win's (of Burma) thefts of state resources, along with the depredations, defalcations, and peculations of the likes of Sani Abacha in Nigeria, Omar al-Bashir in Sudan, Daniel arap Moi in Kenya, Siaka Stevens in Sierra Leone, Charles Taylor in Liberia, and many others in the developing world, gave implicit if not explicit unholy license to middle- and low-ranking officials in their countries to follow suit. The silken web of deceit throughout much of Africa and Asia enveloped and affirmatively sanctioned the behavior of those who wanted to do what others were doing (and to get what they were getting). The tentacles of corruption thus encompassed all parts of their societies, and encouraged law-breaking in every conceivable fashion.

Lee believed that once a pattern of corrupt behavior develops—once leaders enrich clients and followers corruptly in order to buttress their own rule and prominence—then those loyal followers have continually to be fed with cash, jobs, mistresses, concubines, and the like, a path dependency. Over time, corruption becomes accepted at all levels of society. It is the role of leaders to disrupt such patterns or never to allow them to begin. Lee's leadership trajectory showed that leaders can make a difference and can stanch corruption even when it is well entrenched *if* they exercise political will and demonstrate personal integrity (which equates with legitimacy) and institute a credible enforcement capability. But, possibly, Lee and Khama are outliers. It is with the ongoing examples of Kagame, Xi, and Buhari that we can best test the proposition that leaders can constrain corruption at any point in a national cycle, even after its rot has spread widely and deeply infected every pore of the afflicted state. To do so, they need both to inspire and coerce.

Contrary to what readers might assume, leaders who succeed need be authoritative, creative, courageous, and exemplary in their personal character, but not necessarily charismatic. None of the anticorruption leadership successes were or are charismatic: not Khama, Lee, MacLehose, or Masire. Nor was Kufuor or is Johnson-Sirleaf. Buhari is not traditionally charismatic either, although some Rwandans might assert that Kagame was charismatic. Mandela was charismatic, but was not especially helpful in curbing corruption in South Africa. The special quality of charisma is neither necessary nor common among leaders who disrupt the prevalence of corruption in their countries.[75]

President John Magufuli, who took office in Tanzania in late 2015, is another leader to watch. He literally and personally swept a clean broom against Dar es Salaam's accumulated trash and filth, immediately after entering office made examples of bureaucrats and hospital directors who showed up to work late, and promised to end corruption. He banned most official overseas travel—a profitable perquisite—for politicians and bureaucrats, and preached meaningful austerity. When Magufuli paid his first state visit, to Rwanda, he drove there to save air travel costs.

Magufuli criticized the nation's judges for their partiality, for being on the take, and for their failure to help root out corruption. Distrusting them, he created a special court to deal only with corrupt public persons. Soon, 596 cases were before the court. Magufuli also sacked a number of senior officials in the Tanzania Revenue Authority who had shifted funds illicitly overseas, suspended bureaucrats in the Tanzania Ports Authority who had given importers special "considerations" on at least $40 million in import taxes, and fired the director general of the Prevention and Combating of Corruption Bureau (PCCB). The last had "overlooked" the scandal in the ports authority. (For more on the PCCB, see chapter 5.)

In early 2016, the head of the country's identity card program was accused of taking bribes and relieved of his responsibilities.[76] Subsequently, in 2016, Magufuli ordered an audit of the official employment rolls. That turned up 10,000 public sector ghost workers (of a reputed total of about 550,000 employees) who were costing the government more than $2 million a month, and profiting mid-level and upper-level bureaucrats and politicians. "We intend to have workers in government who are honest, accountable, and hardworking," said Prime Minister Kassim Majaliwa.[77] Magufuli insists that all of his ministers sign a special integrity pledge and declare their assets (or forfeit their portfolios).

Whether Magufuli, known as "the bulldozer," effectively manages to reduce rampant Tanzanian corruption from the top down will be another clear test of the importance of human agency in battling corruption. In his case, there was no evidence beforehand that the ruling Chama Cha Mapinduzi's (Party of the Revolution) compromise presidential candidate would have behaved so innovatively against the long-engrained and long-enshrined corrupt practices of his party and his peers. But, personally outraged by his government's long failure to serve the people, Magufuli immediately grasped the obvious nettle of reform—becoming immensely popular overnight. But, he may not be tackling his country's structural foundation of corruption and his political party's continuing reputation for "thuggishness" and for its failure to pay its bills.[78] However, if his initiative lasts, and succeeds, Tanzania could prove another (large) African country where committed leadership makes a positive difference.

All kinds of examples of leadership initiatives for evil and good abound in Africa and Asia, but a laborious case-by-case analysis of how corruption grew in country after country (and even in the Americas under Carlos Menem in Argentina, Hugo Chavez in Venezuela, and Dilma Rousseff in Brazil) in the twentieth century and since would show that leaders gave implicit permission, indulged themselves and their coteries, robbed their nations, and smiled their way to offshore banks while simultaneously diminishing national GDPs per capita and making inequality more severe. "As long as top government officials are thought to be corrupt [by their underlings and by citizens], nothing done at lower levels will effectively curtail corruption."[79]

Who leads matters. This book's final chapter will return to the impressive role that exemplary leadership can play in winning the battle against domestic corruption.

IX

People Power, Social Media, and Corporate Rigor

Too few political leaders in the developing world exert themselves responsibly and effectively against corruption. It is not that they try to reduce corruption and their policies receive too little support or that they choose poor policies; instead, for most leaders and aspirant leaders in the developing world, battling corruption has no interest. It is not a rational choice. For the most part transactionalists, these men and women are more often concerned with maintaining power and privilege than with effecting social change. Many of their kind enter public service and public office primarily to strengthen themselves politically and enrich their families and associates, lineages, or ethnic groups—not to help their people improve their livelihoods and better the human condition.

Given such existing cynicism about corrupt regimes on the part of many citizenries throughout the developing world, given prevailing beliefs that nearly all politicians refuse to deliver or are incapable of delivering corruption-free societies, and given abundant citizen frustration regarding the desire and ability of so many political leadership classes to do much more than pay lip service to anticorruption rhetoric, it is hardly surprising that citizenries writ large and civil societies in a number of developing countries have actively attempted over many years to influence individual leaders to do more.

In South Cyprus, for example, a public opinion survey carried out by Nicosia University and a local firm revealed that 46 percent of those assessed believed that the Republic of Cyprus "had been turned into a 'Banana Republic'" because of wholesale bribery. Thirty-five percent of the respondents said that they had little confidence in obtaining justice. In a separate poll, 83 percent of Greek-speaking Cypriots believed that corruption was a major problem. A full 50 percent said that they had personally witnessed an incident of corruption.[1] Finding avenues of positive change thus blocked, and its efforts derided, civil society in many ordinarily passive countries has on a number of occasions engaged in direct action—protest movements, crowd-sourced reports, political party mobilizations, and electoral contestations—all primarily to achieve anticorruption objectives.

The power and number of a society's civil organizations per capita are strongly correlated with the curbing of corruption, especially when controlled for GDP per capita and Human Development Index levels.[2] People power, in other words, can (if but rarely) shift political debates in favor of corruption reduction initiatives or actually make signal differences that lead to improved national outcomes.[3]

Some civil society efforts involve, even depend upon, the use of modern technology, especially dash cams, handheld telephones, and texting devices. Social media is also a valuable method both to arouse concern about corruption and to mobilize citizens to do something about it. So are a variety of ingenious experimental designs. But each new venture depends upon spontaneously erupting group leaderships that arouse blocs of citizens to attempt to effect change for good through consciousness-raising, sit-ins and other forms of peaceful attention seeking, and by taking to the streets in protest.

This chapter is about the many old and new ways that citizens can make a direct positive difference in the battle against corruption. It is also about how multinational firms can become better corporate citizens and cease corrupting (usually) developing countries.

Using New Technologies

The ubiquity of mobile telephones (and the Internet) in the developing world permits civil society consisting of citizens and nongovernmental organizations (NGOs) to play major roles in combating corruption. At least two-thirds of all sub-Saharan Africans have 2G or 3G handheld devices, although only 19 percent currently have access to broadband and the Internet using personal computers. The text-messaging and photographic capabilities of mobile telephones allow individual interactions with corrupt public officials to be aggregated and documented. Even if authorities do not immediately act on such crowd-sourced evidence, and NGOs do not always know exactly how to translate those kinds of documentation into action, the sheer ability to record corrupt incidents is empowering, and, in at least some instances, capable of being assembled to activate antagonism to corruption.[4] This combination has been particularly powerful in India and Pakistan, in Central Asia, and in sections of sub-Saharan Africa where, for example, Ushahidi ("Testimony") and Frontline SMS have long been employed to manage crises and disasters, track human rights violations and violators, note violent acts in real time, and reveal security breaches. Bribespot.com (which originated in Estonia) receives anonymous texts reporting bribes in eight languages, with additional languages and nations coming. In Nigeria, Tracka allows citizens to report projects where funds are being embezzled, and BudgIT permits citizens to follow how national and state budgets are spent.

In future years, more and more governments and civil society operatives will increasingly utilize handheld instruments to empower anticorruption endeavors. As smart telephones get smarter—as 4G, 5G, and 6G are extended and become much more powerful—so those technological advances will become more widely available and less expensive. Their deployment will hence make it possible to disseminate information about corruption widely and intensively and to collect hard data about corruption and corrupt acts almost instantaneously. In Afghanistan, the United States Agency for International Development (USAID) is sponsoring an extensive scheme to track and monitor financial transactions via mobile telephone technology so as to deter corrupt dealings.

When official data of all kinds becomes available, then thoughtful civil society analysts can do ingenious data mining and disclose information about corruption that is otherwise unavailable. In Mexico, for example, a think tank examined the rolls of the nation's educational establishment and discovered more than 1,400 teachers born on the same day in a single year. Those ghost teachers were purged from the rolls, depriving officials who had been pocketing their pay of easy money. In Nigeria, investigators discovered evidence of serious money laundering by poring over property and company registers. Tax authorities in many countries are able to discover the real owners of more than 85 million companies worldwide by searching OpenCorporates, a British-originated web compendium of property registers from more than 105 nations and political entities. The more data appear online, the more they can be explored to obtain information capable of hindering the proliferation of corrupt practices.[5]

Opinion polling is also increasingly important in discovering how citizens evaluate their own national environments of corruption and whether they report making progress in any battles against corrupt dealings that are joined by governments or social movements. Transparency International's Corruption Barometer Survey (see chapter 2) already performs this function in a number of countries. Latinobarometro and Afrobarometer both also ascertain citizen views on their continents. Some of their regular polling results, and national surveys such as Gilani in Pakistan, reflect degrees of satisfaction with corruption or proxies for corruption, with national leadership accomplishments, and with many other issues that are valuable in assessing and confronting corruption in individual states.[6] Specialized surveys for other purposes, or specifically about bribery as in Cyprus, also provide information that assists civil societies, governments, and donors in assessing the extent of and varieties of corrupt behavior in a particular political jurisdiction. Oxfam, the international charity, provides trusted surveys about public services that help to deter the proliferation of corrupt practices.

There is no end to the relevant and helpful data that can be accumulated through judicious polling of mobile telephone subscribers, citizens on the street, persons shopping in the markets of the developing world, and individuals gathered around a village water pipe. In society after society, such accumulated data provides abundant evidence of public discontent with the corrupt practices of those who rule—with societies smothered by the sleaze and alarmed by the stench of corruption. The question for civil society and political reformers in each of those affected nation-states hence quickly becomes how best to transform mass resentment and mass resignation (or resilience) into the kinds of actions that will bring about meaningful change for the better.

PUTTING BUREAUCRATIC INTERACTIONS ONLINE

The simplest and most direct use of modern technology to moderate or defeat petty corruption follows decisions to avoid most, if not all, face-to-face contact between a bureaucrat and a citizen. If interactions are online, completed via user-friendly interfaces (preferably on a mobile telephone), a client can obtain birth certificates, marriage licenses, and all kinds of documents from what in India they call the permitting Raj without being hit up for bribes or "tea money." In theory, all supplicants wanting some kind of bureaucratic action would be treated equally—by an algorithm or a computer. Because none could be favored, no applicant could be speeded up or slowed down without interfering with a computer application or program, a task that would be hard for the ordinary civil servant. Applicants could also file for a permit using a number, which would mean that it would be even harder to discriminate for or against a particular person.

If everything relatively routine were turned into a machine-moderated transaction that could be overseen remotely and technologically, the ability to act by a bureaucrat in a less than even-handed manner would be reduced. This method of state officials dealing with clients and consumers could be extended to the immigration and customs hall, where categories and classes could be (admittedly with some difficulty and ingenuity) reduced to algorithms hard to manipulate in favor of that importer and not this importer. Advanced modern computer programs permit discretion to be limited, if not removed, for most interactions between the state and its citizens. Binomial decision-making would end many requirements for human intervention and thus largely eliminate human discrimination.

Extortionate efforts by hospital clerks to admit an injured person for a fee, a principal to permit a pupil to enroll, or a policeman to wave a car with bald tires through a barrier might also, with some clever technological adaptations and the use of handheld devices, be reduced, if not eliminated—given sufficient political will from above. Petty corruption could be overwhelmed and subsequently be greatly reduced if available modern technical resources were employed to replace face-to-face encounters.

INDIA AND IPAIDABRIBE.COM

India is a massive nation where people have taken matters into their own hands, seemingly successfully. Corruption is endemic in India, and has been since about the fourth century BC, when a social critic wrote about the forty ways to embezzle. More recently, the 1,000-year old *Ramayana* epic described how the evil giant Ravana bribed a guardian of hell to avoid punishment.[7] But very little was ever done by their divine rulers in the various princely states, by British colonial overlords, or by India's first independent governments to reduce corruption there.[8] Now, every day, in almost every imaginable circumstance, Indians pay extra for what is theirs by right—a driving license, a marriage certificate, admission to a state hospital, and so on. In India, as in all of South Asia, people report to survey compilers that the most corrupt operators are the police, the courts, and the administrators of land registers.[9] These practices continue in India despite well-drafted, tough-sounding laws against corruption, an Anti-Corruption Bureau, the police Central Bureau of Investigation, the Central Vigilance Commission (to oversee federal-level corrupt crimes), the Directorate of Enforcement, and the Financial Intelligence Unit.[10]

According to T. R. Raghunandan, an anticorruption activist and one of the founders of the Delhi-based Janaagraha Center for Citizenship and Democracy, the problem is that in a massive society such as India (and elsewhere in the developing world) corruption imposes huge economic costs and makes legitimate transactions difficult. It "perpetuates mis-governance" by reducing any incentive to abolish red tape. Thus, the systems are slow, and public servants can easily demand bribes to accelerate consideration. But Raghunandan also asserts that because lubricating or petty corruption "breaks the spirit" of ordinary Indians and they become accustomed over and over to "enduring bad services," they pay bribes and learn to distrust themselves as well as the various governmental jurisdictions whose servants regularly penalize their lives.[11]

Marriage certificates, say, cost 6000 rupees ($130). "Agents outside the marriage certificate office roam around. Those are the ones you pay." Another resident reported, "When I was departing . . . from Mumbai Airport [a] customs officer requested $100 because my wife's last name was not changed to mine in her passport. I opted to bribe because it was 1 a.m." From yet another: "You do it because everyone does it. . . . Say you need some building permits, if you pay 10,000 rupees ($220) you'll get it in two days, if you don't . . . you spend months trying to fight them."[12]

In Tamil Nadu, in 2007, two local social entrepreneurs closely involved in the national Right to Information movement created the 5th Pillar movement to "realize freedom from corruption," a national culture of civic responsibility, "and intolerance of graft." A 5th Pillar was needed, the founders agreed, to underscore the importance of civil society in battling corruption alongside the four standard pillars of democracy: the executive, the legislature, the judiciary, and the media. Vijay Anand, one of the founders of the 5th Pillar, and an American-based Internet technology entrepreneur, believed rather romantically that if Indians "collectively as a nation [said] no to bribe, eventually it will end" and the national system of corruption would collapse.[13]

Initially, the 5th Pillar focused on instilling anticorruption ethics via training programs for citizens and impeding graft and bribery in Tamil Nadu. It made presentations to civic groups and chambers of commerce, printed its own magazines, and produced a weekly television show about governance and citizen rights in Tamil Nadu. It sought to eliminate India being enslaved by corruption. The 5th Pillar assisted citizens from many challenged backgrounds to approach the government, and to file complaints, protest against specific examples of corruption, and report instances of extortion. It tried to empower whistleblowers. It initiated a Students against Corruption movement and held Freedom from Corruption training workshops in about 1,600 colleges and universities. But the 5th Pillar became better known for employing a number of nonviolent Gandhian tactics to mobilize large numbers of citizens to confront the Tamil Nadu state government regarding freedom of information and corruption issues, and for its efforts to bring about meaningful positive change.

When it began, Anand and the 5th Pillar staff could hardly have expected to end or even to minimize corruption in their massive South Indian state. But they assisted a number of individual citizens to rectify corrupt wrongs, and helped to reform the manner in which citizens interacted with the Regional Transportation Office, where licenses and permits had customarily been provided only after the payment of steep, illegal, extra fees. As an NGO challenging endemic corruption at the state level, the 5th Pillar provided practical ways for people "to say no to extortion."[14] In 2015 and 2016, it could claim no major societal transformations, no sustainable reductions in corrupt practice at the state level. But, along with other Indian movements, it offered (as do the analogous Central Asian efforts, described below) a steady critique of corruption in the world's second most populous nation.

The daily abuses of Indians by public officials were long tolerated elsewhere in the world's largest democracy with a rueful shrug until high profile national scandals of a venal kind mobilized campaigners like Raghunandan and a widespread army of disgruntled Indians of all backgrounds. Those scandals included the mismanagement and profiteering that accompanied the Indian staging of the Commonwealth Games of 2010 and a fraudulent sale of mobile telephone licenses and mobile telephone frequency bands of the electronic spectrum that cost the nation as much as $39 billion in revenues foregone. A Transparency International study of Indian corruption found that 62 percent of all citizens had paid bribes in 2004–2005. In 2010, India ranked 87th of 178 countries on the Corruption Perceptions Index of that year, level with Albania and well below China and below its own ratings in 2009 and 1999. In 2015, India was listed in the same index in 76th place of 168 countries, a slight improvement.[15]

Many such analyses of corrupt ills are carried out all over the world. But, in India, Raghunandan and several local colleagues decided to move beyond criticism to action. In 2008, they began thinking about and later experimenting with a web-enabled method of listing and reporting bribes. Initially, they sought to invent a simple way of tracking the costs to consumers of lubricating corruption—a price-predicting mechanism. By 2010, they had created ipaidabribe.com, which logged more than 14,000 self-reports in the first year from individuals in 453 Indian cities who had paid out about $10 million in bribes. Those reports were at first in English, but the website was soon configured to receive reports in all of the major Indian languages, and from mobile telephones as well as laptop computers. The initial reports were of incidents, but in time the ipaidabribe site was able to receive lengthy content, stories, and more. Doing so enabled those who had launched ipaidabribe to understand to which institutions Indians paid the greatest proportion of bribes (the police, followed by the registry), how bribes flowed and to where, and which kinds of processes attracted the largest number of bribers. This accomplishment was all the more remarkable across the many disparate Indias within India, especially given the challenges posed by a weak technological infrastructure.

But ipaidabribe was designed to be diagnostic and reformist as well as to provide details on a set of pursuits that all Indians condemned and still felt compelled to practice. It was also intended to be educational—to offer citizens a full understanding that they were not alone in facing corruption, and of their rights vis-à-vis the government. With these data—numbers of incidents and a thick description of how the corrupt transactions occurred and why—Raghunandan and his colleagues could suggest which were the best public service processes to simplify in order to reduce corrupt temptations, and how citizens could refuse to give bribes. Ipaidabribe also disseminated a "ten commandments" list of the best ways to confront corruption. Its creators prided themselves on having enabled a "swarm-like" resistance to corrupt practices.

CENTRAL ASIAN DASH CAMS

Despots rule the former Soviet satraphies in Central Asia. But tight control in those stans has not completely dampened protest movements employing up-to-date technology. In Kazakhstan, drivers have mounted dash cams on their automobiles in order to film traffic police shakedowns in real time. The resulting videos have been uploaded to YouTube. In Tajikistan, drivers take movies of police activity at roadblocks and then show the videos on local television. In Kyrgyzstan, religious activists have posted bloody selfies after being harshly interrogated by state security services.

Corruption has run wild in Central Asia for generations. "You can finish school by buying your diploma. You can bribe your professors to pass exams." Moreover, the "majority don't believe they can change anything."[16] But now, at least, Central Asians can confront state security actions by filming extortionists or recording the effects of beatings. Although further punishments often follow, such interventions make "the scourge of police corruption harder for governments to deny."[17] Most of the self-documentations are done by ordinary citizens who mostly want the state and its policemen to follow the law.

When Kazakhstan's Driver Defense Society posts videos of corrupt cops to a central YouTube channel and to Facebook, its stated purpose is to encourage educated police officers just to obey the law and for drivers to know their rights. The Driver Defense Society seeks accountability and positions itself against arbitrary and thus illegal police-state brutality. It receives videos from the aggrieved public and posts them for all to see, so as to shame the state. A similar operation is underway in Kyrgyzstan, where a 2015 video that went viral showed a traffic policeman soliciting a bribe and then attacking the driver when he realized that he was being filmed.

In neighboring Uzbekistan, the Neighborhood Watch movement posts complaints to Facebook about the failure of local officials to deliver basic services such as natural gas or electrical power. Another online group in Tashkent, the capital, employs dashboard cameras to document incidents of extortion on the roads. Uzbek lawyers run a website called Tashabbus (Initiative). It dispenses free legal advice about how to avoid paying bribes, deal with corrupt bureaucrats, and cope with the heavy hand of the thoroughly corrupt Uzbek government. Its overriding goal is to strengthen the local rule of law and align the government with the state's constitution—and to help Uzbeks imagine a corruption-free society.

KENYAN METHODS

The ipaidabribe movement soon spread from India to several other countries where corruption has long seriously undermined public life and prevented consumers from obtaining services from governments at nominal cost. In Kenya, Anthony Ragui in 2011 invited citizens to follow the Indian example and list their corrupt encounters with the police and with ministries and municipalities. Many thousands immediately sent texts describing how much they had paid and to whom, but despite the sophistication of Kenyan mobile telephone users, within its first years only 7 percent of eligible Kenyans were reporting bribes on the local ipaidabribe site, possibly because of justifiable fears that their anonymity would not be maintained. "Not in My Country," another site, is specifically for reports of corruption in the Kenyan schools.

In 2013, two years after the Kenyan ipaidabribe website was installed—and after two years during which many millions in bribes (one estimate was that 125,584,333 Kenyan shillings, or about $1.3 million, had changed hands)— President Uhuru Kenyatta even launched an official website so that Kenyans could tell his government directly about bribery and graft. Citizens were invited to fill out online forms, upload photos or videos, or report corruption via text messages. They could do so anonymously, and by text message as well as on the web.[18]

All accounts of corrupt behavior, both the taking and giving of bribes, are important. Quantifying helps to illustrate and strengthen the case against corruption more vividly than the accumulations of anecdotes. But verifying each incident is impossible; those who provide reports on the ipaidabribe or other websites, especially including President Kenyatta's, may or may not be dishonest or have hidden agendas. But the mass of numbers over time reveal insights into the character and extent of corruption within countries and across those countries. Indeed, such an aggregation of incidents provides a formidable platform for remedial action.

But there is one critical aspect of corruption that these kinds of sites, as helpful as they are, cannot readily capture. Venal corruption or big-ticket corruption—the major scams—are not easily reported by individuals with direct knowledge of the vast crore of rupees, yen, pounds, euros, or dollars that have been paid to get access to lucrative developing world contracts, to arms transfers, and to profitable construction opportunities. In some ways, lubricating or petty corruption constitutes low-hanging fruit; large-scale (venal) corruption is a much greater danger to the nation-state, to the economy, and to citizens. Different kinds of sleuthing are required to uncover the big frauds. Sometimes forensic accounting does so, sometimes individual whistleblowers

unveil gross acts, and sometimes investigators from commissions or departments of justice zero in on accused individuals and corporations. If sufficient
political will is available, exposures and prosecutions can follow.

Social Auditing

Data-gathering websites, dash cam agitation, opinion polls, special surveys
and the like all are forms of social auditing. Another type of social audit that
can reveal corrupt activity by public servants is carried out by organizing a
direct feedback mechanism of the kind that most of us employ whenever we
want to ascertain if work is being performed properly.

PAKISTANI TELEPHONE CHECKS

In Pakistan, after bribe solicitations began to annoy him more than they usually did, Zubair Bhatti, an official in charge of a district in Punjab Province,
decided to take several simple but connected actions. He compelled registration officers to record the mobile telephone numbers of everyone with whom
they conducted business daily, and then to forward those lists to his office.
He dialed some of those numbers randomly, inquiring about the respondent's
experiences before the registry officers. By employing this fundamental
method of inquiry, the senior official found that many supplicants were illiter-
ate and that few knew the variety of fees that they were required to pay, or
even the total amounts. As in India, these citizens were dependent upon "deed
writers" who loitered around district offices and "helped" those who came to
register their properties or do other business with the federal government.
The deed writers were inflating the fees required by the registry, keeping the
difference, and paying kickbacks to the property registration clerks.

Once having gathered evidence in this manner of the many ways by which
the registration clerks mistreated their clients, Bhatti introduced a simple reform procedure: the registration clerks were henceforth obliged to issue receipts, to sign their own names, and to report the amounts collected by the
deed writers. Bhatti then called clients by telephone to verify what he had
been told. This tactic is a variation of the service delivery survey instrument
method oft-used elsewhere, sometimes called citizen report cards, especially
in Europe and India.[19]

Bhatti next introduced to other districts under his purview what he came
to call his Citizen Feedback Monitoring Program (CFMP) methodology. Everyone engaged in public service, from office clerks to livestock extension
workers, was now compelled to record every public visitor's mobile phone
number so that Bhatti could continue to make follow-up calls, thereby generating goodwill for the government and for officialdom, and simultaneously

soliciting information about how service providers were performing (or not performing).

These innovations, especially reaching out to the public, drew national press coverage and the notice of the chief minister of the Punjab.[20] He wanted to expand the social audit model across the entire province of ninety-five million people and its thirty-six districts, and to use it to reduce petty corruption. At that point in 2010, half of all Punjabis polled had paid bribes for public services during the prior year, despite the existence of a well-established National Accountability Bureau.[21] But gaining credibility among citizens for the social audit model meant actually employing the information received by telephone call-backs to remove corrupt officials or otherwise to act decisively against corruption. That was hard.

Meanwhile, Bhatti left the district administrative service and joined the Asia Foundation's office in Islamabad. From there he persuaded the chief minister of the Punjab to scale up the CFMP, with Bhatti in charge. He did not want an electronic citizen complaint channel so much as a mechanism to elicit positive and negative feedback from customers. Bhatti's design was intended less to catch corrupt offenders and more to improve administrative functioning—to change management practices or to transfer or remove weak officials. Incidentally, a proper CFMP would also marginalize petty corruption, and lead (as it inevitably did) to arrests.

Within a year, after the CFMP had expanded and operating it manually had become burdensome and inefficient, the World Bank helped the Punjab to set up a call center. It later employed robocalls (from the chief minister), an automated text messaging service to send and receive, an online system for capturing information, and the use of a dashboard to display feedback. A website was also created. Using the much more efficient text messaging capabilities of mobile telephones, citizens could "press 1 for corruption" or "press 2 for no corruption" and then leave detailed responses.[22]

From 2011 to the end of 2012, the CFMP sent 1.5 million text messages to Punjabis, who received them well. The chief minister also directed those at district coordination meetings throughout the province to pay close attention on a monthly basis to citizen feedback, especially newly prepared bar graphs that displayed increasing or decreasing amounts of reported corruption. By late 2013, the monthly total of mobile numbers contacted from the central call center averaged 280,000; in early 2014 it averaged 333,000. A high percentage of the text message replies by that point reported various kinds of corrupt practices, and those reports could be quantified. By 2014, 30 percent of the users and text messagers surveyed believed that corruption had been reduced as a result of the CFMP and the attention that it had generated. Seventy percent said that they were confident that these methods would further reduce corruption in the future.[23]

Anything that could contribute even in a limited way to curtailing corrupt behavior in one of the most corrupt countries in the world obviously was welcomed by citizens as well as the leaders of the Punjab. Perhaps the CFMP had indeed lowered the amount (and the perception) of corruption in the Punjab. But from the aggregated Corruption Perceptions Index scores for Pakistan as a whole, it would be difficult to discern any improvement in national ratings, which stayed essentially the same, from 27 in 2011 to 29 in 2014. Those scores ranked Pakistan 136th of 174 nations in 2014, below Mauritania and Vietnam and just above Iran, Nigeria, and Russia.[24] In 2015, Pakistan ranked 117th of 168 countries along with Tanzania, and below Vietnam and Mozambique, with a score of 30. Nevertheless, now that mobile telephones are almost everywhere, the Punjabi method of eliciting consumer feedback by text message, and then removing corrupt middle managers or other service providers, provides a comparatively straightforward, simple, and easily scalable approach to reducing corruption everywhere in the developing world.

PAPUA NEW GUINEA

Papua New Guinea, a very different, less populous, but much wilder and less governed polity than Pakistan, has used similar methods to battle corruption. Well before the Bhatti experiments, its Transparency International local chapter had established a network of community groups across the fractured country that disseminated information about corruption within their micro-local confines and more broadly through existing radio, print, and social media. It also distributed mobile telephones to rural teachers so that those individuals could easily report corrupt behavior by texting to a collecting point in Port Moresby, the capital, or by sending such information directly to the government. Even so, as in Pakistan, it is difficult to gauge the extent to which these superior new abilities to communicate about and pinpoint corrupt infractions actually managed to reduce graft and bribe giving and taking. In 2015, the CPI rated Papua New Guinea 139th on the scale, well below Pakistan.[25]

THE PHILIPPINES

The Philippines' Anti–Red Tape Act of 2007 sought to reduce corrupt opportunities and to make governmental service deliveries more efficient for citizens. But its provisions remained unenforced until mid-2009. For years, Filipinos had complained about the opaque manner in which officials prevented them from easily obtaining the licenses, permits, and other approvals required for everyday life. Each of these difficult transactions provided an opportunity for facilitation payments or other under-the-table exchanges. Civil servants solicited bribes in exchange for limiting paperwork or speeding up processing times. "Fixers" at each location facilitated such payments and colluded with the officials. Bribery and inefficiency in government offices and in any and all interactions between the government and its citizens had come to be considered routine, with corruption rife throughout the governmental apparatus at national and provincial levels. In 2007, 32 percent of citizens and 61 percent of businesses reported paying bribes in these kinds of circumstances.[26] President Ferdinand Marcos had purloined $10 billion of government assets in the 1990s, and his successors had each been tarnished by allegations of massive embezzlement and extortion. Moreover, the Office of the Ombudsman, the country's primary anticorruption agency, was focused more on venal graft, not on lower-level forms of corrupt dealing. Before 2007, and even to this day, a culture of impunity pervaded much of the country, impeded growth, and prevented national progress.

The 2007 act required all government offices to post a list of their procedures so that the public could learn how to apply for services and learn what an official could and could not require. It limited processing times and the number of required approvals. It also instituted jail terms for bribes. But, without citizen feedback, the Filipino government would never know whether the act was being implemented well or poorly, or whether the drive for efficiency was being accomplished.

The Civil Service Commission (CSM) for many years had possessed a mechanism to receive notices of corrupt activity and other complaints from citizens, but it was little used since it relied on the initiatives of the citizens themselves. In order to determine whether the 2007 act was producing the desired results, the CSM designed and introduced a social audit instrument that was intended to elicit feedback in the usual manner, but additionally to help to shift the mindset of civil servants without raising their hackles. Many of the questions asked, usually indirectly, about the corrupt activities of "facilitators" and other hustlers who took bribes to speed up attention by officials. The CSM also decided to conduct unannounced, undercover, inspections of government offices to invigilate the manner in which the law was being followed.

The CSM's representative sample survey of high-density service delivery offices, with the multiple interactions between bureaucrats and citizens, rated every office's fulfillment of the requirements of the 2007 act, published the results in the national press (thus shaming some of the offices and their managers), and then awarded a Citizen Satisfaction Center Seal of Excellence, together with a small cash prize, to the best performing office each year. Particularly, that last effort promoted healthy competition among government agencies, and obviously benefited the public.[27]

This carrot strategy was subsequently extended by the Philippines Department of the Interior and Local Government (in cooperation with the CSM) to give Seals of Good Housekeeping, with monetary rewards, to those provincial and municipal-level administrations that satisfied service requirements similar to those for nationally run offices, disclosed their finances transparently, passed reviews by the national Commission on Audit, and reduced the number of days it took to open a new business (presumably stimulated by the World Bank's long attention to this aspect of the permitting process). More recently, the government of President Benigno Aquino III gave performance-based bonuses to individual officials whose agencies performed well on the CSM survey, met a set of good governance criteria, and carried out their duties impeccably.

This important diagnostic exercise was even more relevant—in terms of improving service to the public and reducing bribery—for agencies that received failing grades. The Anti–Red Tape remedial team from the CSM set about retraining the staff in those offices. "We hand-hold agencies to help them streamline their processes . . . and [to] develop [their] capabilities [as] frontline service providers," the head of the team explained.[28]

Surprise inspections, carried out at midday to snare offices that violated a mandate that they stay open over the lunch hour, also helped to reform the manner in which public servants fulfilled their responsibilities to Filipinos. (President John Magufuli in Tanzania has instituted similar checks on bureaucratic performance and attention to duty. See chapter 8.)

Another initiative, begun in 2014, sought to strengthen the struggle against corrupt practices by rewriting the survey instrument and including new and better questions about bribe taking and graft. One question asked citizens to estimate how long transactions with bureaucrats took, thus indirectly inquiring whether illicit payments smoothed transactions.

These diverse social audit measures may have reformed the ways in which many civil servants conducted business with the public that they were obliged to serve. But, evaluations by the CSM itself suggested that after its first seven years, awareness by citizens of the prompt and free attention that they should be expecting from interactions with the administration was still a work in progress. Citizens were not routinely holding civil servants accountable or filing complaints of poor service. Comparatively few Filipinos used the national hotline to raise serious service issues, but a critical NGO head said that the reforms had developed new levels of trust among citizens. According to the CSM's own data, the number of offices with failing grades from 2011 to 2014 fell from 27 percent of the total to 4 percent. "Excellent" designations rose from 4 percent to 26 percent in the same period.[29]

According to the Corruption Perceptions Index, Filipino scores improved significantly, from 24 in 2007 to 38 in 2014 (with a 2014 global ranking of 85, well above China but below Malaysia and Mongolia). Businesses also reported fewer bribe solicitations by public servants. But anticorruption activists and other local observers could not necessarily credit the social audit effort with the country's improved anticorruption standing. The nature of Aquino's leadership, and his insistence on better governance, may have contributed more to the perception of reduced corruption in the Philippines. (Aquino became president in 2010.) In 2015, the Philippines' CPI scores and rankings fell to 95th place (along with Mexico) with a score of 35.

The new (in 2016) president of the Philippines—Rodrigo Duterte—has a "tough on crime" reputation and a self-promoted disdain for civil liberties and civil rights. He threatens to assassinate thieves and other miscreants and to attack crime with brutal measures. The barons of sleaze—the corrupters—within his country may conceivably retreat before his draconian efforts. He may also reinforce the more gentle CSM approach to tackling corruption. But as of late 2016, Duterte has inspired a largely brutal and minimally legalistic vigilante effort against the merchants of corruption and drugs.

TRACKING SURVEYS

Public expenditure tracking and quantitative service delivery surveys, expensive as they are to undertake, offer additional clever methods of gaining the information required to estimate likely impacts of corruption in developing societies and unmask ways governments might intercede somewhere along the various chains of peculation and abuse. Those kinds of surveys trace resource flow directions and pinpoint the scale and possible location of diversions. They permit governments (if political will exists), donors, and civil society to ameliorate practices that are likely corrupt, and to alter the arrangements and procedures that facilitate such developmentally deleterious pursuits.[30]

OPINION POLLS

As in the Philippines, polling citizens can provide key details about how a country's informal sector—its corruption nexus—operates, the extent to which it endangers a nation's growth and social prospects, and the quality of its governance. Provinces in China now have social research centers that survey their inhabitants on a variety of governance issues. Many cities in China employ consumer satisfaction surveys to measure how well each jurisdiction is delivering services to its inhabitants. University departments often conduct surveys, and there are national and provincial government websites to solicit feedback from the Chinese citizenry. Commercial survey firms also elicit opinions on a range of subjects, some touchy. One asked respondents whether persons convicted of corruption should receive the death penalty; 75 percent said "yes." This answer supplemented polls over several years that found that the failure of China's national government to come down hard on corruption (which President Xi Jinping's administration is now doing—see chapter 8) bothered a majority of those who responded to the survey.[31]

Where mobile telephones and social media are available, it is now possible to gauge how satisfied citizens are or are not with anticorruption crusades, with other governmental service improvements that decrease opportunities for corruption, and with particular institutions within the public service—the police, the birth registry, the licensing office, or whatever. Mobile telephone text inquiries (much more than over the Internet) permit regular and persistent feedback on a variety of subjects that directly or indirectly improve the awareness of corruption's impact on a community or of the success of remedial initiatives. These feedback channels via text messaging are also an opportunity to upload direct observations of corrupt interchanges, as discussed at length earlier.

These social audit, social media, and citizen action interventions all help to bring petty corruption out of the closet. They allow citizens to vent, and in democratic or quasi-democratic states, to nudge police establishments or bureaucracies to abuse their customers less. But corruption has largely continued. Only in some rare instances (see below) have these social movements contributed, by themselves, to sustainably reduced levels of state or local corruption.

Civil Society

All of these new methods of ascertaining who is corrupting whom and why and how, and how much corruption exists within a community, are valuable. But only rarely have such innovative methods led to concerted, mass action capable of toppling the very pillars of corruption, or at least threatening their routine existence. Aroused masses howled in 2015 at the sheer effrontery of their corrupt political masters in India, where all manner of corruption has long corroded society; in Guatemala, Honduras, and Mexico, where massive street protests against outright political theft echoed the fervor of Tunisian and Egyptian civil movements during the Arab Spring; and even in Malaysia, where $681 million from a state sovereign wealth fund found its way into the prime minister's personal bank account.[32] These movements of protest (and earlier ones in Bulgaria, Brazil, Moldova, Turkey, and Ukraine and 2016 actions in Brazil, Lebanon, Papua New Guinea, and Zimbabwe) have at least put rulers on notice, forced some of the highly placed miscreants to leave office, and widened the opening for effective civil society action.

In the arena of wildlife protection, a West African organization called the Eco Activists for Governance and Law Enforcement, assisted by the Great Apes Survival Partnership and law enforcement agencies in Guinea and in

Paris (Interpol), built a case against Guinea's chief wildlife protector and saw him jailed. He was charged with corruptly conducting international trade in chimpanzees, bonobos, and gorillas.[33] There may be other instances in which governments have moved against corrupt, illegal trade in live fauna, as well as tusks and horns (as in Tanzania), but the arrest in Guinea marks one of the first times a civil society organization has helped track down violations and enforce actions against corrupt behavior in the wildlife arena. (The Zambian actions against poachers discussed in chapter 5 occurred because of official commission scrutiny.)

The UN Office on Drugs and Crime also published an innovative report linking corruption to the destruction of more than 7,000 species of endangered fauna and flora. It said explicitly that the illicit trade in rhino horn and elephant ivory, and of pangolin scales, could not exist without the kinds of corruption that permit the movement of such contraband across borders, largely from Africa to Asia.[34]

INDIA

In India, with the ipaidabribe movement having resonated well with the public and having aroused consciences politically and socially, the groundswell of support for anticorruption initiatives eventually morphed into the establishment of an effective political experiment. Drawing on the much earlier and much revered models of protest pioneered by Mohandas K. Gandhi in the 1920s and 1930s and a massive 1975 anticorruption march on Parliament led by Jayaprakash Narayan, in early 2011 Ana Hazare, a frail seventy-four-year-old former soldier, military driver, and social activist dressed in Gandhian homespun white cotton began fasting in front of television cameras to persuade Parliament to pass anticorruption legislation and to institute a powerful office of an anticorruption ombudsman. Hazare proposed giving the ombudsman's office, or Jan Lokpal, full authority to investigate and prosecute the corrupt acts of prime ministers, parliamentarians, judges, and bureaucrats. That is, Hazare advocated overturning the privileges and rigid operations of one of the world's largest and most dense regulatory regimes by force of individual sacrifice and social media.

Boosted by a mobilizing effort on Facebook spearheaded by Hazare's "India against Corruption" movement, his personal anticorruption initiative stimulated protest marches in sixty Indian cities and towns. (Anand's 5th Pillar movement supported Hazare.) By mid-2011, 12 million people had registered their support of Hazare and his movement by ringing a campaign hotline. Another 60,000 persons sent emails to national government officials. Most knowledgeable local commentators suggested that Hazare's backers belonged predominantly to the 160 million-strong and growing middle-class—

largely literate and educated persons long exercised by exactions imposed by the regulatory raj. One prominent lawmaker called Hazare's plea and the support that he had aroused "the first step in a painful process of transforming the entire nature of government in India." It would be resisted, he predicted, by "the whole political class and the bureaucratic class. . . . They will see it as a death sentence." Hazare himself supposed that "the fire will spread" because "people power [was] bigger than everything." He continued, "The middle class has always had a much higher tolerance because it could pay the bribes. This has now broken. Enough is enough."[35]

Finally, in September 2011, Parliament resolved to support Hazare and the protest movement that he had aroused. Hazare ended his hunger strike. Parliamentary committees began to meet to assess how they could accommodate Hazare's demands and maintain their own and the government's control and authority. One of the main ministerial objections to Hazare's anticorruption approach was the obvious need for an enlarged bureaucracy—the mooted office of an ombudsman—to enforce the provisions of any new act. Some legislators also feared that any new office could itself run amok. Its operations, they said (fearfully), required parliamentary oversight.

In the end, neither Prime Minister Manmohan Singh nor his ruling All-India Congress Party really favored a serious version of the Hazare reform proposal. At the end of 2011, the Lok Sabha (lower house of Parliament) did pass a bill that embodied some of the content that Hazare wanted. But it reserved to the Congress–led government final control over the ombudsman; Hazare had wanted that new institution to be independent and capable of bringing ministers and parliamentarians to book. The Lok Sabha sent the weakened bill to the Rajya Sabha (India's upper house), which was so divided that the proposed legislation was referred to a select committee, which took it up only in late May 2012. Although Hazare felt compelled because of these prolonged ponderings of his anticorruption proposals to launch an indefinite hunger strike and to lead protests outside the prime ministerial residence, the bill only came out of committee in September 2012 and was delivered to the full Rajya Sabha in November. The cabinet of Singh's government next reviewed the proposed legislation, by now amended, and approved it with major weakening amendments in early 2013.

Hazare rejected the new draft of the Jan Lokpal amended bill and promised further rounds of agitation, given Parliament's procrastination, inertia, and evident hostility to his reforms. The bill languished until the end of 2013, only being approved in its adulterated form by the Lok Sabha in December, after Hazare again fasted, this time for nine days. But even after the passage of a Jan Lokpal office with reduced powers, no ombudsman and no institution capable of investigating parliamentarians and bureaucrats was established.

By then Hazare was ready to enter the direct political arena—not to form a political party but to urge followers to vote only for the "right" candidates, whom he would select.

PAPUA NEW GUINEA

Civil society initiatives regarding corruption in the developing world often take much less ambitious forms than those pursued, Gandhian style, by Hazare. In Papua New Guinea, for example, informed citizen participation in reform efforts depends on broad educational campaigns that emphasize the dangers of corruption and teach individuals how to recognize subtle as well as obvious instances of corrupt behavior. Papua New Guinea has a low adult literacy rate of 57 percent; only 55 percent of children are enrolled in primary school. Those numbers mean that to develop participatory and strong civil society platforms capable of combating corruption and the country's rampantly corrupt politicians, civil society must work energetically and persistently over many years to raise the consciousness first of urban and then— much more difficult—rural (jungle-dwelling) Papua New Guineans to understand and then oppose corruption.

Given that context, hardly unique in the developing world, if corrupt practices are to be opposed by an effective civil society and effective NGOs, required is "the explicit facilitation of the growth and proliferation of organized . . . grassroots women's groups, faith-based groups, self-help groups, lending and saving groups, umbrella groups, and others [especially community-based organizations] that bring together people with a common purpose," as in nineteenth-century Sweden.[36] A group, even a bible study group, may meet without an explicit anticorruption agenda, but still turn incidentally to examinations of corruption and its curbing. Liberalization of difficult political arenas may come from civil society groupings that are active for other reasons. In Papua New Guinea, for example, environmentally focused groups are particularly active in opposing corruption because its existence impedes good land husbandry and the protection of avifauna and other wildlife.

MEXICO

In Mexico, where corruption and narco-trafficking have saturated every nook and cranny of the country for decades, several important initiatives are taking root. Corruption is believed to cost Mexico as much as 10 percent of GDP annually. From 2000 to 2013, forty-one state governors were party to corruption investigations. Their offices and many others throughout the federal system and the states are, in effect, auctioned to the highest bidders. The winners in turn extort payments from contractors, narcotics traffickers, and organized crime. In other words, it is still business as usual in Mexico.[37]

According to the Mexican Institute for Competitiveness, nearly all corruption crimes go unpunished. Of more than 400 cases sent to the federal attorney general's office between 1998 and 2012 (already an astonishing limited number), only seven culprits faced charges. The head of the institute remarked that "you cannot sustain a political system where people have enough information to know the extent of corruption but the state institutions are totally incapable of prosecuting it." Furthermore, he lamented, "How can you solve the problem of violence and organized crime if you don't solve the problem of corruption?"[38]

But, thanks to an aroused and increasingly articulate civil society backed by the Roman Catholic Archdiocese in Mexico City, several promising new approaches may make being corrupt more costly and more dangerous for politicians and state employees.

A nascent civil society movement in 2015 lobbied successfully for a new law giving greater access to official information. It also created what has been called a civil observatory to monitor governmental projects that conceivably could be carried out corruptly. One is a very large airport for Mexico City that is being built with $11 billion in rather murky government funds.

One of the more prominent civil action organizations is called ¿Como Vamos? Or "How Are We Doing?" It documents which of Mexico's states have or have not instituted anticorruption reforms that subject their operations to federal audits. So far, public pressure and the awareness provided by ¿Como Vamos? led to the ratification of this protocol by ten of the country's thirty-two states.

Two other NGOs have created a platform named Three Out of Three that encourages candidates in elections to publish their assets, financial interests, and proof of tax payments. They urge voters to tell candidates that they will receive their votes only if the candidates reveal such hitherto unavailable information. In late 2016, federal legislators were still deciding whether to agree to declare their own assets.

NGOs throughout the Mexican universe of the corrupt have rallied citizens against potential presidential conflicts of interest and financial improprieties. One longtime leader of a think tank suggested that anticorruption civil society campaigners should not just "help to write good laws but also to make sure they are implemented [with] support from social and mainstream media." Another leader echoed that approach: "We have a voice. But the press and social media are our megaphone."[39]

After Joaquin Guzman Loera, head of the notorious Sinaloa narcotics cartel, escaped in 2015, maybe by tunnel, probably by corruption, from Mexico's toughest prison, NGOs and other social critics redoubled their frustration with a society that many call infinitely corrupt. (Seven prison officials, including two from the Mexican secret service, were charged in connection with the escape.) "For years it has been clear that justice does not exist," said a prominent political cartoonist accustomed to the madness of Mexican peculation and the widespread abuse of power. "There is nothing left for people to do but to make up alternative realities."[40]

Yet, in late 2016, the impunity for criminals and corrupt officials that has long plagued the Mexican judicial system was hampered with the supposed scrapping of the prevailing Napoleonic inquisitorial system in favor of a North American adversarial model. Whereas the old practice relied largely on confessions frequently obtain punitively from supposed perpetrators, the new reform presumes innocence (a novel feature for Mexico), excludes confessions obtained improperly, and provides lawyers for those on trial. With the intent of abrogating judicial corrupt dealings, it also triples the number of judges who will hear cases: one to ensure the rights of the accused before a trial; a second to preside; a third to make sure that any sentence is carried out correctly.[41] These reforms may make corrupting judges that much harder, but there is still room for cabals and conspiracies and for those who seek to induce judges to do so.

Civil society efforts, and the initiatives of citizen petitioners, were also rewarded in late 2016 by sweeping proposed improvements to the nation's anticorruption regime. President Enrique Peña Nieto announced a new law creating the country's first independent anticorruption prosecuting authority. It also gives protection to whistleblowers. Most important, it mandates cooperation across federal, state, and municipal enforcement levels, and with U.S. agencies. However, the new law does not require recipients of government contracts to divulge their tax information or reveal the assets or conflicts of interest. But it does provide for significant criminal and administrative sanctions for those who bribe, rig bids, peddle influence, and misuse official resources.

CENTRAL AMERICA

"We can't take it anymore," a Honduran salesman and protest marcher said as he joined thousands of others holding bamboo torches and parading weekly through the streets of Tegucigalpa, the country's capital, in 2015. Grotesque levels of corruption, long tolerated in Honduras and in neighboring El Salvador and Guatemala, finally seemed too much to endure.

In Honduras, the eruption of civil society followed journalistic revelations of lavish lifestyles enjoyed by health officials, thanks to $300 million in bribes paid by local and foreign suppliers of medicines and medical devices. The country's ruling National Party benefited from this chicanery through shell companies created to obscure the inflated payments that were part and parcel of the bribery scheme. (The president of Honduras when much of the falsification and peculation occurred was implicated in the affair and admitted that the National Party received the monies in question.) The marchers sought President Juan Orlando Hernandez's ouster, despite a term that officially ends only in 2018. He refused and instead offered dialogue and a new, unspecified, anticorruption system to eliminate graft and corruption in the courts and in politics—panaceas that the protesters refused to accept.

Guatemala's protests in 2015 were larger and more agitated. Every Saturday beginning in April, thousands of citizens poured into the central Constitution Square in Guatemala City to demand the removal of President Otto Perez Molina, a former chief of military intelligence during the country's long war against left-leaning insurgents at the end of the last century and early in this one. These protestors took to the streets when the UN-created International Commission against Impunity in Guatemala reported that the state's customs agency had received millions of dollars in kickbacks in exchange for reducing import duties for a range of local companies, and had funneled those hefty bribes to the vice president and president. The commission further discovered that drug traffickers were financing politicians and political campaigns and that the state's social security scheme was riddled with suspect payments and fraud. It alleged that the head of the state's central bank and the leading vice presidential candidate in the September 2015 presidential election had used his position to protect corporations laundering large amounts of cash.[42]

According to the commission, those in charge of the national health system had skimmed millions of dollars off a contract meant to provide dialysis treatment for patients with kidney problems. More than thirteen patients died as a result of negligent treatment, connecting Guatemalan upper level corruption to the brutal loss of lives.[43]

Three ministers, the heads of the central bank and the Social Security Institute, and the sitting vice president all lost their jobs. Fourteen implicated cabinet ministers resigned. President Perez was not a candidate in the September poll and was scheduled anyway to vacate his office in January 2016, but the marchers in Guatemala City nevertheless demanded his head because he "must have known about" and facilitated the widespread corruption uncovered and documented by the UN Commission (acting as an investigatory commission such as those discussed in chapters 4 and 5).[44] After more than 100,000 Guatemalans marched on Congress urging Perez's resignation, its members voted unanimously to strip Perez of immunity, sending his case to the courts. (Thanks to the ubiquity of smartphones, the marchers were subsequently mobilized via a Facebook page into a movement of continuing social protest and pressure called Justicia Ya, or Justice Now.) Perez resigned the next day and was quickly jailed to await trial on fraud and bribery charges.

Ivan Velasquez, the Colombian head of the UN Commission, later said that no other cause could have united so many Guatemalans: "Because there has been much division within civil society and among people who view others' activities with mistrust," having a common cause was greatly beneficial. "The issue of corruption managed to bring people together for nearly twenty weeks, leading to what you could call public manifestations en masse in a country that has experienced a lot of apathy"—and a long acceptance of corruption.[45]

In the presidential election first round, 70 percent of Guatemalans cast ballots, a record turnout. With 24 percent of the vote, Jimmy Morales, a television comedian, surprisingly led; his campaign slogan had been "Not corrupt, not a thief." In the second round, Morales originally faced a former first lady and a key member of Perez's party, both of whom received almost 20 percent of the vote.[46] But then the Perez follower dropped out. Morales won overwhelmingly.

Morales' victory and the emergence of Justicia Ya strengthened the case that corruption and widespread tax evasion by wealthy elites contributed mightily to Guatemala's heavy inequality; 60 percent of all Guatemalans live in poverty and 50 percent of all children suffer from chronic malnutrition. The leader of the Foundation for the Development of Guatemala (Fundesa), a research organization affiliated with the national chamber of commerce, agreed that Guatemala's biggest problem was corruption. "There is no problem of resources," he said. "We believe that 30 percent of the budget is lost to corruption."[47]

The UN's Guatemalan Commission was established in 2007 and began operating in 2008 in the wake of the country's long and brutal civil war as a tightly negotiated partnership between the UN and the government of Guatemala. Its mandate was to "strengthen and assist" Guatemalan institutions in identifying, investigating, prosecuting, and dismantling domestic illegal security apparatuses and clandestine security organizations, i.e., the shadowy government-linked bodies that had terrorized much of the country in past times and the criminal gangs that were responsible for high levels of mayhem in contemporary Guatemala.

The commission continued its investigations even after Morales was elected, in mid-2016 revealing that the kickback scheme over which Perez had presided was just the most obvious part of a much larger arrangement to run all of Guatemala for personal benefit. After Perez won a presidential election in 2011, the commission charged, he and his cronies signed at least 450 contracts intended to be licenses for the buyers to skim more than $65 million from the state, with sizable kickbacks for Perez and his Patriotic Party. The party, declared the commission, was more a criminal gang than a political party. Its role was to "rob the state."[48] In Guatemala, elites (especially the fifty-eight prominent politicians and military personnel indicted by the commission) constituted a criminal organization—a kleptocratic conspiracy capable of capturing a national revenue stream, a mafia running a state.

In chaotic and murderous El Salvador, which rejected the establishment of its own Commission against Impunity, civil society agitation nevertheless encouraged the attorney general to investigate and prosecute a judicial bribery ring, eventually arresting twelve officials (including three sitting judges and two state prosecutors). In 2012, 80 percent of the country's judges were allegedly under investigation for corruption, but few arrests were made. In 2015, however, the attorney general made a strong case against the members of the ring; they had connived to absolve murderers, extortionists, drug traffickers, and money launderers from punishment.[49]

Clearly, as in India and a few other corrupt jurisdictions such as Moldova, an aroused civil society can at least put ruling parties and ruling classes on notice that corruption is unacceptable. Corrupt behavior in Honduras and Guatemala is not for the fainthearted, since both countries are among the most crime-ridden and murderous on earth, but the steady marches in the capitals of both countries and risk-taking on the part of popular organizers upended political complacency in both nations. Whether corrupt dealings now descend farther underground in Central America, or are significantly modified for the better over the near- and medium-terms, remains to be seen.

What is more certain is the demonstrated value of externally authorized and externally financed, staffed, and run investigative commissions. Guatemala's has been headed by a succession of esteemed South and Central American judges and attorneys general. Even before 2015, the commission was producing results, turning over decisive investigations to the national judiciary for successful prosecution and conviction in Guatemala's courts. Its 2015 and 2016 its reports were incendiary, however, confirming what most Guatemalans suspected (rampant high-level corruption) and leading, via protest marches, to increased societal condemnation of corrupt behavior by national officials and politicians hitherto regarded as untouchable. Similar UN-mounted operations in other strategically important countries could likewise put venal political operations on notice, and potentially even lead to diminutions of corrupt practice.

UGANDA

The National Foundation for Democracy and Human Rights in Uganda (NAFODU) realized about 2007 that the country's police patrols regularly demanded "fees" from Ugandans to register cases, to find "missing" files about cases, and to pay for other services that were nominally free. In the eyes of many Ugandan citizens, the police were "armed robbers in uniform" and police stations were regarded as "extortion and exploitation grounds." A Transparency International local index of bribery found that the Ugandan police led the pack.[50] Often, distrust of the police has forced citizens to take vigilante action.

NAFODU created the Police-Community Partnership Forum in 2009 and forged a memorandum of understanding with the law enforcement authorities. They were at first reluctant to cooperate, but once presented by NAFODU with evidence from surveys, radio shows, and vast raft of complaints, senior police officials participated in a variety of citizen-police meetings throughout the nation and appeared on local radio shows to respond to called-in reports of infractions. The police also received mobile telephone text messages detailing bribe requests and other illegal acts, forwarded by the forum. NAFODU mounted a number of ethics training programs for the police, too. At the end of each session the police were asked to sign an integrity pledge that had been developed by the police themselves.

NAFODU's efforts led to a reduction in incidents of police extortion as conveyed by text messaging, feedback at community meetings, call-ins broadcast by radio, and complaints to the district offices of the NGO. By late 2010, according to NAFODU, there was a "perceptible change in police behavior."[51] By then, the country's law enforcement leadership at the local level was also using its association with the forum to request help in persuading the national government to improve conditions of service and salaries for the police force. The police establishment had appreciated that citizen voices could join their own in bringing attention to grievances and, just possibly, employing civil society action for its own betterment. But the forum exhausted its internal funding, an external grant was not received and, after 2011, many police renewed their requests for "fees" with much of their former insistence.

From Protest to Politics

The failure of the Hazare reforms in India energized Arvind Kejriwal, a young former tax inspector, mechanical engineer, and close aide of Hazare, to break with his mentor and shift the energies that Hazare had tapped from a focus on protest to a readiness for serious politics. (Hazare eventually felt that the movement should remain neutral, politically.) Kejriwal, who had been battling corruption as a social activist since 2000, and who had been awarded the prestigious Ramon Magsaysay Asian leadership prize in 2006 for his efforts to promote transparency and the "right to information," in 2012 formed the Aam Aadmi [Common Man] Party (AAP) to mobilize voters (not just middle-class protestors) against corruption. He and his party first entered regional elections in late 2013, winning twenty-eight seats in Delhi State and forming a government there with the help of the Congress party. But after only forty-nine days in office he resigned because opponents blocked a bill that would have created an independent body modeled on the proposed Jan Lokpal legislation, with power to investigate politicians and civil servants suspected of corruption in Delhi. Next, Kejriwal put his party up against Narendra Modi's Bharatiya Janata Party in the 2014 national general elections, contesting 400 constituencies across the nation and forecasting that the AAP would win 100 seats. Unfortunately for his claims and his reputation, Kejriwal's party won but four seats and nearly all of its other candidates lost their electoral deposits. Modi himself routed Kejriwal in Varanasi by more than 300,000 votes.

That could easily have constituted the end of the Hazare/Kejriwal anticorruption crusade in India. Instead, in early 2015, in another round of regional elections, the AAP astonished nearly everyone by winning sixty-seven of the seventy seats in the Delhi state assembly. Kejriwal, who again became chief minister, had promised voters action against corruption, housing for the poor, better availability of affordable, clean water, lower electrical utility bills, free wifi, protection and greater safety for women, and full attention to all of Delhi's developmental needs. It was a winning message, transforming civil society and middle class protests into an electoral triumph and a new platform for working class reform in a complex state (really a megacity) of 17 million people. "Our mission," said a senior AAP official, is "to change the political culture" in Delhi, to "provide a model where an ordinary common man is encouraged to become a stakeholder in our democracy."[52]

In its first weeks in office, the AAP government established thirty-eight patient welfare committees in all government hospitals to hear and then attempt to ameliorate public grievances. Each is headed by the legislative assembly member from the local area around the hospital in question. The incoming Delhi minister of health promised that each committee would facilitate the participation of the relevant patient and local communities and monitor how each hospital functioned. Day to day grievances were intended to be resolved at the local level—an innovation for India—and each of the committees was empowered by the minister to make decisions about cleanliness, availability of medicines, and even treatment issues on the spot. Another of the health minister's reforms was a massive deworming program for all of Delhi's students, public and private.[53]

Saying that after elections in India "leaders turn into gods and misuse public funds," Kejriwal decided to try to change the way democracy was practiced by engaging in a series of participatory budget exercises with members of the Delhi public. This was his way of bringing government back to the people. Residents in several districts of Delhi were gathered together and issued paper and pens so that they could offer Kejriwal's AAP government suggestions and air complaints. Kejriwal declaimed that decisions taken in the usual manner, inside closed rooms, reeked of fraud, whereas decisions arrived at in the open were credible. He hoped to consult in this manner with all of the seventy constituencies within Delhi state.[54]

These attempts to engage India's citizens in the democratic process build upon World Bank and U.S. presidential attempts to make budgetary processes more transparent and parallel similar contemporary initiatives in Argentina; Boston and Cambridge, Mass.; Cameroon; Greece; Tasmania; and Tunisia. In Argentina, citizens were asked via a new web application to evaluate sixteen legislative bills and then to choose the three most important for online debate. Then, approximately 7,000 citizens gave strong or lukewarm support to those bills, and parliamentarians presumably paid attention. In Boston, high school students were gathered in a number of assemblies to recommend ideas and projects to be incorporated into the city's budget. In Greece, a web application gave citizens in the birthplace of democracy the opportunity to question their national political representatives, to monitor their voting behavior, to crowdsource opinions, and to chat live with other concerned citizens. A "candidate watch" function made it possible for constituents to interact directly with politicians. Tasmania brought focus groups together to provide advice on bioethics and medical concerns. In Tunisia, members of the constitution-writing constituent assembly met with 300 civil society organizations and more than 5,000 individual citizens to help critique constitutional draft proposals.[55]

One further AAP initiative in India built upon the party's earlier origins. It began creating a mobile telephone application to enable Delhi residents and other users to make secret video and audio recordings of corrupt dealings. The application enables someone suspecting an illicit request or some other indication of fraud to start recording with the knowledge that the screen of the mobile telephone would immediately go dark and appear to be switched off. The application links the mobile telephone to a secure governmental server where the data are stored and employed for investigations. The application supplements the AAP's existing hotline, on which citizens notify the authorities that they are being harassed for a bribe.[56]

Finally, in June 2015, Kejriwal introduced into the Delhi assembly a Jan Lokpal bill similar to the one he was not allowed to introduce in 2014 and for which Hazare had fasted and aroused his followers.

Time will tell whether Kejriwal and the AAP will succeed in reducing corruption in Delhi, and whether their efforts prove a model of citizen engagement and citizen action for the developing world. The Indian government claims that the AAP does little for the citizens of Delhi; Kejriwal claims that the central government hamstrings all of his initiatives and harasses him and his assistants, including a key aide jailed for corruption.[57] But it is the only explicit anticorruption initiative that has ever succeeded at the ballot box, unless one counts the election of Morales in Guatemala and Muhammadu Buhari in Nigeria.

This variety of successful people power was much more decisive in mobilizing Indians against corruption than the civil resistance efforts of Gandhi or Hazare. Although it is true that "mobilized citizens engaging in nonviolent tactics make up a social force that can exert pressure on the state," and that nonviolent resistance can employ extra-institutional methods to disrupt corrupt and unaccountable institutions, and perhaps whole societies, thus far aroused civil societies have curtailed corruption in a sustainable manner in very few instances.[58] Nor have the protest movements of Central America or elsewhere as yet led to effective political mobilizations and victories for anticorruption activists at the ballot box. Furthermore, it is too soon—alas—to claim that aroused civil societies can curb corruption sustainably.

Taming the Corporate World

Since a preponderance of the venal or large-scale bribing that occurs across the globe is initiated by corporations, in many instances foreign firms attempting to sell products (guns and butter) or gain access to profitable mining and other resource opportunities in the developing world, and since the Extractive Industries Transparency Initiative (discussed in chapter 2) and the UN, OECD, and U.S. laws and strictures against corrupt behavior overseas (see chapter 3) only inhibit corporate corruption marginally, what else can be done to manage the big bribers and to prevent them from tempting poorer but equally avaricious bribe-takers?

When Johnson & Johnson, the massive American pharmaceutical multinational, considered terminating a corrupt distributor in Greece, senior executives at home argued that choices were limited. "We would lose half our business," they feared. Johnson & Johnson bribed in Greece (and elsewhere overseas) because everyone else was doing it, and the ends justified the means. Executives of Siemens, Germany's largest industrial conglomerate, believed paying bribes overseas was essential. "We thought we had to do it. Otherwise we'd ruin the company." In Mexico, Walmart executives were under enormous pressure from the home office to do whatever was necessary to obtain permits to open more and more stores. GlaxoSmithKline bribed doctors and hospital directors in China because their headquarters in Britain set such high sales targets that every means to fulfill them seemed legitimate. In low-integrity regions, "a lethal mix of end users" embodies corrupt intent and everyone plays unfair. Sales and marketing teams at trade shows and in hotel bars share boastful stories about their biggest bribes.[59] Competition, healthy or unhealthy, understandably drives corporate mendacity.

Escalation of commitment is natural, given pressures to perform and an anxiety to please a supervisor and not to fail. "[T]he closer a project is to completion the more likely decision makers are to exhibit escalation," and to indulge in "bribing not to lose," even though experience shows that continuing to court an overseas politician or official in a low integrity region is patently unwise.[60]

One thought leader in this arena of corporate best practices affirms that relying on legal sanctions, on fear of punitive measures against individuals and corporations, is insufficient to reframe the way big companies and bribers with large caches of cash do business in the developing world. "In a large organization, adherence to legal and ethical rules is critical, and a deterrence culture that is based on a fear of being caught and punished must be real." But, he argues that such a punitive-inspired approach should be supplanted by "an affirmative culture" where employees and managers all behave correctly and anticorruptly because they know that such behavior is right, expected, and a best practice.[61]

Leadership is key. A firm's CEO—and it is essentially up to the CEO and his legal team—needs to articulate and nurture an ethos that is fundamentally opposed to any forms of corrupt behavior in all aspects of corporate endeavor. That means not only absolute prohibitions against bribing to get business, but also a well-understood refusal to countenance indulging in the kinds of influence peddling and influence dealing that are permitted (on a very small scale) by the U.S. Foreign Corrupt Practices Act. Employees at all levels must be held accountable for any deviations from what should become the corporate culture regarding corruption. Zero intolerance can become a norm for one firm after another, but only if such zero intolerance is fundamental to management's method of doing business.

These practices, "performance with integrity," need to be uniform across the globe. Core rules should not vary according to different business or extractive opportunities or different operational constraints. A decentralization of company values—as in the Siemens case and as appears to occur almost daily, according to the reports of several integrity blogs—may be at the root of this failure in many cases to project a leader's words into complementary practices wherever that multinational firm does business.

Responsible leadership is crucial. "Only the CEO can affirmatively create the culture and drive fusion of high performance with high integrity."[62] Corporate boards of directors have strong roles to play as well. But their most important function is to compensate only for performance with integrity and to ensure that such an anticorruption message permeates the firm.

Several obvious steps are helpful in establishing an enduring culture that protects a corporation, particularly a large one that operates on many continents and in many countries. The CEO and his or her deputies must "provide consistent and committed leadership." To do so, they need to exude integrity themselves and take direct responsibility for setting the corporate tone and style. That implies a corporate culture that never cuts corners, that rewards those in the ranks who behave ethically, and that never forgives lapses even when large profits may have resulted from questionable or borderline procedures.

That is tough talk. But it permits the conscious construction within a company of an integrity infrastructure that motivates the ostensibly purely profit-driven components of any enterprise. A key to such an infrastructure is risk assessment—to anticipate proactively potential corruption issues and problems and to invent methods of preventing profit from trumping corruption, no matter what. Managing subsidiaries, partners, and distant associates is fundamental to a full-bore assessment of potential risks to an integrity infrastructure. It also means putting in place procedures that are consistent across all of a multinational's regions and all of its component businesses. The existence of the FCPA and similar legislation plus the great risks of public exposure have altered the nature of the anticorruption discourse from "punishment *ex post* to prevention and compliance *ex ante*." Within the corporation, this discourse should encourage multinational enterprises to alter their internal cultures.[63]

The gold standard in all of these matters has been translated into the areas of life and corporate endeavor that are most easily susceptible to varieties of petty corruption and that could easily develop into venal, prosecutable corrupt behaviors. One big American corporation with tentacles across the globe had "a broad policy that its employees and third parties should not bribe or give in to extortion whatever their nationality," nor should they succumb to corrupt local customs or locally permissive laws. "What is right" was the ultimate corporate question and practice. The policy imposed rigid protocols for travel, specifying what was acceptable and unacceptable; all travel was required to have a legitimate business purpose and be approved beforehand by senior management. The giving and receiving of gifts of more than nominal amounts was prohibited, even if such gifts were culturally required. Strict recordkeeping and a solid auditable trail were required.[64] This company imposed upon management the responsibility not only of articulating such rules of integrity but of fostering employee awareness and a broad internalization of the corporate ethic. What made this approach particularly powerful was the notion that compensation from the top of the corporation down through line managers and beyond was based not only on performance (the usual criterion) but on performance with integrity, especially in emerging markets.

Because multinational corporations have often provided the funds with which to corrupt susceptible politicians and officials in developing countries, because obtaining business by whatever means is the nature of many transactions between large transnational firms and large as well as small emerging states, and because until recently few effective legal barriers inhibited the offering and taking of inducements in the developing world, almost every firm that has operated overseas offered bribes for business because its competitors did, and because in-country nationals required it. But now that stricter enforcement of prohibitions against bribery is becoming the norm and firms are regularly being prosecuted (even in China), the practices of the most punctilious multinational entities may be more widely emulated. Those practices and company rules are capable of being shared across the corporate universe, backed as they are by obligations to the EITI, UN guidelines, and OECD, British, Canadian, and American legislation.

Even Ukraine, a notoriously corrupt state in the midst of turmoil and transition, in 2015 made it mandatory for companies hoping to compete for public contracts to draft codes of conduct for employees, develop programs to acquaint employees with anticorruption ethics and procedures, appoint anticorruption compliance officers reporting to shareholders, and to protect whistleblowers. The absence of an anticorruption corporate plan will enable courts to presume guilt, as does the United Kingdom Bribery Act, should actions be brought against such a firm. (In 2015, too, the president of Ukraine appointed a former prosecutor to head the country's new Anti-Corruption Bureau. That appointee promised to investigate serious misconduct by politicians and judges, as well as businessmen.)[65]

In the United States, Leslie Caldwell, the chief of the Department of Justice's Criminal Division, made it clear that American or foreign firms suspected of violating the Foreign Corrupt Practices Act (FCPA) (see chapter 3) could gain credit by conducting thorough internal investigations and turning over evidence of wrongdoing to the division in a timely manner. "We expect cooperating companies to identify culpable individuals," even senior executives, she said. The penalty for not fully assisting the division was apparent when it charged Alstrom, the French power and transportation corporation, and four senior executives (three of whom pleaded guilty) with violating the Foreign Corrupt Practices Act. The Department of Justice ended up collecting from Alstrom $772 million, one of the largest criminal penalties ever levied in an FCPA case.[66]

Another salutary and far-reaching FCPA-related case broke in 2015 when the FBI and Swiss police arrested the top executives of the Football International Federation Association (FIFA) for putting up for sale the supposedly objective decisions about which countries would gain much coveted rights to hold the most important international tournaments (the football World Cup) and regional football competitions like the European Cup. The scheme had long been rumored and was obvious. FIFA, nominally an international NGO that operated successfully for decades as if it were a multinational corporation, controlled and could divvy up golden chances for city-states like Qatar and nations like Brazil, Germany, Russia, and South Africa to hold the globe's most popular athletic events, hence to gain prestige and glory and to share in ample television transmission proceeds. Prospective host countries learned over the years that FIFA often selected those nations that were prepared to reward members of its executive body well. The price of a vote of a single key FIFA board member in favor of South Africa (host in 2010) was a cool $10 million. Presumably the price for Qatar (host in 2022) was much higher. And for Russia in 2018?

The U.S. Department of Justice charged FIFA's high-level officials with "corrupting the enterprise." These officials had abused the international conduct of football (soccer) and had damaged FIFA and the regional bodies with which the fourteen indicted perpetrators were also affiliated. Subsequently, the Federation itself suspended its long-time chairman, the head of its European component, and the chair's chief deputy for being parties to corruption. The Department of Justice addressed the fact that FIFA is not a governmental body, and that bribery is a crime only when public servants are involved, by alleging that those who were in charge of FIFA and took bribes were victimizing the organization and football more generally. Commercial bribery is illegal only if it "goes against the interests of an employer." A lawyer believes that the U.S. was "trying to save FIFA from itself."[67]

Not a day goes by when the FCPA blog fails to report guilty pleas by individuals and companies who gained advantages overseas by bribing officials and politicians for mining concessions or access to petroleum drilling contracts (as in Petrobras or Pemex), for lower import tariffs, as in Guatemala, or for substantial sums to expedite the entry of containers, say, into the hideously congested ports of St. Petersburg or Lagos. Any revolution in multinational corporate behavior, such as is advocated above, is still not at hand. Nor have there been consumer boycotts of companies paying bribes in contravention of the FCPA, OECD regulations, or various domestic barriers. Even the Guatemalan, Honduran, and Indian protests are against local rulers who skim and steal, not against the foreigners (and the domestic businesses) who pay to play. But as civil society movements against corruption swell in number and increase in effectiveness, protests and political action will possibly focus on both the supply and demand sides of the corruption equation.

Under President Obama and his two attorneys general, the U.S. has intensified its attack on corporate, sovereign wealth fund, and individual corruption because it is wrong, but also because the Department of Justice believes that such corruption is a major cause of global instability, a severe hindrance to economic development everywhere, a major creator of poverty, and a critical abuse of national social contracts. Funds pilfered abroad—as in the Malaysian government sovereign wealth fund case, where more than $3 billion was misappropriated—also distorts real estate markets and the overall American economy (witness Miami and New York). For all of those reasons and more, corruption is a "threat to American national security."[68] At the end of 2016, Congress also gave U.S. presidents the power through the Global Magnitsky Human Rights Accountability Act to prevent corrupt leaders from any country from traveling to the United States and to freeze their American assets. But even such American efforts will hardly daunt those corporations, funds, and individuals who are corrupt and who corrupt others until international agreements and legislation eliminate banking secrecy and the protection that many countries and some American states give to those who obscure property ownership registrations. There is still much to be done to level the global playing field—to shift even corporate and sovereign wealth fund behavior from particularism to ethical universalism.

Curing Corruption

LESSONS, METHODS, AND BEST PRACTICES

Ferreting out and chastising culprits of corruption was easy in medieval times. In at least some towns in England, politicians publicly weighed themselves annually. If waistlines had enlarged and girths expanded, holders of public office were assumed to have grown fat at the expense of taxpayers and citizens. Shrinking size, or at least a steady state, was seen as an emblem of responsibility, "suggesting that a leader had been working hard on the people's behalf."[1] An elaborate ceremony culminated with all occupants of official positions standing on the scales of justice, with the assembled crowd cheering those who had gained no weight (and were therefore presumed to be honest workers) and castigating (and flinging rotten fruit at) those who had grown large and had therefore, obviously, abused their positions. Some were even driven from office. Thus was accountability served, and corrupt dealings kept in reasonable check by the employment of objective measures . . . and measurements. Excess avoirdupois signaled untrammeled greed at public expense.

Today's times are more complex. But corruption can still be reduced by well-crafted and well-targeted anticorruption institutional re-engineering efforts, by limitations of discretion and other restrictions on temptation, by opening the affairs of government and bureaucracy to bursts of sunshine and transparency, by unbridling and enabling civil society, and by encouraging and rewarding the exercise of responsible political will on the part of elected political leaders. Dislodging kleptocrats and disturbing their vertically arranged networks doubtless helps. So does the forcible shutting of offshore accounts and closing access to secret banking arrangements.

Battling corrupt tendencies in all societies is unremitting, but the good news is that it can be done. Anticorruption can succeed. The lives of the least favored can thus be improved; development efforts may no longer be undercut by theft from the public purse. If a few contemporary international jurisdictions have succeeded in rejecting corruption, and others did so decades ago, so can the stain of corruption be erased systematically from more and more of the globe's beleaguered and mostly fragile states. The key ingredient is determined leadership exercised on behalf of, and in service of, a public responsive collectively to such new initiatives. Leaders can embolden middle classes and citizenries generally to take charge, and can rein in their own regime's propensities for grasping avarice. Most of all, leaders can provide the kinds of behavioral integrity and behavioral bright lines that, over time, shift prevailing political cultures from acceptance of corruption to rejection of corruption. Given commitment and an ethical bearing, beating back the merchants of entrenched mendacity can indeed be accomplished.

The evidence presented in earlier chapters of this book shows that combating the cancer of corruption globally and in selected nation-states is a constant work in progress. Just like cancer in human cells, corruption is insidious, metastasizing readily and easily, and resistant to first-order remedies. In many places perceived as rampantly corrupt, the disease has been accepted as a chronic illness, the pains and troubles of which simply must be endured. In those many infected countries—comprising perhaps three-quarters of the planet—it is the rare public official who rejects bribes, refuses to extort, refrains from stealing state resources when he or she has a chance, and is slow to abuse citizens. But the most potent cure for such debilitating and tempting profiteering involves whole societies, not merely individuals. Corruption is a collective infection. Sustainable recovery involves strengthening the immune systems—the ethical spines—of entire political cultures.

Laws and Investigations

Many initiatives to moderate the curse of corruption within a nation-state, including good laws and adequate sanctions, effective investigative operations, apparatuses to develop information and prepare indictments, well-motivated and carefully prepared prosecutors, impartial and intelligent judges, and the full armaments of modern systems of justice are necessary to combat corruption effectively. So are instruments of accountability, such as a vigilant, observant, and free media capable of exposing potential abusers and incidents of abuse; auditors general with keen forensic capabilities; ombudsmen to receive and delve deeply into citizen complaints; and unintimidated civil societies that can operate as energetic and scalpel-sharp tribunes of the people. Any innovation that improves transparency is valuable. So is the removal of red tape (minimizing individual discretion), enabling businesses to operate with fewer permits and licensing checks, the abolition or flattening of tariffs, and any and all measures that empower citizens facing bureaucratic inertia and recalcitrance. Putting such interactions online also reduces the ability of corrupt public servants to impose their personal will on transactions with citizens. The less discretionary judgment, the fewer the opportunities for corruption.

Each of these improved instruments is important, but none on its own can curb corruption completely. Even an overall goal of improving political institutions, a positive aim, is necessary but rarely sufficient. Whole societies, not their various parts, must be transformed if ethical universalism and a norm of noncorruption are to replace the many kinds of compromises that permit or facilitate the corrupt default impulse to take hold or to remain embedded in today's nation-state.

Individual national legal frameworks are usually secure enough to ensnare all manner of corrupt schemes. Most prohibit public servants from receiving gratuities, favors, or fees to exercise influence for or against decisions. Any deviations from impartiality or neutrality are specified as infractions against written or customary codes of conduct for public officials. In a number of jurisdictions, too, employees of private concerns are banned from taking bribes to influence commercial considerations of almost any kind, or to bend the manner in which a corporation competes in the marketplace. Almost all relevant statutes define corruption as some variant of abusing public office or public position for private gain. Some spell out in great detail each of the offenses that qualify.

The legal mesh against corruption has few loopholes, and little of it suffers from ambiguity or possible misinterpretation. Moreover, many of the existing anticorruption statutes, worldwide, specifically permit wide-ranging searches and seizures of suspects. The more imaginative and far-entangling examples also permit authorities to infer corrupt behavior if public servants live visibly beyond their means or cannot readily explain how they came to possess expensive jewelry, fancy motorcars, or lavish houses and other property in distant lands. Bank accounts may be examined and residences searched. In other words, nearly all countries where corruption is rated prevalent possess laws sufficiently powerful to arraign suspected offenders and prosecute them to excellent effect. It is not because of weak legal systems that corruption flourishes.

International legislation has also made it much easier in this decade than before to contain corruption. The U.S. Foreign Corrupt Practices Act, the British Anti-Bribery Act, the OECD Code against Corruption, and the UN Covenant against Corruption, plus several additional national and regional pacts, all target external suppliers of corrupt inducement, effectively inhibiting multinational corporations from exchanging cash for contracts and concessions. The Extractive Industries Transparency Initiative and new Securities and Exchange Commission guidelines, with their emphasis on full disclosure of the proceeds of payments to exploit the precious resources of countries that are already corrupt, attempt to make the supply side of corruption that much more transparent. On the demand side, an International Anti-Corruption Court could investigate, judge, and punish corrupters, especially those who orchestrate grand corruption endeavors in weak states lacking independent judiciaries.

The FCPA is the most powerful of these transnational instruments; its clauses and U.S. legal practice permit prosecutors to pursue any person, corporation, or NGO that has passed its funds through the American banking system or has offices or operations within the United States. Tax evasion and money laundering are major crimes, and those who are venally corrupt often cross such red lines. The long reach of American jurisdiction, the centrality of the U.S. dollar and U.S. banks to the global financial system, plus a willingness in this century actively to pursue extraterritorial corruption, has made even strictly local and internal instances of venal corruption easier than ever to trace and to prosecute. Switzerland and a few other popular hiding holes for hot money are also cooperating nowadays with European, American, and local investigators. More ways than ever exist to trace the proceeds of venal corruption back to its sources and, as the Panama Papers disclosed, to find the bolt-holes into which illicit proceeds are deposited.

Likewise, the conditionality (positive incentives) imposed on newer nation-states by the European Commission regarding admission to the European Union and by the Millennium Challenge Corporation (MCC) regarding eligibility for significant cash inflows from that American source, have encouraged local attacks on corrupt practices, many of which have managed to reduce corrosive behavior. But in only a few of those European "successes" have the improvements proven sustainable, in those cases largely because of domestic agency. Similarly, at least several of those African low-income countries that became eligible for MCC have curbed corruption only temporarily. In a related finding, "higher per capita funding [from overseas] does not seem to produce any statistically significant improvements in the governance scores of . . . partner states."[2]

Nearly all heavily corrupt jurisdictions have long-established investigatory bodies, national auditing offices, and mechanisms to receive and process citizen complaints. Allegations are capable of being pursued, convoluted schemes unraveled, and possible perpetrators questioned. In some countries, too, the media are inquisitive and free, which helps to uncover and publicize potential abuses of public or private office. Civil society can be active, too, in highlighting systematic or specific kinds of service delivery failures and likely corruption. In today's world, the use of mobile telephone texting and dash cam videos have opened up additional avenues of disclosure and, with photographic evidence transmitted electronically, become capable of offering direct confirmation of illicit dealings. Social media are also employed to mobilize mass citizen awareness and to engender protests against those who persist in corrupt practices. Nearly all forms of corruption are subject, more than ever before, to being exposed by citizens and investigators. Mass protests often follow, as in China, Guatemala, Honduras, Kazakhstan, Kenya, Lebanon, Malaysia, Moldova, Nigeria, and Zimbabwe.

A Bureaucratic Pathology

Researchers who label political corruption a "bureaucratic pathology" suggest that a possible answer to the temptations of corruption is to centralize administrations in graft-prone areas. A centralized public service has clearer lines of authority than a decentralized one, despite the latter's ability to empower numerous watchdogs. Centralized systems are also more accountable than decentralized ones because the lines of authority are more transparent and less secret. To the extent that a country's corruption reflects poor methods of public administration, with citizens being compelled to lubricate faltering procedures and to pay bribes to jump interminable queues, then improving lines of authority and narrowing channels of discretion could conceivably alleviate pressures to trade cash for services.[3] But if the bureaucrats are in fact pathologically corrupt, they will continue to use their public positions to extract private payments whether reporting in a centralized or a decentralized fashion. Since corruption starts from the top, fiddling with administrative reporting alterations for public officials will hardly help except at the margin.

Defining the problem of corruption purely as a matter of ferreting out and punishing crime—treating corruption as social deviance—fails to appreciate how deeply most kinds of corruption are embedded in national, even criminalized, norms.[4] It also neglects to appreciate the extent to which most developing world investigative bodies and judges are thoroughly compromised. In those common circumstances, where the law has little credibility and serves the interests of prevailing corrupt practices, improving methods of punishment may accomplish little. Once a society has tipped itself deeply into corruption, imprisoning individuals obscures a pervasive disease affecting the whole society.

Many argue persuasively that anticorruption efforts succeed only when local civil society is strong—when citizens "are able to build inter-group coordination mechanisms" and foster "elite accountability" sufficient to swell social trust and inhibit the corrupt behavior of persons in political and economic power.[5] An inclusive and well-led civil society grows the kinds of cross-ethnic trust that can be utilized, as in India, to build effective movements of protest and thus to persuade those in positions of national and state influence to cease so cavalierly tolerating corruption at many levels. Unfortunately, in the global battle against corruption, civil society in many nations is still weak and easily manipulated by heads of state and parliamentarians. A supporting civil society contributes mightily, but only over the medium-run, to comprehensive cures of the corruption malady.

Schools and teachers can also proselytize against corruption by discouraging bribe giving and supporting text-messaging reporting campaigns. Such educational efforts are valuable at all levels, but particularly promising is a nascent program to warn budding African businessmen and entrepreneurs about the intricacies of corrupt practice and to urge them to join the civil battle against its spread. (The World Bank also conducts a series of salutary integrity training schemes for public officials worldwide.) Using a UN toolkit tested at fourteen graduate business schools in Africa, Europe, India, and South America, three African university business schools emphasize in special short courses ethics training for future managers and for working executives. Nigeria's Lagos Business School integrates the lessons of the toolkit into its regular MBA curriculum, South Africa's Stellenbosch University Business School translates the toolkit into an ethics course for managers, and Tanzania's Mzumbe University discusses solving cross-cultural ethical dilemmas and about how an East Africa that is integrating can reduce corruption.[6] More of these kinds of corruption-arousal endeavors must obviously erode the inevitably of corruption within whole societies and entire professions, but, again, such helpful initiatives assist at the margin until entire cultures are inspired to overcome corruption.

If the constituents of a state want to reduce the impress of corruption, they must be able to access most, if not all, of the available institutions and instruments of reform. But merely establishing such mechanisms often has little effect on the amount or frequency of corruption within a society. Many African and Asian states tried to replicate the success of the Hong Kong Independent Commission against Corruption (ICAC) but could not, in considerable part because of problems of design and human resource weaknesses, but more completely because key stakeholders—the leaders of the nations concerned—exerted little political will in favor of such independent anticorruption action. In case after case examined in chapter 5, and in one of the key cases in chapter 4, the national executive either directly obstructed the manner in which investigative commissions functioned or, even more damaging, failed credibly to commit to enterprises that were, it became apparent, intended to be more expressive than instrumental. Unlike in Croatia, Hong Kong, and Singapore, elsewhere the executive almost always and almost ev-

erywhere also deprived commissions of adequate budgets, adequate personnel, and adequate office accommodations.

A president and a legislature may have established an investigative commission with a mandate to reduce corruption, but without the ongoing, real,
support of politicians. In all of those cases, corrupt activity persisted despite
the often well-intended but poorly-backed efforts of the commissioners and
their staffs. The well-run original Zambian Anti-Corruption Commission, for
example, faltered when a new national president decided that its actions were
obstructing his own determination to loot the state.

Because of such institutional deficiencies, nearly all of the investigative
commissions examined in earlier chapters could not accomplish their mandates with the efficacy demonstrated in Hong Kong. There, desperate to recover from decades of seamy corruption and several major scandals, a British
governor created and imposed the ICAC. He obtained the needed legislative
support in the form of enabling and punitive laws and then set about recruiting capable directors and personnel to carry out his wishes. What was essential then, and what was lacking subsequently elsewhere, was the provision of
adequate financial resources that gave the governor's efforts credibility and
the ICAC stature and, in time, legitimacy. The governor also made it clear, as
too few other leaders have done, that no offender—no matter how close to his
office or him personally—would be spared investigation and prosecution. Singapore, Botswana, and Rwanda did the same. Thus, anticorruption efforts in
those countries, and in few others, early appeared as initiatives of integrity.
Not only was the absolutely essential element of political will demonstrated
month after month and year after year—the executives in each case clearly
impressed citizens with how sincere they were in their attempts to create new,
less abusive, national political cultures—but they each played no favorites.
These leaders refused to protect political cronies or ruling political party operatives, as the presidents did on repeated occasions, for example, in Kenya,
Malawi, and Uganda. They did not shield political party fund-raising mechanisms, often an excuse and a motivator of corrupt practices, from scrutiny, as
the recent Brazilian and Guatemalan scandals (and many others, such as those
in South Africa and Zimbabwe) illustrate.

In those many jurisdictions where corruption is entrenched, even being
criminal in its scope and reach, and where locally authorized and administered investigatory operations are bound to be more cosmetic and futile than
effective, the Guatemalan model provides an innovative answer. There, from
2007 to 2015 (see chapter 9), an externally run and funded, UN-authorized
operation (the Commission against Impunity) unearthed evidence of venal
fraud and culpability at the highest political level and supervised indictments
and prosecutions. Its efforts led to major shifts in political leadership and, at
the very least, to a greater societal awareness of the sweep of corrupt prac-

tices. Whether this effective assault on impunity provides an enduring cure for one of Guatemala's main ills is as yet unknown. But creating such UN-backed investigatory commissions to probe corrupt dealings and end impunity in such benighted and fragile places as Angola, the Democratic Republic of the Congo, Myanmar (Burma), South Sudan, and Sudan would greatly assist the global crusade to moderate corrupt behavior.

Political Leadership

Political will is the single most critical variable in any effective campaign against corruption. Without the signals that determined political leaders can send to their disparate peoples and variegated constituencies—even in a nation as populous and complex as China—there is almost no chance that corrupt behavior can be modified, much less reformed. Those signals—the exercise of firm and exemplary political will—need to be strong and clear if they are to compel people to cease profiting in the way "everyone else" is profiting. To achieve a collective response that is positive, a leader's commitment must be credible and her or his personal behavior appropriately chaste. Personal compromise and hypocrisy condemns many anticorruption campaigns to failure.

In each of the significant positive sustained examples in this book, the executive believed in the anticorruption objective and used investigative commissions, prosecutors, attorneys general, and the courts to advance, not to frustrate, that mission. In those cases, the executive was sufficiently secure in its leadership and authority to resist the inevitable pushback from those many politicians, bureaucrats, and security officials who were enmeshed in corrupt practice and addicted to its rewards.

The more completely a ruler and a regime have allowed themselves to be seduced by the wages of corruption, the harder it is to retrieve integrity for public servants or to regain a national moral high ground. A full embrace of corruption by ruling elites, no matter if nominally democratic or not, greatly alters governmental priorities across the board for the worse and accentuates a society's sense of spiritual decay. That is why it takes gargantuan efforts on the part of leaders, preferably with the backing of an aroused civil society and an observant media, to beat back the powerful forces of entropy—in this case representing those who are profiting well from corruption—and to start afresh. These newly emboldened leaders require all instruments, institutions, and sanctions available, and abundant courage and determination. They also need a vision of a better and more prosperous future around which they can forge a constituent consensus against continued corruption. Ultimately, for anticorruption drives to succeed and be sustained, leaders must persuade most of their followers that the state will no longer allow high-level public officials to loot and enjoy the proceeds (witness President Jacob Zuma's new "secure" and expensive mansion, or Gabon President Ali Bongo's thirty-nine villas in Paris and an unusually large one in Libreville), and will also crack down mercilessly on those who exact annoying petty bribes.

Of great significance, the executives in Singapore, Hong Kong, and the rest of the high performing countries were able to accomplish such reorientations of their societies and to guide them toward an embrace of ethical universalism. They engaged their citizens, consciously or not, in a process of gradual socialization against corruption throughout admittedly contained domains. Hong Kong's ICAC, from its inception, took a genuine anticorruption message to every governmental ministry, to customs and excise offices, to businesses, and to schools. These outreach efforts actually altered attitudes. The efforts of the ICAC, overall, but especially its educational and preventive sections, gradually revamped norms. Rather than corrupt practices being accepted as something unpleasant to be tolerated, as vexing but accustomed procedural complexities, the ICAC's endeavors persistently and ineluctably established a new normative framework for the colony that has endured despite a major change of administration. Singapore accomplished the same transformation in about the same length of time, as has Rwanda more recently, and as did Botswana from its inception. Croatia, pulled by Europe and impassioned local leaders, may have done the same. China may be on the way to the same goal. In each case, once the venal corrupters as well as the petty corrupters realize that corruption is going out of style—that ceasing indulging in corruption is what everyone else is doing—solving for the collective action endeavor becomes much easier. Possibly this constitutes the "critical mass" that tips existing equilibria away from particularism toward ethical universalism.[7] But to initiate and embolden such an important shift, revolutionary leadership must be in the vanguard.

Hong Kong's ICAC, and Lee Kuan Yew, Sir Seretse Khama, and Paul Kagame ultimately—using several persuasive and sometimes coercive means—convinced their countrymen of three propositions: that a nation-state free of corruption would prosper much more than one replete with corruption; that what was good for the state would be good for the individual; and, critically, that an individual's renouncing of corruption would coincide with renunciations from everyone else. Society—the collective—would be the winner. Everyone would "get to yes" together.

Clearly, changing individual incentive structures is essential to accomplishing collective results. The sharp stick and the mailed fist are insufficient, but nevertheless required. Lee Kuan Yew would not have so dramatically rescued Singapore from its massively corrupt past if he had done so too gently and irresolutely. He had to preach a committed message and show symbolically that he truly meant to cleanse his city-state's Augean Stables, removing from office anyone, even close colleagues, who took advantage of their official positions for private gain. His son, now Singapore's prime minister, hardly has to use the same draconian tactics today since, for many years now, Singapore's entire national value system—its political culture—has tolerated no corrupt practices, no matter how mild and inconsequential.

Kagame undertook the same kind of attitudinal and cultural revolutions in Rwanda when he erected billboards forbidding further corruption and sacked close associates who were indulging themselves financially at the expense of their constituents. Khama started Botswana off on the same track in the 1960s and thus avoided the kinds of early outbreaks of embezzlement, extortion, and bribery that bedeviled the administrations of even the most well-meaning and benevolent of his African peers. When his successors in Botswana suffered a regression to that corrupt African mean, they were soon able to reestablish the prevailing national anticorrupt norm using tactics reminiscent of Hong Kong and Singapore.

The key ingredient in any recipe for corruption reduction is consummate, resolute, political leadership. Entire societies obtain behavioral cues from those who govern them. In small, fragile societies particularly, it desperately matters who leads and how they lead. It matters even more conclusively with regard to corruption, the prevalence of which always is influenced materially by what is happening at the apex of the local community and society. Cabinet ministers look to their presidents and former presidents for implicit authority to misappropriate funds, to demand kickbacks for large contracts, and to approve mining or similar concessions only after arranging special gratuities for themselves (or for the ruling political party). If the prevailing climate is ripe, legislators likewise employ what power they have to approve new laws or budgets only when those who need such actions make it worth a parliamentarian's while. Military generals sell promotions or put ghost soldiers on profitable payrolls (as in Afghanistan and Nigeria). Police superintendents establish a payment schedule for "extra sums" to be received from lower-ranking officers. The young patrolman on the beat or manning a traffic control barrier sees his superiors eating at the communal trough of corruption. So he or she wants to "eat" as well. "If you get into a state institution . . . you go there and eat. You eat, you yourself. Your family. . . . You eat on your behalf, but also let some crumbs fall." Why should middle-ranking or low-ranking civil servants or their military equivalents refuse to do what everyone else is doing, and what their superiors and role models are doing? "Everybody does it, so whether it is bad or good everybody does it anyway."[8] The pustules of corruption are best cured from the top—from the site of the infection—not from some distantly related appendage.

In the battle to cure corruption, sensitive and honest political leadership, like esteemed medical leadership (possessing knowledgeable diagnostic abilities and talented surgical hands) is key. But the objective of effective leadership action is less the sidelining or imprisonment of sets of alleged offenders than it is the wholesale transformation of a society from tolerance to intolerance of corruption. This disruptive, normative narrative was responsible more than legal instruments, stronger institutions, and fuller accountability for the transformation of Denmark, Sweden, Norway, Finland, New Zealand, Australia, the Netherlands, Prussia, Britain, Switzerland, and Canada from corrupt to noncorrupt in and after the nineteenth century, for ending Tammany Hall's reign in New York City at the beginning of the twentieth century, and for the kinds of wholesale anticorruption investigations now taking place in Brazil, Croatia, Guatemala, Bulgaria, Romania, and a host of unrelated countries. Corruption only ends when the collective consciousness eschews corrupt behavior—when from a societal point of view episodes of graft and extortion become shameful rather than commonplace.

Hong Kong, by prosecuting, by reaching out across the colony with a strong ethical message, and by proactively reducing bureaucratic or procedural preferences for corruption in governmental agencies, during but a brief few decades converted an outpost of seething gratuity peddling into a city proud of its new probity. The work of the ICAC and steady doses of political will changed the colony's expectations of proper bureaucratic and even corporate behavior profoundly. Singapore did the same, based on a similar strong prosecutorial base, and because corrupt practices were eventually believed by its citizens to be inimical to development and obstacles to prosperity. In both entrepreneurial city-states, political cultures were vastly reconfigured and corruption became mostly an archaic pursuit.

What is happening in China today, and what could still happen in Nigeria under a strong-willed President Muhammadu Buhari, shows that prevailing norms can give way. That is what occurred, strikingly, in Rwanda in recent years. As in Singapore and Hong Kong, being corrupt and being codependent with corrupt politicians and bureaucrats became outmoded and dangerously out of step.

In Botswana, leaders were never especially coercive in transforming their societies from corrupt to noncorrupt. Hong Kong achieved major sustainable changes by being firm but without being overly punitive. But the others, such as China, depend on an aggressive leadership action allied to unremitting coercion to accomplish societal transformation. Clearly, a signal measure of coercion exerted over at least a generation—a willingness to jail miscreants and provide heavy penalties for corrupt culprits—is helpful if norms are to be modified and reforms to take hold (as they never did in Bolivia or South Africa). Determined leadership, in other words, succeeds in curbing corrupt practices if it is forceful, consistent, clear about goals, and—preferably—very even-handed and legitimated. By such means, societal and citizenry behaviors can be reconfigured and new norms evolved.

Another way of making that same point emphasizes the critical importance of anticorruption victories as enduring ones. Scattershot assaults are valuable, especially if they moderate particularly odious practices of corruption, but only broad-based endeavors as in Hong Kong, Singapore, Botswana, and Rwanda (and perhaps in today's China) deeply engage citizens and are therefore able to sustain their results over several generations and to socialize whole societies effectively.

Whether this transferring of norms can occur in large societies as well as small ones, where more constituents can be reached more easily and less expensively, obviously is a central question. Rwanda, with twelve million citizens, is much more populous than Hong Kong, Singapore, or Botswana, but it is also mainland Africa's most densely settled country. China (and perhaps Nigeria) is the consummate test since the Indian initiative is ongoing and, so far, is effectively limited to one (admittedly large) state.

No effective campaign against corruption succeeds without visionary, committed leaders. China is reducing graft and fraud because President Xi Jinping believes that it is in the interest of the ruling Communist Party, the Central Committee of the party, and himself as supreme leader to create a cleaner ruling echelon and thus to remove the inefficiencies and costs to China of continued, wide-open corrupt practice. Xi may also be removing his enemies and potential enemies under the cover of an anticorruption drive. Nevertheless, if Xi's campaign persists, the long-entrenched impunity of corrupt behavior will have been removed or at least reoriented, and party functionaries and policemen may, as in Hong Kong under the British, appreciate that corruption is harmful to their own futures as citizens of China as well as to the embryonic nation itself.

The significance of political leadership can also be seen, retrospectively, in the Nordic cases and New Zealand. Frederick the Great was influential in Prussia. In Denmark the beneficial role of kings is clear, plus the leadership of particular public intellectuals and political entrepreneurs in the nineteenth century. Sweden and Finland boasted several political operatives during the nineteenth and early twentieth centuries who wore the respective mantles of leadership well, and battled against corruption. New Zealand can point to enlightened leaders who helped to alter the nation from enduringly corrupt to innovatingly anticorrupt. Nothing, to repeat, would have cured corruption there or in any other nation by reforming from the bottom and hoping that a trickle-up effect would end the national malaise.

Since responsible political leadership clearly makes a difference, since no anticorruption effort has succeeded that has not been driven by leaders, from the top, and since communities and societies never reform themselves, how do we nurture those kinds of leaders and orchestrate their political ascents? In some societies in Africa, where the middle class is now growing and becoming more influential, its appreciation of anticorruption endeavors should ensure the selection of candidates (see chapter 11) who are supportive of assertive efforts to transform their nation-states. The universal norm of ethical universalism will spread from established nations in Europe and Asia to those many countries where institutions are still weak and nations are not yet fully built. Civil society in those scattered places will demand sturdier and more anticorrupt leadership than ever before. Educational initiatives will also help.

Nevertheless, as Lee Kuan Yew has proclaimed, leaders are born, not made. Does that mean that social change and the spread of political culture to new states cannot influence and nurture new kinds of leaders? Does it mean that corruption will remain a comfortable antinorm until a person randomly comes along who ascribes to the "big bang" theory and, as in Rwanda in this century, decides to uproot prevailing practices of corruption? To wait, in that way, for a miracle or a rebirth would be disheartening, inconclusive, and unsatisfying.

Instead, since leaders when they come to power have a choice, it falls to electorates and exercised publics to support only those contenders whose hands are clean and who reliably promise to reduce official corruption from the top. Theoretically, whole populations could refuse to pay bribes and petty corruption would cease. That is to some limited extent what Ana Hazare accomplished in India and what the voters in Delhi achieved in 2015. But whether such popular movements, with their own leaders, will succeed any more than Ronald MacLean-Abaroa did as mayor of La Paz is not clear. What we do know is that when committed leaders harness the anticorruption sentiments of citizens and mobilize them behind a vision of positive change, they break communal molds and begin a process that can cleanse large societies of the disfiguring stain of corruption. Encouragingly, battling corruption to a standstill can be a matter of decades, not centuries.

Uncompromising Approaches

Outsiders can assist, too. Although battling corruption is largely an internal task, presidents and prime ministers of more powerful nations can support developing country leaders who are transforming their once corrupt countries by public praise, with project completion funds, and via a host of other initiatives. More signally, powerful nations should shun those who run the most corrupt, criminalized states of the world, refuse to welcome them to foreign shores, certainly downgrade relations as much as possible, and reluctantly but smartly end any and all assistance until such time as the target nation begins to prosecute major corrupt politicians and public servants. "Shunning" can take many public and more pointed private forms. Naming names leads to shame and notoriety. Visas can be denied to the major peculators and influence peddlers, and their daughters and sons. Permits to reside or study abroad can be denied. Arms and other embargoes can be introduced. Military cooperation can be ended. Investors can be urged to avoid the country in question. Tough love, with the possibility of progress, is the object of such initiatives.

An uncompromising approach is essential if campaigns against corruption are to succeed. But local leaders can also marry coercive strategies to programs of positive inducement. They can reduce the temptations of corruption by paying public servants more, thus in theory reducing incentives to extort their clients and to filch from the public purse. In Imperial Qing China, district magistrates were given an extra allowance "to nourish honesty."[9] British India's overlords knew that penury could hardly purchase integrity. In the nineteenth century, Nordic nations and others realized that they had to provide living wages if they expected their public servants to cease stealing. In more modern times, Singapore and Hong Kong have pursued such sensible policies, rewarding their officials generously. But few states other than China have had the wherewithal to provide more than basic wages to their mandarins and others tasked with providing governmental services to the public. Police in Uganda and Kenya (and many other places) blame poor pay for their constant importuning of innocent civilians. In only a limited number of places in Africa, for example, are the bureaucrats and the security officials rewarded commensurately with the private sector (Singapore's goal).

Rather than raising salaries, Romania's prime minister, himself suspected of benefiting from corrupt inducements, suggested that bribery should be legalized. What he apparently meant was that since his government could not pay public servants, particularly physicians in state hospitals, as much as they deserved, and since patients received better service when they slipped envelopes of cash to their doctors, Victor Ponta proposed making those irregular fees regular, declarable, and therefore taxable. In other words, the amount of the "bribes," now "payments" directly to the physicians, would be scheduled according to the medical treatment delivered and listed along with regular fees for all to see. Theoretically, customers would pay less and the doctors would not need to negotiate with each client.[10]

There is every reason to believe that most Asian and African public servants and policemen believe that they are underpaid. They therefore request special fees and "tea money" from those who require their services, and they importune because their overseers are always doing the same. Or, as in Nigeria's main airport, at Indian land registration offices, at almost anywhere a permit or license is dispatched, or at roadblocks across the developing world, public servants arrange to top up their miserable wages with "contributions" from a public that can hardly refuse. The Singaporean and Hong Kong alternatives are better, but few nation-states will be able in coming decades to drive out corruption by raising wages substantially. Anyway, there is no guarantee, and no research, that shows that avarice would not still prevail, absent the kind of bold, reformative leadership that this book advocates. "It is not poverty. It is just a question of greed, just bad manners. Wanting to amass and amass . . . for yourself and . . . your brothers," explained a Kenyan or Ugandan informant.[11]

Among the many other methods explored by practitioners and researchers to curb corruption generally or in particular countries, more democracy is often recommended. As developing states democratize, this proposition assumes, they will naturally reduce corruption levels and push corruption into the national unacceptable column. Common sense certainly suggests that more democracy means less corruption. But research shows that solid democracies may be just as corrupt as wild kleptocracies; democratization need not drive out corruption. Moreover, as the nations of the world have, overall, become slightly more democratic, they have become no less corrupt. For many countries, anyway, becoming more "democratic" may enable more forms of corruption to flourish, not fewer. As indicated in chapter 1, democratic societies are often plagued by absences of inclusion, meaning that they are corrupt. The problem is that not all democracies are pure democracies. Merely holding elections may mean too little. The Zimbabwes of the world hold elections and have political institutions, such as a lively Parliament, but fundamental freedoms are absent and the courts are controlled by the president. Corruption runs rampant there. "What matters . . . is not elections . . . but rather the permanent capacity to ensure that whoever is elected respects individual rights, autonomy, and voice."[12] That capacity is associated with a meaningful control of corruption; it tends toward ethical universalism.

Botswana is a thoroughly democratic country and has been since independence in 1966. It is the least corrupt country in the African Union, according to the Corruption Perceptions Index. Cape Verde and Mauritius, also near the top of the African least-corrupt list, are well-practiced democracies. Rwanda, also with little corruption, and Singapore are nominal democracies, but democracies that are tightly controlled and restrictive. Liberia, the "most improved" nation in the anticorruption sweepstakes for 2004–2014 (see chapter 6), is clearly democratic; its rise in the least-corrupt ratings is associated with more democracy, but also with the gifted and clear-minded leadership of President Ellen Johnson-Sirleaf. More democracy is helpful in the battle against corruption, but increasing supplies of that political good need not by themselves reduce levels of corruption.

In chapter 7, we noted that broad-based universal educational levels were correlated with less societal corruption. At least, expanding educational opportunities assisted Nordic and Antipodean countries, and probably Canada, to shift from a corrupted past to a less corrupt future. Common sense again suggests that better educated persons understand the damage that corruption inflicts on nation-states and, as those nation-states become more literate and their citizens better schooled, corruption levels fall. But no evidence shows that corruption has been reduced in Kenya and Nigeria as its populations have, over the last thirty years, become much better educated, producing many more secondary- and tertiary-level graduates. Well-educated South Africans rob the public purse and abuse their offices no less than their poorly educated countrymen. Nothing in the literature suggests, either, that university-trained persons steal less than persons who only finish high school. Most politicians in most of the globe's determinedly corrupt states are nakedly corrupt, indulging in venal schemes along with their well-educated peers across the globe. (Anecdotal evidence even suggests that better educated politicians purloin much more cleverly than their less well-schooled associates.) Nevertheless, for other developmental reasons, more education is a positive public good. Hong Kong's ICAC experiment has shown dramatically how compellingly educational efforts specifically against corruption can, in a few short years, alter political cultures and greatly reduce behavioral defaults toward corruption.

Civil society in a number of corrupted countries has experimented successfully with varieties of surveillance as a technique to make the practice of corruption by bureaucrats and politicians much more onerous and ruinous. In India, in Mexico, in the Philippines, and elsewhere, as the ninth chapter has demonstrated, the actions of civil society leaders and organizations have at least made corruption more visible and more costly. The widespread availability of mobile telephones and web cams has also given citizens new techniques for reporting corruption by place and time, and often by offender. Anything that names, and possibly shames, bribe takers and bribe givers, plus those who extort, helps at a minimum to publicize corrupt acts and, conceivably, to reduce their number.

Furthermore, machine learning could predict those zones of corruption where investigators and prosecutors could best devote their energies and time. Computer programs can be asked to locate patterns amid masses of big data, thus allowing machines to highlight objectively those human conditions or human behaviors that most bear close surveillance. Algorithms do the work; humans can interpret and act on the outcomes of such data mining. Admittedly, however, employing the results depends on political will, a quality often in short supply.

Overall, removing discretion helps. So does putting transactions between citizens and bureaucrats online. Anything that increases transparency, strengthens public information and public awareness, and narrows the power of individual servants of the state makes corrupt behavior harder and more traceable. Eliminating the reach of the permitting raj reduces opportunities for extortion and graft.

Another almost foolproof method of controlling grand corruption is to mandate compulsory independent, preferably external, audits of a nation's entire governmental apparatus, annually. To do so is expensive, but properly trained auditors can quickly uncover, as in Malawi in 2015, falsified account books, ghost workers, agricultural overpayments, secret slush funds, and the like. Most official national audit offices perform very well under difficult circumstances. But they are almost always obliged to table annual reports in Parliament, where no one needs to act. In capable parliaments, usually where there are sizable oppositions, public accounts committees, theoretically chaired by leaders of an opposition (if there is an opposition party) employ such annual reporting by state auditors as texts to investigate the operations of state or parastatal organizations. In a few places, those legislative invigilations have revealed shoddy management and, occasionally, blatant corrupt dealings.[13] But energetic public accounts committees are few in the parliamentary democracies of Africa and Asia. They usually play catch-up, tracing errors in the past, and—so far—they have only rarely confronted corruption head on. None has been as effective as the Canadian Public Accounts Committee. In many parliaments, too, the reports of the auditors general simply sit in a parliamentary clerk's office, awaiting an inspection that never comes.

More beneficial use could be made in today's battle against corruption of the many offices of ombudsmen that exist in countries that are corrupt. Many sitting ombudsmen are thoughtful and active, like the public protector in South Africa, but in most cases and even in hers, their ability to make a difference is limited to reporting, often to Parliament (where their conclusions again sit, waiting). Only in a few jurisdictions may the office of the ombudsman prepare cases for prosecution. Most ombudsmen are government employees, their emoluments and positions at the disposal of the executive. Few are permitted to talk about their reports to the media; in South Africa the public protector's two reports about President Jacob Zuma's seemingly corrupt use of state resources to construct a secure vacation and retirement home became public, but without any remedial action occurring (as the public protector demanded) until public outcry and constitutional court decisions compelled Zuma to promise token repayments. More can be made of auditors and ombudsmen in the ceaseless struggle against corruption, but to do so would demand exercises of political will and credible commitment to reform on the part of political actors.

An international anticorruption court of the style and with the mandate outlined in chapter 3 would also deter grand corruption by offering a tribunal of final jurisdiction, and ultimate sanction. It would constitute a legitimized venue for prosecuting cases of corruption in every jurisdiction where domestic judges were under the thumb of corrupt and authoritarian executives, or where ombudspersons and auditors were unable to persuade authority figures in their own countries to pay attention. Recall the overriding exemplary impact of the Permanent Court of Arbitration in The Hague when it issued a clear ruling on the rights of those states bordering the South China Sea.[14]

Other strategies to accentuate accountability exist. With committed political will, the media could be encouraged to investigate rumors of corruption and to undertake thorough examinations of anyone in politics or state employ alleged to be abusing her or his official position for private gain. The activities of overseas corporations investing in mining, manufacturing, or agriculture could be scrutinized more completely. The media could follow the money and ask questions about unexpected wealth, ostentation, and other suspicious private and public developments. How did that mega–shopping center get built on state-owned land? How were state facilities and airports illicitly used by private persons connected to the head of state? How is it that in times of acute food scarcity some traders had plentiful stocks of grain, most of it siphoned from governmental warehouses? How is it that illegal narcotics manage to flow so easily through national airports, evading interception? And so on. The media, if left to run free under private owners not controlled by a government, can often do the job of exposure that is best accomplished by the Fourth Estate. In most places, however, such transparency is feared, journalists are hunted and opposed, and whatever openness and scrutiny there is occurs against great odds. Many heads of state persecute and assassinate journalists who expose corruption.

Another innovative suggestion to help reduce graft and money laundering is to reduce the supply of large-denomination currencies, thus making it much harder for criminals and corrupt politicians to move large amounts of cash to safe havens. If bills such as the €100 and $100 are removed from circulation, carrying substantial bribes across borders would require trunks instead of suitcases, and a retinue to make sure the haul arrived at its illicit destination. "Phasing out big bills would make it harder for domestic currency to support corruption abroad. A million dollars in hundred-dollar bills is easy to tote in a shopping bag, but a million in ten-dollar bills weighs an ungainly two hundred and twenty pounds."[15]

Each of these initiatives and endeavors is relevant in lessening the impact and spread of graft and sleaze. Ultimately, however, consummate political leadership enables them and drives all successful attempts to remove the stranglehold of corruption. For that reason, donors who have devoted substantial sums to sponsoring anticorruption investigating commissions modeled on Hong Kong would be well advised henceforth to spend assistance monies on capacity building for leadership—not on anticorruption efforts per se. If a new generation of political leaders can be helped to emerge in the nations most blighted by corrupt behavior, if those leaders can be encouraged through training and other well-established methods to appreciate the importance in their countries of strengthened rules of law and improved transparency and accountability, and if they can be made more aware of how corrupt practices inhibit development and marginalize their own legacies, then foreign assistance funds will be better spent.[16] There is little point, as this book has demonstrated, in spending precious time and expensive capital to upgrade institutions and instruments (such as commissions) when political will is so central to winning the total battle against corruption. Nurturing effective leadership is cost-effective and decisive. Too little foreign assistance in today's philanthropic world is devoted to fostering collective action, strengthening leadership, and supporting the free media.[17]

The Final Battle

Victory is not at hand. Anticorruption campaigners cannot claim more than partial successes. No definitive cure for corruption is apparent. Nor are the aroused citizenries of China, Guatemala, Honduras, India, Malaysia, and Moldova necessarily harbingers of a victorious civil movement against the corrupt behavior of ruling elites. But, as this book has shown, there is much greater intolerance today than a decade ago by publics across the globe of political, bureaucratic, and corporate corrupt misdeeds. As the middle class grows in Africa from one-third to two-thirds of the continent's population, and as Asian and Latin American workers demand better and less-corrupt behavior on the part of their rulers, so the clamor for fundamental change becomes more constant and more shrill. Consequently, because of the power of the ballot box, in nominally democratic societies the lax leadership standards of the past will gradually be superseded by a phalanx of more ethical, much less corrupt parliamentarians, cabinet ministers, prime ministers, and heads of state. In the quasi-democratic and authoritarian corners of the globe, this transition toward a noncorrupt future will take longer and will depend on regime changes and the rise of leaders who understand, in the manner of Lee Kuan Yew, that their own futures and the prosperity of their countries fundamentally depend on weakening the vise of corrupt practice and on ushering in a new norm of ethical universalism. Nirvana is achievable, however long it takes.

Given the increasingly bright light now being focused on illicit, harmful, corrupt behavior from Croatia to Papua New Guinea and from Guatemala to

Brazil and South Africa, corruption can no longer lurk in the shadows, unspoken, unacknowledged, but ever present and ever harmful to national priorities—especially in low income, fragile, states. This naming and shaming is a relatively recent phenomenon, as is international attention to the ills of corrupt behavior. The disease that was little talked about until the middle 1990s is now the central developmental ailment of our times. Fortunately, as this book has shown, we know what it takes to provide remedies, given sufficient political will within nations and across world order. Heads of state and heads of government, assisted by an alert civil society and improved political institutions, and supported if necessary from the outside, are now capable of leading their communities away from the pursuit of insistent peculation toward the embrace of collective probity.

What Works

THE ANTICORRUPTION PROGRAM

1. The nation seeks, elects, or anoints a transformative political leader embodying the new political will; this leader will commit herself or himself to an all-out battle against corruption in and throughout her or his administration. The leader makes advances against corruption a measure by which to evaluate the success, and potential for re-election, of her or his administration, and pledges to seek higher ratings (with specific targets) on the CPI, the WBCC, and other benchmark indexes. Energetic and exemplary leaders of vision and credible integrity are essential. The anticorruption project cannot succeed without someone legitimate and forthright to stimulate such disruptive change.

2. In office, the new leader strategically removes holdover senior ministers and officials who are tainted by corrupt practices and, soon, discharges any of his or her own appointees who lick sticky fingers or trade personal enrichment for the exercise of undue influence. She or he promises to continue to clean the political and bureaucratic stables of anyone, especially police and army commanders, who abuse their public positions.

3. The new executive and the legislature strengthen the legal barriers against corruption and revamp or establish a new anticorruption commission with extensive investigative and prosecutorial prerogatives and a broad mandate to extirpate corruption wherever it is located. The new executive appoints a tough-minded, responsible, experienced prosecutor or lawyer to head the commission, provides

for its financial and personnel needs, and guarantees the commission and its head independence from executive, legislative, or crony interference.

4. As added armament, the executive and legislature provide for a resuscitated or new office of auditor general and appoint a person with skills and vision. It is important that the auditor general and an ombudsperson report to the nation, not just to parliament or the president, and that the auditors have the right and responsibility to investigate the accounts of all governmental and parastatal offices and office holders.

5. The executive and legislature bind the nation to the provisions of the proposed International Anti-Corruption Court, giving citizens added protection and further avenues of appeal against corrupt behaviors.

6. The president or prime minister declares his or her assets, opens them to public scrutiny, and insists that all political appointees, judges, ambassadors, and civil service employees above a certain rank also file elaborate declarations of assets annually, with the auditor general to scrutinize them and report back publicly to the nation.

7. The president appoints life-tenured senior judges with impeccable integrity and establishes an escrow account to pay their salaries, with regular raises, so as to sustain their independence and impartiality.

8. To enhance transparency, the president and the legislature promise to respect press and media freedom. Together, they back a permissive freedom of information law.

9. The national Anticorruption Commission energetically establishes a section within its organization to prevent corruption and another to educate the public about the ills of corruption and the rights of all citizens. The commission sponsors integrity training sessions for corporate as well as public leaders. The object of this portion of the commission's work is to socialize citizens to understand that corrupt practices are no longer to be expected and will not be tolerated. Preventive efforts and educational outreach are designed to create a new national norm of ethical universalism that is antithetical to the practice of corruption.

10. A compendium of rights is posted for public viewing at every office where citizens interact with bureaucrats and seek permits, licenses, and the like. It is also distributed over the Internet and via social media. Further, permitting and licensing activities are shifted online, thus making the exercise of bureaucratic discretion that much more difficult.

11. The Anticorruption Commission establishes hotlines to receive citizen telephonic reports, text messages, videos, or other allegations and

evidence of bribing, extortion, graft, etc. by policemen, customs inspectors, airport security agents, tax officials, or any other public servants. It also welcomes and provides financially rewarding support for whistleblowers and whistleblowing.

12. The Anticorruption Commission adopts advanced quantitative methods and expenditure surveys to measure public works programs and other large-scale spenders of public capital to determine whether state funds are being disbursed and utilized without accompanying graft.

13. The government abolishes a bevy of regulations and simplifies its tariffs to reduce those arenas in which the exercise of human discretion encourages corruption.

14. On behalf of the nation, the president or prime minister and the legislature agree to adhere to the provisions of the Extractive Industries Transparency Initiative and to bring national laws into conformity with the OECD Convention against Bribery and the UN Convention against Corruption, as well as regional anticorruption agreements.

A Research Note and Acknowledgments

The infectious and social fabric–eroding nature of corruption has been inescapable over my working lifetime in Africa, Asia, and the Caribbean. I knew many of the culprits, including some mentioned by name in these pages. I also consorted with those brave leaders and civil society activists who tried to reduce corruption and injustice in their many countries. The intellectual origins of this book are thus deeply rooted in direct personal experiences and in varieties of participatory research in and about some rampantly corrupt and some less corrupt countries across many decades. More consistently, for at least the last sixteen years, I have been thinking, teaching, and writing about how to ameliorate the disease of corruption throughout the developing world. The destiny of almost every field locale—from Fiji to Burma to Kenya and Nigeria and on to Haiti—has been affected by corruption, the fates of their peoples mostly being controlled by corruption, rent seeking, and distorted priorities. How to remove the monkey of corruption from their backs has been a central concern over innumerable decades.

The Corruption Cure is an extension of my earlier writings on comparative politics. My research and writing on governance and on state failure during this period, and my creation of the Index of African Governance (and other measurements of governance), all dealt peripherally but critically with the phenomenon of corruption and the political results of corrupt behavior for the peoples of the developing world. The contents of an edited book, *Corruption, Global Security, and World Order* (2009), and chapters in my *Africa Emerges: Consummate Challenges, Abundant Opportunities* (2013) and *Transformative Political Leadership* (2012) foreshadowed some of what I write about here, especially the fundamental role of political leadership in combating corruption. Several of us, including the president of Namibia, in 2004 established the African Leadership Council under the wise chairmanship of the second president of Botswana in order to strengthen political leadership in sub-Saharan Africa, but in part to combat corruption.

Even more influential in conceptualizing effective anticorruption strategies were classes with Harvard Kennedy School graduate students, especially those in my courses on the politics of the developing world and on the nature of political leadership. Together we explored the insidious nature of corruption and examined potential remedies. The germ of the arguments in these pages will be familiar to those generations of students; appropriately, they can assert co-authorship. So can senior students who participated with me in two courses at the University of Cape Town Summer School. I owe a very large intellectual debt to all of my students and unwitting collaborators, some of whom have gone on to become high officials and presumably noncorrupt ones in their own developing nations.

Equally formative intellectually, and critical in so many other ways, was my year-long fellowship at the Woodrow Wilson International Center for Scholars in 2014–2015. I could not have hoped for a more supportive atmosphere; much of the first draft of this book was written by me in a bare office overlooking Wilson Square, contemplating each of the changing Washington seasons. I am grateful to the Wilson Center, especially to Robert Litwak, Monde Munyangwa, Steve McDonald, Joe Brinley, Lindsay Anderson, Kimberley Connor, and Arlyn Charles for consistent and important backing and critical encouragement, and to the staff of the Wilson Center library for decisive research collaboration. Two assistants, Katharina Krause and Soyeon Kim, cheerfully and industriously facilitated my research endeavors. A significant part of this book rests on their labors. A number of my colleagues as fellows contributed meaningfully throughout our months together; Charles Glaser, Jack Goldstone, Roya Hakakian, Benjamin Hopkins, Joseph Sassoon, James Schear, Matthew Taylor, and Paul Williams all helped in companionable ways to advance the writing of this book.

Outside of the Wilson Center, Paul Russell, vastly experienced in the enduring battle against corrupt politicians, and Diana Cammack were essential guides to political malfeasance in southern Africa. Kimberley Smiddy kindly introduced me to the corrupt and the corruptible in Malawi. Rotimi T. Suberu and Daniel Jordan Smith were expert guides to the Nigerian morass of corruption. Raymond Baker instructed me in the deeper ways of venality. Ben W. Heineman, Jr., my Harvard colleague, kindly tutored me about the better methods of curbing corporate misconduct. Alejandro Ponce helped me to understand the contributions of the World Justice Project Rule of Law Index and to glimpse the innards of Mexican corruption. I am also grateful to Alejandro Lerch for the opportunity to address Mexico's Policia Federale in Los Cabos, and to learn from its officers directly about the mechanisms of corrupt practice.

At the forefront of the assessment of Brazil's massive current corruption scandal is Judge Sérgio Fernando Moro of the Federal Criminal Court in Curitiba, Paraná State. I am grateful for his willingness to discuss, not ongoing cases, but the nature of Brazilian corruption and possible governing theories of anticorruption. Likewise, I am thoroughly appreciative of the unstinting support of Pedro Dallari and Felipe Loureiro during my weeks in Brazil at the International Relations Institute of the University of São Paulo.

In Zimbabwe, where corruption is omnipresent, I have been well guided over several years by Firle Davies and Frances Lovemore, and, before his untimely death, by Eddison Zvobgo, sometime minister of justice, and, unwittingly, by Herbert Murerwa, sometime minister of finance. Johnnie and Anne Carson have over several decades been delightful friends and keen observers of corruption. This book leans on all of these fine people and our shared experiences.

Botswana, Rwanda, and Singapore have each managed to reduce corrupt behavior below the levels exhibited by their neighbors. Well before his death, Sir Seretse Khama of Botswana let me accompany him across a parade ground in Gaborone; he explained why he was determined to deter fellow Tswana from succumbing to the temptations of corruption. Lengthy conversations years later in Gaborone with President Festus Mogae, Foreign Minister Archie Mogwe, and Governor of the Bank of Botswana Quill Hermans were also very formative. Several of my students from and in Rwanda, and local researchers in Kigali, explained what President Paul Kagame (who had spoken of his work several times to groups of us at Harvard University) was attempting to achieve and how he did it. Six hours intensively interviewing Lee Kuan Yew in Singapore in 2006 informed me exactly why he attacked corruption so vigorously in the 1960s, 1970s, and after. Kishore Mahbubani was my guide to Singapore then, and since.

My conversations with politicians in Malawi from 1993 through 2012 often concerned corruption. The late Aleke K. Banda, sometime minister of finance and sometime minister of agriculture, was very clear and forthcoming over the many years of our friendship. So was President Bakili Muluzi, who endlessly promised me that he was about to crack down on corruption, but never did. Discussions in Zambia with President Kenneth D. Kaunda over several decades, the late Arthur Wina, when he was minister of finance, and his brother Sikota Wina, speaker of Parliament and many times a cabinet minister, were also instructive about the real nature of corrupt acts. Mark Chona added to the conversation at a memorable dinner in Lusaka. These friends knew whereof they spoke. My interminable session with President Frederick Chiluba of Zambia in a small library in State House included many fanciful denials of his complicity in corruption. I also spoke with President Michael Sata before his death.

In Arusha one early evening, I was informed by Julius Nyerere, late president of Tanzania, about the dangers of corrupt behavior; he was bemoaning to me his own failures while president to curb corrupt practices. He urged greater attention to reforming the ways in which leadership was developed and exercised. A long, surprisingly candid, private conversation one evening in Addis Ababa with the late Prime Minister Meles Zenawi touched on corrupt dealings and election fraud, with promises to extirpate such illicit operations.

In South Africa, conversations about how deep and how destructive corruption was and is have taken place over decades with such diverse and opposed political personalities as President Thabo Mbeki, Mayor Patricia de Lille, the late Helen Suzman, the late Nthato Motlana, Wilmot James, Alec Boraine, and the late Frederik van zyl Slabbert; with many academic colleagues, especially Roger Southall, André du Toit, and Chris Saunders; and with a host of friends and mentors, including Moeletsi Mbeki, Raymond Louw, Benjamin Pogrund, Jules and Selma Browde, and Benjamin Rabinowitz. I am deeply appreciative of their varied and incisive insights, in some cases conveyed over years and years of friendship. I am also fully indebted to the late, indomitable Helen Suzman—she of the rapier-like ironic parliamentary thrust and consummate intolerance for cant and fraud—for friendship and hospitality, and most of all for penetrating instruction on how best to recognize and then to combat corruption, especially in apartheid and postapartheid South Africa.

I am also immeasurably indebted, as the citations and bibliography make clear, to those who have studied corruption seriously since about 1960, if not before. Mine is a work of primary scholarship and synthesis that relies on an impressive foundation of excellent pioneering research and writing by my many esteemed predecessors: especially Robert Klitgaard, Joseph Nye, Jr., Susan Rose-Ackerman, and James Scott; this foundation further rests on the pathbreaking scholarship of those who are today in the vanguard of thoughtful examinations of corruption theory—in particular Paul M. Heywood, Michael Johnston, Alina Mungiu-Pippidi, Bo Rothstein, Jan Teorell, and Eric Uslaner. Indeed, nothing is more impressive than the research on various aspects of corruption that is being sponsored by the University of Gothenburg's Quality of Government Institute. Many of the insights and propositions in chapters 1 and 7 inevitably lean heavily on the institute's probing formulations and the scholarship that it has inspired. Closer to home, Jennifer Widner's Innovations for Successful Societies project at Princeton University's Woodrow Wilson School has vastly deepened my understanding of how the battle against corruption globally has proceeded in the trenches, sometimes successfully. My intellectual and personal gratitude to all of these persons, and to the many others whose names appear in the endnotes and the bibliography, is large and palpable.

In many significant ways, those of us who try to reduce corruption globally, and write about it, are even more fully indebted to the insights, activism, leadership, and friendship of Peter Eigen, founder of Transparency International and of the Extractive Industries Transparency Initiative. He very early understood the neglected evils of corruption, and what had to be done. He stimulated and advanced some of the globe's most formidable assaults on corruption.

I also dedicate this book to those many indigent farmers and urban workers across the planet who refuse to pay bribes and resist extortionists, and who are today embracing civil protest activities from Malaysia and India to Guatemala and Honduras. They are the daily heroes who merit our support. We attempt to make the world a little less corrupt so that they may enjoy better human outcomes.

—*R. I. R.*
12 January 2017

Notes

Introduction: Beating Back the Varieties of Brigandage

1. For more on Brazil, too late for this volume, see my "The Judge Who Would Remake Brazil: How Sergio Moro Has Tackled Corruption," *Foreign Affairs* blog, Dec. 21, 2016.

2. These numbers are from the Organisation for Economic Co-operation and Development (OECD), CleanGovBiz, "The Rationale for Fighting Corruption," Background Brief, 2014, 2, http://www.cleangovbiz.org/49693613.pdf; http://www.gfintegrity.org/reports, Dec. 8, 2015; Richard Rose and Caryn Peiffer, *Paying Bribes for Public Services: A Global Guide to Grass Roots Corruption* (Basingstoke, Palgrave Macmillan, 2015), xi, 1, 10. Rose and Peiffer calculate their 1.6 billion figure for the total number of persons affected by bribery yearly across the globe by multiplying the Global Corruption Barometer average for bribery by the world's estimated population.

3. Christine Lagarde, quoted in Szu Ping Chan, "Global Corruption Risks Tipping More Countries into Crisis, IMF Warns," *Telegraph*, May 11, 2016.

4. Alina Mungiu-Pippidi, "Some Countries Really Are More Corrupt than Others," http://foreignpolicy.com/2016/05/24, 3.

5. Nelson Mandela, speech at Mafiking in 1997, quoted in Anthony Sampson, *Mandela: The Authorized Biography* (New York, Random House, 1999), 533; Paul Kagame, quoted in Stephen Kinzer, *A Thousand Hills: Rwanda's Rebirth and the Man Who Dreamed It* (Hoboken, Wiley, 2008), 236; James D. Wolfensohn, quoted in Vinay Bhargava, "Curing the Cancer of Corruption," http://www.siteresources.worldbank.org/extaboutus; Catherine Weaver, *Hypocrisy Trap: The World Bank and the Poverty of Reform* (Princeton, Princeton University Press, 2008), 108–109, 121; http://www.worldbank.org/en/news/pressrelease, Dec. 19, 2013; John Kerry, quoted in Stephen Castle and Kimiko de Freytas-Tamura, "Leaders Vow to Thwart Financial Corruption," *New York Times*, May 13, 2016; Thomas Erdbrink, "Iranians React to Nuclear Deal with Elation but Also Skepticism," *New York Times*, April 4, 2015.

6. Juan E. Pardinas, quoted in Kirk Semple, "Grass Roots Anticorruption Drive Puts Heat on Mexican Lawmakers," *New York Times*, May 28, 2016; Sarah Chayes, "Corruption and Terrorism: The Causal Link," http://carnegieendowment.org/2016/05/12.

7. Mungiu-Pippidi, "Some Countries Really Are More Corrupt," 4.

I: The Nature of Corruption

1. See "Political Will" section, below, this chapter.

2. Joseph S. Nye, "Corruption and Political Development: A Cost-Benefit Analysis," *American Political Science Review*, XLI (1967), 419. Nye was drawing in part on Edward C. Banfield, *Political Influence* (Glencoe, IL, Free Press, 1961), 315. For a recent approach to the definitional issue, see Oskar Kurer, "Definitions of Corruption," in Paul M. Heywood (ed.), *Routledge Handbook of Political Corruption* (New York, Routledge, 2015), 30–41.

3. Samuel P. Huntington, "Modernization and Corruption," in his *Political Order in Changing Societies* (New Haven, Yale University Press, 1968), 59.

4. James C. Scott, *Comparative Political Corruption* (Englewood Cliffs, Prentice-Hall, 1972), 3:21.

5. John T. Noonan, Jr., *Bribes* (New York, Macmillan, 1984), xi, 13–14, 702.

6. Susan Rose-Ackerman, *Corruption: A Study in Political Economy* (New York, Academic Press, 1978), 6–7; Rose-Ackerman, *Corruption and Government: Causes, Consequences, and Reform* (New York, Cambridge University Press, 1999), 9; Rose-Ackerman, "The Challenge of Poor Governance and Corruption," http://www.copenhagenconsensus.com/files/filer/cc/papers, 2004; Rose-Ackerman, "Corruption in the Wake of Domestic National Conflict," in Robert I. Rotberg, *Corruption, Global Security, and World Order* (Washington, DC, Brookings, 2009), 66.

7. Robert Klitgaard, *Controlling Corruption* (Berkeley, University of California Press, 1988), 23–24.

8. Henk A. Brasz, "The Sociology of Corruption," in Arnold J. Heidenheimer (ed.), *Political Corruption: Readings in Comparative Analysis* (New York, Holt, Rinehart, and Winston, 1978), 42, originally published as "Some Notes on the Sociology of Corruption," *Sociologica Neerlandica*, I (1963), 111–117.

9. Robert Williams, "Corruption: New Concepts for Old?" *Third World Quarterly*, XX (1999) 503, 510.

10. Robert Harris, *Political Corruption: In and Beyond the Nation State* (London, Routledge, 2003), 6.

11. Laura S. Underkuffler, "Defining Corruption: Implications for Action," in Rotberg (ed.), *Corruption, Global Security, and World Order* (Washington, DC, Brookings, 2009), 27–42; Paul M. Heywood and Joshua Rose, "Curbing Integrity or Promoting Integrity? Probing the Hidden Conceptual Challenge," in Peter Hardi, Paul M. Heywood, and Davide Torsello (eds.), *Debates of Corruption and Integrity* (Basingstoke, Palgrave Macmillan, 2015), 107, 109–110, 112.

12. Daniel Jordan Smith, "The Paradoxes of Popular Participation in Corruption in Nigeria," in Rotberg (ed.), *Corruption*, 283–309.

13. Gunnar Myrdal, "Corruption: Its Causes and Effects," in Heidenheimer, *Readings*, 540, originally in *Asian Drama: An Enquiry into the Poverty of Nations* (New York, Twentieth Century Foundation, 1968), II:951–968.

14. Colin Leys, "What Is the Problem about Corruption?" *Journal of Modern African Studies*, III (1965), 225–226, 229. Earlier Leys had commented on the insufficiency of moralistic explanations for corruption, objecting as did Nye to the approach of Ronald Wraith and Edgar Simpkins, *Corruption in Developing Countries* (London, Allen & Unwin, 1963), 45, which decided that corruption was avarice run amok among people who—whatever their background, ethnicity, or nationality—knew that what they were doing was wrong. Lucy Mair, *The New Nations* (Chicago, University of Chicago Press, 1963), 124–125; Scott, *Comparative Corruption*, 64, 74–75.

15. Bert F. Hoselitz, "Levels of Economic Performance and Bureaucratic Structures," in Joseph La Palombara (ed.), *Bureaucracy and Political Development* (Princeton, Princeton University Press, 1963), 190.

16. Fred W. Riggs, "The 'Sala Model' and Comparative Administration," in Heidenheimer, *Readings*, 214–216, originally in "The Sala Model: An Ecological Approach to the Study of Comparative Administration," *Philippine Journal of Public Administration*, VI (1962), 3–16.

17. Michael Johnston, "The Search for Definitions: The Vitality of Politics and the Issue of Corruption," *International Social Science Journal*, XCIX (1996), 321; Michael Johnston, *Syndromes of Corruption: Wealth, Power, and Democracy* (New York, Cambridge University Press, 2005), 11, 187.

18. Bo Rothstein, *The Quality of Government: Corruption, Social Trust, and Inequality in In-*

ternational Perspective (Chicago, University of Chicago Press, 2011), 14–16, 103; Rothstein, "Anti-Corruption: The Indirect 'Big-Bang' Approach," *Review of International Political Economy*, XVII (2011), 230; Oskar Kurer, "Corruption: An Alternative Approach to Its Definition and Measurement," *Political Studies*, LIII (2005), 223, 236; Rothstein and Jan Teorell, "What Is Quality of Government? A Theory of Impartial Political Institutions," *Governance*, XXI (2008), 165–190.

19. Lee Kuan Yew quoted in "Lee Kuan Yew's Chance of a Lifetime," *Straits Times*, Feb. 16, 2013.

20. Mark E. Warren, "Political Corruption as Duplicitous Exclusion," *PS: Political Science and Politics*, XXXIX (2006), 804; Mark E. Warren, "The Meaning of Corruption in Democracies," in Heywood, *Routledge Handbook*, 43–45; Eric M. Uslaner, *Corruption, Inequality, and the Rule of Law: The Bulging Pocket Makes the Easy Life* (New York, Cambridge University Press, 2008), 5, 9, 243. But see his p. 202.

21. Kurer, "Corruption," 233; Kurer, "Definitions," 38. See also Uslaner, *Corruption*, 6.

22. Alina Mungiu-Pippidi, *The Quest for Good Governance: How Societies Develop Control of Corruption* (New York, Cambridge University Press, 2015), 3, 18.

23. Adam Liptak, "Narrowing Scope for Prosecuting Corruption," *New York Times*, June 28, 2016.

24. Carl Hulse, "Is the Supreme Court Naïve about Corruption? Ask Jack Abramoff," *New York Times*, July 6, 2016.

25. "A Narrow Ruling on Public Corruption," *New York Times*, June 29, 2016.

26. Mungiu-Pippidi, *The Quest*, 5.

27. Rose-Ackerman, *Corruption*, 189–210.

28. See Sarah L. Bracking, "Corruption and Development: The Mutable Edges of Morality in Modern Markets," in Heywood, *Routledge*, 228, 238.

29. Quoted in John Hatchard, "Adopting a Human Rights Approach towards Combating Corruption," in Martine Boersma and Hans Nelen (eds.), *Corruption and Human Rights: Interdisciplinary Perspectives* (Amsterdam, Intersentia, 2010), 7–11, emphasis in the original text.

30. Richard L. Cassin, "Another Reason Why Calling Graft a Victimless Crime Is Dumb," Foreign Corrupt Practices Act (FCPA) Blog, Nov. 23, 2015, http://www.fcpablog.com/blog/2015/11/23/.

31. Matthew Murray and Andrew Spalding, "Freedom from Official Corruption as a Human Right," Brookings Research Paper, 2015; Andrew Spalding, "Is Freedom from Corruption a Human Right?" FCPA Blog, May 26, 2015, http://www.fcpablog.com/blog.

32. See especially the chapters by Matthew Bunn, "Corruption and Nuclear Proliferation," and Jessica C. Teets and Erica Chenoweth, "To Bribe or to Bomb: Do Corruption and Terrorism Go Together?" in Rotberg (ed.), *Corruption*, 124–193.

33. Harris, *Political Corruption*, 169, 196.

34. See Sarah Chayes, *Thieves of State: Why Corruption Threatens Global Security* (New York, Norton, 2015), 11–13, 73, 150. See also Danny Singh, "Corruption and Clientelism in the Lower Levels of the Afghan Police," *Conflict, Security, and Development*, XIV (2014), 621–650; Matthieu Aikens, "The Bidding War: How a Young Afghan Military Contractor Became Spectacularly Rich," *New Yorker*, March 7, 2016, 46–55.

35. Secretary of State John Kerry, "Remarks on Community Building and Countering Violent Extremism," Sokoto, Nigeria, Aug. 23, 2016, http://www.state.gov/secretary/remarks/2016/08/261212.htm.

36. Klitgaard, *Corruption*, 3; John Sydenham Furnivall, *Colonial Policy and Practice: A Comparative Study of Burma and Netherlands India* (Cambridge, Cambridge University Press, 1948), 175–177. The "sentiment" in Burma was said to be culturally particular. See also Scott, *Corruption*, 68–69; Davide Torsello, "Corruption as Social Exchange: The View from Anthropology," in

Peter Hardi, Paul M. Heywood, and Davide Torsello (eds.), *Debates of Corruption and Integrity: Perspectives from Europe and the US* (Basingstoke, Palgrave Macmillan, 2015), 175.

37. Johnston, *Syndromes*, 12, 192.

38. Underkuffler, "Defining," 42.

39. Anna Persson, Bo Rothstein, and Jan Teorell, "Why Anticorruption Reforms Fail—Systemic Corruption as a Collective Action Problem," *Governance*, XXVI (2013), 455; Michael W. Collier, "Explaining Corruption: An Institutional Choice Approach," *Crime, Law, and Social Change*, XXXVIII (2002), 7–12, 26.

40. Jean Pierre Olivier de Sardan, "A Moral Economy of Corruption in Africa?" *Journal of Modern African Studies*, XXXVII (1999), 43. See also Marcel Mauss, *The Gift: The Form and Reason for Exchange in Archaic Societies* (London, Routledge, 1990, orig. pub. 1923), 31.

41. Olivier de Sardan, "Moral Economy,"

42. Ibid., 26.

43. Ibid., 32.

44. Nathaniel H. Leff, "Economic Development through Bureaucratic Corruption," *American Behavioral Scientist*, VII (1964), 11; Huntington, *Political Order*, 386.

45. Richard Rose and Caryn Peiffer, *Paying Bribes for Public Services* (Basingstoke, Palgrave Macmillan, 2015), 5.

46. Heather Marquette and Caryn Peiffer, "Corruption and Collective Action," Developmental Leadership Program, University of Birmingham, Research Paper 32 (January 2015), 8.

47. Ali Mohammad Ali, quoted in Taimoor Shah and Alissa J. Rubin, "Afghan Forces Straining to Repel Taliban Attacks," *New York Times*, Oct. 31, 2015.

48. Raymond W. Baker, *Capitalism's Achilles Heel: Dirty Money and How to Renew the Free-Market System* (Hoboken, Wiley, 2005), 50, 51.

49. Klitgaard, *Corruption*, 42.

50. Mungiu-Pippidi, *The Quest*, 18, 23; see also Rose and Peiffer, *Paying Bribes*, 21–22.

51. Scott, *Corruption*, 66–68, distinguishes clearly.

52. Uslaner, *Corruption*, 11.

53. Some of ideas in this paragraph and several succeeding ones draw upon Robert I. Rotberg, *Africa Emerges: Consummate Challenges, Abundant Opportunities* (Cambridge, Polity, 2013), 97–100. Cf. Uslaner, *Corruption*, 17, 193, 243. He asserts at 17 (on what evidence?) that persons do not lose faith in their fellow citizens from being subjected to petty corruption.

54. Transparency International—Kenya, "Kenya Bribery Index 2008," http://www.tikenya.org/dfocuments/kenyabriberyindex08.

55. Job Oganda, quoted in Derek Kilner, "Watchdog Says Graft Could Cause More Electoral Violence in Kenya," Voice of America (VOA) News, March 9, 2009, http://www.voanews.com.

56. See Charlie J. Hughes, "Reporter's Notebook: Sierra Leone," http://www.globalintegrity.org/sierraleone.

57. Daniel Jordan Smith, "The Paradoxes of Popular Participation in Corruption in Nigeria," in Rotberg (ed.), *Corruption*, 293.

58. Aaron Bornstein, "On the Ground in Cambodia: Was My Anti-bribery Fight Just Dust in the Wind?" FCPA Blog, Aug. 31, 2015, http://www.fcpablog/blog.

59. "Passport Most Corrupt Sector," *Daily Star* (Dhaka), June 30, 2016.

60. UN Office on Drugs and Crime, "The Global Programme against Corruption" (Vienna, 2004, 3rd ed.), chapter 1 (np), citing Rose-Ackerman, "Democracy and 'Grand Corruption'" (Paris, UNESCO, 1996).

61. Uslaner, *Corruption*, 11, 16.

62. Antony Goldman, quoted in "A Man and a Morass," *Economist*, May 28, 2011.

63. International Crisis Group, "Burundi: A Deepening Corruption Crisis," March 21, 2012,

http://www.crisisgroup.org; "'Bongo Funded Sarkozy Campaign': Aide," *Yahoo/News*, November 2011. See also Xavier Harel and Thomas Hofnung, *La scandale des biens mal acquis* (Paris, Broché, 2011).

64. See Chayes, *Thieves*, 96.

65. Human Rights Watch, "Transparency and Accountability in Angola: An Update," April 12, 2010, http://www.hrw.org/news; Padraig Carmody, *The New Scramble for Africa* (Cambridge, Polity, 2011), 121–124; Human Rights Watch, "Well-Oiled: Oil and Human Rights in Equatorial Guinea," July 9, 2009, http://www.hrw.org/news. For Equatorial Guinea and the Riggs Bank scandal, see Baker, *Capitalism's Achilles Heel*; Leslie Wayne, "Shielding Seized Assets from Corruption's Clutches," *New York Times*, Jan. 1, 2017.

66. Walter of Milemete, "On the Nobility, Wisdom, and Prudence of Kings," in Cary J. Nederman (ed. and trans.), *Political Thought in Early Fourteenth-Century England: Treatises by Walter of Milemete, William of Pagula, and William of Ockham* (Tempe, Arizona, Center for Medieval and Renaissance Studies, 2002), 47, artfully used and quoted in Chayes, *Thieves*, 83.

67. Quoted in Chayes, *Thieves*, 77.

68. "Nigeria Sets Up Anti-Corruption Team," BBC News, Aug. 11, 2015. The U.S. Department of Justice has a Kleptocracy Asset Recovery Initiative dedicated to helping to repatriate ill-gotten proceeds.

69. Olivier de Sardan, "Moral Economy," 29.

70. Quamrul Mahmud, "Impact of Corruption on Economic Growth Performance in Developing Countries," http://www.scribd.com/doc/764/analysees-report; Kwabena Gyimah-Brempong, "Corruption, Economic Growth, and Income Inequality in Africa," *Economics of Governance*, III (2002), 183–209; Park Hung Mo, "Corruption and Economic Growth," *Journal of Comparative Economics*, XXIX (2001), 66–79.

71. Edward C. Banfield, *The Moral Basis of a Backward Society* (Glencoe, IL, Free Press, 1958), 17, 33, 83–99.

72. But Heywood and Rose assert that impartiality and ethical universalism "cannot provide a coherent account of the integrity of political systems." Heywood and Rose, "Promoting Integrity?" 111.

73. The phrase is Olivier de Sardan's, "Moral Economy," 29.

74. For a persuasive and pathbreaking explanation of the power of ethical universalism as an organizing and explanatory paradigm, see Mungiu-Pippidi, *The Quest*, 14, 17, 58, 79–80, 86, 116, 163 for quotation, and throughout. Earlier, she advanced her theory of the importance of ethical universalism in "Becoming Denmark: Historical Designs of Corruption Control," *Social Research*, LXXX (2013), 1259–1270, especially 1262; Alina Mungiu-Pippidi, "Controlling Corruption through Collective Action," *Journal of Democracy*, XXIV (2013), 104, 109. She draws conceptually on Talcott Parsons' theories of social action, the ideas of Amartya Sen, *Development as Freedom* (New York, Knopf, 1999), and others. She particularly cites Parsons, *Introduction to Max Weber: The Theory of Social and Economic Organization* (New York, Free Press, 1997), 80–82. Note that Mungiu-Pippidi wants to restrict true ethical universalism to fully democratic states and to non–city states, thus excluding Hong Kong, Singapore, and Rwanda from being considered ethically universalist. She also thinks that Botswana is insufficiently ethically universalist (but see chapter 8). I argue that ethical universalism implies the transformation of political culture and profound normative shifts and that those radical alterations have occurred in the countries mentioned.

75. Johnston, *Syndromes*, 206.

76. Ibid., 207; Robert Legvold, "Corruption, the Criminalized State, and Post-Soviet Transitions," in Rotberg, *Corruption*, 202–216. See also the appendixes at the end of Johnston, *Syndromes*.

77. Chayes, *Thieves*, 118, 122, 124, 126, 130, 145; see also her "The Structure of Corruption: A Systematic Analysis Using Eurasian Cases," Carnegie Endowment for International Peace, published paper, June 30, 2016.

78. Global Witness, report, quoted in Richard C. Paddock, "Cambodian Leader Abused Position, Helping Family Get Rich, Report Says," *New York Times*, July 7, 2016.

79. Karen Dawisha, *Putin's Kleptocracy: Who Owns Russia?* (New York, Simon & Schuster, 2015); see also Carl Gershman, "Unholy Alliance: Kleptocratic Authoritarians and Their Western Enablers," *World Affairs*, http://www.worldaffairsjournal.org/article/unholy-alliance, after June 30, 2016.

80. Mungiu-Pippidi, *The Quest*, 31–32.

81. Robert I. Rotberg, "The Failure and Collapse of Nation-States: Breakdown, Prevention, and Repair," in Robert I. Rotberg (ed.), *When States Fail: Causes and Consequences* (Princeton, Princeton University Press, 2004), 1–50.

82. Furnivall, *Colonial*, 176.

83. Matthew Bunn, "Corruption and Nuclear Proliferation," in Rotberg, *Corruption*, 124–166.

84. Arvind K. Jain, "Corruption: A Review," *Journal of Economic Surveys*, XV (2001), 102.

85. Jan Teorell, "Corruption as an Institution: Rethinking the Nature and Origins of the Grabbing Hand," University of Gothenburg, Quality of Government Institute, Working Paper 2007/5 (2007), 2.

86. Larry Diamond, "A Quarter Century of Promoting Democracy," *Journal of Democracy*, XVIII (2007), 119, calls for "revolutionary change in institutions," but required is a revolution in the societal collective, not in institutions.

87. See above, 33.

88. See also Teorell, 6–7, and the research reviewed there.

89. Persson, Rothstein, and Teorell, "Why Anti-Corruption," 450.

90. Bo Rothstein, "Anti-Corruption: The Indirect 'Big Bang' Approach," *Review of International Political Economy*, XVIII (2011), 230.

91. Philosophers are rethinking the meaning of collective/group action. This is not the place to do more than note the emerging discourse, led by Brian Epstein, *The Ant Trap: Rebuilding the Foundation of the Social Sciences* (New York, Oxford University Press, 2015), 52–53, 247. He takes exception to John R. Searle, *The Construction of Social Reality* (New York, Free Press, 1995), and other writings. This is an ontological debate, but it adds to and complements the emphasis on collective action discussed here and much more fully by Rothstein and Mungiu-Pippidi. For an excellent summary of both the principal-agent and the collective action approaches, see Marquette and Peiffer, "Corruption and Collective Action," 1–8.

92. Pranab Bardhan, "Corruption and Development: A Review of the Issues," *Journal of Economic Literature*, XXXV (1997), 1332.

93. Mungiu-Pippidi, *The Quest*, 117. See also idem, 165.

94. Persson et al., "Reforms Fail," 454, 458.

95. Ibid.

96. "Big bang" is Rothstein's phrase. See Rothstein, *Quality*, 118, and his articles.

97. UK Department of International Development, Research for Development, "Understanding 'Political Will,'" Appendix 3, to "Politicking for the Poor: Senior Leaders Political Management of Pro-Poor Initiatives in an Era of Centrists" (London, 2004), 1.

98. Lori Ann Post, Amber N. W. Raile, and Eric D. Raile, "Defining Political Will," *Politics and Policy*, XXXVIII (2010), 656.

99. For these qualities of leadership, see Robert I. Rotberg, *Transformative Political Leadership: Making Difference in the Developing World* (Chicago, University of Chicago Press, 2012), 21–26.

100. Post et al., "Will," 659.

101. Derick W. Brinkerhoff, "Assessing Political Will for Anti-Corruption Efforts: An Analytic Framework," *Public Administration and Development*, XX (2000), 240, 242.

102. Sahr J. Kpundeh, "Political Will in Fighting Corruption," in Kpundeh and Irene Kors (eds.), *Corruption and Integrity Improvement Initiatives in Developing Countries* (New York, United Nations Development Programme [UNDP], 1998), 68. See also the mixed definitions of political will in John Hatchard, *Combating Corruption: Legal Approaches to Supporting Good Governance and Integrity in Africa* (Cheltenham, Edward Elgar, 2014), 28–30, 234, 238; Letitia Lawson, "The Politics of Anti-Corruption Reform in Africa," *Journal of Modern African Studies*, XLVII (2009), 73–74.

103. Mandela, speaking in Katlehong, 1993, quoted in Stanley B. Greenberg, *Dispatches from the War Room: In the Trenches with Extraordinary Leaders* (New York, Thomas Dunne, 2009), 145. See also L. Log Raditlthokwa, "Corruption in Africa: A Function of Leadership," in Kwame Frimpong and Gloria Jacques (eds.), *Corruption, Democracy, and Good Governance in Africa* (Gaborone, Lightbooks, 1999), 49–55.

104. Anna Persson and Martin Sjöstedt, "Responsive and Responsible Leaders: A Matter of Political Will?" *Perspectives on Politics*, X (2012), 623.

105. Ibid., 626.

106. Post et al., "Will," 663, 664.

107. Quoted in Zephyr Teachout, *Corruption in America: From Benjamin Franklin's Snuff Box to Citizens United* (Cambridge, MA, Harvard University Press, 2014), 185.

II: Measuring and Assessing Corrupt Behavior

1. See Robert I. Rotberg, "The Governance of Nations: Definitions and Measures," in Robert I. Rotberg (ed.), *On Governance: What It Is, What It Measures, and Its Policy Uses* (Waterloo, ON, Centre for International Governance Innovation [CIGI], 2015), 7–17.

2. Of the ninety-three existing indexes of governance, the great majority are subjectively based.

3. Paul M. Heywood and Joshua Rose, "Curbing Corruption or Promoting Integrity? Probing the Hidden Conceptual Challenge," in Peter Hardi, Paul M. Heywood, and Davide Torsello (eds.), *Debates of Corruption and Integrity* (Basingstoke, Palgrave Macmillan, 2015), 105.

4. But see Ben A. Olken, "Corruption Perceptions vs. Corruption Reality," *Journal of Public Economics*, XC (2009), 950–964.

5. Paul M. Heywood and Jonathan Rose, " 'Close but No Cigar': The Measurement of Corruption," *Journal of Public Policy*, XXXIV (2014), 520.

6. Miriam A. Golden and Lucio Picci, "Proposal for a New Measure of Corruption, Illustrated with Italian Data," *Economics and Politics*, XVII (2005), 52–53. Olken tried a similar method to estimate road-building corruption in Indonesia. See his "Corruption Perceptions," 250–264.

7. Stefan Svallfors, "Does Government Quality Matter? Egalitarianism and Attitudes to Taxes and Welfare Policies in Europe," Umea University, Department of Sociology, 2012.

8. Alina Mungiu-Pippidi, *The Quest for Good Governance: How Societies Develop Control of Corruption* (New York, Cambridge University Press, 2015), 42. See also Oskar Kurer, "Definitions of Corruption," in Paul M. Heywood (ed.), *Routledge Handbook of Political Corruption* (New York, Routledge, 2015), 38.

9. Eric M. Uslaner, *Corruption, Inequality, and the Rule of Law: The Bulging Pocket Makes the Easy Life* (New York, Cambridge University Press, 2008), 15. For an excellent discussion of "perceptions" and how best to use them, see Richard Rose and Caryn Peiffer, *Paying Bribes for Public Services: A Global Guide to Grass-Roots Corruption* (Basingstoke, Palgrave Macmillan, 2015), 50–56.

10. For the origins of Transparency International, see Peter Eigen (trans. Joelle Diderich), *The Web of Corruption: How a Global Movement Fights Graft* (Frankfurt/Main, Campus Verlag, 2003), 99–100; Fredrik Galtung and Jeremy Pope, "The Global Coalition against Corruption: Evaluating Transparency International," in Andreas Schedler, Larry Diamond, and Marc F. Plattner (eds.), *The Self-Restraining State: Power and Accountability in New Democracies* (Boulder, Rienner, 1999), 257–259; and on its early impact, Hans Krause Hansen, "The Power of Performance Indices in the Global Politics of Anticorruption," *Journal of International Relations and Development*, XV (2012), 515.

11. Transparency International, CPI website, 2014, http://www.transparency.org.

12. For these and other governance indexes, see Robert I. Rotberg and Aniket Bhushan, "The Indexes of Governance," in Rotberg, *On Governance*, 55–90.

13. Transparency International, "Corruption Perceptions Index 2014: Technical Methodology Note," http://www.transparency.org. For the original methodology, through about 2002, see Johann Graf Lambsdorff, "Measuring Corruption—The Validity and Precision of Subjective Indicators (CPI)," in Charles Sampford, Arthur Shacklock, Carmel Connors, and Fredrik Galtung (eds.), *Measuring Corruption* (Aldershot, Hants., Ashgate, 2006), 81–99.

14. TI, "Corruption Perceptions Index 2014: Full Source Description," http://www.transparency.org; http://data.worldank.org/data-catalog/CPIA.

15. See TI, "Full Source," 12; http://Worldjusticeproject.org/rule-of-law index.

16. Michaela Saisana and Andrea Saltelli, "Corruption Perceptions Index 2012: Statistical Assessment," European Commission, Joint Research Centre Scientific and Policy Reports (Ispra, Italy, 2012), 8. Saisana and Saltelli offer a statistical justification for the CPI, 9.

17. Heywood and Rose, "Cigar," 511.

18. Ibid., 513–516, 518, 526. The reputation study is Leo Huberts, Karin Lasthuizen, and Careel Peeters, "Measuring Corruption: Exploring the Iceberg," in Sampford et al., *Corruption*, 273.

19. Saisana and Saltelli, "Statistical Assessment," 10–15, 19, 21. Saisana and Saltelli applied additional statistical tests to confirm their findings.

20. http://info.worldbank.org/governance/wgi/index, 2015.

21. WGI CC, 2014, http://info.worldbank.org/governance/wgi/.

22. Melissa Thomas, "What do the Worldwide Governance Indicators Measure?" *European Journal of Development Research*, XXII (2010), 39; Laura Langbein and Steve Knack, "The Worldwide Governance Indicators: Six, One, or None?" *Journal of Development Studies*, XLVI (2010), 365.

23. See Nathaniel Heller, "Defining and Measuring Corruption: Where Have We Come From, Where Are We Now, and What Matters for the Future?" in Rotberg, *Corruption*, 51. See also Marianne Irene Camerer, "Measuring Public Integrity," *Journal of Democracy*, XVII (2006), 152–165.

24. http://www.integrity-index.or/methodology. A working paper prepared by Alina Mungiu-Pippidi and Ramin Dadasov, "Measuring Control of Corruption by a New Index of Public Integrity," European Research Centre for Anti-corruption and State Building, Working Paper 48, Hertie School of Governance (April 2016), http://www.againstcorruption.eu, 17–20, 30–34, explains why those six categories were chosen to rate in-country corruption and how each is arrayed.

25. Ibid., 24.

26. http://integrity-index.org.

27. See Global Assessment Portal, 2015, http://www.gaportal.org/global-indicators/.

28. See http://www.globalintegrity.org/data/downloads.cfm.

29. See Heller, "Defining," 52–53.

30. Global Integrity website, 2015, http://www.globalintegrity.org. Those African Integrity Indicators were not published as of 2016.

31. For the underlying plan of the WJI, and explanations and justifications, see Juan C. Botero and Alejandro Ponce, "Measuring the Rule of Law," World Justice Project, Working Paper 1, November 2010 (p. 41 for the quoted question). The other quotations come from http://worldjusticeproject.org/rule-of-law-index, 2014.

32. Michaela Saisana and Andrea Saltelli, "JRC Statistical Audit of the WJP Rule of Law Index 2014," EC Joint Research Centre, working paper for the 2014 Rule of Law Index, http://worldjusticeproject.org/rule-of-law-index, 196–197.

33. http://bpi.transparency.org; http://www.economist.com/node/21536518, Nov. 2, 2011c.

34. Dilyan Donchev and Gergelyh Ujhelyi, "What Do Corruption Indices Measure?" Sept. 25, 2013, 3. Also useful in this arena is the *Economist*'s Crony-Capitalism Index. See "The Party Winds Down," *Economist*, May 7, 2016.

35. Catherine Weaver, *Hypocrisy Trap: The World Bank and the Poverty of Reform* (Princeton, Princeton University Press, 2008), 131.

36. Hansen, "Power," 519–521. On the Lesotho project, see John Hatchard, *Combating Corruption: Legal Approaches to Supporting Good Governance and Integrity* (Cheltenham, Edward Elgar, 2014), 245–253.

37. After SNC-Lavalin withdrew from the Patna Bridge project in 2015, China supplied most of the funds and management expertise to continue constructing that major bridge. For more on Canadian overseas industrial corruption, see articles in a special issue of the *Canadian Foreign Policy Journal*, especially Ellen Gutterman and Andrea Lane, "Beyond LAVs: Corruption and Commercialization and the Canadian Defence Industry," XXIII (2017), 72–92..

38. Quoted in *Huffington Post Canada*, "World Bank's Corrupt Companies Blacklist Dominated by Canada," Sept. 16, 2015. See also Leonard McCarthy, "Spending Development Dollars with Integrity," Oct. 22, 2015, http://www.fcpablog.com/blog/2015/10/22/.

39. Transparency International, Global Corruption Barometer 2013, 3–6, http://www.transparency.org/. For the barometer survey method see Rose and Peiffer, *Paying Bribes*, 8–11, 77–83.

40. Donchev and Ujhelyi, "Corruption Indices," 3. See similar criticisms in Daniel Treisman, "What Does Cross-National Empirical Research Reveal about the Causes of Corruption?" in Heywood, *Routledge Handbook*, 95–109.

41. Donchev and Ujhelyi, "Indices," 27. Similarly excellent critiques of the common measurements of corruption may be found in Paul M. Heywood, "Measuring Corruption: Perspectives, Critiques, and Limits," in Heywood (ed.), *Routledge Handbook*, 137–153.

42. http://www.financialsecrecyindex.com/introduction/methodsand concepts.

43. http://index.baselgovernance.org, 2015.

44. Open Budget Survey and Index, 2012, http://survey.international budget.org/what -we-do. See also Karen Hasse, "Transparency Alone Is Not Enough to Combat Graft," Good Governance Africa, March 31, 2015, http://gga.org/stories/editions/aif-31.

45. http://ati.publishwhatyoufund.org/wp-content/uploads/2016.

46. http://ati.publishwhatyoufund.org/index-2016/results.

47. http://www.revenuewatch.org/rgi, 2015. See also Alexandra Gillies, "The World Bank, Reputational Concerns and the Emergence of Oil Sector Transparency as an International Norm," 2008, unpub. workshop presentation, Cape Town.

48. Lisa Lambert, "SEC Adopts Rule on Oil, Mining Payments to Foreign Governments," *Reuters*, June 27, 2016.

49. For a salutary exposé of some of these predatory companies, see J. R. Mailey, "The Anatomy of the Resource Curse: Predatory Investment in Africa's Extractive Industries," Africa Center for Strategic Studies Special Report 3 (2015).

50. See Peter Eigen, "A Coalition to Combat Corruption: TI, EITI, and Civil Society," in Rotberg, *Corruption*, 425–428.

51. http://eiti.org/implementation, 2015; "Please Don't Expect Miracles," *Economist*, April 11, 2015; "A Fight for Life," *Economist*, Oct. 24, 2015; Global Witness says that $4 billion worth of mineral proceeds were siphoned off to opaque companies connected to politicians and officials in a few murky African countries, notably the Republic of Congo, and in China. See Global Witness, "How to Lose $4 Billion: Credibility Test for Global Transparency Standard," Oct. 16, 2015, http://www.globalwitness.org/reports.

52. Quoted in Emmanuel Asiwe, "Sanitizing Nigeria's Murky Oil Sector," http://www.huhu online.com, June 28, 2015.

53. http://progrep/eiti.org/countries/2015.

54. Till Bruckner, "The Professor, the General, and the World's Fishiest Business," *Foreign Policy*, Aug. 5, 2015, http://foreignpolicy.com/2015/08/05; Robert I. Rotberg, "Chinese Ships Exploit Weak, Poor, Preoccupied Africa," *Globe and Mail*, June 1, 2015.

55. "The Party Winds Down: Our Crony Capitalism Index," *Economist*, May 7, 2016.

III: Strong Laws and Other Watchdogs

1. Jon S. T. Quah, "Combating Corruption in Singapore: What Can Be Learned?" *Journal of Contingencies and Crisis Management*, IX (2001), 29.

2. See also Hilton L. Root, *Small Countries, Big Lessons: Governance and the Rise of East Asia* (Hong Kong, Oxford University Press, 1996), 46.

3. Tan Ah Leak, "The Experience of Singapore in Combating Corruption," in Frederick Stapenhurst and Sahr J. Kpundeh (eds.), *Curbing Corruption: Toward a Model for Building National Integrity* (Washington, DC, World Bank Institute, 1999), 62.

4. Quah, "Combating Corruption in Singapore," 33–34; Tan Ah Leak, "The Experience of Singapore," 61.

5. Chief Justice Sundaresh Menon, quoted in Adrian Tan, "Singapore Sentencing Guidelines: At the Intersection of Public and Private Graft," http://www.fcpablog.com/blog/, May 5, 2015.

6. Elena Chong, "Ex-IT Director, Businesswoman Charged with Graft," *Straits Times*, Sept. 9, 2016. See also Leonie Tear and Sui Yi Siong, "Singapore: Anti-Corruption Compliance and Corporate Practices," white paper, http://www.ethixbase.com, Sept. 9, 2016.

7. From John Hatchard, *Combating Corruption: Legal Approaches to Supporting Good Governance and Integrity in Africa* (Cheltenham, Edward Elgar, 2014), 89. See the lengthy and helpful discussion, too, at 90–92, and of the use of tort provisions at 95–99.

8. Bertrand de Speville, *Hong Kong: Policy Initiatives against Corruption* (Paris, OECD, 1997), 24; Petter Langseth, "Prevention: An Effective Tool to Reduce Corruption," UN Office of Drug Control and Crime Prevention, ISPAC conference, Nov. 19, 1999 (Milan), 32.

9. Choe Sang-Hun, "South Korea Tightens Rules against Gifts to Fight Graft," *New York Times*, March 3, 2015.

10. Kenneth Good, "Corruption and Mismanagement in Botswana: A Best-Case Example?" *Journal of Modern African Studies*, XXXII (1994), 505, 506, 516. See also John D. Holm, "Curbing Corruption through Democratic Accountability: Lessons from Botswana," in Kempe Ronald Hope and Bornwell C. Chikulo (eds.), *Corruption and Development in Africa: Lessons from Country Case-Studies* (Basingstoke, Palgrave, 2000), 292–293; Gabriel Kuris, "Managing Corruption Risk: Botswana Builds an Anti-Graft Agency, 1994–2012," Princeton University, Innovations for Successful Societies Program, 2013, 1–2.

11. Charles Manga Fombad, "Curbing Corruption in Africa: Some Lessons from Botswana's

Experience," *International Social Science Journal*, LI (1999), 241–254; Andrew Briscoe and H.C.L. Hermans, *Combating Corruption in Botswana* (Gaborone, Ebert Foundation, 2001), 16–18.

12. Fombad, "Botswana," 246.

13. Samira Lindner, U4 Anti-Corruption Resource Centre, "Tanzania: Overview of Corruption and Anti-Corruption,
http://www.U4.no, March 7, 2014.

14. Provisions of the Zambian Anti-Corruption Commission Act, http://www.iaaca.org /zambia, accessed Dec. 3, 2014.

15. For a full analysis, see Muna Ndulo, "Review of the Anti-Corruption Legal Framework in Zambia," Southern African Institute for Policy and Research (Lusaka, 2014), 23.

16. Provisions of the South African Act, http://www.iaaca.org/southafrica, accessed Dec. 4, 2014.

17. http://www.iaaca.org/Ghana, accessed Dec. 4, 2014.

18. Freedom House, 2013.

19. Transparency International, 2013; U4 Expert Answer, 2014.

20. U4 Expert Answer, 2014, 8.

21. Erick Kabendera and Mark Anderson, "Tanzanian PM under Pressure to Resign over Alleged Fraudulent Payments," *Guardian*, Dec. 1, 2014; "Tanzania's Kikwete Sacks Tibaijuka amid Corruption Row," BBC News, Dec. 23, 2014; "Tanzania's Energy Minister Quits over Graft Scandal, Denies Wrongdoing," *Reuters*, Jan. 24, 2015.

22. Liberia General Auditing Commission, http://www.gacliberia.com.

23. "Sierra Leone Loses Track of Millions in Ebola Funds," *New York Times*, Feb. 15, 2015.

24. *Mail and Guardian* (Johannesburg), Feb. 5, 2014; Aug. 5, 2014. Roughly, divide by 10 or 11 to obtain U.S. dollar equivalents during that period.

25. "Kenya Audit: Government Accounts 'Disturbing,'" BBC News, July 29, 2015.

26. Mungiu-Pippidi, *The Quest*, 79.

27. John Hatchard, "The Institution of the Ombudsman in Africa . . . ," *International and Comparative Law Quarterly*, XXXV (1986), 255–270. For his more up-to-date view on the role of ombudspersons, see Hatchard, *Combating*, 115–120.

28. *Foreign Policy* (November–December 2014), 66.

29. Quoted in Marianne Merten, " 'Flouting the Law Crux of Nkandla,' " *The Star* (Johannesburg), Aug. 4, 2015.

30. Chief Justice Mogoeng Mogoeng, quoted in Norimitsu Onishi, "Zuma's Spending on Home Is Ruled Unconstitutional," *New York Times*, April 1, 2016.

31. See Marislee Nishijima, Randall P. Ellis, and Regina C. Cati, "Evaluating the Impact of Brazil's Central Audit Program on Municipal Provision of Health Services," unpub. paper, 2016.

32. Mungiu-Pippidi, *The Quest*, 121.

33. Jennifer Widner, "Building Judicial Independence in Common Law Africa," in Andreas Schedler, Larry Diamond, and Marc F. Plattner, *The Self-Restraining State: Power and Accountability in the New Democracies* (Boulder, Rienner, 1999), 177–178; Hatchard, *Combating*, 205–227.

34. Robert I. Rotberg, "Mugabe Takes Zimbabwe further into the Void," *Christian Science Monitor*, February 9, 1999.

35. Quoted in Maya Gainer, "How Kenya Cleaned Up its Courts," *Democracy Lab Weekly Brief*, July 9, 2016.

36. Anne Amadi, quoted in ibid.

37. Buhari, quoted in Nigeria: "Buhari Charges Judiciary to Fight Real, Perceived Corrupt Practices in Judicial System," *Vanguard*, Nov. 23, 2015, http://www.allafrica.com/stories/2015.

38. Chief Justice Francis Nyalali, of Tanzania, quoted in Widner, "Common Law," 184;

observe the judicial discretion dilemmas discussed in Sufian Hemed Bukurura, "The Judiciary and Democratic Governance in Sub-Saharan Africa: The Complexities of Regulating Competing Interests," in Kwame Frimpong and Gloria Jacques (eds.), *Corruption, Democracy, and Good Governance in Africa* (Gaborone, Lightbooks, 1999), 109–121.

39. Robert I. Rotberg, "It's Time for Canada to Back an International Anti-Corruption Court," *Globe & Mail*, April 25, 2016. Some of the prose and concepts in this section of the book draw on my article.

40. See Mark L. Wolf, "The Case for an International Anti-Corruption Court," *Governance Studies at Brookings*, July 2014, for a full discussion of the original idea.

41. Holm, "Corruption," 291. On the significance of press freedom, see Mungiu-Pippidi, *The Quest*, 122.

42. Petter Langseth, "Prevention: An Effective Tool to Reduce Corruption," Global Programme against Corruption, UN Office of Drug Control and Crime Prevention (Vienna, 1999), 10. Some research shows that press freedom need not necessarily be correlated with reduced corruption. Other conditions are critical.

43. The empirical research on these questions is set out in Catharina Lindstadt and Daniel Naurin, "Transparency Is Not Enough: Making Transparency Effective in Reducing Corruption," *International Political Science Review*, XXXI (2010), 302–304.

44. Mungiu-Pippidi, *The Quest*, 167, 169, 173, 181. Mungiu-Pippidi makes the substantial point that the American (more open, more objective) model of media behavior and performance is often opposed or even replaced by a captive media model common to the rest of the world. But because the American model has become the ideal, journalists everywhere strive (if their owners and editors allow them) to conform to the objective model. Ibid., 179.

45. Richard Rose and Caryn Peiffer, *Paying Bribes for Public Services: A Global Guide to Grass-Roots Corruption* (Basingstole, Palgrave Macmillan, 2015), 72.

46. http://Db.nelsonmandela.org/speeches/Prague, May 26, 1992.

47. "Eritrea President Denies Stifling Free Speech," VOA News, April 24, 2012, http://www.voanews.com; BBC News, Dec. 12, 2011; http://www.bbc.co.uk/news.

48. Ayesha Kajee, executive director of the Freedom of Expression Institute in South Africa, quoted in Mohammed Keita, "Across Africa, Governments Criminalize Investigative Reporting," *Attacks on the Press in 2010: A Worldwide Survey by the Committee to Protect Journalists* (New York, 2011), 17.

49. See Robert I. Rotberg, *Africa Emerges* (Cambridge, Polity, 2013), 108.

50. Sammy Darko, "Accused Judges Shown Bribe Videos," BBC News, Sept. 10, 2015, http://www.bbc.com; Clement Sefa-Nyarko, "In Ghana, Will Vast Judicial Corruption Scandal Undo 23 Years of Political Stability?" IPI Global Observatory, Sept. 23, 2015, http://theglobalobservatory.org/2015/09/In-ghana.

51. http://Rsf.org/index/index2016.

52. Karen Hasse, "Corruption Fatigue: Transparency Alone Is Not Enough to Combat Graft," Good Governance Africa (Johannesburg), March 31, 2015.

53. See Hatchard, *Combating*, 143. See also Ben Worthy and Tom McClean, "Freedom of Information and Corruption," in Paul M. Heywood (ed.), *Routledge Handbook of Political Corruption* (New York, Routledge, 2015), 348–349, 353.

54. Chon-Kyun Kim, "Anti-Corruption Initiatives and E-Government: A Cross-National Study," *Public Organization Review*, XIV (2014), 391.

55. Lindstedt and Naurin, "Transparency," 302–305.

56. Mungiu-Pippidi, *The Quest*, 110. This openness is measured in a pioneering manner by the World Justice Project's innovative 2016 Open Government Index. See http://world

justiceproject.org/open-government-index. Sweden, New Zealand, and Norway are the most open; Myanmar, Uzbekistan, and Zimbabwe are the least open, according to the index.

57. Richard L. Cassin, "Country Count for the Corporate Investigations List (October 2016)," FCPA Blog, Oct. 13, 2016, http://www.fcpablog.com.

58. *President William J. Clinton: Statement on Signing the International Anti-Bribery and Fair Competition Act of 1998,* The American Presidency Project (Nov. 10, 1998), http://www .presidency.ucsb.edu/ws/index.php?pid=55254.

59. Transparency International, "Exporting Corruption, Progress Report, 2015," http://www.transparency.org/news/pressrelease, Aug. 20, 2015; Fritz Heimann et al., "Exporting Corruption: Progress Report 2014 . . . ," Transparency International, http://www.transparency .org/exporting_corruption. For TI's methodology, see p. 10. On the OECD Convention, see also Hatchard, *Combating,* 254–257.

60. Abiola O. Makinwa, *Private Remedies for Corruption: Towards an International Frame- work* (Utrecht, Eleven, 2013), 465.

61. Cathalijne van der Plas, "Once a Laggard, the Netherlands Finally Tackles Overseas Bribery," FCPA Blog, Sept. 19, 2016; idem, "The Netherlands: Tougher Bribery Laws (with Gaps), Help for Graft Victims," FCPA Blog, Sept. 22, 2016.

62. Choe Sang-Hun, "Antigraft Law Stirs Up Wariness on Gift-Giving in South Korea," *New York Times,* Sept. 30, 2016; *Korea Herald,* Sept. 8, 2016.

63. http://www.gov.uk/government/news/new-crime-unit, Aug. 9, 2015. For an assessment of the impact of the British law, see Celia Wells, "Enforcing Anti-Bribery Laws against Transnational Corporations—a UK Perspective," in Peter Hardie, Paul M. Heywood, and Davide Torsello (eds.), *Debates of Corruption and Integrity* (Basingstoke, Palgrave Macmillan, 2015), 59–80.

64. http://www.unodc.org/unodc/en/treaties/cac/signatories.

65. A. Keith Thompson, "Does Anti-Corruption Legislation Work?" *World Customs Jour- nal,* VII (2013), 45; Makinwa, *Private,* 476.

66. OECD Foreign Bribery Report, 2014, http://www.oecd-daf/oecd-foreign-bribery -report. But see also "When Companies Come Clean on Bribery," *Christian Science Monitor,* Dec. 2, 2014, http://www.csmonitor.com/commentary.

67. Thompson, "Does Anti-Corruption Legislation Work?" 40. For SEC actions, see also chapter 2.

68. Ibid., 42.

IV: The Virtue of Anticorruption Investigative Commissions: Hong Kong, Singapore, Indonesia

1. John R. Heilbrunn, "Anticorruption Commissions: *Panacea* or Real Medicine to Fight Corruption?" (Washington, DC, World Bank, 2004), 2. See also the similar results in Alina Mungiu-Pippidi, *The Quest for Good Governance: How Societies Develop Control of Corruption* (New York, Cambridge University Press, 2015), 106, 109.

2. Tah Ah Leak, "The Experience of Singapore in Combating Corruption," in Frederick Sta- penhurst and Sahr J. Kpundeh (eds.), *Curbing Corruption: Toward a Model for Building National Integrity* (Washington, DC, World Bank Institute, 1999), 60.

3. Jon S. T. Quah, "Curbing Corruption in Singapore: The Importance of Political Will, Expertise, Enforcement, and Context," in Quah (ed.), *Different Paths to Curbing Corruption: Les- sons from Denmark, Finland, Hong Kong, New Zealand, and Singapore* (Bingley, UK, Emerald, 2013), 149.

4. Chua Cher Yak, "Singapore's Three-Pronged Program to Combat Corruption: Enforcement, Legislation, and Adjudication," 2003, http://unpan1.un.org/intradoc/groups/public /documents/apcity/unpan047818, 2, 3, 5.

5. Henry J. Lethbridge, *Hard Graft in Hong Kong: Scandal, Corruption, the ICAC* (Hong Kong, Oxford University Press, 1985), 24–51.

6. Quoted in Lethbridge, *Graft*, 85. See also, T. Wing Lo, *Corruption and Politics in Hong Kong and China* (Buckingham, Open University Press, 1993), 81–82, 88–89.

7. Mark Hampton, *Hong Kong and British Culture, 1945–97* (Manchester, Manchester University Press, 2016), 145.

8. Bertrand E. D. de Speville, *Hong Kong: Policy Initiatives against Corruption* (Paris, OECD, 1997), 11.

9. Leo Goodstadt, "Squeeze Me, Please," *Far Eastern Economic Review*, June 25, 1970.

10. For details, see Alastair Blair-Kerr, *Second Report of the Commission of Enquiry* (Hong Kong, Govt. Printer, 1973). See also Melanie Manion, *Corruption by Design: Building Clean Government in Mainland China and Hong Kong* (Cambridge, MA, Harvard University Press, 2004), 30.

11. Hampton, *Hong Kong*, 145.

12. Bertrand E. D. de Speville, *Overcoming Corruption: The Essentials* (Kuala Lumpur, Research for Social Advancement, 2010), 58. See also de Speville, "Anticorruption Commissions: The 'Hong Kong Model' Revisited," *Asia-Pacific Review*, XVII (2010), 66.

13. De Speville, *Hong Kong*, 27.

14. Robert Klitgaard, *Controlling Corruption* (Berkeley, University of California Press, 1988), 110.

15. Jin-Wook Choi, "Institutional Structures and Effectiveness of Anticorruption Agencies: A Comparative Analysis of South Korea and Hong Kong," *Asian Journal of Political Science*, XVII (2009), 210, 211; Ian Scott, "Institutional Design and Corruption Prevention in Hong Kong," *Journal of Contemporary China*, XXII (2013), 79.

16. Scott, "Design," 132.

17. Jack Cater, quoted in Lo, *Corruption*, 97.

18. Manion, *Design*, 36.

19. See also de Speville, *Overcoming Corruption*, 52.

20. De Speville, "Hong Kong," 54. See also Manion, *Design*, 46–48.

21. A full account of the Community Relations Department's activities is contained in Ian Scott, "Engaging the Public: Hong Kong's Independent Commission against Corruption's Community Relations Strategy," in Quah, *Different Paths*, 79–108. For the two numbers cited, see 90, 95.

22. Lo, *Corruption*, 111, 113.

23. Choi, "Institutional," 205.

24. Ibid., 216.

25. ICAC, "Facts," http://www.icac.org.hk, Sept. 2014. For more details, see Scott, "Prevention," 85.

26. Lo, *Corruption*, 141–142. See also Manion, *Design*, 56–63, with several charts.

27. Cimigo, "ICAC Annual Survey, 2008."

28. Bertrand E. D. de Speville, "The Experience of Hong Kong, China, in Combating Corruption," in Stapenhurst and Kpundeh, *Curbing*, 52. See also de Speville, *Overcoming Corruption*, 9, 34, 82.

29. Scott, "Prevention," 87.

30. Transparency International, *Corruption Perceptions Index*, 2015; Manion, *Design*, 83.

31. De Speville, *Hong Kong*, 62.

32. Martin Yip, "Can Hong Kong Stay Corruption-Free under China?" BBC News, July 10, 2013, http://www.bbc.com/news/world, accessed Dec. 15, 2014; Scott, "Prevention," 86.

33. ICAC, "Hong Kong: The Facts," http://www.icac.org.hk, Sept. 2014.

34. Michael Forsythe, "Ex-city Official and Property Tycoon Are Convicted in Hong Kong Graft Trial," *New York Times*, Dec. 19, 2014.

35. "Troubled Leaders," *Economist*, Oct. 10, 2015.

36. Corruption Perceptions Index, 2014, http://www.transparency.org/cpi2014.

37. Jane Moir, "Hong Kong's Anti-bribery Laws Should be Expanded to Cover Off-shore Graft," *South China Morning Post*, July 12, 2016. See also Joyce Ng and Niall Fraser, "Turmoil at ICAC after Principal Investigator Becomes Second Departure in Days from Hong Kong Graft-Buster," ibid., July 12, 2016.

38. "The Force Is with Who?" *Economist*, July 23, 2016.

39. But see Niall Fraser, "Hong Kong Anti-Graft Commissioner Defends Its Independence Following Weeks of Top-Level Staffing Turmoil," *South China Morning Post*, Aug. 23, 2016.

40. De Speville, "Anti-Corruption Commissions," 63.

41. For an informative synopsis of the culture of corruption under Sukarno and Suharto, see Raymond W. Baker, *Capitalism's Achilles Heel: Dirty Money and How to Renew the Free-Market System* (Hoboken, Wiley, 2005), 68–76.

42. Quoted in Carol Giacomo, "Indonesia's Corruption Fighters in the Fight of their Lives," *New York Times*, Feb. 19, 2015; quoted in Gabriel Kuris, "Holding High Ground with Public Support: Indonesia's Anticorruption Commission Digs In, 2007–2011," Princeton University, Innovations for Successful Societies, 2012.

43. "Indonesia's Widodo Tested as Anti-Graft Chief Named Suspect in Tit-for-Tat Feud, *Reuters*, Feb. 17, 2015; Joe Cochrane, "Indonesia's Graft Fight Strikes Fear Even among the Honest," *New York Times*, Feb. 11, 2015.

44. http://www.transparency.org/cpi2015/results; http://www.gallup.com/poll/157073.

45. Gabriel Kuris, "Inviting a Tiger into Your Home: Indonesia Creates an Anti-Corruption Commission with Teeth, 2002–2007," Princeton University, Innovations for Successful Societies, 2012, http://www.successfulsocieties.Princeton.edu.

46. Data at http://www.lsi.or.id.

47. Quoted in Kuris, "Holding High Ground," 5.

48. See Kuris, "Holding High Ground," 13.

49. Quoted in Kuris, "Holding High Ground," 17.

50. "KPK Exposes More Corrupt Practices at Supreme Court," *Jakarta Post*, Feb. 14, 2016. The KPK also arrested the businessman offering the bribe and his lawyer.

51. "Jokowi's Moment," Special Report on Indonesia, *Economist*, Feb. 27, 2016, 5.

52. "Time for Tito," *Economist*, June 25, 2016.

53. Quoted in Gabriel Kuris, "The Little Anti-Corruption Agency That Could," *Foreign Policy*, Aug. 7, 2015, 7.

54. Quoted in Francis Chan, "Jokowi Runs out of Patience with Corrupt Officials," *Straits Times*, Oct. 13, 2016.

V: African Investigative Commissions: From Integrity to Interference

1. Samuel Atuobi, "Corruption and State Instability in West Africa: An Examination of Policy Options," Kofi Annan International Peacekeeping Centre (KAIPTC) Occasional Paper, 21 (2007).

2. Alan Doig, David Watt, and Robert Williams, "Measuring 'Success' in Five African Anti-Corruption Commissions," U4 Publications, Transparency International (2005), 6.

3. Quoted in Gabriel Kuris, "Managing Corruption Risks: Botswana Builds an Anti-Graft Agency, 1994–2012," Princeton University, Innovations for Successful Societies, 2013, 13; Kuris also prepared "From a Rocky Start to Regional Leadership: Mauritius' Anti-Corruption Agency," 2012, in the same series.

4. Afrobarometer, "Results: Botswana," http://afrobarometer.org/results, 2012.

5. http://www.transparency.org/cpi2015/results.

6. *The Voice* (Gaborone), July 2013.

7. David Sebudubudu, "Background Paper on Botswana," for Hertie School of Governance and the European Commission, Feb. 28, 2014, 9,13, 19, 20.

8. Sebudubudu, "Background," 10.

9. Daniel Jordan Smith, "The Paradoxes of Popular Participation in Corruption in Nigeria," in Robert I. Rotberg (ed.), *Corruption, Global Security, and World Order* (Washington, DC, Brookings, 2009) 283–284.

10. David Cameron, overheard talking to Queen Elizabeth II, and quoted in Stephen Castle and Kimiko de Freytas-Tamura, "Leaders Vow to Thwart Financial Corruption," *New York Times*, May 13, 2016.

11. Grace Obike, "Nigeria: Buhari Appoints Himself to End Nation's Oil Corruption," *Christian Science Monitor*, Oct. 14, 2015. For Alison-Madueke, see also chapter 6, fn. 2.

12. For the terms, see Inge Amundsen, *Political Corruption: An Introduction to the Issues* (Bergen, Chr. Michaelsen, 1999), 9–10.

13. George Ayittey, "Nigeria's Struggle with Corruption," testimony before the House Subcommittee on Africa, May 18, 2006, quoted in Wale Adebanwi and Ebenezer Obadare, "When Corruption Fights Back: Democracy and Elite Interest in Nigeria's Anti-Corruption War," *Journal of Modern African Studies*, XLIX (2011), 190; Larry Diamond, "Class Formation in the Swollen African State," *Journal of Modern African Studies*, XXV (1987), 567.

14. Tatalo Alamo, a columnist, in *The Nation* (May 18, 2008), and Soyinka, quoted in Rotimi T. Suberu, "The Travails of Nigeria's Anti-Corruption Crusade," in Rotberg, *Corruption*, 264, 266. See also Steven Pierce's long chapter on this ignominious period in Nigeria in his *Moral Economies of Corruption: State Formation and Political Culture in Nigeria* (Durham, Duke University Press, 2016), 105–151.

15. Raymond W. Baker, *Capitalism's Achilles Heel; Dirty Money and How to Renew the Free-Market System* (Hoboken, Wiley, 2005), 57, 63.

16. For his assets and how they were seized, see Hatchard, *Combating*, 300.

17. Paul Okojie and Abubakar Momeh, "Corruption and Reform in Nigeria," in Sarah L. Bracking (ed.), *Corruption and Development: The Anti-Corruption Campaigns* (Basingstoke, Palgrave, 2007), 105.

18. http://www.theguardian.com/world/2012/Oct/05.

19. Adebanwi and Obadare, "Fights Back," 190; Baker, *Achilles Heel*, 51.

20. Constitution of the Federal Republic of Nigeria, 1999, Section 15 (5).

21. Adebanwi and Obadare, "Fights Back," 192; David Uchenna Enwerematu, "The Struggle against Corruption in Nigeria: The Role of the National Anti-Corruption Commission (ICPC) under the Fourth Republic," *Institut Francais de Recherche en Afrique*, special issue 2 (2004), 25, 29.

22. Ibid., 193.

23. For a good description and explanation of the 419 scams, see Baker, *Achilles Heel*, 64–65.

24. Sam Roberts, "Diepreye Alamieyeseigha, 62, Ex-Governor Impeached on Corruption Charge in Nigeria," *New York Times*, Oct. 15, 2015.

25. Suberu, "Travails," 264.

26. The aphorism and much of the preceding several paragraphs draws on Adebanwi and Obadare, "Fights Back," 186, 195–204.

27. http://huhuonline.com/hunew/index.php, Aug. 1, 2016.

28. Raymond Fisman and Edward Miguel, *Economic Gangsters: Corruption, Violence, and the Poverty of Nations* (Princeton, Princeton University Press, 2008), 80.

29. Official audit report, in Emmanuel Asiwe, "Buhari Orders Arrest of Dasuki over Alleged N333bn Bogus Arms Deals," http://huhuonline.com/hunew/index.php, Nov. 18, 2015. Response in Asiwe, "Dasuki Lampoons Presidency: Describes Interim Report as Theatrical & Absurd," http://huhuonline.com, Nov. 19.

30. Sola Akinrinade, quoted in Norimitsu Onishi, "Anti-Graft Drive Hits Nigeria's Luxury Economy," *New York Times*, Oct. 17, 2015.

31. Ayi Kwei Armah, *The Beautyful Ones Are Not Yet Born* (Boston, HMco, 1968); Peter Abrahams, *A Wreath for Udomo* (London, Faber, 1956); Chinua Achebe, *Anthills of the Savannah* (London, Heinemann, 1987), and *A Man of the People* (London, Heinemann, 1966).

32. UN Economic Commission for Africa, "African Governance Report (2005), 37–38.

33. Quoted in Deepa Iyer, "Earning a Reputation for Independence: Ghana's Commission on Human Rights and Administrative Justice, 1993–2003," Princeton University, Innovations for Successful Societies, 2011, 5.

34. Ibid., 7.

35. Ibid., 11.

36. Alan Doig, David Watt, and Robert Williams, "Measuring 'Success' in Five African Anti-Corruption Commissions," Transparency International, Q4 Expert Answer (2005), 35.

37. Ibid., 24.

38. Ibid., 24.

39. Ibid., 9.

40. AllAfrica, 2013; Legal and Human Rights Centre, 2013.

41. BBC News, "Tanzania's Magufuli Scraps Independence Day Celebration," Nov. 24, 2015, http://www.bbc.com/news/; "Tanzania: Outrage in Tanzania Elite as Magufuli Intensifies Rwandanisation," Nov. 23, 2015, http://www.AllAfrica.com/stories/20151123.

42. George Ogalo and Peter Marsden (eds.), *Corruption and Its Consequences in Kenya* (Nairobi, Concordis International, 2013), 9; BBC News, Jan. 23, 2006; Jeffrey Gettleman, "Kenya Struggles over Best Response to Attack," *New York Times*, April 9, 2015.

43. Fergal Keane, "A Fearless Kenyan Whistle-Blower," BBC News, Feb. 9, 2006.

44. Quoted in Fisman and Miguel, *Gangsters*, 42.

45. BBC News, Jan. 23, 2006. See also Fisman and Miguel, *Gangsters*, 208–209. For the full story of the Kenyan saga, see Michela Wrong, *It's Our Turn to Eat: The Story of a Kenyan Whistleblower* (London, Fourth Estate, 2009).

46. Ogalo and Marsden, *Corruption*, 10–11; Isaiah M. Mbiti, "Beyond Laws: Fighting Corruption on Multiple Fronts Needed," *Adli* newsletter (Nairobi), August–September 2013, 1; Dalmas Okendo, "Kenyans Want an Operation Smile: Unleash the Scalpels on the Corrupt," *Adli* newsletter, 7; Ethics and Anti-Corruption Commission, "National Survey on Corruption and Ethics, 2012" (Nairobi, EACC, 2013), 14.

47. Isaiah Mwongela Mbiti, "Beyond Laws: Fighting Corruption on Multiple Fronts Needed," *Adli* (2013), 1, 7; EACC, "Survey," 12.

48. Kempe Ronald Hope, "Tackling the Corruption Epidemic in Kenya: Toward a Policy of More Effective Control," *Journal of Social, Political, and Economic Studies*, XXXVIII (2013), 5.

49. Ogalo and Marsden, *Corruption*, 23; EACC, "Survey, 2012," 44.

50. Githongo and Waqo quoted in "Anti-Graft Chief Says Kenya Needs High-Profile Convictions," *New York Times*, Nov. 18, 2015.

51. See more at: http://www.the-star.co.ke/news/president-uhuru-kenyatta-statement-corruption#sthash.gF4KFehk.dpuf, Nov. 23, 2015.

52. The Proclamation, Section 2a, quoted in UN Economic Commission for Africa, "African Governance Report (2005), 150. See also Arsema Tamyalew, "A Review of the Effectiveness of the Federal Ethics and Anti-Corruption Commission of Ethiopia," World Bank and European Union (Brussels, 2010), 8–10, 15–16.

53. The Proclamation, Section 4.

54. Tamyalew, "Effectiveness," 24.

55. Tewodros Mezmur and Raymond Koen, "The Ethiopian Federal Ethics and Anti-Corruption Commission: A Critical Assessment," *Law, Democracy, and Development*, XV (2011), 229.

56. Tamyalew, "Effectiveness," 29–30, 35.

57. Ibid., 30.

58. http://www.celebritynetworth.com, accessed Jan. 8, 2015; Global Integrity, "Ethiopia: Corruption Notebook" (2006), 2; Mezmur and Koen, "Federal Ethics," 216; UN Economic Commission for Africa, "African Governance Report" (2005), 150.

59. http://www.transparency.org/research/cpi/cpi2002.

60. De Speville, "Anti-Corruption Commissions," 47.

61. Bertelsmann Foundation, "Madagascar Country Report, 2014, http://www.bti-project.org/reports, accessed Nov. 24, 2014; Sofia Wickberg, "Overview of Corruption and Anti-Corruption in Madagascar," Transparency International, Sept. 19, 2014.

62. http://www.transparency.org/cpi2014/results, accessed Feb. 4, 2015; http://www.transparency.org/cpi2015/results, accessed May 20, 2016.

63. *The Amcham Post*, Dec. 15–21, 2014.

64. Russell to RIR, private email, April 20, 2015.

65. *Mufaya Mumbuna v. the People*, judgment 11, Sept. 7, 1984, http://www.zambialii.org/zm/judgment/supreme-court/1984/10.

66. Russell to RIR, private email, Sept. 9, 2015.

67. Lawrence Hansingo, Zambian Anti-Corruption Commission, Statistics 1984–1990, transmitted Oct. 16, 2015, via Paul Russell.

68. Russell to RIR, Oct. 25, 2015.

69. Judgment in the case of *Attorney General of Zambia v. Meer Care & Desai*, quoted in John Hatchard, *Controlling Corruption: Legal Approaches to Supporting Good Governance and Integrity* (Cheltenham, Edward Elgar, 2014), 72. Other relevant material at 34–37, 40. For a Zambian view of corruption in his country during Chiluba's presidency, see Jotham C. Momba, "Economic Reforms, Corruption and the Crises of Governance in Zambia: The Dilemma for the Donor Community," in Kwame Frimpong and Gloria Jacques (eds.), *Corruption, Democracy, and Good Governance in Africa* (Gaborone, Lightbooks, 1999), 195–196.

70. John Hanks, *Operation Lock and the War on Rhino Poaching* (Johannesburg, Penguin, 2015), 33–35, 83–84.

71. Russell to RIR, 36.

72. Testimony of Paul Russell, Cape Town, Jan. 18, 2015. For an informed discussion of the limits of prosecutorial discretion, see Hatchard, *Combating*, 152–161.

73. *Southern Africa Report*, March 6, 2009, 5.

74. See Hatchard, *Combating*, 188–189, 228, on jurists being placed, as in this case, in impossible and vulnerable positions.

75. Charlotte Vaillant, Imran Ahmed, et al., "Joint Evaluation of Support to Anti-Corruption Efforts: Zambia Country Report," 2011, http://www.sida.se/publications, 25–27; See Charlotte Vaillant et al., "Joint Evaluation of Support to Anti-Corruption Efforts: Zambia Country Re-

port," Norwegian Agency for Development Cooperation (NORAD), 2012, 15, http://www.sida .se/contentassets/.

76. Ibid., 41.

77. Daniel Munkombwe, quoted in Linda Kasonde, "The Challenge of Leadership and the Poverty of Ambition," African Leadership Institute newsletter, August 19, 2015.

78. Quoted in John H. Plumb, *Sir Robert Walpole: The King's Minister* (Boston, HMco, 1956), 206.

79. BBC News, "Zambia Election: Michael Sata Takes Presidential Oath," in BBC Africa, Sept. 23, 2011. Mungiu-Pippidi wryly remarks that new heads of state who originally profess anticorruption intentions often develop "a new clientele" that has to be rewarded with corrupt rents; Alina Mungiu-Pippidi, *The Quest for Good Governance: How Societies Develop Control of Corruption* (New York, Cambridge University Press, 2015), 33.

80. Marie Chene, "Zambia: Overview of Corruption and Anti-Corruption," Transparency International, U4 Expert Answer, 7; U4 report on Zambia, 2015, 4.

81. Marie Chene, Transparency International U4 Expert Answer, "Zambia: Overview of Corruption and Anti-Corruption," April 16, 2014, 3.

82. Afrobarometer, 2013, "Trust and Corruption in Zambia."

83. U.S. Department of State, 2013 Country Report on Human Rights Practices.

84. Chene, "Zambia," 7.

85. Bertelsmann Foundation, Zambia Country Report, 2014; Freedom House, *Freedom in the World: Zambia Country Report*, 2013.

86. For the early reception of the ACB, see Isaac C. Lamba, "Controlling Corruption in Africa: The Case of Malawi," in Frimpong and Jacques, *Corruption, Democracy*, 261–264.

87. Hannes Hechler and Bea Parkes, "Annual Review of DFID/RNE Malawi's Anti-Corruption Bureau Support Programme," 2010, 16.

88. Mustafa Hussein, "Combating Corruption in Malawi: An Assessment of the Enforcing Mechanisms," *African Security Review*, XIV (2005), 4.

89. ACB, "Investigations Report on Petroleum Control Commission," 42–45.

90. ACB, "A Report on Allegations of Corruption in the Award of a Pre-shipment Inspection Contract," 18.

91. David Hall-Matthews, "Tickling Donors and Tackling Opponents: The Anti-Corruption Campaign in Malawi," in Sarah L. Bracking (ed.), *Corruption and Development* (New York, Palgrave Macmillan, 2007), 86–87; Associated Press, Sept. 8, 2002.

92. Hussein, "Combating Corruption in Malawi," 3.

93. Nixon S. Khembo, "National Integrity Systems: Malawi 2004," Transparency International Country Report, 2004, 9.

94. Millennium Consulting Group, "Governance and Corruption Baseline Survey, Malawi, 2005" (Lilongwe, 2006), 7. UN Economic Commission for Africa, "African Governance Report" (2005), 150.

95. Quoted in Hall-Matthews, "Tickling Donors," 77.

96. Hall-Matthews, "Tickling Donors," 83.

97. PricewaterhouseCoopers audit report, http://malawi24.com/wp-content/uploads/2015 /06/Malawi-audit-report-MK92-billion-cashgate-scandal.pdf.

98. Rex Chikoko, "Malawi 'Theft' Balloons to R540m," *Mail & Guardian*, Feb. 13–19, 2015; Godfrey Mapondera and David Smith, "Malawi President Sacks Cabinet over Corruption Scandal," *Guardian*, Oct. 13, 2013.

99. Jimmy Kainja, "What Drives Corruption and Why It Won't Disappear Soon," *The Conversation*, Oct. 1, 2015.

100. Peter Mutharika, official transcript, speaking to the Council on Foreign Relations, New York, Sept. 24, 2015.

101. Hechler and Parkes, "Annual Review," 26.

102. Q4 (2005) 23. For a thorough review of the mandate of anticorruption commissions in Africa, especially their legal underpinnings, see Hatchard, *Combating*, 180–188, 191–200.

VI: The Most Improved: Results

1. "Latest Corruption Allegations against Dominica PM Mirror US Report in 2009," *Caribbean News Now*, Jan. 21, 2016. http://www.caribbeannewsnow.com. I tried personally to elicit Skerrit's views on these allegations on several occasions throughout 2015 and 2016, through his nation's embassy in Washington and by direct contact—all to no avail. No one responded to seven inquiries.

2. See the chart in Alina Mungiu-Pippidi, *The Quest for Good Governance: How Societies Develop Control of Corruption* (New York, Cambridge University Press, 2015), 133; http://www.transparency.org/, CPI for 2004 and 2014. Chile and Uruguay are top performers, according also to a corruption victimization scale, with only about 5 percent of Chileans being affected, on average, in contrast to 67 percent of Haitians, 25 percent of Hondurans, and 15 percent of Venezuelans—all in 2012. See Brian M. Faughnan and Mitchell A. Selgison, "Corruption in Latin America: A View from the Americas Barometer," in Paul M. Heywood (ed.), *Routledge Handbook of Political Corruption* (New York, Routledge, 2015), 212–224.

3. John Gerring and Strom C. Thacker, "Political Institutions and Corruption: The Role of Unitarism and Parliamentarism," *British Journal of Political Science*, XXXIV (2004), 302.

4. Global Integrity, cited in Mungiu-Pippidi, *The Quest*, 196.

5. Roy Godson et al., "Building Societal Support for the Rule of Law in Georgia," *Trends in Organized Crime*, VIII (2004), 9; Christoph H. Stefes, *Understanding Post-Soviet Transitions: Corruption, Collusion, and Clientelism* (London, Palgrave, 2006), 95.

6. Londa Esadze, "Organized Nature of Corruption and Public Administration in Transition Countries: A Case Study of Georgia," Workshop, 2003, European Group of Public Administration (EGPA) annual conference, 3; Rebecca S. Katz, *The Georgian Regime Crisis of 2003–2004: A Case Study in Post-Soviet Media Representation of Politics, Crime, and Corruption* (Stuttgart, ibidem-Verlag, 2006), 116.

7. Christofer Berglund and Johan Engvall, "How Georgia Stamped Out Corruption on Campus," *Foreign Policy*, Sept. 3, 2015, 1.

8. Alexander Kupatze, "Explaining Georgia's Anti-Corruption Drive," *European Security*, XXI (2012), 17, 19; William A. Clark, *Crime and Punishment in Soviet Officialdom: Combating Corruption in the Political Elite, 1965–1990* (Armonk, M. E. Sharpe, 1993), 86; Louise Shelley, "Georgian Organized Crime," in Louise Shelley, Erik R. Scott, and Anthony Latta (eds.), *Organized Crime and Corruption in Georgia* (New York, Routledge, 2007), 52; Pavel K. Baev, "Civil Wars in Georgia: Corruption Breeds Violence," in Jan Koehler and Christoph Zurcher (eds.), *Potentials of Disorder: Explaining Conflict and Stability in the Caucasus and in the Former Yugoslavia* (Manchester, Manchester University Press, 2003), 127–144.

9. BBC monitoring service, Sept. 19, 2001, quoted in Kupatze, "Explaining," 20. See also Robert Legvold, "Corruption, the Criminalized State, and Post-Soviet Transitions," in Robert I. Rotberg (ed.), *Corruption, Global Security, and World Order* (Washington, DC, 2009), 220–222.

10. See Richard Bennet, "Delivering on the Hope of the Rose Revolution: Public Sector Reform in Georgia, 2004–2009," Princeton University, Innovations for Successful Societies, http://www.Princeton.edu/successfulsocieties.

11. Berglund and Engvall, "Georgia," 5.

12. Matthew Devlin, "Seizing the Reform Moment: Rebuilding Georgia's Police, 2004–2006," Princeton University, Innovations for Successful Societies.

13. Andrew Schalkwyk, "Rejuvenating the Public Registry: Republic of Georgia, 2006–2008," Princeton University, Innovations for Successful Societies.

14. For more on the conflicts of interest question, see Staffan Andersson and Frank Anechiarico, "The Political Economy of Conflicts of Interest in an Era of Public-Private Governance," in Paul M. Heywood (ed.), *Routledge Handbook of Political Corruption* (New York, Routledge, 2015), 253–269.

15. Lili Di Puppo, "Anti-corruption Intervention in Georgia," *Global Crime*, XI (2010), 224.

16. Freedom House, "Nations in Transit—Georgia," 2010; Transparency International, Global Corruption Barometer, 2010.

17. Global Integrity Report, 2011, http://www.globalintegrity.org/report/2011. See also Johan Engvall, "Against the Grain: How Georgia Fought Corruption and What It Means," Central-Asia Caucasus Institute and Silk Road Studies Program (SAIS and the Stockholm Institute for Security and Development Policy), Occasional Paper, 2012, 57–61.

18. Quoted in Stephen Kinzer, *A Thousand Hills: Rwanda's Rebirth and the Man Who Dreamed It* (New York, Wiley, 2009), 236.

19. "A Pioneer with a Mountain to Climb," *Economist* (Sept. 27, 2008).

20. Global Integrity, "Rwanda Country Report," 2009.

21. Quoted in Marie Chene, "Overview of Corruption in Rwanda," U4 Expert Answer, Transparency International, April 16, 2008.

22. Global Corruption Barometer, 2013.

23. Kinzer, *Thousand Hills*, 236.

24. See Monica A. Clark, "Combating Corruption in Liberia," *Journal of Development and Social Transformation*, V (2008), 25–29; Matt Chessen and Robert Krech, "Post-War Reconstruction in Liberia," http://www.mattlesnake.com/gemap, 3–15; William Reno, "Anti-corruption Efforts in Liberia: Are They Aimed at the Right Targets?" *International Peacekeeping*, XV (2008) 387–389.

25. Franziska Zanker, "A Decade of Police Reform in Liberia: Perceptions, Challenges and Ways Ahead," Policy Brief, Centre for Security Governance (Kitchener), Security Sector Reform, 2.0, September 2015.

26. See more at: http://www.fcpablog.com/blog/2016/5/27/liberias-best-connected-lawyer-arrested-in-uk-linked-bribe-p.html#sthash.O2t97mfN.dpuf.

27. Quoted in "Top Liberian Politician Arrested in Corruption Scandal," *Guardian*, May 25, 2016. For the full account see http://www.globalwitness.org/thedeceivers, May 13, 2016.

28. TI, Global Corruption Barometer, 2013.

29. Bertelsmann Foundation, Bertelsmann Transformation Index 2014, Macedonia Country Report. See also Analytico, "Mechanisms for Fighting Police Corruption in the Republic of Macedonia—Legal and Institutional Set Up," 2013, 6, http://www.analyticaamk.org; http://www.dcaf.ch/Region/Southeast-Europe/Projects/Regional-Training-on-Police-Corruption-Research-April-to-June-2013.

30. See Maria Koinova, *Ethnonationalist Conflict in Postcommunist States: Varieties of Governance in Bulgaria, Macedonia, and Kosovo* (Philadelphia, University of Pennsylvania Press, 2013), 123, 188–189.

31. Quoted in Tinatin Ninua, "Former Yugoslav Republic of Macedonia: Overview of Political Corruption," Transparency International, March 31, 2014, 7–8.

32. United Nations Development Programme (UNDP), "Fighting Corruption to Improve Governance in FYR Macedonia," 2014, http://www.undp.org/content/undp/en/home/ourwork/.

33. *Southeast European Times*, June 24, 2013; Analytico, "Mechanisms," 9, 17.

34. GRECO and the Council of Europe, "Compliance Report on the Former Yugoslav Republic of Macedonia," March 23, 2012, 4.

35. Global Integrity Report, 2011, http://www.globalintegrity.org/report.

36. DIFI (Direktoratet for forvaltning og IKT—Agency for Public Management and eGovernment), "Macedonia—Building Integrity in Defence: An Analysis of Institutional Risk Factors," 2015, 2.

37. Organized Crime and Corruption Reporting Project, "Macedonia Rapped for High-Level Political Corruption and Restricted Press," http://www.occrp.org/en/daily/4597.

38. European Commission, "Report from the Commission to the European Parliament and the Council on Montenegro's Progress in the Implementation of Reforms," May 22, 2012.

39. See EC, "Report," 3.

40. EC, "Report," 8.

41. Samridhi Shukla, "Montenegro: Overview of Political Corruption," Transparency International, May 20, 2014; Freedom House, *Freedom in the World: Montenegro*, 2013; Montenegro's Network for the Affirmation of the NGO Sector (MANS), "Winning Elections in Montenegro," 2013, https://dgap.org/sites/default/files/.

42. EC, "Report," 5–6.

43. See Ana Selic et al., "Analysis of the Effects of Anti-Corruption Policies in Montenegro," Euroblok, 2011, http://pdc.ceu.hu/archive/00006833/.

44. DIFI, "Montenegro–Building Integrity in the Defence Sector," 2015, 2.

45. Kagame, speech of Nov. 7, 2014, on http://presidency.gov.rw/index.

VII: Nordic, Antipodean, and Other Exceptionalism: How Did Anticorruption Take Root?

1. http://www.transparency.org/cpi2015/results/.

2. Singapore is an unexpected 17th on the Legatum list, after Luxembourg, Germany, the United Kingdom, and Austria. See http://www.li.com/programmes/prosperity-index.

3. Quoted in Gardiner Harris, "Obama Easily Warms to Nordic Heads of State," *New York Times*, May 14, 2016.

4. But see the suggestion that there is something sticky about CPI's longitudinal scores (II, 12).

5. Jan Delhey and Kenneth Newton, "Social Trust: Global Pattern or Nordic Exceptionalism," Wissenschaftszentrum Berlin für Sozialforschung, Discussion Paper, June 2004, 24–28.

6. The others of historical accomplishment could include Andorra, Austria, Bavaria, Britain, France, Lichtenstein, Luxembourg, Prussia, and Switzerland. The last, and Britain and Luxembourg, are included in the top ten on the CPI in 2015. But earlier CPI rankings did not necessarily include any of those three nations.

7. Mette Frisk Jensen, "The Question of How Denmark Got to Be Denmark—Establishing the Rule of Law and Fighting Corruption in the State of Denmark 1660–1900," University of Gothenburg Quality of Government Institute, Working Paper 2014:06 (2014), 4.

8. Tine Damsholt, "'Hand of King and Voice of the People': Gruntvig on Democracy and the Responsibility of the Self," in John A. Hall, Ove Korsgaard, and Ove K. Pedersen (eds.), *Building the Nation: N.F.S. Gruntvig and Danish National Identity* (Montreal, McGill-Queen's University Press, 2015), 153, drawing on Gruntvig and Jens Arup Seip, "Teorien om det opinionsstyrte enevaelde [Theory of Opinion-Guided Absolutism]," *Norsk Historisk Tidsskrift*, XXXVIII (1958), 397–463. See also Korsgaard, "How Gruntvig Became a Nation Builder," in Hall et al., *Building*, 196–197.

9. Frisk Jensen, "Denmark," 6.

10. For the English experience, see Linda Levy Peck, *Court Patronage and Corruption in Early Stuart England* (Boston, Unwin Hyman, 1990; London, Routledge, 1993); Alastair Bellany, *The Politics of Court Scandal in Early Modern England: News Culture and the Overbury Affair, 1603–1660* (Cambridge, Cambridge University Press, 2002).

11. Frisk Jensen, "Denmark," 7.

12. Ibid., 10.

13. Ibid., 13.

14. Alina Mungiu-Pippidi, "Becoming Denmark: Understanding Good Governance Historical Achievers," unpub.? draft, 2013, 26, suggests that the audits were a key element in returning Denmark to its prewar anticorruption posture. This draft chapter may have been intended for what became the author's *The Quest for Good Governance*, but the full chapter did not appear there.

15. On this last point, see Michael Johnston, "The Great Danes: Successes and Subtleties of Corruption Control in Denmark," in Jon S. T. Quah (ed.), *Different Paths to Curbing Corruption: Lessons from Denmark, Finland, Hong Kong, New Zealand and Singapore* (Bingley, UK, Emerald, 2013), 26.

16. See Korsgaard, "Gruntvig," in Hall et al., *Building a Nation*, 204.

17. Nikolai F. S. Grundtvig, 1849, quoted in Michael Boss, "Between Tradition and Modernity: Grundtvig and Cultural Nationalism," in Hall et al., *Building a Nation*, 85.

18. The discussion of Sweden draws heavily on Jan Teorell and Bo Rothstein, "Getting to Sweden: Malfeasance and Bureaucratic Reforms, 1720–1850," University of Gothenburg Quality of Government Institute, Working Paper 2012:18 (2012), 15–18, where the numbers may be found as well. The authors suggest that there may have been an "increased awareness" of corrupt practices rather than an actual rise in corrupt behavior.

19. In an earlier publication, Rothstein called Sweden and Denmark in the early nineteenth century "thoroughly corrupt," in his "Anti-corruption: The Indirect 'Big Bang' Approach," *Review of International Political Economy*, XVIII (2011), 240.

20. Teorell and Rothstein, "Getting to Sweden," 22.

21. Ibid., 24.

22. Knot Wichman, *Karl XIV Johans Regering och den Liberala Oppositionen* (Goteberg, Pehrsons Forlag, 1927), quoted in Teorell and Rothstein, "Getting to Sweden," 29. Rothstein and Uslaner also assert that "Swedish political culture [benefited from] universalizing the egalitarianism of the peasant community." Swedish peasants, they say, had not been subject to feudalism. Bo Rothstein and Eric M. Uslaner, "All for All: Equality, Corruption, and Social Trust," *World Politics*, LVIII (2005), 43.

23. Emil Hildebrand, quoted in Rothstein, "Big Bang," 243.

24. Lars Pettersson, "In Search of Respectability: Popular Movements in Scandinavian Democratization—From Voluntary Associations to Mass Organizations," in Lars Rudebeck and Olle Törnquist (eds.), *Democratization in the Third World: Concrete Cases in Comparative and Theoretical Perspective* (New York, St. Martins, 1998), 99.

25. Ibid., 245; Uslaner, *Corruption*, 245. See also the checklist in Rothstein, *Quality of Government*, 113–114.

26. Paula Tiihonen, "Good Governance and Corruption in Finland," in Seppo Tiihonen, *The History of Corruption in Central Government* (Amsterdam, IOS Press, 2003), 104–105.

27. Ari Salminen, "Control of Corruption: The Case of Finland," in Quah, *Different Paths*, 65; Salminen, Olli-Pekka Viinamaki, and Rinna Ikola-Norrbacka, "The Control of Corruption in Finland," *Administraie Si Management Public*, IX (2007), 88.

28. Tiinonen, "Corruption in Finland," 109.

29. Darren C. Zook, "The Curious Case of Finland's Clean Politics," *Journal of Democracy*, XX (2009), 163, 167.

30. Leslie Lipson, *The Politics of Equality: New Zealand's Adventures in Democracy* (Chicago, University of Chicago Press, 1948), 17.

31. Raymond Joseph Polaschek, *Government Administration in New Zealand* (Wellington, Oxford University Press, 1958), 96. This book's index has no entry for "corruption." Nor for "bribery," "embezzlement," or "fraud."

32. *Parliamentary Debates*, 1879, quoted in Lipson, *Politics*, 158.

33. Lipson, *Politics*, 159. See also the discussion of the spoils system in Lipson, *Politics*, 422–435. In this index, too, there is no entry for "corruption" or any of those other indicative nouns.

34. Sidney and Beatrice Webb, "Impressions of a Tour of New Zealand," cited in Polaschek, *Administration*, 105. Earlier quotations at the beginning of the paragraph from ibid., 100–102. The latter quotations are from Sidney Webb to William Pember Reeves, sometime cabinet minister in New Zealand and then agent general in London, August 27, 1898; Beatrice Webb to Catherine (Kate) Courtney, August 24, 1898, both in Norman Mackenzie (ed.), *The Letters of Sidney and Beatrice Webb* (Cambridge, Cambridge University Press, 1978), II, 76–79.

35. M. P. Keith Sorrenson, "New Zealand: Maori and Pakeha," in William S. Livingston and William Roger Louis (eds.), *Australia, New Zealand, and the Pacific Islands since the First World War* (Austin, University of Texas Press, 1979), 170; John A. Williams, *Politics of the New Zealand Maori: Protest and Cooperation, 1891–1909* (Seattle, University of Washington Press, 1969), 14–18, 23.

36. Lipson, *Politics*, 482, 488–489; see also Erik Olssen, "Towards a New Society," in Geoffrey W. Rice (ed.), *The Oxford History of New Zealand* (Auckland, Oxford University Press, 1992, 2nd ed.), 259–261.

37. Robert Gregory and Daniel Zirker, "Clean and Green with Deepening Shadows? A Non-complacent View of Corruption in New Zealand," in Quah, *Different Paths*, 119.

38. Lipson, *Politics*, 479.

39. Polaschek, *Administration*, 283.

40. Gregory and Zirker, "Clean and Green," 117–118.

41. For details, see Ross Curnow, "What's Past Is Prologue: Administrative Corruption in Australia," in Tiihonen, *History of Corruption*, 46–49.

42. Antoon D. N. Kerkhoff, Michel P. Hoenderboom, D. B. Ronald Kroeze, and F. Pieter Wagenaar, "Dutch Political Corruption in Historical Perspective," in Niels Grüne and Simona Slanička, *Korruption: Historische Annäherungen an eine Grundfigur Politischer Kommunikation* (Gottingen, Vandenhoeck & Ruprecht, 2010), 450.

43. Frits M. van der Meer and Jos C. N. Raadschelders, "Maladministration in the Netherlands in the 19th and 20th Centuries," in Tiihonen, *History of Corruption*, 190–193.

44. Quoted in Kenneth Kernaghan, "Corruption and Public Service in Canada: Conceptual and Practical Dimensions," in Tiihonen, *History of Corruption*, 87–88.

45. Sharon Sutherland, "The Canadian Federal Government," in John W. Langford and Allan Tupper (eds.), *Corruption, Character, and Conduct: Essays on Canadian Government Ethics* (Toronto, Oxford University Press, 1993), 114; but see Kenneth McNaught, *The Penguin History of Canada* (London, Penguin, 1988, orig. pub. 1969), 151–152.

46. Robert Bothwell, Ian Drummond, and John English, *Canada, 1900–1945* (Toronto, University of Toronto Press, 1987), 52.

47. Martin Robin, "British Columbia: The Politics of Class Conflict," in Robin (ed.), *Canadian Provincial Politics* (Toronto, Prentice Hall, 1978), 40.

48. Kenneth M. Gibbons, "The Political Culture of Corruption in Canada," in Gibbons and Donald C. Rowat (eds.), *Political Corruption in Canada: Cases, Causes, and Cures* (Toronto, McClelland and Stewart, 1976), 239–244; Ralph Heintzman, "Politics and Corruption in Quebec," in ibid., 217–224; Peter Bruton, John Downing, and Fraser Kelly, "Graft Never Hurt a Politician

at the Polls," in ibid., 226; S.J.R. Noel, *The Politics of Newfoundland* (Toronto, University of Toronto Press, 1971), 162–170.

49. See Donald MacDonald, quoted in ibid., 230.

50. Quoted in Kenneth Kernaghan, "The Ethical Conduct of Public Servants," in Gibbons and Rowat, *Political*, 160. For more on Canadian corruption, see Robert I. Rotberg, "Canada's Corruption at Home and Abroad: An Introduction to the Special Issue," *Canadian Foreign Policy Journal*, XXIII (2017), 1–14.

51. Sutherland, "Federal Government," 115–116.

52. Sutherland, "Federal Government," 140.

53. Benjamin T. Jones, *Republicanism and Responsible Government: The Shaping of Democracy in Australia and Canada* (Montreal, McGill-Queens, 2014), 19.

54. Ibid., 8.

55. Robert Neild, *Public Corruption: The Dark Side of Social Evolution* (London, Anthem, 2002), 11.

56. Eric M. Uslaner and Bo Rothstein, "Mass Education, State-Building and Equality: Searching for the Roots of Corruption," University of Gothenburg Quality of Government Institute, Working Paper 2012:5, 2012, 3.

57. Ibid., 7–8, 17.

58. Mungiu-Pippidi, *The Quest*, 23.

59. Mungiu-Pippidi, *The Quest*, 10.

VIII: The Gift of Political Will and Leadership

1. Jean Tirole, "A Theory of Collective Reputations with Applications to the Persistence of Corruption and to Firm Quality," *Review of Economic Studies*, LXIII (1996), 3; Amr G. E. Sabet, "Corruption, Governance and Collective Sanctions: Can a Wicked Problem Be Tamed?" *Studies of Changing Societies*, I (2012), 83.

2. Robert I. Rotberg, "Leadership Alters Corrupt Behavior," in Robert I. Rotberg (ed.), *Corruption, Global Security, and World Order* (Washington, DC, Brookings, 2009), 342.

3. Alina Mungiu-Pippidi, *The Quest for Good Governance: How Societies Develop Control of Corruption* (New York, Cambridge University Press, 2015), 208, also 115.

4. See the argument advanced at length in Robert I. Rotberg, *Transformative Political Leadership: Making a Difference in the Developing World* (Chicago, University of Chicago Press, 2012). See also Eric M. Uslaner, *Corruption, Inequality, and the Rule of Law: The Bulging Pocket Makes the Easy Life* (New York, Cambridge, 2008), 183, 204.

5. See Robert I. Rotberg and Aniket Bhushan, "The Indexes of Governance," in Robert I. Rotberg (ed.), *On Governance: What It Is, How It Is Measured, and Its Policy Uses* (Waterloo, ON, Centre for International Governance Innovation [CIGI], 2015); Rotberg, *Transformative*, 13.

6. Uslaner, *Corruption*, 211.

7. Mungiu-Pippidi, *The Quest*, 85.

8. Deng Xiaoping, quoted in Orville Schell, "Lee Kuan Yew, the Man Who Remade Asia," *Wall Street Journal*, March 27, 2015.

9. Samuel P. Huntington, *Political Order in Changing Societies* (New Haven, Yale University Press, 1968), 68; Rajeev K. Goel and Michael A. Nelson, "Corruption and Government Size: A Disaggregated Analysis," *Public Choice*, LXXXXVII (1998), 114–117.

10. See Bo Rothstein, "Anti-Corruption: The Indirect 'Big Bang' Approach," *Review of International Political Economy*, XVIII (2011), 236.

11. For the distinction between transactional and transformational leadership, see Rotberg, *Transformative*, 22.

12. Rotberg, *Transformative*, 6, 17.

13. Rotberg, *Transformative*, 11–12; Ann Ruth Willner, *The Spellbinders: Charismatic Political Leadership* (New Haven, Yale University Press, 1984), 46–47.

14. Benjamin F. Jones and Benjamin A. Olken, "Do Leaders Matter? National Leadership and Growth since World War II," *Quarterly Journal of Economics*, CXX (2005), 835–864. See Rotberg, "Leadership Alters," 344.

15. James C. Scott, *Comparative Political Corruption* (Englewood Cliffs, Prentice Hall, 1972), 19. See also Peter John Perry, *Political Corruption and Political Geography* (Brookfield, VT, Ashgate, 1997), 121.

16. Mungiu-Pippidi, *The Quest*, 131–132, prefers to exclude Singapore from her list of "contemporary achievers" successfully curbing corruption because it is an "authoritarian achiever," like the United Arab Emirates or Qatar. Such polities "do not qualify," she writes, "as ruled by ethical universalism" even if they know how to control bribery, etc. Reducing corruption must come about by thoroughly democratic means to count, she believes.

17. Jon S. T. Quah, "Combating Corruption in Singapore: What Can Be Learned?" *Journal of Contingencies and Crisis Management*, IX (2001), 29; Quah, "Curbing Corruption in Singapore: The Importance of Political Will, Expertise, Enforcement, and Context," in Quah (ed.), *Different Paths to Curbing Corruption: Lessons from Denmark, Finland, Hong Kong, New Zealand, and Singapore* (Bingley, UK, Emerald, 2013), 145.

18. For much more in this vein and a fuller exposition of how Lee led, and why, see Rotberg, *Transformative*, 106–120.

19. See Lee Kuan Yew, *From Third World to First: The Singapore Story, 1965–2000* (New York, Harper, 2000), 157.

20. Ibid., 163.

21. Rotberg, "Leadership Alters," 347.

22. Francis T. Seow, *To Catch a Tartar: A Dissident in Lee Kuan Yew's Prison* (New Haven, Yale University Press, 1994), 20.

23. I say "semi-authoritarian" because as brusque, clear-minded, and forceful as Lee was, and as much as he always managed to get his own way and preside authoritatively, he was fair-minded, believed in the full participation of citizens, and curtailed free speech almost entirely by the exercise of punitive libel judgments. A fuller discussion is contained in my *Transformative Political Leadership*. Michael D. Barr, in several books and his "Singapore's Lee Kuan Yew: Traveling Light, Traveling Fast" in Ramachandra Guha (ed.), *Makers of Modern Asia* (Cambridge, MA, Harvard University Press, 2014), 151, is harsher. He calls Lee's regime a clever "marriage of repression and capitalism." The repression was heavy in the 1970s, when Lee detained dissidents, beat them, and humiliated them in confinement in many other ways. See also Barr, *Lee Kuan Yew: The Beliefs behind the Man* (London, Curzon, 2000); idem, *The Ruling Elite of Singapore: Networks of Power and Influence* (London, Tauris, 2014).

24. Quoted in Syed Hussein Alatas, "The Problem of Corruption," in Kernial Singh Sandhu and Paul Wheatley (eds.), *Management of Success: The Moulding of Modern Singapore* (Singapore, Institute of Southeast Asian Studies, 1989), 993.

25. Kishore Mahbubani, paraphrased in David Pilling, "Pragmatic Singapore Can Afford a Little Poetry," *Financial Times*, Aug. 6, 2015.

26. Quoted in Hilton L. Root, *Small Countries, Big Lessons: Governance and the Rise of East Asia* (Hong Kong, Oxford University Press, 1996), 47.

27. Uslaner, *Corruption*, 244; See also the important commentary by Brian Epstein, "When Local Models Fail," *Philosophy of the Social Sciences*, XXXVIII (2008), 3–24.

28. Ouyang Huan Yan worked for the Lees for more than forty years. She watched Lee "hold his children's hands, and felt that he was more like a friendly friend, a patient father, and 'someone you can trust and be at ease with.'" She said Lee "had no airs about him and was friendly and

humble to the servants." Even after Lee became prime minister in 1959, she remembered that "he remained a modest and simple man [who] stuck to his [daily] breakfast of a glass of Ovaltine, two pieces of bread and two eggs." *The New Paper online*, April 2, 2015, http://www.tnp.sg/news /mr-lee-kuan-yews-maid-40-years-says-lee-family-they-had-no-airs#sthash.u44ztQk6.dpuf.

29. Barr, "Singapore's Lee Kuan Yew," 254.

30. See, for example, the experience of Francis T. Seow, as related in his major critique of Lee: *To Catch a Tartar*; "The Wise Man of the East," *Economist*, March 28, 2015. For more on this subject, see Rotberg, *Transformative*, 114–115.

31. http://www.transparency.org/cpi2015/results.

32. http://www.indexmundi.com/g/r-aspx?v=67. These are purchasing power parity (PPP) numbers. By this measure, Singapore was the sixth wealthiest place in the world, after Lichtenstein, Qatar, Luxembourg, Bermuda, and Monaco.

33. See Chia Siow Yue, "The Character and Progress of Industrialization," in Sandhu and Wheatley, *Success*, 250–279. For Lee on why air-conditioning was imperative, see his *Singapore*, 316.

34. James Minchin, *No Man Is an Island: A Portrait of Singapore's Lee Kuan Yew* (London, Unwin Hyman, 1990, orig. pub. 1986), 317.

35. Thomas Tlou, Neil Parsons, and Willie Henderson, *Seretse Khama, 1921–80* (Gaborone, Botswana Society, 1995), 49, 53.

36. Quoted in Tlou et al., *Seretse*, 252.

37. Khama, speaking in New York, quoted in Tlou et al., *Seretse*, 360.

38. Quett Ketumile Joni Masire, "Economic Opportunities and Disparities," in Stephen R. Lewis (ed.), *Very Brave or Very Foolish? Memoirs of an African Democrat* (Gaborone, Palgrave Macmillan, 2006), 239.

39. Masire, *Very Brave*, 103.

40. Mungiu-Pippidi, *The Quest*, 147, calls Botswana "an enlightened monarchy," but that is a great misreading of how Botswana works.

41. Masire, *Very Brave*, 240.

42. For Prussia, see John R. Gillis, *The Prussian Bureaucracy in Crisis, 1840–1860: Origins of an Administrative Ethos* (Berkeley, Cambridge University Press, 1971), 25.

43. Masire, *Very Brave*, 240.

44. Mungiu-Pippidi, *The Quest*, 145, 149, believes that Botswana achieved no ethical universalism. She writes that material resources, and corruption temptations, were too high. But that is a misreading of what a reformed political culture meant for the country and ultimately for Africa.

45. Daron Acemoglu, Simon Johnson, and James A. Robinson, "An African Success Story: Botswana," in Dani Rodrik (ed.), *In Search of Prosperity: Analytic Narratives on Economic Growth* (Princeton, Princeton University Press, 2003), 85–88, 104–106.

46. This paragraph draws on the detailed argument contained in Rotberg, *Transformative*, 26–29.

47. Ibid., 28.

48. Quoted in Rosabeth Moss Kanter, "Leadership in a Globalizing World," in Nitin Nohria and Rakesh Khurana (eds.), *Handbook of Leadership Theory and Practice* (Boston, Harvard Business Review Press, 2010), 589.

49. Jay A. Conger and Rabindra N. Kanungo, *Charismatic Leadership in Organizations* (Thousand Oaks, Sage, 1998), 213.

50. For definitions and discussion, see Rotberg, *Transformative*, 30–32.

51. See Robert I. Rotberg and Rachel M. Gisselquist, *Strengthening African Governance: The Index of African Governance, Results and Rankings* (Cambridge, MA, Kennedy School of Government, Harvard University, and World Peace Foundation, 2009).

52. http://www.transparency.org/cpi2014/results.

53. http://www.indexmundi.com/g/r-aspx?v=67.

54. Masire, *Very Brave*, 241, 242.

55. Afrobarometer, 2005 and 2012, http://afrobarometer.org/results.

56. Quoted in Evan Osnos, "Born Red," *New Yorker*, April 6, 2015, 42; Reuters, "China to Implement New Anti-graft Law," March 8, 2015.

57. But see Ezra Vogel, *Deng Xiaoping and the Transformation of China* (Cambridge, MA, Harvard University Press, 2011), 468, 470, 553, 707–709. See also Ting Gong, "Forms and Characteristics of China's Corruption in the 1990s: Change with Continuity," *Communist and Post-Communist Studies*, XXX (1997), 277–288.

58. Osnos, "Red," 44–45.

59. Several China watchers quoted in Gordon G. Chang, "Xi's Purge: Anticorruption or Loyalty-Based? Is It Finished Yet?" *World Affairs Journal*, June 22, 2015, http://www.worldaffairs journal.org.

60. "No Ordinary Zhou," *Economist*, Aug. 2, 2014.

61. Chinese Central Commission for Discipline Inspection, cited in "Xi Turns Sights On Wayward Senior Leaders in China Graft Fight," *Bloomberg News*, Nov. 2, 2016; Frank Langfitt, "China's Fierce Anti-Corruption Crackdown: An Insider's View," NPR, Dec. 24, 2014, http://www.npr.org/blogs/parallels; Macabe Keller and Hsinchao Wu, "How to Discipline 90 Million People," *Atlantic*, April 2015. For China's anticorruption strategies in their fullest context, see Melanie Manion, "Institutional Design and Anti-Corruption in Mainland China," in Paul M. Heywood (ed.), *Routledge Handbook of Political Corruption* (New York, Routledge, 2015), 243–249.

62. See Stephanie Saul and Dan Levin, "Charged with Graft in China, Finding Life of Luxury in U.S.," *New York Times*, May 16, 2015; "Anti-graft Net Recovers Assets," *China Daily*, Dec. 9–11, 2016.

63. "No Ordinary Zhou," 50; Richard L. Cassin and Hui Zhi, "Can Corrupt Armies Win Wars?" FCPA Blog, Aug. 25, 2015; "Chinese Woman Convicted of Graft," *New York Times*, Dec. 12, 2014; Michael Forsythe, "China Sentences 2 Former Communist Officials," *New York Times*, Oct. 15, 2015.

64. Michael Forsythe, "Chinese Ex-General, Charged with Corruption, Dies," *New York Times*, March 16, 2015; Chris Buckley, "China Arrests Ex-Chief of Domestic Security in Graft Case," *New York Times*, December 6, 2014. See also "Rank and Vile," *Economist*, Feb. 14, 2015.

65. Squire Patton Boggs, "Monthly China Anti-Bribery Update Report, February 2015," http://www.anticorruptionblog.com.

66. Dan Levin, "China Names 14 Generals Suspected of Corruption," *New York Times*, March 3, 2015.

67. Jerry Fang, "Scoreboard: Tigers Falling Fast in Anti-Graft Campaign," Oct. 19, 2015, http://www.fcpablog.com/2015/10/19.

68. Langfitt, "China's Fierce," http://www.npr.org.

69. Tania Branigan, "Politburo, Army, Casinos: China's Corruption Crackdown Spreads," *Guardian*, Feb. 14, 2015.

70. "China Wants Military to Be on Guard against 'Liberalism,' " *Malay Mail Online*, April 16, 2015, http://www.themalaymailonline.com/print/world/china.

71. Simon Denyer, "China's Leader Institutes Ban, Kicks Golf to the Curb," *Boston Globe*, Oct. 23, 2015.

72. http://www.transparency.org/cpi2015/results.

73. Quoted in Adam Nossiter, "Nigerian President-Elect Sets out His Agenda," *New York Times*, April 2, 1915.

74. The La Paz case is discussed in Phyllis Dininio, "The Risks of Recorruption," in Bertram

I. Spector (ed.), *Fighting Corruption in Developing Countries: Strategies and Analysis* (Bloomfield, CT, Kumarian Press, 2005), 239–240.

75. For a skeptical analytical view of the relationship between transformative political leadership and charisma, see Rotberg, *Transformative*, 36–38.

76. See Fred Muvunyi, "Tanzania's Magufuli Leads Fight against Corruption," Deutsche Welle, May 12, 2016, http://www.dw.com/en/tanzanias-magufuli; Michael Jennings, "Will Magufuli's Popular Anti-Corruption Drive in Tanzania Last?" *World Politics Review*, April 1, 2016, http://www.worldpoliticsreview.com/articles/18367; Robert I. Rotberg, "Africa's New Broom Cleans House," *Globe & Mail*, Dec. 29, 2015.

77. "Tanzania Purges 10,000 'Ghost Workers' in Anti-Corruption Drive," BBC News, May 17, 2016.

78. "Government by Gesture," *Economist*, May 28, 2016.

79. Raymond W. Baker, *Capitalism's Achilles Heel: Dirty Money and How to Renew the Free-Market System* (Hoboken, Wiley, 2005), 251.

IX: People Power, Social Media, and Corporate Rigor

1. Reported in *Simerini* (Nicosia), April 20, 2015; Transparency International—Cyprus poll reported on Sept. 7, 2015, in TRNC News, online blog.

2. Alina Mungiu-Pippidi, *The Quest for Good Governance: How Societies Develop Control of Corruption* (New York, Cambridge University Press, 2015), 167, 169–170.

3. For more on people power, especially in Brazil in 2016, see Robert I. Rotberg, "The Judge Who Could Remake Brazil: How Sergio Moro Has Tackled Corruption," *Foreign Affairs* blog, Dec. 21, 2016, www.foreignaffairs.com/articles/2016-12-21

4. See Rotberg, "Mobile Phones Propelling Africa's Renaissance," *Diplomat & International Canada*, April–June 2015, 33–35.

5. See https://opencorporates.com, and click on each country. For Mexico, see Carin Zissis, "Explainer: The Case of the Ongoing Teacher Protests in Mexico," http://www.as-coa.org/articles/explainer, July 6, 2015.

6. For details about surveys, see chapter 3, and Richard Rose and Caryn Peiffer, *Paying Bribes for Public Services: A Global Guide to Grass-Roots Corruption* (Basingstoke, UK, Palgrave Macmillan, 2015), 76–83.

7. R. P. Kangle, *The Kautiliya Arthasastra* (Mumbai, University of Bombay, 1972), 91.

8. For the British looting of India under the East India Company and after, see John S. Furnivall, *Colonial Policy and Practice: A Comparative Study of Burma and Netherlands India* (Cambridge, Cambridge University Press, 1948), 27.

9. See Gopakumar K. Thampi and Sita Sekhar, "Citizen Report Cards," in Charles Sampford, Arthur Shacklock, Carmel Connors, and Fredrik Galtung (eds.), *Measuring Corruption* (Aldershot, Hants., Ashgate, 2006), 245.

10. For the origin of these well-meant institutions, and their inability to stem Indian corruption, see Shiladitya Chakraborty, *Public Service Reforms in India: A Fight against Corruption* (Calcutta, Towards Freedom, 2013).

11. Quoted in Asia, Sept. 21, 2011, http://asiafoundation.org/in-asia/2011/09/21. For Bangladesh, see chapter 1, 30.

12. Quoted in Paul de Bendern, "Insight: Anti-Corruption Campaign Awakens India's Middle Class," Reuters, Aug. 24, 2011, http://www.reuters.com/article/2011/08/24.

13. Quoted in Shaazka Beyerle, *Curtailing Corruption: People Power for Accountability and Justice* (Boulder, Rienner, 2014), 140–141.

14. Ibid., 166.

15. http://www.transparency.org/cpi2015/results.

16. Dina Baidildayeva, quoted in Sarah Kendzior and Noah Tucker, "Dashcams for Freedom," *Foreign Policy*, Aug. 5, 2015.

17. Ibid.

18. Jessica McKenzie, "Tell President Kenyatta You Paid a Bribe," Oct. 31, 2013, http://tech president.com/news/wegov/.

19. For the concept, see Petter Langseth, "Measuring Corruption," in Sampford et al., *Measuring Corruption*, 24–27.

20. See "Eureka Moments," *Economist*, Sept. 24, 2009, http://www.economist.com/node /14483872.

21. http://www.transparency.org/country#Pak_PublicOpinion.

22. Mohammad Omar Masud, "Calling the Public to Empower the State: Pakistan's Citizen Feedback Monitoring Program, 2008–2014," Princeton University, Innovations for Successful Societies, February 2015, 7–9.

23. Ibid., 14–15.

24. http://www.transparency.org/cpi2014/results.

25. http://www.transparency/org/cpi2015/results. PNG ranked equally with Guinea, Kenya, Uganda, Bangladesh, and Laos.

26. Maya Gainer, "Listening to the Public: A Citizen Scorecard in the Philippines, 2010–2014," Princeton University, Innovations for Successful Societies, 2015, http://www.suc cessfulsocieties.Princeton.edu.

27. Gainer, "Listening," 8.

28. Ibid., 9.

29. Ibid., 15.

30. For more details, see http://World Bank.org/wbsite/external/topics/extsocialdevelop ment/ and . . . /extpoverty/.

31. "The Critical Masses," *Economist*, April 11, 2015.

32. Because some of the payments to the prime minister of Malaysia passed through a bank in New York, the prime minister's receipt of funds from the sovereign wealth fund triggered a Department of Justice inquiry. Some of the funds may have purchased real estate in New York. Illicit monies flow across national boundaries.

33. James Gorman, "Enforcing Conservation in Africa," *New York Times*, Oct. 13, 2015.

34. Yury Fedotov and John E. Scanlon, "Tackling Corruption Will Deal a Lethal Blow to the Illegal Wildlife Trade," *Guardian*, Sept. 19, 2016.

35. Quoted in Simon Denyer, "India's Anti-Corruption Movement Aims to Galvanize Democracy," *Washington Post*, Aug. 12, 2011; de Bendern, "Insight."

36. Sarah Dix and Emmanuel Pok, "Combating Corruption in Traditional Societies: Papua New Guinea," in Rotberg, *Corruption*, 253.

37. Findings prepared by IMCO, a Mexican think tank, cited in "The Mexican Blues," *Economist*, June 11, 2016.

38. Juan E. Pardinas, quoted in Kirk Semple, "Grass Roots Anti-Corruption Drive Puts Heat on Mexican Lawmakers," *New York Times*, May 28, 2016.

39. Luis Rubio and Viridiana Rios, quoted in "The New Movers and Shakers," *Economist*, May 2, 2015.

40. Rafael Pineda, quoted in William Neuman, "Mexicans Aren't Buying Official Account of 'El Chapo' Escape," *New York Times*, August 5, 2015.

41. "Trials and Errors," *Economist*, June 18, 2016.

42. "A Central American Spring?" *Economist*, Aug. 15, 2015.

43. Azam Ahmed, "Guatemala's Corruption Investigations Make Quick Strides," *New York Times*, Aug. 26, 2015.

44. Rick Messick, "Tackling Grand Corruption: Guatemala's Successful Experiment," *The Global Corruption Blog*, June 24, 2015; Elisabeth Malkin and Azam Ahmed, "Guatemala Votes to Strip Its President of Immunity," *New York Times*, Sept. 1, 2015.

45. Valasquez, interviewed in *El Faro* and trans. and ed. in Gabriel Labrador, "Head of Guatemala's CICIG Reflects on Past Victories, Challenges Ahead," InSight Crime, Nov. 17, 2015,

46. Elisabeth Malkin, "Guatemalan Comedian Wins First Round of Presidential Vote," *New York Times*, Sept. 7, 2015.

47. Juan Carlos Zapata, quoted in Elisabeth Malkin, "Toppling a President, Then Pursuing Deeper Changes," *New York Times*, Sept. 16, 2015.

48. Plaza Publico, a Guatemalan news website, quoted in "Bad Apples Everywhere," *Economist*, June 11, 2016.

49. Mimi Yagoub, "El Salvador Judges Accused of Stealing Seized Cash," *InSight Crime*, Nov. 26, 2015, http://www.insightcrime.org/news.

50. Both quoted in Beyerle, *Curtailing*, 188–189.

51. Ibid., 196.

52. Quoted in Samira Shackle, "What Is Behind the Resurgence of the AAP, India's Radical Anti-Corruption Movement?" *New Statesman*, Feb. 13, 2015.

53. "Delhi: AAP Government to Set Up Patient Welfare Committees in Hospitals," PTI Agency, April 16, 2015, http://www.dnaindia.com/india/report-delhi-aap.

54. "AAP Government Kicks Off 'Participatory Budget' Exercise," PTI Agency, April 19, 2015, http://www.dnaindia.com/india/report-aap.

55. See Participedia, http://www.challengestodemocracy.us/home/looking-for-inspiration-five-innovations-in-public-participation/#sthash.1RYoJJxa.dpuf; http://demos.legislatura.gov.ar; vouliwatch.gr.

56. "Aam Aadmi Party's 'Sting App' to help Fight Corruption," Press Trust of India, April 3, 2015, http://www.ndtv.com/delhi-news.

57. "Delhi CM Kejriwal Has Not Done Anything since Coming to Power: Congress," *Indian Express*, July 8, 2016.

58. Beyerle, *Curtailing*, 31.

59. All quoted in Alison Taylor, "Does Competition Cause Corruption?" FCPA Blog, June 22, 2015, http://www.fcpablog.com/blog/2015/6/22; Richard Bistrong, "When Corruption Becomes Normal," FCPA Blog, June 29, 2015, http://www.fcpablog.com/blog.

60. Richard Bistrong, "When the Finish Line Is Close, the Pressure to Bribe Increases," FCPA Blog, Oct. 15, 2015, http://www.fcpablog.com/blog.

61. Ben W. Heineman, Jr., "The Role of the Multi-National Corporation in the Long War against Corruption," in Rotberg, *Corruption*, 362.

62. Ben W. Heineman, Jr., *High Performance with High Integrity* (Boston, HBS Press, 2008), 12.

63. Abiola O. Makinwa, *Private Remedies for Corruption: Towards an International Framework* (Utrecht, Eleven, 2013), 465, 466.

64. Heineman, "Multi-National," 366; See also Mike Scher, "A Board-Backed Code of Ethics Is a Cornerstone of Compliance 2.0," FCPA Blog, Nov. 9, 2015, http://www.fcpablog.com, /blog/2015.

65. http://www.fcpablog.com/blog/2015/4/22/compliance-officers-required-under-new-ukraine-anti-corrupti.html#sthash.QylFipLG.dpuf.

66. Richard L. Cassin, "Resource Alert: This Is What Cooperation with the DOJ Looks Like," FCPA Blog, April 20, 2015, http://www.fcpablog.com/blog/2015/4/20/resource-alert00.

67. Marc A. Agnifilo, quoted in Rebecca R. Ruiz, "Justice Dept. Sees FIFA as Victim and Group's Leaders as Wrongdoers," *New York Times*, Oct. 10, 2015.

68. Editorial, "America's Global Corruption Crusade," *New York Times*, Aug. 1, 2016.

X: Curing Corruption: Lessons, Methods, and Best Practices

1. Kimiko de Freytas-Tamura, "With Scales, British Town Weighs Officials' Merits," *New York Times*, May 19, 2016.

2. Alina Mungiu-Pippidi, *The Quest for Good Governance: How Societies Develop Control of Corruption* (New York, Cambridge University Press, 2015), 203.

3. John Gerring and Strom C. Thacker, "Political Institutions and Corruption: The Role of Unitarism and Parliamentarism," *British Journal of Political Science*, XXXIV (2004), 324–325.

4. Michael Johnston, "Why Do So Many Anti-Corruption Efforts Fail?" *NYU Annual Survey of American Law*, LXVII (2012), 476. On corruption as a criminal enterprise, see Sarah Chayes, *Thieves of State* (New York, Norton, 2015), 96–98.

5. Michael W. Collier, "Explaining Corruption: An Institutional Choice Approach," *Crime, Law, and Social Change*, XXXVIII (2002), 18–19, citing Mitchell Seligson, "Nicaraguans Talk about Corruption: A Follow-up Study of Public Opinion," Casals & Associates, Arlington, VA, 1999; Michael Johnston, "Fighting Systemic Corruption: Social Foundations for Institutional Reform," *European Journal of Development Research*, X (1998), 85–87.

6. Shiv Tripathi and Ganka Daniel Nyamsogoro, "Africa's Business Schools Must Champion Anti-Corruption Education," *The Conversation*, Aug. 3, 2015, https://theconversation.com /africas-business-schools.

7. Alina Mungiu-Pippidi, "Controlling Corruption through Collective Action," *Journal of Democracy*, XXIV (2013), 109.

8. Quotations from unnamed interviewees in Anna Persson, Bo Rothstein, and Jan Teorell, "Why Anti-Corruption Reforms Fail—Systemic Corruption as a Collective Action Problem," *Governance*, XXVI (2013), 448–459

9. Robert E. Klitgaard, *Controlling Corruption* (Berkeley, University of California Press, 1988), 81.

10. Leonid Bershidsky, "Stop Bribery by Legalizing It," *Bloomberg View*, Aug. 31, 2015, http://www.bloombergview.com.

11. Quoted in Klitgaard, *Corruption*, 462.

12. Torsten Persson and Guido E. Tabellini, *The Economic Effects of Constitutions* (Cambridge, MA, Massachusetts Institute of Technology, 2003), 173.

13. See Robert I. Rotberg and Jennifer Erin Salahub, "African Legislative Effectiveness," *North-South Institute* (Ottawa) report, October 2013, for a discussion of how public accounts committees can make a difference.

14. Simon Denyer and Emily Rauhala, "Beijing's Claims to South China Sea Rejected by International Tribunal," *Washington Post*, July 12, 2016.

15. Nathan Heller, citing the work of Kenneth Rogoff, "Imagining a Cashless World," *New York Times*, Oct. 10, 2016. India and Venezuela tried something similar in late 2016, to disastrous effect.

16. On focusing foreign assistance on the training of political leaders, see Michael Lund, "Intrastate Conflicts and the Problem of Political Will," in Lund and Steve McDonald (eds.), *Across the Lines of Conflict: Facilitating Cooperation to Build Peace* (New York, Columbia, 2015), 11. See also the recommendations for capacity building in L. Log Raditlhokwa, "Corruption in Africa: A Function of the Crisis of Leadership," in Kwame Frimpong and Gloria Jacques (eds.), *Corruption, Democracy, and Good Governance in Africa: Essays on Accountability and Ethical Behaviour* (Gaborone, Lightbooks, 1999), 54.

17. Mungiu-Pippidi, *The Quest*, 172.

Select Bibliography

ESSENTIAL READINGS ON CORRUPTION AND ANTICORRUPTION

Books

Amundsen, Inge, *Political Corruption: An Introduction to the Issues* (Bergen, Chr. Michelsen Institute, 1999)

Baker, Raymond W., *Capitalism's Achilles Heel: Dirty Money and How to Renew the Free-Market System* (Hoboken, Wiley, 2005)

Banfield, Edward C., *The Moral Basis of a Backward Society* (Glencoe, Free Press, 1958)

———, *Political Influence* (Glencoe, Free Press, 1961)

Barr, Michael D., *Lee Kuan Yew: The Beliefs Behind the Man* (London, Curzon, 2000)

———, *The Ruling Elite of Singapore: Networks of Power and Influence* (London, Tauris, 2014)

Bellany, Alastair, *The Politics of Court Scandal in Early Modern England: News, Culture, and the Overbury Affair, 1603–1660* (New York, Cambridge University Press, 2002)

Beyerle, Shaazka, *Curtailing Corruption: People Power for Accountability and Justice* (Boulder, Rienner, 2014)

Boersma, Martine, and Hans Nelen (eds.), *Corruption and Human Rights: Interdisciplinary Perspectives* (Amsterdam, Intersentia, 2010)

Bracking, Sarah L. (ed.), *Corruption and Development: The Anti-Corruption Campaigns* (Basingstoke, Palgrave, 2007)

Briscoe, Andrew, and H.C.L. Hermans, *Combating Corruption in Botswana: A Review of the Relevant Policies, Laws, and Institutional Capacity to Combat Corruption in Botswana* (Gaborone, Ebert Foundation, 2001)

Carmody, Padraig, *The New Scramble for Africa* (Cambridge, Polity, 2011)

Chakraborty, Shiladitya, *Public Service Reforms in India: A Fight against Corruption* (Calcutta, Towards Freedom, 2013)

Chayes, Sarah, *Thieves of State: Why Corruption Threatens Global Security* (New York, Norton, 2015)

Clark, William A., *Crime and Punishment in Soviet Officialdom: Combating Corruption in the Political Elite, 1965–1990* (Armonk, NY, M. E. Sharpe, 1993)

Dawisha, Karen, *Putin's Kleptocracy: Who Owns Russia?* (New York, Simon & Schuster, 2015)

de Speville, Bertrand E. D., *Hong Kong: Policy Initiatives against Corruption* (Paris, Organisation for Economic Co-operation and Development [OECD], 1997)

———, *Overcoming Corruption: The Essentials* (Kuala Lumpur, Research for Social Advancement, 2010)

Eigen, Peter (trans. Joelle Diderich), *The Web of Corruption: How a Global Movement Fights Graft* (Frankfurt/Main, Campus Verlag, 2003)

Ellis, Stephen, *This Present Darkness: A History of Nigerian Organized Crime* (New York, Oxford University Press, 2016)

Fisman, Raymond, and Miriam A. Golden, *Corruption: What Everyone Needs to Know* (New York, Oxford University Press, 2017)

Fisman, Raymond, and Edward Miguel, *Economic Gangsters: Corruption, Violence, and the Poverty of Nations* (Princeton, Princeton University Press, 2008)

Frimpong, Kwame, and Gloria Jacques (eds.), *Corruption, Democracy, and Good Governance in Africa* (Gaborone, Lightbooks, 1999)

Furnivall, John Sydenham, *Colonial Policy and Practice: A Comparative Study of Burma and Netherlands India* (Cambridge, Cambridge University Press, 1948)

Gibbons, Kenneth M., and Donald C. Rowat (eds.), *Political Corruption in Canada: Cases, Causes, and Cures* (Toronto, McClelland and Stewart, 1976)

Gillis, John R., *The Prussian Bureaucracy in Crisis, 1840–1860: Origins of an Administrative Ethos* (Berkeley, University of California Press, 1971)

Hall, John A., Ove Korsgaard, and Ove K. Pedersen (eds.), *Building the Nation: N.F.S. Gruntvig and Danish National Identity* (Montreal, McGill-Queens University Press, 2015)

Hampton, Mark, *Hong Kong and British Culture, 1945–97* (Manchester, Manchester University Press, 2016)

Hanks, John, *Operation Lock and the War on Rhino Poaching* (Johannesburg, Penguin, 2015)

Hardi, Peter, Paul M. Heywood, and Davide Torsello (eds.), *Debates of Corruption and Integrity: Perspectives from Europe and the U.S.* (Basingstoke, Palgrave Macmillan, 2015)

Harel, Xavier, and Thomas Hofnung, *La scandale des biens mal acquis* [*The Scandal of Ill-gotten Gains*] (Paris, Broché, 2011)

Harris, Robert, *Political Corruption: In and Beyond the Nation State* (London, Routledge, 2003)

Hatchard, John, *Combating Corruption: Legal Approaches to Supporting Good Governance and Integrity* (Cheltenham, Edward Elgar, 2014)

Heidenheimer, Arnold J., and Michael Johnston (eds.), *Political Corruption: Concepts and Contexts*, 3rd ed. (New Brunswick, Transaction, 2002)

Heineman, Ben W., Jr., *High Performance with High Integrity* (Boston, Harvard Business Review Press, 2008)

Heywood, Paul M. (ed.), *Routledge Handbook of Political Corruption* (New York, Routledge, 2015)

Hirschfeld, Katherine, *Gangster States: Organized Crime, Kleptocracy, and Political Collapse* (Basingstoke, Palgrave Macmillan, 2015)

Hope, Kempe Ronald (ed.), *Police Corruption and Police Reforms in Developing Societies* (Boca Raton, CRC Press, 2015)

Hope, Kempe Ronald, and Bornwell C. Chikulo (eds.), *Corruption and Development in Africa: Lessons from Country Case-Studies* (Basingstoke, Palgrave, 2000)

Huntington, Samuel P., *Political Order in Changing Societies* (New Haven, Yale University Press, 1968)

Johnston, Michael, *Syndromes of Corruption: Wealth, Power, and Democracy* (New York, Cambridge University Press, 2005)

———, Victor T. LeVine, and Arnold J. Heidenheimer (eds.), *Political Corruption: Readings in Comparative Analysis* (New Brunswick, Transaction, 1970)

Jones, Benjamin T., *Republicanism and Responsible Government: The Shaping of Democracy in Australia and Canada* (Montreal, McGill-Queen's University Press, 2014)

Katz, Rebecca S., *The Georgian Regime Crisis of 2003–2004: A Case Study in Post-Soviet Media Representation of Politics, Crime, and Corruption* (Stuttgart, ibidem-Verlag, 2006)

Kinzer, Stephen, *A Thousand Hills: Rwanda's Rebirth and the Man who Dreamed It* (Hoboken, Wiley, 2008)

Klitgaard, Robert, *Controlling Corruption* (Berkeley, University of California Press, 1988)

———, *Tropical Gangsters: One Man's Experience with Development and Decadence in Deepest Africa* (New York, Basic Books, 1990)

Koehler, Jan, and Christoph Zurcher (eds.), *Potentials of Disorder: Explaining Conflict and Stabil-*

ity in the Caucasus and in the Former Yugoslavia (Manchester, Manchester University Press, 2003)

Koinova, Maria, *Ethnonationalist Conflict in Postcommunist States: Varieties of Governance in Bulgaria, Macedonia, and Kosovo* (Philadelphia, University of Pennsylvania Press, 2013)

Kpundeh, Sahr J., and Irene Kors (eds.), *Corruption and Integrity Improvement Initiatives in Developing Countries* (New York, United Nations Development Programme [UNDP], 1998)

Langford, John W., and Allan Tupper (eds.), *Corruption, Character, and Conduct: Essays on Canadian Government Ethics* (Toronto, Oxford University Press, 1993)

Lee Kuan Yew, *From Third World to First: The Singapore Story, 1965–2000* (New York, Harper, 2000)

Lethbridge, Henry J., *Hard Graft in Hong Kong: Scandal, Corruption, the ICAC* (Hong Kong, Oxford University Press, 1985)

Lipson, Leslie, *The Politics of Equality: New Zealand's Adventures in Democracy* (Chicago, University of Chicago Press, 1948)

Lo, T. Wing, *Corruption and Politics in Hong Kong and China* (Buckingham, Open University Press, 1993)

MacMullen, Ramsay, *Corruption and the Decline of Rome* (New Haven, Yale University Press, 1988)

Makinwa, Abiola O., *Private Remedies for Corruption: Towards an International Framework* (Utrecht, Eleven, 2013)

Manion, Melanie, *Corruption by Design: Building Clean Government in Mainland China and Hong Kong* (Cambridge, MA, Harvard University Press, 2004)

Masire, Quett Ketumile Joni (ed. Stephen R. Lewis), *Very Brave or Very Foolish? Memoirs of an African Democrat* (Gaborone, Palgrave Macmillan, 2006)

Mauss, Marcel, *The Gift: The Form and Reason for Exchange in Archaic Societies* (London, Routledge, 1990, orig. pub. 1923)

Minchin, James, *No Man is an Island: A Portrait of Singapore's Lee Kuan Yew* (London, Unwin Hyman, 1990, orig. pub. 1986)

Mungiu-Pippidi, Alina, *The Quest for Good Governance: How Societies Develop Control of Corruption* (New York, Cambridge University Press, 2015)

Neild, Robert, *Public Corruption: The Dark Side of Social Evolution* (London, Anthem Press, 2002)

Noonan, John T., Jr., *Bribes* (New York, Macmillan, 1984)

Ogalo, George, and Peter Marsden (eds.), *Corruption and its Consequences in Kenya* (Nairobi, Concordis International, 2013)

Peck, Linda Levy, *Court Patronage and Corruption in Early Stuart England* (Boston, Unwin Hyman, 1990)

Perry, Peter John, *Political Corruption and Political Geography* (Aldershot, Hants., Ashgate, 1997)

Persson, Torsten, and Guido E. Tabellini, *The Economic Effects of Constitutions* (Cambridge, MA, Massachusetts Institute of Technology [MIT], 2003)

Pierce, Steven, *Moral Economies of Corruption: State Formation and Political Culture in Nigeria* (Durham, Duke University Press, 2016)

Polaschek, Raymond Joseph, *Government Administration in New Zealand* (Wellington, Oxford University Press, 1958)

Power, Timothy J., and Matthew M. Taylor (eds.), *Corruption and Democracy in Brazil: The Struggle for Accountability* (Notre Dame, IN, Notre Dame Press, 2011)

Quah, Jon S. T. (ed.), *Different Paths to Curbing Corruption: Lessons from Denmark, Finland, Hong Kong, New Zealand, and Singapore* (Bingley, UK, Emerald, 2013)

Root, Hilton L., *Small Countries, Big Lessons: Governance and the Rise of East Asia* (Hong Kong, Oxford University Press, 1996)

Rose, Richard, and Caryn Peiffer, *Paying Bribes for Public Services: A Global Guide to Grass-Roots Corruption* (Basingstoke, UK, Palgrave Macmillan, 2015)

Rose-Ackerman, Susan, *Corruption: A Study in Political Economy* (New York, Academic Press, 1978)

————, *Corruption and Government: Causes, Consequences, and Reform* (New York, Cambridge University Press, 1999, 2nd ed. 2016)

Rotberg, Robert I., *Africa Emerges: Consummate Challenges, Abundant Opportunities* (Cambridge, Polity, 2013)

————, *Transformative Political Leadership: Making a Difference in the Developing World* (Chicago, University of Chicago Press, 2012)

———— (ed.), *Corruption, Global Security, and World Order* (Washington, DC, Brookings, 2009)

———— (ed.), *Governance and Innovation in Africa: South Africa after Mandela* (Waterloo, ON, Centre for International Governance Innovation [CIGI], 2014)

———— (ed.), *On Governance: What it Is, What it Measures, and Its Policy Uses* (Waterloo, ON, CIGI, 2015)

———— (ed.), *When States Fail: Causes and Consequences* (Princeton, Princeton University Press, 2004)

————, and Rachel M. Gisselquist, *Strengthening African Governance: The Index of African Governance, Results and Rankings* (Cambridge, MA, Kennedy School of Government, Harvard University, and World Peace Foundation, 2009)

Rothstein, Bo, *The Quality of Government: Corruption, Social Trust, and Inequality in International Perspective* (Chicago, University of Chicago Press, 2011)

Rudebeck, Lars, and Olle Törnquist (eds.), *Democratization in the Third World: Concrete Cases in Comparative and Theoretical Perspective* (New York, St. Martin's Press, 1998)

Sampford, Charles, Arthur Shacklock, Carmel Connors, and Fredrik Galtung (eds.), *Measuring Corruption* (Aldershot, Hants., Ashgate, 2006)

Sampson, Anthony, *Mandela: The Authorized Biography* (New York, Random House, 1999)

Schedler, Andreas, Larry Diamond, and Marc F. Plattner (eds.), *The Self-Restraining State: Power and Accountability in New Democracies* (Boulder, Rienner, 1999)

Scott, James C., *Comparative Political Corruption* (Englewood Cliffs, Prentice Hall, 1972)

Shelley, Louise, Erik R. Scott, and Anthony Latta (eds.), *Organized Crime and Corruption in Georgia* (New York, Routledge, 2007)

Spector, Bertram I. (ed.), *Fighting Corruption in Developing Countries: Strategies and Analysis* (Bloomfield, CT, Kumarian Press, 2005)

Stapenhurst, Frederick, and Sahr J. Kpundeh (eds.), *Curbing Corruption: Toward a Model for Building National Integrity* (Washington, DC, World Bank Institute, 1999)

Stefes, Christoph H., *Understanding Post-Soviet Transitions: Corruption, Collusion, and Clientelism* (London, Palgrave, 2006)

Teachout, Zephyr, *Corruption in America: From Benjamin Franklin's Snuff Box to Citizens United* (Cambridge, MA, Harvard University Press, 2014)

Tiihonen, Seppo (ed.), *The History of Corruption in Central Government* (Amsterdam, IOS Press, 2003)

Tlou, Thomas, and Neil Parsons, Willie Henderson, *Seretse Khama, 1921–80* (Gaborone, Botswana Society, 1995)

Uslaner, Eric M., *Corruption, Inequality, and the Rule of Law: The Bulging Pocket Makes the Easy Life* (New York, Cambridge University Press, 2008)

Waal, Alex de, *The Real Politics of the Horn of Africa: Money, War, and the Business of Power* (Cambridge, Polity, 2015)

Weaver, Caroline, *Hypocrisy Trap: The World Bank and the Poverty of Reform* (Princeton, Princeton University Press, 2008)

Wraith, Ronald, and Edgar Simpkins, *Corruption in Developing Countries* (London, Allen & Unwin, 1963)

Wrong, Michaela, *It's Our Turn to Eat: The Story of a Kenyan Whistleblower* (London, Fourth Estate, 2009)

Articles, Chapters, and Reports

(but omitting material in the notes from the media or blogs)

Acemoglu, Daron, Simon Johnson, and James A. Robinson, "An African Success Story: Botswana," in Dani Rodrik (ed.), *In Search of Prosperity: Analytic Narratives on Economic Growth* (Princeton, Princeton University Press, 2003), 85–106

Adebanwi, Wale, and Ebenezer Obadare, "When Corruption Fights Back: Democracy and Elite Interest in Nigeria's Anticorruption War," *Journal of Modern African Studies*, XLIX (2011), 185–213

Alatas, Syed Hussein, "The Problem of Corruption," in Kernial Singh Sandhu and Paul Wheatley (eds.), *Management of Success: The Moulding of Modern Singapore* (Singapore, Institute for Southeast Asian Studies, 1989), 985–1002

Alence, Rod, "Political Institutions and Developmental Governance in Sub-Saharan Africa," *Journal of Modern African Studies*, XLII (2004), 163–187

Atuobi, Samuel, "Corruption and State Instability in West Africa: An Examination of Policy Options," Kofi Annan International Peacekeeping Training Centre (KAIPTC) Occasional Paper, 21 (2007)

Baev, Pavel K., "Civil Wars in Georgia: Corruption Breeds Violence," in Jan Koehler and Christoph Zurcher (eds.), *Potentials of Disorder* (Manchester, Manchester University Press, 2003), 127–144

Bardhan, Pranab, "Corruption and Development: A Review of Issues," *Journal of Economic Literature*, XXXV (1997), 1320–1346

Barr, Michael D., "Singapore's Lee Kuan Yew: Traveling Light, Traveling Fast," in Ramachandra Guha (ed.), *Makers of Modern Asia* (Cambridge, MA, Harvard University Press, 2014), 244–266

Becker, Gary S., and George J. Stigler, "Law Enforcement, Malfeasance, and Compensation of Enforcers," *Journal of Legal Studies*, III (1974), 1–18

Bennet, Richard, "Delivering on the Hope of the Rose Revolution: Public Sector Reform in Georgia, 2004–2009," Princeton University Innovations for Successful Societies

Bracking, Sarah L., "Corruption and Development: The Mutable Edges of Morality in Modern Markets," in Paul M. Heywood (ed.), *Routledge Handbook of Political Corruption* (New York, Routledge, 2015), 225–241

Brasz, Henk A. "Some Notes on the Sociology of Corruption," *Sociologica Neerlandica*, I (1963), 111–117.

Brinkerhoff, Derick W., "Assessing Political Will for Anti-Corruption Efforts: An Analytic Framework," *Public Administration and Development*, XX (2000), 239–252.

Bruton, Peter, John Downing, and Fraser Kelly, "Graft Never Hurt a Politician at the Polls," in Kenneth M. Gibbons and Donald C. Rowat (eds.), *Political Corruption in Canada: Cases, Causes, and Cures* (Toronto, McClelland and Stewart, 1976), 239–244

Bukurura, Sufian Hemed, "The Judiciary and Democratic Governance in Sub-Saharan Africa: The Complexities of Regulating Competing Interests," in Kwame Frimpong and Gloria Jacques (eds.), *Corruption, Democracy, and Good Governance in Africa* (Gaborone, Lightbooks, 1999), 109–121

Bunn, Matthew, "Corruption and Nuclear Proliferation," in Robert I. Rotberg (ed.), *Corruption, Global Security, and World Order* (Washington, DC, Brookings, 2009), 124–166

Camerer, Marianne Irene, "Measuring Public Integrity," *Journal of Democracy*, XVII (2006), 152–165

Chang, Gordon G., "Xi's Purge: Anticorruption or Loyalty-Based? Is it Finished Yet?" *World Affairs Journal*, June 22, 2015, http://www.worldaffairsjournal.org

Chayes, Sarah, "The Structure of Corruption: A Systematic Analysis Using Eurasian Cases," Carnegie Endowment for International Peace, published paper, June 30, 2016

Clark, Monica A., "Combating Corruption in Liberia: Assessing the Impact of the Governance and Economic Management Assistance Program (GEMAP)," *Journal of Development and Social Transformation*, V (2008), 25–32

Collier, Michael W., "Explaining Corruption: An Institutional Choice Approach," *Crime, Law, and Social Change*, XXXVIII (2002), 1–32

Curnow, Ross, "What's Past is Prologue: Administrative Corruption in Australia," in Tiihonen, *History of Corruption* (2003), 37–64

Delhey, Jan, and Kenneth Newton, "Social Trust: Global Pattern or Nordic Exceptionalism," Wissenschaftszentrum Berlin für Sozialforschung, Discussion Paper, June 2004

de Speville, Bertrand E. M., "Anticorruption Commissions: The 'Hong Kong Model' Revisited," *Asia-Pacific Review*, XVII (2010), 47–71

Devlin, Matthew, "Seizing the Reform Moment: Rebuilding Georgia's Police, 2004–2006," Princeton University, Innovations for Successful Societies

Diamond, Larry, "Class Formation in the Swollen African State," *Journal of Modern African Studies*, XXV (1987), 567–596

———, "A Quarter Century of Promoting Democracy," *Journal of Democracy*, XVIII (2007), 118–120

Dininio, Phyllis, "The Risks of Recorruption," in Bertram I. Spector (ed.), *Fighting Corruption in Developing Countries: Strategies and Analysis* (Bloomfield, CT, Kumarian Press, 2005), 233–249

Di Puppo, Lili, "Anti-Corruption Interventions in Georgia," *Global Crime*, XI (2010), 220–236

Dix, Sarah, and Emmanuel Pok, "Combating Corruption in Traditional Societies: Papua New Guinea," in Rotberg, *Corruption*, 239–259

Doig, Alan, David Watt, and Robert Williams, "Measuring 'Success' in Five African Anti-Corruption Commissions," U4 Publications, Transparency International (2005)

Donchev, Dilyan, and Gergely Ujhelyi, "What Do Corruption Indices Measure?" *Economics and Politics*, XXVI (2014), 309–331

Economic Commission for Africa, "Assessing the Efficiency and Impact of National Anti-Corruption Institutions in Africa" (Addis Ababa, Economic Commission for Africa, 2010)

Eigen, Peter, "A Coalition to Combat Corruption: TI, EITI, and Civil Society," in Rotberg, *Corruption*, 416–429

Engvall, Johan, "Against the Grain: How Georgia Fought Corruption and What It Means," Central-Asia Caucasus Institute and Silk Road Studies Program (Stockholm, SAIS and the Stockholm Institute for Security and Development Policy, 2012), Occasional Paper, 5–61.

Enweremadu, David Uchenna, "The Struggle against Corruption in Nigeria: The Role of the National Anti-Corruption Commission (ICPC) under the Fourth Republic," *Institut Francais de Recherche en Afrique*, special issue 2 (2004), 41–66

Epstein, Brian, "When Local Models Fail," *Philosophy of the Social Sciences*, XXXVIII (2008), 3–24

Fombad, Charles Manga, "Curbing Corruption in Africa: Some Lessons from Botswana's Experience," *International Social Science Journal*, LI (1999), 241–254

Frisk Jensen, Mette, "Fighting Corruption in Modernity: A Literature Review," unpub., 2012

———, "The Question of How Denmark Got to Be Denmark—Establishing the Rule of Law and Fighting Corruption in the State of Denmark 1660–1900," University of Gothenburg Quality of Government Institute, working paper, 2014:06 (2014)

Gainer, Maya, "Listening to the Public: A Citizen Scorecard in the Philippines, 2010–2014," Princeton University, Innovations for Successful Societies, 2015, http://www.successful societies.Princeton.edu

Galtung, Fredrik, and Jeremy Pope, "The Global Coalition against Corruption: Evaluating Transparency International," in Andreas Schedler, Larry Diamond, and Marc F. Plattner (eds.), *The Self-Restraining State: Power and Accountability in New Democracies* (Boulder, Rienner, 1999), 257–284

Gerring, John, and Strom C. Thacker, "Political Institutions and Corruption: The Role of Unitarism and Parliamentarism," *British Journal of Political Science*, XXXIV (2004), 295–330

Gibbons, Kenneth M., "The Political Culture of Corruption in Canada," in Kenneth Gibbons and Donald C. Rowat (eds.), *Political Corruption in Canada: Cases, Causes, and Cures* (Toronto, McClelland and Stewart, 1976), 239–244

Godson, Roy, et al., "Building Societal Support for the Rule of Law in Georgia," *Trends in Organized Crime*, VIII (2004), 5–27

Goel, Rajeev K., and Michael A. Nelson, "Corruption and Government Size: A Disaggregated Analysis," *Public Choice*, XCVII (1998), 107–120

Golden, Miriam A., and Lucio Picci, "Proposal for a New Measure of Corruption, Illustrated with Italian Data," *Economics and Politics*, XVII (2005), 37–75

Good, Kenneth, "Corruption and Mismanagement in Botswana: A Best-Case Example?" *Journal of Modern African Studies*, XXXII (1994), 499–521

Gregory, Robert, "Assessing 'Good Governance' and Corruption in New Zealand: Scientific Measurement, Political Discourse, and Historical Narrative," Victoria University of Wellington Institute for Governance and Policy Studies, Working Paper 13/03, 2013

Gregory, Robert, and Daniel Zirker, "Clean and Green with Deepening Shadows? A Non-Complacent View of Corruption in New Zealand," in Jon S. T. Quah (ed.), *Different Paths to Curbing Corruption: Lessons from Denmark, Finland, Hong Kong, New Zealand, and Singapore* (Bingley, UK, Emerald, 2013), 109–136

Gyimah-Brempong, Kwabena, "Corruption, Economic Growth, and Income Inequality in Africa," *Economics of Governance*, III (2002), 183–209

Hall-Matthews, David, "Tickling Donors and Tackling Opponents: The Anti-Corruption Campaign in Malawi," in Sarah L. Bracking (ed.), *Corruption and Development: The Anti-Corruption Campaigns* (New York, Palgrave Macmillan, 2007), 77–102

Hansen, Hans Krause, "The Power of Performance Indices in the Global Politics of Anti-Corruption," *Journal of International Relations and Development*, XV (2012), 506–531

Hatchard, John, "Adopting a Human Rights Approach towards Combating Corruption," in Martine Boersma and Hans Nelen (eds.), *Corruption and Human Rights: Interdisciplinary Perspectives* (Amsterdam, Intersentia, 2010), 7–23

———, "The Institution of the Ombudsman in Africa with Special Reference to Zimbabwe," *International and Comparative Law Quarterly*, XXXV (1986), 255–270

Heilbrunn, John R., "Anti-Corruption Commissions: *Panacea* or Real Medicine to Fight Corruption?" (Washington, DC, World Bank Institute, 2004)

Heineman, Ben W., Jr., "The Role of the Multi-National Corporation in the Long War against Corruption," in Rotberg, *Corruption*, 359–387

Heintzman, Ralph, "Politics and Corruption in Quebec," in Gibbons and Rowat, *Political Corruption in Canada*, 217–224

Heller, Nathaniel, "Defining and Measuring Corruption: Where Have We Come From, Where Are We Now, and What Matters for the Future?" in Rotberg, *Corruption*, 47–65

Hellman, Deborah, "Defining Corruption and Constitutionalizing Democracy," *Michigan Law Review*, CXI (2013), 1385–1422

Heywood, Paul M., "Measuring Corruption: Perspectives, Critiques, and Limits," in Heywood, *Routledge Handbook*, 137–153

Heywood, Paul M., and Joshua Rose, "'Close but No Cigar': The Measurement of Corruption," *Journal of Public Policy*, XXXIV (2014), 507–529

———, "Curbing Corruption or Promoting Integrity? Probing the Hidden Conceptual Challenge," in Peter Hardi, Paul M. Heywood, and Davide Torsello (eds.), *Debates of Corruption and Integrity: Perspectives from Europe and the US* (Basingstoke, Palgrave Macmillan, 2015), 102–119

Holm, John D. "Curbing Corruption through Democratic Accountability: Lessons from Botswana," in Kempe Ronald Hope and Bornwell C. Chikulo (eds.), *Corruption and Development in Africa: Lessons from Country Case-Studies* (Basingstoke, Palgrave, 2000), 288–304

Hope, Kempe Ronald, Sr., "Tackling the Corruption Epidemic in Kenya: Toward a Policy of More Effective Control," *Journal of Social, Political, and Economic Studies*, XXXVIII (2013), 287–316

Hoselitz, Bert F., "Levels of Economic Performance and Bureaucratic Structures," in Joseph La Palombara (ed.), *Bureaucracy and Political Development* (Princeton, Princeton University Press, 1963), 168–198

Huberts, Leo, Karin Lasthuizen, and Careel Peeters, "Measuring Corruption: Exploring the Iceberg," in Sampford et al., *Corruption*, 273, 265–294

Hussein, Mustafa, "Combating Corruption in Malawi: An Assessment of the Enforcing Mechanisms," *African Security Review*, XIV (2005), http://www.isssafrica.org/topics/corruption-and-governance/01-dec-2005

Iyer, Deepa, "Earning a Reputation for Independence: Ghana's Commission on Human Rights and Administrative Justice, 1993–2003," Princeton University, Innovations for Successful Societies, 2011

Jain, Arvind K., "Corruption: A Review," *Journal of Economic Surveys*, XV (2001), 71–121

Jin-Wook Choi, "Institutional Structures and Effectiveness of Anticorruption Agencies: A Comparative Analysis of South Korea and Hong Kong," *Asian Journal of Political Science*, XVII (2009), 195–214

Johnston, Michael, "Fighting Systemic Corruption: Social Foundations for Institutional Reform," *European Journal of Development Research*, X (1998), 85–104

———, "The Great Danes: Successes and Subtleties of Corruption Control in Denmark," in Jon S. T. Quah (ed.), *Different Paths to Curbing Corruption: Lessons from Denmark, Finland, Hong Kong, New Zealand and Singapore* (Bingley, UK, Emerald, 2013), 23–56

———, "Reflection and Reassessment: The Emerging Agenda of Corruption Research," in Heywood, *Routledge Handbook*, 273–287

———, "The Search for Definitions: The Vitality of Politics and the Issue of Corruption," *International Social Science Journal*, XLIX (1996), 321–335

———, "Why Do So Many Anti-Corruption Efforts Fail?" *NYU Annual Survey of American Law*, LXVII (2012), 467–496

Jones, Benjamin F., and Benjamin A. Olken, "Do Leaders Matter? National Leadership and Growth since World War II," *Quarterly Journal of Economics*, CXX (2005), 835–864

Kerkhoff, Antoon D., Michel P. Hoenderboom, D. B. Ronald Kroeze, and F. Pieter Wagenaar, "Dutch Political Corruption in Historical Perspective," in Niels Grüne and Simona Slanička, *Korruption: Historische Annäherungen an eine Grundfigur Politischer Kommunication* (Göttingen, Vandenhoeck & Ruprecht, 2010), 443–467

Kernaghan, Kenneth, "Corruption and Public Service in Canada: Conceptual and Practical Dimensions," in Tiihonen, *History of Corruption*, 83–98

———, "The Ethical Conduct of Public Servants," in Gibbons and Rowat, *Political Corruption in Canada*, 159–170

———, "Rules Are Not Enough: Ethics, Politics, and Public Service in Ontario," in Langford and Tupper, *Corruption, Character, and Conduct*, 174–196

Kim, Chon-Kyun, "Anti-Corruption Initiatives and E-Government: A Cross-National Study," *Public Organization Review*, XIV (2014), 385–396

Kpundeh, Sahr J., "Political Will in Fighting Corruption," in Kpundeh and Irene Hors (eds.), *Corruption and Integrity Improvement Initiatives in Developing Countries* (New York, UNDP, 1998), 91–110

Kupatze, Alexander, "Explaining Georgia's Anti-Corruption Drive," *European Security*, XXI (2012), 16–36

Kurer, Oskar, "Corruption: An Alternative Approach to Its Definition and Measurement," *Political Studies*, LIII (2005), 222–239

———, "Definitions of Corruption," in Paul M. Heywood (ed.), *Routledge Handbook of Political Corruption* (New York, Routledge, 2015), 30–41

Kuris, Gabriel, "From a Rocky Start to Regional Leadership: Mauritius's Anti-Corruption Agency, 2006–2012," Princeton University, Innovations for Successful Societies, 2013, http://successfulsocieties.Princeton.edu

———, "From Underdogs to Watchdogs: How Anti-Corruption Agencies Can Hold Off Potent Adversaries," Princeton University, Innovations for Successful Societies, 2014

———, "Holding High Ground with Public Support: Indonesia's Anti-Corruption Commission Digs In, 2007–2011," Princeton University, Innovations for Successful Societies, 2012

———, " 'Inviting a Tiger into Your Home': Indonesia Creates an Anti-Corruption Commission with Teeth, 2002–2007," Princeton University, Innovations for Successful Societies, 2012

———, "Managing Corruption Risks: Botswana Builds an Anti-Graft Agency, 1994–2012," Princeton University, Innovations for Successful Societies Program, 2013

Lamba, Isaac C., "Controlling Corruption in Africa: The Case of Malawi," in Frimpong and Jacques, *Corruption, Democracy*, 258–267

Lambsdorff, Johann Graf, "Measuring Corruption—The Validity and Precision of Subjective Indicators (CPI)," in Charles Sampford, Arthur Shacklock, Carmel Connors, and Fredrik Galtung (eds.), *Measuring Corruption* (Aldershot, Hants., Ashgate, 2006), 81–99

———, "The Organization of Anti-Corruption: Getting the Incentives Right," in Rotberg, *Corruption, Global Security, and World Order*, 389–415

Langseth, Petter, "Measuring Corruption," in Sampford et al., *Measuring Corruption*, 7–44

———, "Prevention: An Effective Tool to Reduce Corruption," UN Office of Drug Control and Crime Prevention, International Scientific and Professional Advisory Council (ISPAC) conference, Nov. 19, 1999 (Milan), 1–38

———, Frederick Stapenhurst, and Jeremy Pope, "National Integrity Systems," in Stapenhurst and Kpundeh, *Curbing Corruption*, 127–150

Lawson, Letitia, "The Politics of Anti-Corruption Reform in Africa," *Journal of Modern African Studies*, XLVII (2009), 73–100

Leff, Nathaniel H., "Economic Development through Bureaucratic Corruption," *American Behavioral Scientist*, VIII (1964), 8–14

Legvold, Robert, "Corruption, the Criminalized State, and Post-Soviet Transitions," in Rotberg, *Corruption*, 194–238

Leys, Colin, "What Is the Problem about Corruption?" *Journal of Modern African Studies*, III (1965), 215–230

Lindstadt, Catharina, and Daniel Naurin, "Transparency Is Not Enough: Making Transparency Effective in Reducing Corruption," *International Political Science Review*, XXXI (2010), 301–322

Mahmud, Quamrul, "Impact of Corruption on Economic Growth Performance in Developing Countries," http://www.scribd.com/doc/764/analysees-report

Mailey, J. R., "The Anatomy of the Resource Curse: Predatory Investment in Africa's Extractive Industries," Africa Center for Strategic Studies, Special Report 3 (2015)

Manion, Melanie, "Institutional Design and Anti-Corruption in Mainland China," in Heywood, *Routledge Handbook*, 242–252

Marquette, Heather, and Caryn Peiffer, "Corruption and Collective Action," Developmental Leadership Program, University of Birmingham, Research Paper 32 (January 2015)

Masud, Mohammad Omar, "Calling the Public to Empower the State: Pakistan's Citizen Feedback Monitoring Program, 2008–2014," Princeton University, Innovations for Successful Societies, 2015

Mauro, Paolo, "The Effects of Corruption on Growth, Investment, and Government Expenditure," IMF, Working Paper/96/98, 1996

McLaughlin, Erin, "Culture and Corruption: An Explanation of the Differences between Scandinavia and Africa," *American Journal of Research in Humanities, Arts, and Social Sciences*, II (2013), 85–91

Meer, Frits M. van der, and Jos C. N. Raadschelders, "Maladministration in the Netherlands in the 19th and 20th Centuries," in Tiihonen, *History of Corruption*, 179–196

Mezmur, Tewodros, and Raymond Koen, "The Ethiopian Federal Ethics and Anti-Corruption Commission: A Critical Assessment," *Law, Democracy, and Development*, XV (2011), 215–243

Momba, Jotham C., "Economic Reforms, Corruption and the Crises of Governance in Zambia: The Dilemma for the Donor Community," in Kwame Frimpong and Gloria Jacques (eds.), *Corruption, Democracy, and Good Governance in Africa* (Gaborone, Lightbooks, 1999), 193–200

Mungiu-Pippidi, Alina, "Becoming Denmark: Historical Designs of Corruption Control," *Social Research*, LXXX (2013), 1259–1286

———, "Becoming Denmark: Understanding Good Governance Historical Achievers," unpub.? draft, 2013

———, "Controlling Corruption through Collective Action," *Journal of Democracy*, XXIV (2013), 101–115

———, "The Quest for Good Governance: Learning from Virtuous Circles," *Journal of Democracy*, XXVII (2016), 95–109

Murray, Matthew, and Andrew Spalding, "Freedom from Official Corruption as a Human Right," Brookings Research Paper, 2015

Myrdal, Gunnar, "Corruption: Its Causes and Effects," in Myrdal, *Asian Drama: An Enquiry into the Poverty of Nations* (New York, Twentieth Century Foundation, 1968), II, 951–968

Ndulo, Muna, "Review of the Anti-Corruption Legal Framework in Zambia," Southern African Institute for Policy and Research (Lusaka, 2014), 7–81

Nye, Joseph S., Jr., "Corruption and Political Development: A Cost-Benefit Analysis," *American Political Science Review*, XLI (1967), 417–427

Okojie, Paul, and Abubakar Momoh, "Corruption and Reform in Nigeria," in Sarah L. Bracking (ed.), *Corruption and Development: The Anti-Corruption Campaigns* (Basingstoke, Palgrave, 2007), 103–120

Olivier de Sardan, Jean Pierre, "A Moral Economy of Corruption in Africa?" *Journal of Modern African Studies*, XXXVII (1999), 25–52

Olken, Ben A., "Corruption Perceptions vs. Corruption Reality," *Journal of Public Economics*, XC (2009), 950–964

Osnos, Evan, "Born Red," *New Yorker*, April 6, 2015, 42–55

Park Hung Mo, "Corruption and Economic Growth," *Journal of Comparative Economics*, XXIX (2001), 66–79.

Peiffer, Caryn, and Linda Alvarez, "Who Will Be the 'Principled Principals'? The Determinants of Active Opposition to Corruption," Developmental Leadership Program, University of Birmingham, Research Paper 31 (October, 2014)

———, "Who Will Be the 'Principled-Principals'? Perceptions of Corruption and Willingness to Engage in Anticorruption Activism," *Governance*, XXIX (2016), 351–369

Persson, Anna, and Martin Sjöstedt, "Responsive and Responsible Leaders: A Matter of Political Will?" *Perspectives on Politics*, X (2012), 617–632

Persson, Anna, Bo Rothstein, and Jan Teorell, "Why Anticorruption Reforms Fail—Systemic Corruption as a Collective Action Problem," *Governance*, XXVI (2013), 449–471

Pettersson, Lars, "In Search of Respectability: Popular Movements in Scandinavian Democratization—From Voluntary Associations to Mass Organizations," in Lars Rudebeck and Olle Törnquist (eds.), *Democratization in the Third World: Concrete Cases in Comparative and Theoretical Perspective* (New York, St. Martin's Press, 1998), 85–106

Post, Lori Ann, Amber N. W. Raile, and Eric D. Raile, "Defining Political Will," *Politics and Policy*, XXXVIII (2010), 653–676

Quah, Jon S. T., "Combating Corruption in Singapore: What Can Be Learned?" *Journal of Contingencies and Crisis Management*, IX (2001), 29–35

———, "Combating Corruption in the Asia-Pacific Countries: What We Know and What Needs to Be Done," *International Public Management Review*, X (2009), 5–33

———, "Curbing Corruption in Singapore: The Importance of Political Will, Expertise, Enforcement, and Context," in Quah (ed.), *Different Paths to Curbing Corruption: Lessons from Denmark, Finland, Hong Kong, New Zealand, and Singapore* (Bingley, UK, Emerald, 2013), 137–166

Raditlthokwa, L. Log, "Corruption in Africa: A Function of Leadership," in Kwame Frimpong and Gloria Jacques (eds.), *Corruption, Democracy, and Good Governance in Africa* (Gaborone, Lightbooks, 1999), 49–55

Reno, William, "Anti-Corruption Efforts in Liberia: Are they Aimed at the Right Targets?" *International Peacekeeping*, XV (2008), 387–404

Riak, Maker Mayek, "Reversing the Trend of Corruption in South Sudan: Is Rwanda a Suitable Model?" *Journal of Developing Societies*, XXIX (2013), 487–501

Riggs, Fred W., "The Sala Model: An Ecological Approach to the Study of Comparative Administration," *Philippine Journal of Public Administration*, VI (1962), 3–16

Robin, Martin, "British Columbia: The Politics of Class Conflict," in Martin Robin (ed.), *Canadian Provincial Politics: The Party Systems of the Ten Provinces* (Toronto, Prentice Hall, 1978), 27–68

Rose-Ackerman, Susan, "Corruption in the Wake of Domestic National Conflict," in Robert I. Rotberg, *Corruption, Global Security, and World Order* (Washington, DC, 2009), 66–95

Rotberg, Robert I., "Canada's Corruption at Home and Abroad: An Introduction to the Special Issue," *Canadian Journal of Foreign Policy*, XXIII (2017), 1–14

———, "The Failure and Collapse of Nation-States: Breakdown, Prevention, and Repair," in

Robert I. Rotberg (ed.), *When States Fail: Causes and Consequences* (Princeton, Princeton University Press, 2004), 1–50

———, "The Judge Who Could Remake Brazil: How Sergio Moro Has Tackled Corruption," *Foreign Affairs* blog, Dec. 21, 2016, www.foreignaffairs.com/articles/2016-12-21

———, "Leadership Alters Corrupt Behavior," in Robert I. Rotberg (ed.), *Corruption, Global Security, and World Order* (Washington, DC, 2009), 341–358

———, "Mobile Phones Propelling Africa's Renaissance," *Diplomat & International Canada*, April–June 2015, 33–35

———, and Aniket Bhushan, "The Indexes of Governance," in Robert I. Rotberg (ed.), *On Governance: What It Is, How It Is Measured, and Its Policy Uses* (Waterloo, ON, CIGI, 2015), 55–90

———, and Jennifer Erin Salahub, "African Legislative Effectiveness," *North-South Institute* (Ottawa) report, October 2013

Rothstein, Bo, "Anti-corruption: The Indirect 'Big Bang' Approach," *Review of International Political Economy*, XVIII (2011), 228–250

———, "Conceptualizing QoG," in Nicholas Charron, Victor Lapuente, and Bo Rothstein (eds.), *Quality of Government from a European Perspective: A Comparative Study of Good Government in EU Regions* (Cheltenham, Edward Elgar, 2013), 16–36

———, and Eric M. Uslaner, "All for One: Equality, Corruption, and Social Trust," *World Politics*, LVIII (2005), 41–72

———, and Jan Teorell, "Causes of Corruption," in Paul M. Heywood (ed.), *Routledge Handbook of Political Corruption* (New York, Routledge, 2015), 79–94

———, and Jan Teorell, "What Is Quality of Government?: A Theory of Impartial Political Institutions" *Governance*, XXI (2008), 165–190

Sabet, Amr G. E., "Corruption, Governance and Collective Sanctions: Can a Wicked Problem Be Tamed?" *Studies of Changing Societies*, I (2012), 67–104

Salminen, Ari, "Control of Corruption: The Case of Finland," in Quah, *Different Paths*, 57–77

———, Olli-Pekka Viinamaki, and Rinna Ikola-Norrbacka, "The Control of Corruption in Finland," *Administratie Si Management Public*, IX (2007), 81–95

Schalkwyk, Andrew, "Rejuvenating the Public Registry: Republic of Georgia, 2006–2008," Princeton University, Innovations for Successful Societies, 2009

Scott, Ian, "Engaging the Public: Hong Kong's Independent Commission against Corruption's Community Relations Strategy," in Jon S. T. Quah, *Different Paths to Curbing Corruption: Lessons from Denmark, Finland, Hong Kong, New Zealand, and Singapore* (Bingley, UK, Emerald, 2013), 79–108.

———, "Institutional Design and Corruption Prevention in Hong Kong," *Journal of Contemporary China*, XXII (2013), 77–92

Sebududubudu, David, "The Evolving State of Corruption and Anti-Corruption Debates in Botswana: Issues in Good Governance," German Institute of Global and Area Studies, Background Paper, 2014

Selic, Ana, et al., "Analysis of the Effects of Anti-Corruption Policies in Montenegro, and Recommendation for their Improvement" (Podgorica, Centra za Monitoring, 2011)

Shelley, Louise, "Georgian Organized Crime," in Louise Shelley, Erik R. Scott, and Anthony Latta (eds.), *Organized Crime and Corruption in Georgia* (New York, 2007), 50–68

Singh, Danny, "Corruption and Clientelism in the Lower Levels of the Afghan Police," *Conflict, Security, and Development*, XIV (2014), 621–650

Smith, Daniel Jordan, "The Paradoxes of Popular Participation in Corruption in Nigeria," in Rotberg, *Corruption*, 283–309

Sorrenson, M. P. Keith, "New Zealand: Maori and Pakeha," in William S. Livingston and William

Roger Louis (eds.), *Australia, New Zealand, and the Pacific Islands since the First World War* (Austin, University of Texas Press, 1979), 168–185

Suberu, Rotimi S., "The Travails of Nigeria's Anti-Corruption Crusade," in Rotberg (ed.), *Corruption, Global Security, and World Order* (Washington, DC, Brookings, 2009), 260–282

Sutherland, Sharon, "The Canadian Federal Government," in John W. Langford and Allan Tupper (eds.), *Corruption, Character, and Conduct: Essays on Canadian Government Ethics* (Toronto, Oxford University Press, 1993), 113–150

Svallfors, Stefan, "Does Government Quality Matter? Egalitarianism and Attitudes to Taxes and Welfare Policies in Europe," Umea University, Department of Sociology, 2012

Tamyalew, Arsema, "A Review of the Effectiveness of the Federal Ethics and Anti-Corruption Commission of Ethiopia," European Commission, EuropeAid Cooperation Office, 2010

Tan Ah Leak, "The Experience of Singapore in Combating Corruption," in Frederick Stapenhurst and Sahr J. Kpundeh (eds.), *Curbing Corruption: Toward a Model for Building National Integrity* (Washington, DC, World Bank Institute, 1999), 59–65

Tanzi, Vito, "Corruption around the World: Causes, Consequences, Scope, and Cures," International Monetary Fund (IMF), Working Paper WP/98, 63, 1998

Teets, Jessica C., and Erica Chenoweth, "To Bribe or to Bomb: Do Corruption and Terrorism Go Together?" in Rotberg (ed.), *Corruption*, 167–193

Teorell, Jan, "Corruption as an Institution: Rethinking the Nature and Origins of the Grabbing Hand," University of Gothenburg, Quality of Government Institute, Working Paper 2007/5 (2007)

Teorell, Jan, and Bo Rothstein, "Getting to Sweden: Malfeasance and Bureaucratic Reforms, 1720–1850," University of Gothenburg Quality of Government Institute, Working Paper 2012:18 (2012)

Thampi, Gopakumar K., and Sita Sekhar, "Citizen Report Cards," in Charles Sampford, Arthur Shacklock, Carmel Connors, and Fredrik Galtung (eds.), *Measuring Corruption* (Aldershot, Hants., Ashgate, 2006), 233–250

Thompson, A. Keith, "Does Anti-Corruption Legislation Work?" *World Customs Journal*, VII (2013), 39–64

Tiihonen, Paula, "Good Government and Corruption in Finland," in Tiihonen, *History of Corruption*, 99–118

Ting Gong, "Forms and Characteristics of China's Corruption in the 1990s: Change with Continuity," *Communist and Post-Communist Studies*, XXX (1997), 277–288

Tirole, Jean, "A Theory of Collective Reputations with Applications to the Persistence of Corruption and to Firm Quality," *Review of Economic Studies*, LXIII (1996), 1–22

Torsello, Davide, "Corruption as Social Exchange: The View from Anthropology," in Hardi, Heywood, and Torsello (eds.), *Debates of Corruption and Integrity*, 159–183

Treisman, Daniel, "What Does Cross-National Empirical Research Reveal about the Causes of Corruption?" in Heywood, *Routledge Handbook*, 95–109

UK Department of International Development, Research for Development, "Understanding 'Political Will,'" Appendix 3 to "Politiking for the Poor: Senior Leaders Political Management of Pro-poor Initiatives in an Era of Centrists" (London, 2004)

Underkuffler, Laura S., "Defining Corruption: Implications for Action," in Robert I. Rotberg (ed.), *Corruption, Global Security, and World Order* (Washington, DC, 2009), 27–46

UN Office on Drugs and Crime, "Corruption in the Former Yugoslav Republic of Macedonia: Bribery as Experienced by the Population" (Vienna, 2011)

———, "The Global Programme against Corruption: UN Anti-Corruption Toolkit" (Vienna, 2004, 3rd ed.)

Uslaner, Eric M., "Inequality and Corruption," in Hardi, Heywood, and Torsello (eds.), *Debates of Corruption and Integrity*, 120–134

Uslaner, Eric M., and Bo Rothstein, "Mass Education, State-Building and Equality: Searching for the Roots of Corruption" (University of Gothenburg Quality of Government Institute, Working Paper 2012:5, 2012)

Warren, Mark E., "The Meaning of Corruption in Democracies," in Paul M. Heywood, *Routledge Handbook*, 42–55

———, "Political Corruption as Duplicitous Exclusion," *PS: Political Science and Politics*, XXXIX (2006), 803–807

Wells, Celia, "Enforcing Anti-Bribery Laws against Transnational Corporations—a UK Perspective," in Peter Hardi, Paul M. Heywood, and Davide Torsello (eds.), *Debates of Corruption and Integrity* (Basingstoke, Palgrave Macmillan, 2015), 59–80

Widner, Jennifer, "Building Judicial Independence in Common Law Africa," in Andreas Schedler, Larry Diamond, and Marc F. Plattner, *The Self-Restraining State: Power and Accountability in the New Democracies* (Boulder, Rienner, 1999), 177–194

Worthy, Ben, and Tom McClean, "Freedom of Information and Corruption," in Heywood, *Routledge Handbook*, 347–358

Zook, Darren C., "The Curious Case of Finland's Clean Politics," *Journal of Democracy*, XX (2009), 157–168

INDEX

A NOTE ON THE TYPE

This book has been composed in Adobe Text and Gotham. Adobe Text, designed by Robert Slimbach for Adobe, bridges the gap between fifteenth- and sixteenth-century calligraphic and eighteenth-century Modern styles. Gotham, inspired by New York street signs, was designed by Tobias Frere-Jones for Hoefler & Co.